# WILLIAM WRIGHT

SIMON & SCHUSTER

*New York•London•Toront*

*Sydney•Tokyo•Singapore*

# ALL THE PAIN THAT MONEY CAN BUY

## the

## life

## of

# Christina Onassis

Simon & Schuster
1230 Avenue of the Americas
New York, NY  10020

Simon & Schuster and colophon are registered trademarks
of Simon & Schuster Inc.

Designed by Barbara M. Bachman
Picture section designed by Caroline Cunningham

Manufactured in the United States of America

10 9 8 7 6 5 4 3 2 1

*Library of Congress Cataloging-In-Publication Data*

Wright, William, date—
All the pain that money can buy: the life of Christina Onassis/William Wright.
    p.      cm.
  1. Onassis, Christina.  2. Greece—Biography.  3. Celebrities—Greece—Biography.
4. Upper classes—Greece—Biography.
I. Title
CT1118.053W75   1991

949.507'092—dc20
[B]                        90-20347
                                 CIP

ISBN 0-7432-1163-4

*to Betty Comden, with love*

# CONTENTS

# CONTENTS

# PREFACE

Since most lives are confined by unyielding economic realities, many of us feel a curiosity about the lives of those who, by virtue of great wealth, are free of such restraints. As with other advantages—such as rare intellect or athletic talent—we enjoy seeing how these inherited wild cards might be played, experiencing vicariously lives of vastly expanded boundaries, and perhaps, in the process, envisioning our own possibilities.

When contemplating the very rich, however, we find our natural curiosity checked by the equally natural reaction of envy. Isn't it bad enough they have the mansions and yachts that we lack? Do we have to read about their personal lives as well? A compromise to this conflict of impulses is frequently worked out: we will examine their bounteous lives on the modest condition that they suffer and come to a bad end.

If these are the requirements, Christina Onassis handily meets them. On the brighter side, as a case history for revealing the possibilities of unlimited wealth, she has considerable potential. Only twenty-four when she inherited her fortune, she was spirited, romantic, at times attractive, reasonably bright, and reasonably sane. She was obliged to answer to no relative, spouse, or trustee. Far from being oppressed or embarrassed by her astounding wealth, she had a zest for the fast-paced life of almost unimaginable luxury that it permitted. She had roisterous adventures, a good number of pain-free love affairs, some heady good times. She could also take satisfaction in some major accomplishments, primarily the successful administration of the shipping empire she had inherited from her flamboyant father, Aristotle Onassis.

Even with these positive aspects, however, her brief adulthood was a constant and losing quest for the fixed, reliable love that her childhood lacked. When she died, suddenly and unexpectedly, at the age of thirty-seven, she had finally realized, with the birth three years before of her daughter, the one solid and fulfilling human bond she had ever known. In Christina's struggle for a portion of happiness, she drew regularly on the Aladdin's lamp of her fortune, attempting imaginative and sometimes eccentric strategies, and, like a one-woman welfare state, throwing ever larger amounts of money against the problems that plagued her. If Christina Onassis's life provides a window into the abstruse precincts of the very rich, it is as an individual drama—with its dizzying swings between grief and joy, weakness and strength, selfishness and heroism—that her story makes the greatest claim for examination.

# 1

# A FORTUNE SHIFTS

*O*n the damp, chill day of Aristotle Onassis's funeral in March of 1975, the sea around his island of Skorpios was choppy and dark. Most of the mourners who had flown in from the world's capitals had seen this stretch of water only in the summer, when it was of a sun-charged blueness none but the very rich could afford. On this day it was gray and agitated with whitecaps, a meteorological sign that nothing would be as before, everything would be different.

In the past twenty-three months, Christina Onassis had lost her mother, her brother, and now her father. Before adjusting to one unexpected death, she was slammed with another. She was the last of a family that, for all its social prowess, had been isolated by its wealth and the magnetic force of its central figure, the fortune's creator, who was now being buried. At the age of twenty-four, she felt very, very alone.

So many thoughts crowded her mind she paid little attention to the intimacy forced on her by protocol with the stepmother she detested. On other occasions when she had been compelled to appear with the woman whom she had called "my father's unfortunate obsession," she could think of nothing but her revulsion. Today it was just one of many jarring affronts. As the two women came off the Olympic 727 from Paris at the Greek military airport at Aktion to waiting crowds of photographers and reporters, Jacqueline Onassis, in a black leather trench coat and a black Valentino dress ordered in anticipation of her husband's death, took Christina's arm and walked, as though they were two sisters on a holiday, across the tarmac to the limousine that would follow the hearse to the launch dock at Nidri.

A month of sitting by her father's bed watching him die had taken a physical as well as psychological toll on Christina; she was as thin as she had been for years, and an expression of stunned grief was fixed on her face. Yet the absence of makeup softened and enhanced her large dark eyes and strong Mediterranean features, as did her straight black hair, which she had not thought to have dressed. For once, she was, if not a match for, at least in the same species with the sleek woman at her side, this mannequin-thin style-setter who always made her feel so gauche, so unfeminine, so coarse, so *fat*— and who now clutched her arm reassuringly.

Was this affectionate gesture intended to expunge the ill will between them, the mutual dislike that Jackie refused to acknowledge except in rare private outbursts? Was it a demonstration of family solidarity, a denial of hostility for the benefit of the world press? This woman, for years the wife of an Irish politician, was versed in subtle public signals intended to mislead. Christina was not. She was a Greek.

But she paid little attention to this latest offense from the woman whose invasion of her family had, she was convinced, never been anything but a business venture and who had made her father's last years a public humiliation and a private torment. Christina would not know until some days later when she saw press photos of the funeral that, as they walked from the plane, Jackie had flashed photographers smiles of an almost demented inappropriateness. She might just as well have clasped her hands over her head like a title-winning prize fighter.

A seaplane or helicopter usually ferried Christina from the airport to Skorpios; only for funerals did she make the journey by car, but it was becoming hauntingly familiar. She had made it two years earlier when she followed the casket of her much-loved brother, Alexander, whose grave on Skorpios was alongside the one that had been readied for her father. After years as wary strangers, Christina and her

brother had been brought close by their father's relentless machinations. She had found in him a very special ally, had come to love
him, only to have him snatched from her abruptly when he was
twenty-four. Older than Christina and male, he rather than she
would have been burdened with the responsibility for the vast Onassis empire. Her mother, too, had died mysteriously only five months
earlier: the lovely Tina—so delicate, so refined, everything Christina
was not—whose divorce from her father fifteen years earlier Christina had never been able to accept as anything more than a temporary interruption of an idealized family life that had never been.

Now it struck Christina, she would later tell friends, that each of
them—her mother, her brother, and herself—had done the same
bizarre thing. They had each chosen the partners most calculated to
infuriate the man who she was convinced they loved more than
anyone else in the world. Alexander had been deeply involved with
the Baroness Fiona Thyssen, a woman who was anathema to Onassis
because she was worldly, non-Greek, and sixteen years older than his
teen-aged son. As the former wife of one of the world's richest men,
Fiona was vulnerable to the suspicion of money lust, a suspicion
Aristotle Onassis held, to varying degrees, about anyone who showed
interest in his children.

Christina's choice had been an even greater outrage: Joseph
Bolker, a Los Angeles real-estate man who was not rich enough by
Onassis standards, twenty-nine years older than she, and, worst of
all because of Onassis's extensive dealings with the Saudi Arabians,
a Jew. But the most telling affront was Tina's. She had married the
one person Onassis most hated in the world: his long-time rival,
Stavros Niarchos, a man he suspected of murdering his son and his
sister-in-law, and of providing the U.S. Justice Department with the
information that brought about his 1954 indictment for illegally owning American surplus vessels.

There they all were, feverishly bedding down whoever would most
outrage Aristotle Onassis. Had the course of each of their lives been
dictated either by Onassis's wishes or their clumsy attempts to flout
them? Had they been allowed no wants or desires of their own, desires free of his influence or omnipotent will? Now Christina alone
survived, but would she be free to take her own course or would she
continue to veer according to his magnetic field? Christina had

longed to put an end to their lethal family games, to prove that she had loved him the most and would do whatever he wished. But he had died and, feeling more than ever that she was merely an extension of his will, she had wanted to die with him.

But she had never been very good at killing herself; her death impulses came over her without warning—four years ago in Los Angeles, when she realized how furious her marriage had made her father, then in London only a year earlier when Peter Goulandris had broken off their relationship. These attempts were not the culmination of weeks of mounting despondency, but rather sudden fits of Greek passion and despair—hysterical impulses that were just as quickly countermanded by a stronger wish to live.

Christina's snarled thoughts, only partially dulled by the two Seconals she had taken before leaving Paris, were abruptly penetrated by the high, nasal voice of Senator Ted Kennedy, the only other passenger seated with her and Jackie in the limousine that led the cortège from Aktion to Nidri. Steeled as she was to a day of pain and inconsequential horrors, she was stunned out of her torpor and resignation by the brutal insensitivity of Kennedy's words.

"Listen, Christina," the senator said with the nonchalant voice of one experienced in public rituals, who knows they are staged for others and not taken too seriously by the participants, "since we may not have much time alone, I think we should talk about Jackie's future."

With memories hammering her brain of tangled and unresolved family loves and battles, of the important things unsaid to the man just dead, Christina was shocked at the assault on her consciousness by this gross and unfeeling attempt to discuss Jackie's finances. Could this woman or her functionaries not give her obsession for money a rest for the few hours of the funeral? Couldn't she pretend for just this brief period of orchestrated grief that there had also been some feeling or respect?

"Stop the car!" Christina yelled at the astonished driver. The hundreds of onlookers who lined the road from Aktion to Nidri and the mourners from the windows of the other cars, now stopped, stared dumfounded, as the door of the lead car opened and Christina jumped out. Everyone knew this limousine contained Onassis's world-famous widow. Pushing away tears of rage and leaving the door for Senator Kennedy to pull shut, Christina walked to the second limousine, that of her aunts, Artemis and Merope. Once she was in their car and with the door closed, the cortège proceeded.

Although Christina later related the events of that day to close friends, she remembered little about the crossing to Skorpios in a launch or about the burial itself. She was aware of rows of white lilies in wicker baskets, of crying servants, of her stepbrother John Kennedy, an embarrassed teenager standing awkwardly at his mother's side, and of Caroline Kennedy looking as though she would have preferred to be anywhere else in the world. The grave site was circled by grim-faced old men Christina had known all her life: Greek men who had come up from nothing with her father, men who knew every one of her childhood pranks and blunders, who had laughed and joked with her father about them—and who would now have to call her master.

When the ceremony ended and the crowd was milling aimlessly, waiting for a prompting sign from Christina, she told her father's closest aide, Costa Gratsos, that she wanted the island's staff and the ship's crew to assemble on the deck of the *Christina*, where she would speak to them. As word passed around quickly, the relatives and friends, most of whom would have followed her into the frigid sea at that moment, assumed they were also wanted and moved silently and somewhat shyly toward the yacht. Their role as principals suddenly ended, the Kennedy contingent trailed along, not knowing what bizarre Greek ritual was still to come.

Sleek and of an even more dazzling whiteness in the gloomy day, the *Christina* sat serenely in the deep-water harbor that Onassis had dredged to berth her. This incredible vessel, a 325-foot seagoing estate, had once enthralled the world with its size and opulence. On it, Onassis had entertained the most famous people of his day—Winston Churchill, Greta Garbo, Grace Kelly—and courted Maria llas and Jacqueline Kennedy. Throughout these glittering years, Christina had lurked in the background, a plain little girl with a Levantine nose and dark-circled eyes, a sour reminder of human imperfection at a jamboree of gilded immortals. As she grew, she began viewing with sullen detachment the antics of the mighty who held her parents' attention; she became an unimpressed and disdainful observer, a teen-aged Rosenkrantz or Guildenstern, monitoring the grandiose doings at Elsinore.

Now, with the magus who had willed the yacht into being lying dead nearby, the ship seemed outsize, ostentatious, absurd. On the aft deck, Christina stopped and the mourners crowded around her. She began to speak, but realizing that many of the large crowd packed into the space could not see her, she started to climb by way of a banquette onto a large table. A flutter of arms shot out to steady her, but with a flat-of-the-hand gesture of dismissal, she mounted the table unaided.

She knew that everyone expected to hear a daughter's homage to the father who had affected all their lives, a tribute to the man who had seized the world's attention with his brilliant rise from poverty to the pinnacle of a great fortune, his one-man battles against vindictive corporations and jealous governments, his intimacy with great artists and world leaders. They expected her to pass quickly over these well-known qualities and stress instead his Greekness, his big-heartedness, his sense of fun—the human attributes so often overshadowed by his reputation for publicity coups and business cunning.

Christina said something quite different and, because she said it in Greek, few of the fashionable guests realized that she made no mention of the man they had come great distances to honor. Speaking in a coarse voice that did not have to strain to be loud, she said, "This island, this boat, everything you see. It is all mine. You are all my people now."

Thirteen years later, a hearse rushed Christina's body through the streets of Buenos Aires to the Ezeiza airport, the start of her own final journey to Greece. A dozen motorcycle police cleared the way down the broad avenues that, in a procedure usually reserved for heads of state, had been closed off to traffic. The angry horns of blocked cars echoed throughout the city and mingled with the police sirens to create a pandemic cacophony of the kind that usually marks a historic event—the end of a war, the birth of a sovereign.

In Athens several hundred mourners crowded into St. Fontini Cathedral, while five thousand people filled the surrounding streets. As the funeral procession left Athens and headed toward Nidri, farmers and peasants lined the road in silent acknowledgment of her death. At the dock where the launch waited to carry her remains to Skorpios, police struggled to restrain black-clad local women, who wailed loudly, threw flowers, and tried to touch the coffin. Over a hundred fishing boats and pleasure craft followed Christina's funeral launch to her island, an impromptu nautical escort of respect and grief, whose down-throttled motors filled the air with a low, monotone moan.

Newspapers around the world ran lengthy accounts of Christina's death, most of them on front pages. Television news shows quickly assembled picture histories of her life, and for the next few weeks, newspapers and magazines published provocative stories about the circumstances of her death, the disposition of her fortune, and the future of her only child, the three-year-old Athina. What had Christina Onassis done to deserve such universal grief, such world-wide attention? She was very rich, she ran companies, and the foundation she headed gave away millions each year. But others with similar histories died each year with scant notice. What was there about Christina Onassis that touched and moved so many people?

Was it merely that she was so rich and so young that made her death so affecting to millions who had never known her? If those two attributes, when combined, hold out the promise of great happiness, did that make her death a poignant reminder of the baleful reality that lay behind a favorite fantasy? Or did the public, knowing only of her troubled marriages and suicide attempts, conceive of her as a lovable human shambles in the Judy Garland vein, an epic sufferer who, in the big romantic sweepstakes, was born to lose? Was it that her generosity and big-heartedness were recognized in spite of her lackluster record of philanthropy? Or was it simply that the frequent press coverage of the events of her life had turned her into a figure that the media had persuaded the public it knew and cared about, and that her loss was the loss of, if not a friend, at least a well-liked acquaintance? Perhaps the public accepted her death at thirty-seven as confirmation of comforting beliefs about the inevitability of grief for the very rich.

All of these elements probably applied to the public perception of Christina Onassis. And they applied as well to the perception of her held by those close to her. As her friends, lovers, relatives, and business associates stared grief-stricken at the closed ebony-and-silver casket, surrounded by mounds of white daisies, a cross of pink roses on top, many of them surely reflected on their own dramas with

Christina, most of which involved money, either directly or as an unarticulated subtext.

Throughout her life, the abstract concept of big money surrounded Christina like an aura, an invisible force field that affected all who ventured within it. The emanating rays made those who came near her, she well knew, act in different ways. It altered aims, needs, and scruples. It dominated opinions of Christina, overruling whatever else might have been thought about her—whether favorable or unfavorable—and changed her from a person into an emblem, an embodiment of what almost all of them most wanted, a minor god of a savage religion. When she proved to be mortal like everyone else, it was momentarily jarring to their theological fantasies. They would have played her hand differently, they reassured themselves, and continued to believe.

Christina was entombed in a white marble sarcophagus in the small chapel on Skorpios built by Onassis for the remains of his son Alexander. Greek Orthodox tradition forbids burial inside a church for any but saints, which was a claim no one, not even his father, ever made for Alexander. Paying lip service to this rule, Onassis had had his beloved son buried just outside the chapel. Then, in a typical Onassian combination of loophole-seeking deviousness and God-cheating arrogance, he had extended the chapel to incorporate Alexander's grave. Even in his deepest grief and up against divine law, Onassis had pulled off a slick deal.

Once Alexander had established a beachhead inside the church, Christina had not hesitated to place her father's body alongside her brother's, which was consistent with Onassis's lifelong habit of penetrating forbidden enclaves. Now, she too was laid to rest in this privileged, sacrosanct space. After a tearful Thierry Roussel read a eulogy to his former wife and the mother of one of his three children, the priests sprinkled a few drops of oil on the coffin to symbolize Christina's attainment of eternal rest.

The Onassis sunburst was over. Christina was the last to have the name, which had lodged in the public's consciousness ever since the early 1950s, when her father bought control of Monte Carlo, thereby achieving international prominence as a tycoon of flamboyance and grandiosity. He continued to hold the public's attention with his ever more lavish style of living, with his affair with Maria Callas and his marriage to Jacqueline Kennedy.

Christina fell heir to both his money and the public curiosity he had connived to maintain. For a brief thirteen years, she had presided over the billion-dollar fortune, half of it in trust to the philanthropic foundation she headed, half of it hers to spend as she liked. Because she was a young woman, little attention was paid to her successful administration of a vast shipping empire and her shrewd management of her wealth, but considerable notice was given to her failed marriages, her abortive love affairs, her excess weight, her bouts with depression, her suicide attempts.

With the few glimpses she allowed of her opulent manner of living, the public was in part disgusted, in part enthralled. Her energy, her dauntless enthusiasm, and her unapologetic self-indulgences added new dimensions to the Aladdin-like wish fantasies of limitless wealth. As the public requires with its favorites among the rich, she contributed substantially and colorfully to the hefty file of evidence on the near impossibility for those of great wealth, particularly women, to achieve happiness.

Like so many of her sister heiresses, Christina saw her wealth as an enhancement of her feminine allure. She did not realize that to most male egos her money was a circle of fire through which only the most highly—and impurely—motivated would pass and risk the searing and unmanning heat. Unaware that the psychic odds were insurmountable, she gamely sought to overcome them. And in that effort she also had to contend with the psychological impairments of her tempestuous and love-starved childhood, and with the many self-destructive personality traits that resulted—impulsiveness, impatience, rapaciousness.

She put up a good fight. She had much grief, but she also had many moments of exhilarating happiness, rollicking adventures, and fun of a privileged headiness experienced by few. And finally she had a brief, but life-changing, taste of a profound joy available to most men and women, the birth of a child, who quickly and effortlessly replaced Christina as the center of her own universe. But her salvation arrived too late. She almost made it, but in the end she lost the fight.

# 2

# THE MAKING OF A BILLIONAIRE

$C$hristina was two years old when her father, already one of the world's leading independent tanker owners, bought controlling interest in La Société des Bains de Mer, the company that owned the Casino of Monte Carlo and most of the principality's main resort facilities, including the world-famous Hôtel de Paris. He was, in effect, the owner of Monaco. In the same year, he held his daughter in his arms before a crowd of thousands at a Hamburg shipyard so she could release the bottle of champagne to christen his newest ship, the *Tina Onassis*, not only the largest oil tanker ever built, but the largest cargo ship as well.

When she was three, Onassis took her to another German shipyard and pointed to the 325-foot yacht he had refurbished into the world's most luxurious private vessel. He told her that he had named the glistening ship after her and that from then on it would be her principal home. Also during that year, 1953, his whaling fleet, a highly lucrative sideline from his tanker business, was accused of whaling illegally within Peruvian waters and was impounded, thus putting Onassis virtually at war with Peru.

Toward the end of the same year, he announced an agreement with Saudi Arabia to transport the oil that the Saudis would, under the agreement, produce on their own, pulling the rug out from under the foreign companies then producing the oil. It was a business coup of unimaginable proportions, one with profound international implications, and an intolerable body blow to Aramco, the immensely powerful consortium of American oil companies that until then had controlled Saudi Arabian oil production and shipment.

Onassis's plan, which came to be known as the Jiddah Agreement, would enable the Saudis to expel the Americans from their rich Arabian oil fiefdom. The threat of completing this deal put Onassis at war with the United States, almost as much as with Peru. He had already accomplished the most difficult step, winning the agreement of King Ibn Saud. If he could withstand the forces aligned to stop him and push the accord to a reality, it would make him far and away the richest, most powerful private individual in the world. These were the great years of Aristotle Onassis, the years when, after two decades of struggle to become a major international financial power, he had arrived—and was out to let the world know, not only of his arrival, but of his determination to proceed to even greater heights.

Aristotle Onassis loved his two children. He lavished on them every conceivable luxury, plus some luxuries, like the clothes made for Christina's dolls by Christian Dior, that were of an extravagance inconceivable to many. He ensconced his family in palaces on the sea, a penthouse in Paris, a town house in New York, and finally his ocean-going yacht of stupefying luxury. For their recreation and education, he hired governesses, tutors, sports instructors, playmates. What he could not give them—nor did he feel it necessary considering all he was lavishing upon them—was his time and attention.

It was not simply that he was single-handedly running a number of very complicated enterprises and that he would often work until four in the morning, sleep two or three hours, then return to work. The problem was one of priorities. He was now rich enough to do whatever he pleased, and for a man of his imagination and audacity it was an intoxicating prospect. While still in his forties, he had arrived atop an astonishing pinnacle of wealth. He knew he had the vision and daring to do something memorable with this financial muscle, not just hoard his winnings and live like those with inherited money whom he despised, but spend lavishly, live lavishly—and, to him the highest form of recreation, earn even more lavishly. He loved his hard-won position and knew he could make of it something few others could. Every minute was precious for fashioning deals, furthering social contacts that might be converted into business ones, learning about developments in the world that might open opportunities for more fortunes.

All those who came into contact with Onassis, but especially his children, found him exciting, stimulating, and, above all, great fun. No matter whom he was dealing with at any particular moment— world leaders, secretaries, barbers, his children—they were treated to his outgoing personality, lively curiosity, and unpredictable humor. The guaranteed delight of his appearances only made Christina and Alexander's sense of deprivation at his many absences keener and more painful. Although he would frequently shoot off for a day or two in New York, Buenos Aires, or Tokyo, the separations were not necessarily geographical; the children could be aboard the *Christina* with him and not see him for days as he kept himself closeted in his front-bridge office only to emerge to dine in state with his celebrated guests at adults-only dinner parties.

Onassis was not the kind of parent who makes brutal, psyche-bashing mistakes and thereby traumatizes and alienates his children. To be sure, he wreaked psychic damage on both Alexander and Christina, but not for the usual reasons of insufficient love or unresolved battles that molder into permanent resentments. When they were infants he smothered them with love, and they adored him. When he was around, things were exciting and alive. When he was not around—and that was most of the time—life collapsed into dull routines administered by indifferent servants.

As children, they were puzzled that, although he seemed to love them as a father should and enjoyed being with them, yet he chose not to be with them much of the time. They began to see the absences as somehow their fault. Not surprisingly, the first symptoms of psychological trouble in both Alexander and Christina were classic attention-getting ploys: Alexander's dangerous recklessness and Christina's mutism, her decision at age three to stop talking.

Yet for people of any age, winning the attention of Aristotle Onassis was not easy. He was too enthralled with his own swashbuckling saga, which began with selling neckties on the streets of Buenos

Aires and which was approaching a world-rocking climax just as his children were emerging into awareness of their own identities. He had unlocked secrets of the economic universe and was in the midst of exploiting his arcane knowledge. Christina and Alexander came along at the peak of the heady dénouement of his rare success. They found, to their dismay, that they had been born into a Radio City Musical Hall extravaganza, a Greek tycoon follies with opulent sets and a cast of thousands, the principals and supporting players world famous, the rest employees. For him, having children was fine and good, a graceful embellishment to his achievements, but nothing especially rare. His success, on the other hand, was extremely rare. Much as he loved his children, he saw them as appropriate milestones in his manly progress, but as for their place in the sweep of his saga, they were, like their mother, mere ornaments to it, not major figures.

Like so many others whose early life becomes a matter of interest to the world at large, Aristotle Onassis was given to dramatizing and embellishing his history. His tallest tales tended to cast doubt on the true ones, which were dramatic enough. Most of those people in a position to challenge the truth of his account of the early days in Turkey, Greece, and Argentina were fierce loyalists—his sisters, his cousins who had followed him to Argentina and ended up working for him, his close friend and right-hand man, Costa Gratsos; they might have smiled at the embroideries but would never have contradicted them. Fortunately, there were a few others less loyal who knew him in the early days and who have tempered his version and filled in some, but not all, of the omitted pieces.

Another who could, and did, debunk his most self-aggrandizing stories was Onassis himself. Late in the evening at a nightclub after many drinks, he would admit to a reporter various exaggerations in the legend and quash apocryphal episodes that had long stood undenied. For instance, as a young man in Argentina, he would confess, he never had a string of call girls that featured Evita Perón as its star. Sometimes his motive for this sort of breast-cleaning admission was to plant the story for the first time—denials of sensational rumors often being, for reporters, gasoline on smoking gossip—but

other times he was motivated by an attack of boredom with the lies
that he may have initiated but that now stuck to him like a bad
haircut. More often than not, there was some calculation or other
behind the additions and corrections to whatever tale he was emend-
ing. Onassis had a fine-tuned sense of his audience that enabled him,
almost on contact, to determine what they wanted him to be, and
then to become it.

He did not begin his life in poverty. His father, Socrates Onassis,
was a prosperous Greek tobacco merchant operating in the coastal
Turkish city that was, at the time of Onassis's birth in 1900, called
Smyrna. When his mother, Penelope, died in 1912, his father remar-
ried and had two more daughters, Calliroe and Merope. These two
women, along with Aristotle's sister, Artemis, born two years before
him, would be Christina's aunts and the Onassis relatives with whom
she remained very close throughout her life. The girls of the family
were obedient and carefully brought up. Aristotle was a good ath-
lete but a bad student; an unruly nature got him expelled from a
number of the area's private schools, causing mounting friction between him and his father. He eventually dropped out of high school
altogether.

For most of Aristotle's youth, the family prospered in a period of
political stability. As a result of the Treaty of Versailles in 1919, the
region around Smyrna had been annexed by the Greeks, enhancing
life for the Onassis family and the other Greek residents. But Socrates had always tried to maintain an aloofness from politics and combative nationalism so that, regardless of which flag flew over the city,
he could operate his business undisturbed. The strategy worked well
for many years, but failed to protect him when, in 1922, the Turks
reoccupied Smyrna. Socrates Onassis was imprisoned on trumped-
up charges of anti-Turk activities, and the rest of the family—Aristotle's sister, Artemis; his two half-sisters; and his stepmother Elena
—managed to escape to Greece. Aristotle stayed behind to work for
his father's release.

The large Onassis home was requisitioned by the occupying Turkish general, whose adjutant, a young lieutenant, took a fancy to
Aristotle and kept him on as his batman and, shortly, his lover.
Although young Aristotle had some years before established his credentials as an enthusiastic heterosexual in the red-light district of

Smyrna, the relationship, by Onassis's own account, was not one of mere expedience but a mutually satisfying friendship.

Because of frequent visits to his father, the prison authorities decided young Onassis was plotting mischief, which of course he was, and were about to arrest him. With the aid of the American consul, Aristotle escaped from Smyrna and joined his stepmother and sisters in Greece.

He continued to work for his father's release. At the age of twenty-three, Onassis journeyed to Constantinople, where his father had friends and business contacts. They advised him whom to bribe to obtain his father's release. His risky efforts succeeded after he handed over a large amount of cash to a complaisant Minister of Prisons. But his father, when reunited with his family, was outraged that his son had squandered a large portion of the family's remaining capital, arguing that he had been acquitted of the charges and would have been released in any case.

Whatever the rights and wrongs of Aristotle's ransom payment, he was overwhelmed by a sense of ingratitude and injustice. He felt he had risked his life to save his father's. Everyone in the family should be aware, he said, that the danger from the Turks was real; his father's brother, his much-loved Uncle Alexander, had been executed by them. For his father to quibble over the $25,000 spent to save him from a similar end, when they were all now safe together in Greece and by no means destitute, was for Aristotle the culmination of years of unfair disapproval from his father. No matter what he did—even, it now appeared, saving his life—it brought only one reaction: scornful censure. Thoroughly embittered, he asked for $250 of the remaining money and set out for the country Greeks then saw as the land of opportunity, Argentina.

Alone in South America, Onassis's only asset was an aptitude for languages and his nationality, which provided an instant support network. Local Greeks congregated around favored cafés and restaurants, offering new arrivals advice on getting settled and, most important, tips about jobs. Through that ad hoc employment service, Onassis found himself a job going through the streets of Buenos Aires pushing a wheelbarrow filled with sand, from which children, for a price, could rummage for gifts. After another stint selling neckties, he got a well-paying job with the telephone company as a switchboard operator. Because of his linguistic prowess—he now spoke Greek, Turkish, Spanish, and passable English and French—he specialized in international calls. He didn't yet know how he would achieve it, but he was determined to be rich.

When he had saved a few hundred dollars, Onassis began making investments based on overheard phone conversations between businessmen, and scored a number of modest killings. Trying to look richer than he was, he invested his profits in appearances—new suits, visits to fashionable night spots, a club membership—and launched a lifelong habit of putting himself in the path of the rich and powerful.

Playing on a hunch about the vogue for the Mideast spawned by Rudolph Valentino's *The Sheik*, he decided to become an importer of mild Turkish tobacco, using his father as a supplier. When he couldn't persuade any cigarette manufacturers to buy his product, he decided to invest all of his modest savings in manufacturing his own. With only a few employees, he produced a high-priced cigarette with a sales pitch—milder tobacco and a sexy Arabian-nights aura—that he was convinced would induce Argentinean women to break with tradition and smoke in public, a change he believed with equally strong conviction was historically imminent. If he could bring about such a major revolution in local mores, he would open for himself a huge market for his product.

He worked frantically, quickly going through his savings and borrowing more. Sharp setbacks in a highly competitive and bare-fisted business brought Onassis's unscrupulous side quickly to the fore. He marketed a cigarette under the name Bis, which also happened to be the name of one of the city's most popular brands. In addition, he injected bales of other competitors' tobacco with a chemical that gave it a sickening stench when burned. With much hard work and occasional dirty tricks, his company eventually did well enough for him to quit his telephone-company job. In his mid-twenties, he was at last, if only on a modest scale, a full-fledged capitalist. Except during his foray into the whaling business many years later, he would play pretty much by the rules for the rest of his career. He was indefatigable and ingenious in finding legal ways to circumvent the rules, but when this proved impossible, he lived with them.

Throughout the career of Aristotle Onassis, his involvements with judiciously selected women played a major part in his rise and, later, his expanding glory. With many men who use their amatory prowess for some end other than the one in sight, romance and love-making are thought to be givens of little intrinsic significance, but facets of their makeup that can be enlisted in the pursuit of other, more important interests. With Onassis it was just the opposite. For him, it was so easy to become smitten with a broad range of women, and to fan momentary enthusiasms into grand passions, that he learned at an early age to harness this rampant predilection to his quest for greater goals. He hated diverting time from pursuing his ambitions; with the right romance, he didn't have to.

For the millions who knew Aristotle Onassis only through the press coverage of the last twenty years of his life, it was difficult to think of him as a formidable Romeo. The tired, gross features that peered from magazines and newspapers spoke of hangdog decadence and bloodlines that reached deep into the seamy sooks of Asia Minor. In fact, Onassis, as a young man, was quite good looking. He was short but muscularly built, and his face, while not handsome by conventional standards, had a full-blooded sensuality and smoldering intensity. His features, which he would pass along to Christina, were dominated by a large nose, but also by large, lash-ringed eyes that were striking and soulful. As with many people who in their youth possess strong, dramatic features, the positive aspects of his looks, with age, eroded into negative ones. The nose became more prominent and the seductive eyes of his youth disintegrated in Dorian-Gray fashion into the heavy, lascivious glower of a dissipated old man.

Whatever assets the face of the young Onassis possessed, its frequent broad smiles and bursts of laughter went far to overcome its deficiencies. He was also extremely self-confident and, when the occasion demanded, audacious. He had another quality not frequently found in men who amass great fortunes: charm. He was gregarious, tended to like other people, and was imaginative in ingratiating himself. All of these attributes combined to make him a formidable ladies' man.

His first significant affair was with an opera star, Claudia Muzio. This now seems highly ironic, given his unshakable antipathy to opera and his world-famous liaison thirty years later with Maria Callas. While he may not have liked the music, he responded deeply to the hard work and courage it so obviously required to sing it. When he first saw Claudia Muzio perform, she was young and attractive; she was also an important international star and the toast of Buenos Aires. Onassis, who was a fledgling businessman on the brink of an early ruin, won a meeting through a heavy investment in roses, and shortly thereafter won Muzio herself.

Muzio's beauty and panache might have been sufficient to fire Onassis's ardor, but her success and fame were strong additional attractions. He soon put them to use. He asked then pleaded with Muzio to light a cigarette conspicuously in Buenos Aires's leading nightclub. She agreed and the resulting sensation had the desired effect on the habits of the city's women. The spurt in the sales of Onassis's cigarettes gave him a considerable boost in his climb to wealth. The popularity of his exotic cigarettes was only temporary, however, and losses forced him eventually to close down his manufacturing operation. Happily, the tobacco-importing side of his business flourished through the many contacts he had made trying to launch his manufacturing operation, and by the mid-1930s Onassis had acquired his first million.

As his fortunes rose, Onassis became increasingly fascinated by the shipping business. It was a Greek specialty, to be sure, but not just any Greeks could jump in. A handful of dynasties had long dominated the field—Kulukundis, Goulandris, Livanos—families not known for lavishing welcoming warmth on those who aspired to their ranks, regardless of nationality. But Onassis was determined. In his importing business, he was dismayed to see how much of his profits went to the shippers. If business was bad, they still got paid—and in relation to the capital they had invested, the profits were enormous.

It was no coincidence that the two most important friendships Onassis formed in these years were with individuals who had ties to the shipping world. His closest male friend, the young Greek Costa Gratsos, who, like himself, had come to Argentina in quest of his fortune, had shipowning relatives in Greece. Onassis bombarded Gratsos with questions about the business. The answers were aimed at discouraging Onassis from his wild ambition. As a client of shippers, Onassis saw only the large shipping fees, Gratsos admonished him; he did not see the problems: the costly days and weeks when no cargo could be found, the endless maintenance expenses, the hefty insurance premiums, which didn't begin to cover all the risks.

With each new discouraging fact, Onassis's enthusiasm grew. What were these dangers in a business where you could, if all went normally, earn back your capital investment in two or three years? While it did not take Onassis long to learn everything Gratsos had to teach about shipping, Gratsos remained a close friend throughout Onassis's life, perhaps his closest, providing a prime example of his loyal affection for those who were most useful to him. At all times, Gratsos was the Onassis empire's number-two man, until, after Onassis's death in 1975, he and Christina had an irreconcilable falling-out.

The other advantageous friendship Onassis formed at this time was with a wealthy Norwegian, Ingeborg Dedichen, whom he met on a Europe-bound ship when he was returning for his father's funeral in 1934. She was beautiful, worldly, and aristocratic; her father, Ingevald Bryde, was one of the most prominent shipowners in Norway, a country that then dominated shipping even more than the Greeks, and among the group with whom Ingeborg was traveling were some of the top men in Scandinavian shipping.

With whatever mixture of motives, Onassis fell resoundingly in love with Dedichen, and she with him. They became lovers and would have married except that Dedichen was still legally married during the early period of their relationship, when Onassis's passion might have overruled his single-minded ambition. But Dedichen remained an emotional anchor in his life for many years, and as long as she lived, Onassis supported her financially, leaving no doubt of the sincerity of his feelings for her. Still, at the time they became involved, Dedichen was a well-connected insider in the closed shipping world to which Onassis strongly aspired.

Also during the year 1934 Onassis met a man who made a substantial and ongoing contribution to his success, although in a highly perverse way, and whose life would remain intricately involved with Onassis's and that of his daughter. Stavros Niarchos was a Greek, two years younger than Onassis, from a well-to-do Athens merchant family. Like Onassis, he had no shipping connections but saw ships as the means to the great wealth he hungered for. At first, but only briefly, Onassis and Niarchos were friends, as they both sought to gain footholds in the shipping business. That accomplished, they would become competitors and, finally, bitter enemies in a rivalry that at times turned quite sinister. It is doubtful if any two heterosexual men have ever had such a dominating influence on each other's lives, and their feud would profoundly touch every member of both families.

Stopping off in London after his trip to Greece for his father's funeral, Onassis put the word out among his contacts that he was in the market to buy ships. During those Depression years, buyers of any sort were in short supply, and word moved quickly. He learned that a Canadian company was selling ten freighters at the distressed price of $30,000 apiece. In the company of a marine engineer he had hired, Onassis journeyed to Canada to see the ships. After examining every bulkhead, pipe, and valve over a period of some ten days, he went to banks to obtain loans to buy the ships. Because of his inexperience in shipping and the business's unpredictability, he was turned down. Using his own money, he offered to buy six of the vessels at $20,000 apiece. Begrudgingly, his low offer was accepted.

Although he was now in the shipping business, the tobacco-importing operation would remain the main source of his wealth for several more years. To run his Buenos Aires business during his absences, he had hired two first cousins from Smyrna, Costa and Nicos Konialidis. These young men—sons of his father's sister, Maria—had followed him to South America in the hopes of finding similar good fortune. The Konialidis brothers would remain closely involved with Onassis throughout his life; Nicos would eventually marry Onassis's half-sister, Merope, and in the 1960s and '70s each brother would have a turn running Olympic Airlines, which had been founded and was owned outright by Onassis. After Onassis's death, Nicos Konialidis, angered at not receiving a large bequest, threatened to contest Onassis's will, inducing Christina to pay him a substantial amount to withdraw his claim.

Even though Onassis was new to the shipping business, he soon began to display the imaginative deftness in overcoming obstacles at which he excelled and which contributed greatly to his astounding rise. In London, Onassis received a call from the Greek consul in Rotterdam, informing him that an Onassis freighter recently arrived there was being impounded. A cook had fallen ill and had been taken to the hospital. Because the ship was under Greek registry, the cook had to be replaced with a Greek national, no one else, and could not depart until one was found. Onassis rushed to Rotterdam and pleaded with the consul. He was on a tight schedule. Cargo was due immediately in Copenhagen. Since there were no airline connections, it could take a week to bring a cook from Greece. He would fill the job himself. Could the consul not allow the ship to proceed to Copenhagen, a half-day's voyage, to unload the rest of its cargo? No, the consul was adamant.

The next day Onassis, brimming with good will, invited the consul to visit him aboard the ship to see that the problem was solved. Once he was aboard, Onassis offered the man a glass of champagne and told him he was now a guest on a Panamanian ship. Overnight Onassis had managed to change the registration and was no longer under Greek jurisdiction. While others had flirted with the idea of flags of convenience, soon to be a shipping commonplace, Onassis was the first to use them in a major way, and the first to use the ploy so suddenly in order to wriggle out of a tight spot.

Another Onassis innovation, one entirely his, permanently changed the ways ships could be financed. While a somewhat technical breakthrough, it was perhaps more responsible for Onassis's rise to enormous wealth than any of his more flamboyant schemes. When in the 1950s Onassis was prompted by shipping conditions to expand his fleet by ordering construction of his own ships, financing was extremely difficult for him to obtain, as it was for all shipowners. Banks and other financial institutions knew, from sorry experience, the unpredictability of the shipping business.

Onassis argued that he was not, like some shipowners, reduced to picking up spot cargoes here and there, but had a long-term contract with the Sun Oil Company for transporting their oil. Well and good, responded the financiers, but what if a ship breaks down, has a spill, or experiences any of many other unforeseen eventualities that would place it "offhire," a shipping term for a period during which the charterer does not have to pay? With the ships earning nothing, the owner would probably default on loan payments.

Onassis, knowing this was technically true, understood the money men's fears. He also knew, however, that the chances of prolonged offhire were minimal and that his insurance covered offhires of over three months. Instead of wasting his energy on further pleading with the banks, he went to the oil company and made an offer. If Sunoco would guarantee in its contracts to continue paying throughout any offhire period that might occur, he would make the time up at the end of the contract *and* give Sunoco a comparable amount of time gratis. In other words, a month of paid offhire during the contract period would get the company two free months at the end. Sunoco quickly agreed.

What made the ploy so ingenious was the manner in which it satisfied all three parties. The banks were delighted; the contracts from a most solid business, an oil company, guaranteed income for their loan payments no matter what befell the ship. The executives of Sunoco, who, like Onassis but unlike the banks, knew the chances of offhire were slim, now stood to gain, should one occur.

Onassis knew that he could now obtain unlimited financing for however many ships he wanted to build, provided he had shipping contracts. But for him the sweetest aspect of all was that the ships usually paid for themselves within a few years, then continued to make large amounts of money for twenty or thirty more years. Since most of his contracts were of three to five years' duration, his plan risked no more than a possible two or three free months *after* the ship had paid for itself. And these were free months taken from *decades* of enormous profits. It was a modest concession, to be sure, but one nobody had thought of before and one that released many millions of loan dollars to Onassis and other shippers for the construction of ships.

If a single talent stood out from the others in contributing to Onassis's meteoric rise to the highest echelons of international finance, it was, as it has been for many businessmen, his ability to foresee trends and to act upon them. In 1937 when he ordered his first tanker to be built in Sweden, it was by no means clear that oil would take supremacy over coal as the world's principal fuel. Nor did many agree with his belief that one gigantic ship was a better potential moneymaker than two smaller ones. By ordering the construction of the fifteen-thousand-ton *Ariston*, Onassis was betting on both hunches. He also dazzled onlookers by ordering that his new tanker be fitted with such unheard-of amenities as a swimming pool and two luxurious owner's suites. Such flourishes, which proportionally added little to the overall construction cost, became a hallmark of his style, but were greeted with glum headshakes by established Greek shipping tycoons. When Onassis's new ship was launched in 1938, he took his sisters and some friends on a leisurely cruise from Sweden to San Francisco. He now had seven ships, and this last one, the most costly, paid for itself within a year.

When World War II broke out, a number of Onassis's ships were impounded in Scandinavia and he took sizable losses. Since his operations were so geographically diffuse, as they would remain, there was no place that required his presence more than another. In normal times it made equal sense for him to live in New York, London, Paris, or Athens. Since the European war had shut down the Atlantic for commercial shipping, he moved for a time to Los Angeles and concentrated on Pacific shipping until the attack on Pearl Harbor. Even with the reduced operations the war caused, he was doing well enough in ships to close down his tobacco-importing business. And as a stripling millionaire in Los Angeles, Onassis quickly found his way to Hollywood's most recherché watering places. As a single man rumored to be rich, he had no trouble making friends with the celebrated and glamorous people he aspired to know.

For many years the great Greek shipping families had made London their base of operations, more from an admiration of the high life as practiced by the English than from any tactical necessity. In the 1940s, most of the big operators moved to New York to wait out the war and plan their strategies for the postwar period. Onassis did the same. He took an apartment at the Ritz Tower at Fifty-seventh Street and Park Avenue, on the same floor as Greta Garbo, who would become a close friend years after he left the building. He also rented a weekend house at Center Island on Long Island's north shore, and there he settled Ingeborg.

One of the patriarchs of Greek shipping, Stavros Livanos, lived in the Plaza Hotel, where he kept a salon for his fellow Greeks in exile, which soon became a social center for the Greek shipping fraternity, of whom Onassis and Niarchos were fledgling members. Livanos had two pretty daughters, Athina, whom everyone called Tina, and

Eugenie. When Onassis first saw Tina in 1943, she was thirteen with her leg in a cast, having broken it falling from a horse in Central Park. On the spot, he later claimed, he resolved that eventually he would marry her.

Tina was pretty, agreeable, and enormously rich. She was also Greek and a blood member of the tanker aristocracy to which Onassis aspired. Her broken leg would turn out to have been an omen: throughout her life, she would demonstrate an alarming proneness to accidents, including several broken bones, that had a curious way of presaging new romances. Her lineage and beauty were perfectly suited to Onassis's ambitions, but in other ways Tina displayed an all-around fragility that made her, emotionally and physically, a poor match for the Onassis juggernaut.

When several years later Onassis made his matrimonial intentions clear, Stavros Livanos was unenthusiastic. He, after all, was third-generation shipping, the aging period required for families to enjoy full membership in the fraternity. Onassis and his pal Niarchos were upstarts. In addition, Tina was Livanos's younger daughter. Tradition demanded the older daughter should be married first. Fired with ardor and his burgeoning success, Onassis was in no mood to compromise; he wanted Tina. His determination won the day, as it usually did, and he and Tina were married in a splashy Manhattan wedding on December 28, 1946. Onassis was forty-six and Tina seventeen. Unable to stop Onassis, Livanos decided to endorse him handsomely. A notorious skinflint, he gave the couple two princely wedding gifts: a medium-sized tanker and a jewel-like town house at the east end of Fifty-seventh Street, number 16 Sutton Place.

Intelligent and sensitive, Tina had never been given a chance to grow up. She might have become a fulfilled and well-rounded person, but neither her father nor her mother, Arietta, who was a fervent believer in the Greek tradition of male domination, had any interest in her development beyond turning her into docile wife material for a rich and pampering husband. Onassis fully met those expectations. He hired people to do everything for Tina—even tasks generally deemed appropriate for the wives of rich men, such as running the house and planning the parties—and discouraged any activity that was not considered suitable for a spoiled, rich *girl*.

Tina had a lively wit and a self-awareness that is often the sign of a ripening intellect. Having attended top schools in England and America—she spoke with a British accent—she was far better educated than her dropout husband. What she lacked was the strength and resolve needed to withstand the cabal of older, wiser heads who determined her medieval fate. Adding to her undoing was a strong predilection for the things she *was* allowed, the clothes, jewels, and beautiful homes that seduced her into passivity and made her, finally, a collaborator in her incapacitation.

By the time Tina realized how badly she had been stunted by the coddling—how she had been bribed and distracted, in effect, from becoming an adult—it was too late to remedy her plight, and she turned first to affairs, then to drugs. Tina Livanos was a woman of considerable potential who grew up in the shadow of a powerful man, her father; approaching adulthood and possible liberation, she was steam-rollered by an even more powerful one.

With the end of the war, Onassis's fortunes soared. Although his impounded ships had made him no money for four years, they were still afloat, as many of his competitors' were not. With a fleet of ships at the ready, he was positioned to take advantage of the postwar boom in shipping, which once again he predicted, while more experienced shippers hunkered down for a long, slow recovery to normal business conditions. His nose for opportunity made him move quickly when the U.S. government offered for sale at giveaway prices large numbers of liberty ships, cargo vessels that had been hastily constructed to meet the wartime emergency.

The ships were to be offered by lot through Allied governments. Onassis urged the Greeks to buy every one they could get. Other Greek shippers disagreed. The ships had been built too fast to be any good. His colleagues were wrong, Onassis said. He had examined the ships and they were better built, he insisted, than the ships their belittlers so proudly owned. When Onassis finally convinced his compatriots they were passing up an excellent deal and they scrambled to buy, the Union of Greek Ship Owners, which was brokering the purchases for the Greek government, turned down his request for thirteen of the ships. Because his fleet flew the Panamanian flag, he was informed, he was disqualified to partake in Greece's allocation. It was just one more in a series of snubs and exclusions that infuriated Onassis and hardened his resolve to become richer and more powerful than those who, so unjustly in his eyes, obstructed him.

He eventually bought sixteen of the ships directly, but on far less advantageous financing terms than those offered through the Greek government. He was also eager to get his hands on a number of the larger T2 tankers, which were also for sale, but, because they were considered to have a militarily strategic value in the event of another war, they were being offered to U.S. citizens only. Onassis hired a top New York lawyer, Herbert Brownell, who helped him work out a scheme of dummy American corporations, and bought four of the valuable T2s. With this increase in his holdings, the cascade of money flowing to Onassis grew to a Niagara.

The first years of Aristotle and Tina's married life were made up of a round of socializing with other newly rich newcomers to Manhattan and Long Island. Tina was allowed a hand in decorating the Sutton Place house, which was soon heavy with period French furniture and capped by a small Renoir. Onassis established an office on Wall Street but preferred to work, as he always would, from his home. Like most attractive people with money who appear suddenly in Manhattan as if from nowhere, Tina and Onassis had no trouble luring famous and glamorous people to their frequent large parties. Old New York society was not yet eager to embrace just anyone with a fat checkbook, but to the extent he noticed, that didn't bother Onassis in the least. Because he was coming to be known as a wily but reasonably reputable businessman with a knack for making millions, he had no trouble meeting, on whatever level he wanted, other top businessmen, regardless of their social standing or their opinion of his. As for Tina, because she was charming, outgoing, and always stunningly turned out, she was, at the age of eighteen, becoming one of the most admired young hostesses in Manhattan.

On April 30, 1948, Tina gave birth to a son in New York's Harkness Pavilion. He was named Alexander after Onassis's much-loved uncle who had been executed by the Turks. When, a short time later, a friend asked the perfunctory question whether Tina and Ari planned to have more children, the friend was taken aback to hear Tina say, "No."

"Why not?" the friend asked.

"Ari thinks more than one child clouds the issue."

Onassis's subsequent behavior substantiated his tepid interest in offspring. Years later some close Greek friends asked why he did not have another son, as insurance against Alexander's choosing not to take over the businesses or in case something should happen to him. Onassis responded with a similar statement, to the effect that he didn't want a lot of Onassises running around confusing everyone, diluting the name's impact. Then, when he and Maria Callas were very much in love and she desperately wanted a child, Onassis did everything he could do to avoid even discussing the subject. Still, it seemed odd for a robust and wealthy couple, as Onassis and Tina were in 1948, to sign off with one child—assuming they were happy. Close friends took the strange announcement as evidence that the marriage was not the success it appeared.

In the year following Alexander's birth, Tina had several abortions, but when she became pregnant again in the spring of 1950, she put off repeating the procedure, even though she and Onassis had agreed that she would. Onassis, who was around less and less, was exasperated, then infuriated by her procrastinating. On his sporadic stops in New York they had fierce battles about her stubborn pregnancy, battles that turned violent when he was drunk and attempted to abort the child himself. (In another context Onassis once said, "All Greek men beat their wives—no exceptions.") His brutal efforts were not successful and the pregnancy went to term. Christina Onassis came into the world on December 11, 1950, not because her mother had a change of heart and looked forward to another child, but because she was afraid of what an abortion would do to her health.

The cottage at Center Island that had served as Onassis's love nest with Ingeborg Dedichen, who had retired discreetly to Paris, was no longer grand enough to reflect the massive fortune he was building with such speed. Also, with two children who needed space for play, more time would have to be spent outside the city, and the cottage had no room for nurses, tutors, doting relatives, and all the other elements in the support systems for rich Greek children. And because of Onassis's love of the sea, the idea of a house near the water was appealing.

The Riviera was enjoying a glittering postwar boom and, since both Tina and Onassis were first and foremost Europeans, he Greek and she more British than anything else, they decided to find a place in the south of France. Onassis made the choice, which appeared to have more to do with grandiosity than with need for nurses' rooms or the love of open water. When the chosen villa, the famous Château de la Croe, was first seen by Tina, she couldn't believe it: forty-two palatial rooms on twenty-five magnificently landscaped acres that covered the tip of Cap d'Antibes. It had all the glories of a luxurious French château—formal gardens, statuary, fountains— but with views of the sea from all sides and such modern flourishes as an enormous swimming pool, two tennis courts, and a ceiling in the huge main salon that rolled back electrically at night to reveal starry skies. It was one of Europe's most splendid houses and had, at one time or another, been home to three reigning monarchs: Leopold of Belgium, Umberto of Italy, Farouk of Egypt, and one who had abdicated his throne, the Duke of Windsor and his Duchess.

As Tina ran from room to room gasping with delight at the magnificence of it all, she was no longer a woman born to wealth, but a normal twenty-one-year-old reacting to a beauty and opulence even she had never seen before. Her ingenuous enthusiasm would be echoed by Christina nearly four decades later, the summer before she died, when, in a desperate attempt to keep at her side a husband who had already left, she leased a similarly magnificent Riviera showplace, the Villa Trianon. Passing from one princely room to another with visiting friends, all of whom were overcome with pity for the miserable treatment Christina was receiving from the man she loved, she would forget for a moment the painful devastation of her household and remember that people who lived in such places are generally envied. With pride and excitement Christina would ask her friends, "How do you like my house?"

Tina adored the Château de la Croe and was equally enthusiastic about the dazzling social life that went with it. She and her husband knew a few prominent people in the area, mostly from his bachelor days in Hollywood, and the burgeoning Onassis legend made other social powers curious to meet him. For many Riviera socialites, however, the address on the Onassis invitations was enough to guarantee their acceptance.

With the frequent parties of the first summers, when the Riviera had emerged from its wartime hibernation to all-out international social frenzy, Onassis gave full play to his taste for famous guests. Not only was he motivated by the glory reflected from the recognizable faces illuminating his table, he was also driven by his competitive streak, which was rarely at rest. What was it about these world-renowned people, he was eager to discover, that made them special? Did they have secrets he should learn? Or were they just lucky?

In many ways Tina loved the tableau that she graced — a young, beautiful woman in couturier dresses moving ethereally through palatial settings greeting the world's most beautiful and celebrated people—but she quickly came to realize that she was just another ornament on the Onassis estate. Far from being able to take credit for the palace of perfection over which she presided, she had been stripped of even the responsibility for running the house and overseeing the large staff. To fill that function, Onassis had hired a manager.

Lacking much to do, Tina spent a good deal of time with her two children, but the normal gratifications of motherhood could not alleviate the psychological problems that were beginning to torment her and that her marriage exacerbated. Onassis was warm and outgoing most of the time, but his hot temper could erupt at any moment and in any circumstances, and often the temper was aimed at her. She knew her husband expected her to shine, not just look ravishing—little problem given her soft blond hair, fine features, and supple figure, as well as the time and money she spent adorning and enhancing her assets—but to reign over his dazzling parties with assurance and aplomb. This in itself created tensions, as did the high-powered company. Tina was forced to entertain many with whom she had little in common and who, for good reason, intimidated her. Surrounded by the overbearing luminaries drawn to her house by her husband's wealth and fame, she was inclined to feel herself inadequate, a feeling that began to ripen and grow.

As she became more unhappy, Onassis became more displeased with her, and her attention drifted more and more away from her children. She began to develop an attitude toward them that would remain throughout her short life: she loved them, wanted nothing but good things for them, but had no confidence in her ability to provide the tangible manifestations of love and support she knew that children needed. From time to time she tried to be a good mother, but her efforts were undermined by a nagging suspicion that she was bad at the game, that she was doing more harm than good. To a growing degree she became too wrapped up in her own problems to worry overlong about those of her children.

When Christina was three, Tina suffered a mild nervous breakdown. Tolerance for psychological malfunctions was not a strong point of the Greek husband and Onassis was no exception. While he went along with what had to be done in terms of doctors and bed rest, he could muster little sympathy for the distress of a wife who he felt had everything a woman could want. As for Tina herself, rather than seeing her collapse as a warning sign of growing desperation with her ornamental role, she took it as further proof of her own inadequacy.

Christina and Alexander, therefore, grew up in the atmosphere created by a fragile, elusive mother on one side and, on the other, a tempestuous and exacting father, who had to be pleased at all costs but who was rarely around so they might make stabs at doing so. They had too much respect for one parent and not enough for the other; one inspired fear, the other a pity that would escalate until it approached contempt. And both parents, for wildly different reasons, had their own pressing agendas, ones in which children played no part.

# 3

# PLAIN LITTLE RICH GIRL

Among the opulent fittings of the *Christina*, which would be the principal home of the Onassis family during the 1950s, there was a large room, first called the Nursery, then changed to the Children's Room when Alexander and Christina grew old enough to protest. The walls were covered with murals by Ludwig Bemelmans, the creator of the charming Madeline series of children's books; his paintings for the yacht depicted Paris street scenes involving a similar little French girl. Other features of the room were an electric organ, a small table and chairs of bright yellow lacquer, and cupboards full of expensive toys. As other children browsed in geography books, Christina and Alexander might glance from the yacht and see Greece, Italy, Egypt, Spain, Havana, or New York. It was at the yellow table in this room that Alexander and Christina had their meals and conferred about their father's illustrious guests, for them either objects of derision for their grandiose airs or, more likely, resentment for the parental attention they stole.

In the winters, Christina and her brother attended school in Paris, staying at their father's Avenue Foch apartment if he was in town, but more often nearby with their Livanos grandparents, who, since the end of the war, had made Paris their base. As much as possible, Onassis wanted his children with him, if only then to ignore them for days. He desired their presence, not to create an appearance of dutiful parenting, but more as props for stability to be called on when he needed such bolstering. Onassis never knew when the parenting impulse would strike and he wanted his family nearby—just as he wanted his Piaggio seaplane, his communications systems, and his Greek chef close at hand and ready to gratify other impulses. Onassis's mealtime preference was for French and Italian cooking, but if he had a sudden craving for Greek food he didn't want to wait to gratify the nostalgic urge. Similarly, Christina and Alexander were kept nearby in case he felt like being a father.

Shortly after the *Christina* was delivered in 1954 and received the finishing decorating touches under Tina's supervision, it gradually became Onassis's principal residence, with his wife and children paying him frequent visits from the Château de la Croe. His shipping headquarters were now in Monaco, so he could oversee both his primary business interests and his Monte Carlo plaything from the magnificent vessel, which, because of its conspicuousness, was also a promotional tool of stunning appropriateness for both Onassis and the principality.

Apart from such calculations, Onassis preferred the ship to any of his other residences. Its mobility appealed to his restlessness, its ocean-going capability suited his love of the sea as well as his self-view as a nautical man, and its attention-winning splendor fed his monumental ego. Other tycoons owned estates, châteaux, and triplex penthouses, but he would be the only one with a 325-foot ship with nine large guest cabins—some with separate sitting rooms—a temperature-controlled swimming pool, and a crew that fluctuated between forty and sixty—"More than it takes to run a 30,000-ton tanker," Onassis bragged.

To create this fantasy home, he had converted one of the bargain Canadian freighters, this one having cost $50,000, and had installed such nonbargain luxuries as air-conditioning, a lapis lazuli fireplace, a vitrine-lined circular staircase, a mosaic-floor to the swimming pool, which could be raised hydraulically to serve as a dance floor, and the most advanced radar and communications systems. The main saloon had an El Greco, "The Ascension," and was large enough to be converted to a movie theater for after-dinner entertainment at sea. The walls of the all-white dining room were covered with murals commissioned from Marcel Vertes—which everyone agreed were the least successful aspect of the décor. The stools in the barroom, upholstered in whale scrotums, were the yacht's most exuberant burst of rough-diamond vulgarity.

While the *Christina* came to symbolize the most zestful, high-flying period in Onassis's extraordinary life, the ship was for his daughter just the most elaborate in a series of animate and inanimate rivals for her father's attention. She would later say that the period during which the *Christina* was her principal home was the least happy of her childhood. Years later, when she inherited the ship, she had no interest in keeping it and gave it away, saying, "she didn't much care for boats." But it was a half-hearted attempt to obscure her strongly negative feelings about that particular boat.

Aboard the *Christina*, her parents were more distracted than ever, she was surrounded by strangers, and perhaps worst of all, she had no one her own age to play with. For Onassis, who could easily have flown in all of her Parisian classmates to divert his daughter, having no playmates was not an important deprivation for a child with so many other, rarer distractions. Playmates from "outside" would simply put ideas in Christina's head, corrupt her, perhaps pass along pernicious gossip about her father. It was another eccentricity of Onassis's that would have an effect on Christina's life. When she became a mother herself, she went to considerable pains to provide her own daughter with companions of the same age, determined to spare her the friendless, relentlessly adult world in which she herself had spent her childhood.

In spite of Christina and Alexander's shared isolation in their father's adults-only milieu, they did not become close, but from a young age set out on diverse behavioral paths to deal with the same predicament. She was quiet, withdrawn, and well behaved; he was brash and rebellious. As soon as he could walk, Alexander became mischief-prone and quickly developed into the kind of untamed hellion for whom younger sisters are less than worthless.

On one occasion, Alexander had a tantrum in which he took a stick and broke all the ground-floor windows of the Château de la Croe, which cost thousands of dollars to replace. Another time he was tooling around the grounds of the château in a child's motorized automobile when he spotted his father strolling in the gardens with a guest. With no hesitation, Alexander wheeled the car around and headed directly for the stranger. Had the man not jumped away in time, he could have been seriously hurt. The prank might have been mere showing off, but it also might have been a murderous impulse toward the faceless parade of people who were stealing his father's attention.

Late in 1954, Onassis had much on his mind besides his children's discontents. Although the tanker business was making money at an incredible rate and his whaling fleet was showing even more spectacular profits, serious trouble had surfaced from an unexpected quarter: the U.S. Attorney General's office. Official United States concern about the activities of a Greek shipper came about in a curious manner, one that illustrated the way apolitical, supernational operators like Onassis could become casualties of the highly political battles of a particular nation. Shortly after the Republicans regained the White House in 1952, they launched investigations into the business dealings of top Truman Administration Democrats. Although political vendetta was their motive, the trail soon led to Stavros Niarchos and a complicated moneymaking plan he had set up for Edward Stettinius and other prominent Democrats.

The plan involved the liberty ships that the U.S. Government had sold so cheaply after the war to Niarchos and, to an even greater degree, Onassis. The law governing the sale of those ships had stipulated that they must be owned by Americans or American corporations. Suddenly the investigative attention shifted from profiteering Democrats to the many foreigners who now appeared to own these ships. Onassis, on the advice of his American lawyer at the time, Herbert Brownell, had set up dummy American corporations, the majority of the stock held by complaisant friends and associates with U.S. citizenship. That made the purchases, according to Brownell, perfectly legal. Now elements in the U.S. Government were outraged at the spectacle of foreigners earning fortunes from ships built with American tax dollars, and they sent the Attorney General's office after them.

By one of the oddest quirks of corporate fate, the U.S. Attorney General was now Onassis's old lawyer, Herbert Brownell, who of course knew better than anyone else the details of Onassis's cosmetic corporations, having himself devised the plan and having charged Onassis handsomely for it. Without a qualm, Brownell handed down a sealed indictment of first Niarchos and then, in October 1953, of Onassis. With Washington already angry at Onassis's shrewd acquisition of U.S. ships, the added discovery of his attempted grab of America's rich oil preserve in Saudi Arabia elevated him to a top place on the enemies list and brought all of the government's might together in a determined effort to crush him.

Onassis was infuriated at Brownell's duplicity and had no stomach for lessons in business ethics from a man whose ethics he considered contemptible. Convinced he had done nothing wrong, he ignored his lawyers' advice to stay away from America, sent Tina and the children to St. Moritz, then flew to New York at the beginning of February 1954. When he passed through customs without incident, he sent a note to the Attorney General's office announcing that he was in New York and at their service. While having lunch the next day at the ultra-fashionable Colony restaurant, Onassis was informed by the maître d' that two U.S. marshals wished to speak with him. He was not arrested at his table, as was reported at the time, but was given the option of finishing his lunch, which he declined, then left the restaurant with the two agents. Although everything took place in a dignified manner, the press furor over the incident was as if Onassis had resisted arrest and exchanged gunfire with the law enforcers.

The government knew it had a thin legal case against Onassis—and no moral one—so it imposed some face-saving fines and demanded he divest himself of his American-made ships. He obliged this requirement with a slight expansion of the original ownership setup. He placed the ships in trusts for Christina and Alexander, both of whom were American citizens, to be held until they reached their majority (when each trust would be worth about $75 million). This ploy would later take on unexpected significance when it threatened to give Christina independence from her father at a time in her life when he was doing his utmost to bring her to heel. Until she did as he wished, divorce her first husband, he would blithely and predictably withhold the money, making a mockery of her "ownership" of the entity, which was called Victory Carriers. Even retaining this right to withdraw her ships (a right Christina could probably have challenged in court), Onassis probably would not have made Christina independently wealthy at so young an age, if he hadn't been placed in a tight spot by the U.S. Government.

His public arrest, which resulted in Onassis's spending less than an hour in jail, was responsible to a large degree for the impression many Americans had of Onassis as a shady character, some sort of high-rolling outlaw. In fact, once Onassis started making money, which was very early, he discovered how to make obscene amounts while remaining well within the law. At various times, however, he did some highly reprehensible things—his rule-breaking slaughter of whales about this time was perhaps the most flagrant—but his purchase of American surplus ships was legal. Indeed, the Truman Administration had previously examined his ownership and found nothing improper in it. If anyone behaved reprehensibly in the matter, it was the Attorney General's office and, in particular, the side-switching Attorney General Brownell. Onassis was bitter about the action against him, which he saw as an unprincipled persecution, and he always remained mistrustful of Americans and somewhat hostile to them, an attitude that was inherited to a degree by his two children.

When Christina was five years old, she stood on the deck of her father's yacht and watched Grace Kelly sail into the Monte Carlo harbor for her marriage to the principality's ruler, Prince Rainier III. The film star had been picked up from the liner that had brought her across the Atlantic by her husband-to-be's far smaller yacht, which had been a gift from Onassis, and, accompanied by many other boats, had proceeded to port. From the ramparts of the Grimaldi Palace, cannons boomed and rifles saluted, while in the harbor below fireboats sent up jets of water, sirens whined, and foghorns bellowed. From the sky thousands of red and white carnations rained down on the nautical procession from Onassis's private plane.

Onassis had every reason to be happy about the marriage. Since Rainier had already shown a taste for actresses, Onassis had hatched the scheme for him to marry a world-famous one to bring attention and excitement to the moribund principality. Rainier agreed to the plan, and while Onassis was off trying to sign up Marilyn Monroe, who met the proposition with interest but asked where Monaco was, Rainier took the scheme in his own direction by courting and winning Grace Kelly, an altogether happier choice. During the euphoric days of the royal wedding, the decks of the *Christina* were crawling with film stars, Hollywood producers, and assorted royals. Retreating to the Château de la Croe for a peaceful respite from the toxic doses of glamour, Tina and the children found two Arabian horses had arrived, a gift from the king of Saudi Arabia. These were heady days for the Onassis family.

As the world around Christina became ever more wondrous and dreamlike, she was growing into a particularly awkward and odd-looking little girl. She had a prominent nose and dark, deep-set circles under her eyes, which emphasized the sadness of her expression. The overall effect was not ugliness, but rather the eccentric cuteness of a Walt Disney forest creature. However Christina's looks might have been categorized—bizarre or just plain ugly—they were jarringly out of place in the sleek perfection of her parents' settings. Most of the time she was sullen and mild-mannered, but she had picked up Alexander's knack for tantrums, and occasionally she would rivet those around her with alarming explosions of pent-up anger and frustration. Her rages were sporadic but would occur from time to time, even as an adult.

Most of Christina and Alexander's childhood was spent with servants, none of whom they much liked or respected. And since their parents put little pressure on them to behave appropriately with their hired overseers—in fact, Onassis quietly condoned his children's insurrections against them—the household staff usually came to dislike the two Onassis children as much as they were disliked in return. The result was a disagreeable and loveless atmosphere in which to spend a childhood.

Occasionally Onassis would shatter the grumpy monotony of their lives by a sudden appearance, when he had decided to take a ferocious interest in their development. He might make a great display of teaching Alexander to swim or showing Christina how to cook Greek food. In these fits of fatherhood, however, Onassis spent far more time with Alexander, and went to pains to teach his son Greek. Christina was never very fluent in Greek, a lifelong reminder of her father's neglect.

For the two children, Onassis was a godlike creature who burst upon them without warning and invariably with some new trick to dazzle them. And just when they were growing accustomed to one of his astounding stunts—landing by seaplane next to the yacht, for example—he would come up with some breath-taking new trick, such as water skiing while being towed by his plane. Such feats impressed even the blasé adults of the Riviera; to his six- and eight-year-old children, they were the deeds of a superman.

Stories began circulating that the beautiful Tina had no love for her odd-looking daughter, indeed was ashamed of her. Friends who witnessed the always impeccable Tina reprimanding Christina for a dirtied dress or mussed hair came to that conclusion. They were the kind of criticisms any mother might make of her child in front of others, but coming from the chic and immaculate Tina to her plain and unkempt daughter, the reproaches were taken as an absence of mother love. In fact, Tina had very deep feelings for both Christina and Alexander. As a mother, Tina was inept and inadequate, not because she didn't love her two children, but because she didn't know *how* to love them. Still, her preference for Alexander was obvious, and from Christina's point of view that may have been as hurtful as no love at all.

One day, without preliminary incident, Christina stopped talking. No one—her mother, her father, her governess—could induce her to utter a word. Suddenly there was considerable screeching of brakes in the fast-paced activities at the Château de la Croe and aboard the *Christina*, and for many days Christina was the center of all attention. The most alarmed was Tina, who flew with her daughter to see a top psychologist in Zürich. The diagnosis was "mercurial mutism" which translated into what they all already knew, a sudden and unexpected silence. The doctor went on to explain that the syndrome often appeared in overprotected children, which had the ring of a good guess on the part of a doctor facing one of the world's richest families, about whom he knew nothing. Had he been familiar with their lives, he might also have seen it as a desperate bid for more parental attention.

As an adult, Christina had no recollection of this period and dismissed it with "Maybe I didn't have anything to say." When her remark found its way back to Tina, she snapped, "If she had just said 'Hello,' it would have saved us $25,000."

Eventually Christina resumed talking, but the most likely cause of her crisis, parental neglect, did not change. None of the professionals who examined Christina suggested the blame lay with Onassis and his wife. Perhaps no one dared. Eventually, they dismissed her alarming behavior as a fluke. With such unmistakable cries for help going unheeded, Alexander and Christina continued to muddle on through their childhood, making more-routine bids for attention, sometimes the loving acts of dutiful children, at other times the angry acts of rebellious ones.

Like their mother, they saw themselves as supporting players in an elaborate and complicated spectacle, a spectacle they had no part in creating and which they little understood. Rather than being lulled into contentment by the lavish treats and privileges that came with the spectacle, they were instead beset with anxieties about whether or not they measured up to whatever were their intended roles. That they drew so little of their father's attention, and not much more of their mother's, seemed proof that they did not measure up.

To exacerbate Christina's and Alexander's feelings of unworthiness they were constantly reminded by servants, their parents' friends, and sometimes their parents that they were extremely fortunate to have so much that other children did not have. Even with their isolation from more normal worlds, however, they were beginning to realize that other children had a lot of fundamental things lacking in the Onassis households, things for which Christina and Alexander longed and which no amount of motorized toys or Dior dolls could replace.

As for the adults who were constants in their lives, the two governesses and the servants assigned to them, Christina was particularly unsuccessful at getting along with them. She rejected them as surrogate parents, seeing them instead as hired disciplinarians lacking the attendant love that balances and, in a sense, empowers discipline. Her relations with the people hired to look after her were never good, and she developed a lifelong coldness and indifference to those who worked for her. There were a handful of exceptions in later years, but for the most part she viewed servants and other employees as alien presences with whom friendship was hypocritical and futile. It appeared a kind of snobbery at odds with her outgoing and good-hearted nature and probably stemmed from the mistrust and resentment of servants she felt during her childhood when they were instruments of her parents' neglect.

For the most part, Christina was a well-behaved and unobtrusive walk-on in the Onassis spectacular. But her sporadic tantrums kept those around her on edge and surely contributed to their lack of affection for her. On some occasions the outbursts were aimed directly at her mother and father. A business acquaintance of Onassis, Tassos Fondaris, a top Niarchos executive, recalled an episode crossing the Atlantic on the *Queen Mary* in 1958. Fondaris was headed into the first-class dining room for dinner when he saw Onassis, forlorn and glum, sitting alone on a banquette outside the entrance. Fondaris noted that Onassis was wearing the expected black tie, perfect in every detail—boiled shirt, sapphire studs, black satin cummerbund—except for a jarring incongruity: bright yellow loafers.

"Hey, Ari," Fondaris greeted him, "I think you've made a mistake. Look at your shoes."

"No mistake," Onassis replied, grim-jawed. "Christina was bad today, so Tina and I locked her in our stateroom. The kid got revenge by throwing all our shoes out the porthole."

If the episode had occurred a few years later, Onassis might have simply radioed for his Piaggio seaplane to airlift a four-day supply of suitable shoes to the ship, but in those days, when they still lived somewhat like ordinary mortals, Christina's shoe toss was a disaster for the very stylish Onassises. So often the victim of her father's self-absorbed whims, tempers, and indulgences, Christina did manage a few licks herself. But once his anger at her antics wore off, Onassis undoubtedly admired such shows of spirit.

Unless isolated at sea with his family, however, Onassis was invariably embroiled in business complexities that continued to divert his attention away from whatever problems may have been festering in his homes. As a result of his near grand slam with the Jiddah Agreement to transport Saudi oil, a plot that was foiled when the Americans had a brass-tacks chat with King Ibn Saud, Onassis was branded a pariah in the international oil business and soon found himself boycotted by the large American and British companies that had previously been his most stable customers.

Many of his ships were lying idle, accumulating vast losses, and he was reduced to finding spot cargoes where he could. It began to be clear his enemies were out not merely to punish him but to destroy him for having come so close to usurping their domination of Mideastern oil. In fact, they were well on their way to succeeding in their aim of annihilating the Onassis empire. Facing the destruction of everything he had built, Onassis had little time for the feelings of emptiness besetting his pampered wife or the spats with governesses of his spoiled children.

When in October of 1956 Egypt's Gamal Abdel Nasser nationalized the Suez Canal and then obstructed it by sinking ships in the channels, it was for Onassis a glorious reprieve, a *deus ex machina* in the grand Greek tradition. No longer able to use the canal to transport oil from the Persian Gulf, the world's oil producers were in desperate need of ships, the largest ships possible, to transport the oil around Africa. Since delivery would take over twice as long, twice as many ships were suddenly required. Unfortunately for the oil companies, most of the world's tonnage was tied up in long-term agreements. One of the few people who had ships, many ships, available was the boycotted Onassis, who immediately went from pariah to most popular man in the business.

Not only were his tankers available, they were, unlike his competitors', unfettered by contracts. New contracts would have to be drawn up on rather more difficult terms. The result of Nasser's opportune action was that all of Onassis's ships were now in service and at a far higher rate than those of his competitors. These men, who only weeks before had been gleefully watching his destruction, could do nothing but rub their eyes and acknowledge that fate was insisting that Aristotle Onassis be an enormously rich man.

Just as the crisis of imminent bankruptcy kept Onassis's attention from his domestic ferment, so did the frenzied deal making of his business turn-around. When he did find time for his family, it was to make trouble, primarily in his ever more frequent battles with Tina. Alexander and Christina's feelings that they were not worthy of their glamorous father's attention were now coupled with the more common childhood distress of battling parents. Onassis was not the sort of man to conceal his angers behind closed doors. His blowups at Tina were often witnessed by both children, who were terrorized at what appeared to be the rancorous collapse of their world, bizarre and unstable as it was.

In 1957 hostilities escalated after Tina entered their white-and-gold bedroom at the Château de la Croe and found her husband in bed with an old friend of hers from boarding school, Jeanne Rhinelander from New York, who had a house nearby in Grasse. For Tina, who was still in her twenties, this was a wrenching crisis. During the ensuing recriminations she learned that her husband was regularly amusing himself with other women, indeed had done so little to conceal his affairs that they had become common knowledge among their friends.

Other marriages that are rife with infidelities survive through a modest regard for appearances, especially if there are children. Because the usually wily Onassis was indifferent to Tina's or anyone else's learning of his escapades, it may all have been done *for* Tina, an elaborate mating ritual akin to the beatings he would give her before making love. Tina may have understood that, but still chose to withdraw from the game, not only because she was humiliated by his public affairs or exasperated by his vulgar lack of discretion, but for the very sound reason that she was unhappy in the marriage even during its best moments. Onassis was counting on Tina to recognize the inconsequentiality of his peccadilloes and their lack of threat to her position. He miscalculated because he didn't have an inkling of what was really troubling her.

For Tina the marriage had more serious problems than infidelity. She complained bitterly that Onassis never gave her the least credit for the contribution she made to his life—her struggles to be an admired hostess, her efforts to turn herself out in a way to do him credit, even her stabs at being a mother. The expensive gifts of furs and jewels he tossed her way were, she knew, signals to the world of his wealth and generosity, not tokens of love and gratitude. She felt more and more unappreciated and useless. The more discontented she grew, the more angry it made him.

If exciting Tina and bringing her to heel was what Onassis had in mind by flaunting his infidelity, the plan backfired and drove her further from him. Stepping up her independent social life, she wasted little time in finding diversions for herself, and soon developed a keen taste for handsome boys barely out of their teens. Tina's flings didn't bother Onassis as long as she kept them under control, that is to say, did not become deeply involved with anyone.

She began casual dalliances with a ski instructor or two and flirted with the many eligible men she met on the social circuit, some of whom she would be seen dining with in London or Paris. To one of her loves she delivered a line that was heavy with Colette-like ennui and showed her to be the most self-aware and reflective of all the characters in the Onassis drama. "I conceal the unhappiness in my life with a great deal of pleasure."

At a Rothschild ball in Paris, Tina met a handsome Venezuelan, Reinaldo Herrera, who was eighteen, eight years her junior. They began an affair and soon found themselves in love. Herrera asked her to marry him and, to his surprise, she accepted. She asked Onassis for a divorce, and in a fury he refused. When he calmed down, Onassis confessed, according to Herrera, that he was going through a period of impotence and was not fulfilling his conjugal obligations. He insisted, however, that the problem was temporary, and in time he would again be a good husband to Tina. For the moment, they should work something out along civilized lines.

He acquiesced to their affair, even permitting it to take place on the *Christina* in his presence and that of his children. To the degree anyone thought about it, the assumption was that Christina and Alexander were too young to understand what was going on. But it was not hard for them to figure out that the good-looking young man who was constantly at their mother's side and from whom she could not take her eyes, was something more than a friend. Onassis's reasons for obstructing a divorce were that he still had feelings for Tina and she was the mother of his children. And surely part of his calculation was Tina's wealth, which, in the event of future business disasters, could provide Onassis with a convenient backstop.

Even more at work was Onassis's ego. Approaching his mid-fifties, he dreaded the public humiliation of losing his twenty-six-year-old wife to her handsome young lover. In the eyes of the world, it would be a major defeat, and defeats of any kind, but particularly sexual ones, were not helpful to the image of invincibility he was working so hard to project. From his subsequent actions, it was clear that Onassis wanted to hang on to Tina in order to buy time, time enough for him to line up a replacement so that he could do to her what she had almost done to him. He, in fact, said as much to Costa Gratsos: "I want to leave her before she leaves me." It was the realistic remark of a worldly middle-aged man who knows how things go with beautiful young wives, but he didn't add that Tina had already tried to do that very thing, and would have had he not pulled every trick from his bag to stop her.

Onassis might even have feigned impotence to excuse his neglect of Tina. It would have been typical of his knack for inventing whatever ploy was necessary to have his way, even a confession so embarrassing to one who styled himself a womanizer. By pleading sexual affliction, he was able to win sympathy, create confusion, and gain the time he so badly needed to wrest the advantage from Tina. It also absolved him of suspicions of infidelity. He was determined that if there was to be a scandal he would emerge the winner, Tina the loser. As usual, his wishes prevailed, and the marriage eventually ended on his, rather than Tina's, terms. After a period of gamely attempting to pursue their affair under Onassis's nose, Tina and Herrera gave up. The bizarre openness of it all had a chilling effect on both of them and Herrera eventually withdrew from the field.

While the odd ménage à trois was unraveling, Onassis was taking advantage of the time he had won to regroup with stepped-up social activity. At a party Elsa Maxwell gave in Venice in the early summer of 1957, he met Maria Callas, then the most celebrated diva in the world. The encounter was brief and unremarkable but managed to inflame Onassis with the woman herself, and even more with the idea of the world's two most famous Greeks in a full-blown, widely publicized love affair. This did not mean he did not love Callas; he had loved them all—Claudia Muzio, Ingeborg Dedichen, Tina Livanos—but they all had served a further purpose. He simply held his emotions in reserve until they were triggered by someone who, while filling his emotional and sexual needs, could fill others as well.

What better way to publicly end his lame-duck marriage than in the press explosion over a love affair with the celebrated Maria Callas? His image, put in such jeopardy by Tina's ludicrous attempt at freedom, could now be not only saved from a cuckold's disgrace but elevated to new levels of glory and celebrity. He would await the moment, then, having been rudely shoved by Tina's insurrectionist gambit, move majestically, spectacularly, triumphantly on to the next stage of his dazzling saga. What the scandal would do to his wife and children was of no concern. He never pretended that such sentimental matters touched on his decisions of state.

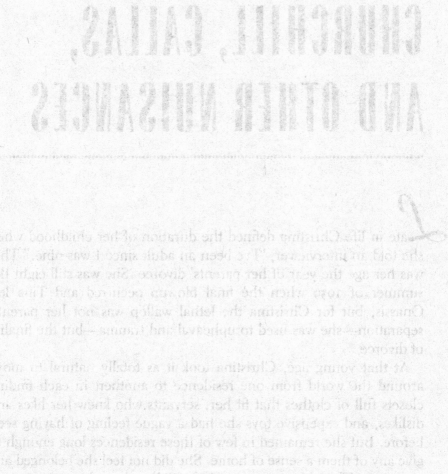

4

CHURCHILL, CALLAS,
AND OTHER NUISANCES

*L*ate in life Christina defined the duration of her childhood when she told an interviewer, "I've been an adult since I was nine." That was her age the year of her parents' divorce. She was still eight the summer of 1959 when the final blowup occurred and Tina left Onassis, but for Christina the lethal wallop was not her parents' separation—she was used to upheaval and trauma—but the finality of divorce.

At that young age, Christina took it as totally natural to move around the world from one residence to another, in each finding closets full of clothes that fit her, servants who knew her likes and dislikes, and expensive toys she had a vague feeling of having seen before. But she remained in few of these residences long enough to give any of them a sense of home. She did not feel she belonged any one place. The only constant in her childhood was her parents, and she had come to see the link between them, however tempestuous and fragile, as her one claim to family. When that shaky partnership was legally ended, Christina felt her childhood was over. Now her family was as fragmented and scattered as her residences had always been. She was, in an emotional sense, on her own.

. . .

Maria Callas had been born in Brooklyn in 1923 to a Greek family who had emigrated from Greece earlier the same year. When she was thirteen, her mother, disenchanted with both America and her husband, took Maria back to Athens to develop her vocal talent. Maria spent the rest of her girlhood in Greece, including the grim years of World War II, when Aristotle Onassis was romping in New York and Hollywood. Callas was a willing Trilby to her driven Svengali of a stage mother and grew up thinking of nothing but a singing career and her development as an artist.

Struggling to make a name for herself in the world of opera, Callas landed a few roles in second-string houses and was eventually asked to sing at the prestigious Arena of Verona. While there she met a wealthy local brick manufacturer and builder twenty years her senior named Giovanni Battista Meneghini, who was an opera aficionado with excellent connections in the world of Italian opera. At the time, Callas was far from a star, but rather a promising young singer living from role to role. Meneghini, fascinated by both the woman and her talent, took over her career, helped her financially, taught her how to dress, how to eat, the people to cultivate. He soon became her manager and played a major role in her rise to the awesome pinnacle she achieved in international opera.

When in 1949 they married, it was more a legitimization of Meneghini's all-inclusive mentor role in her life, the role previously filled by her mother. And as she evolved into the world's greatest opera star, Meneghini offered the total dedication she required, becoming, like her mother, an essential adjunct to her career. Had Callas been happily married to a handsome young man when Onassis met her, he still might not have hesitated to pursue her, but perhaps she would not have been so receptive to the idea of romance. She was thirty-six, one of the world's most famous women, and had never experienced a love affair.

After the 1957 introduction, Onassis did not see Callas again until her Paris debut in December 1958, when, with a barrage of roses, he signaled an interest that seemed to exceed that of an ardent fan. Their next encounter was in the spring of 1959, when he and Tina attended Countess Castelbarco's season-opening ball in Venice. This time he made his intentions clear to Callas—as he did to everyone at the party, including Tina. Oblivious of his marriage as well as of hers, Onassis fawned over Callas as if he were an eighteen-year-old meeting the girl of his dreams at a debutante ball. In the days following the party, the roses that had won him an opera singer thirty years earlier would arrive under the nose of Meneghini. When Callas and her husband were invited on a cruise aboard the *Christina*, Meneghini acquiesced to his wife's wishes and accompanied her like a man on the way to the gallows. For the cruise, Onassis secured the jewels of his collection, Sir Winston and Lady Churchill. The other guests were Churchill's secretary, Anthony Montague Browne, and his wife, Nonie; Churchill's physician, Lord Moran; Onassis's sister Artemis and her husband, Professor Theodore Garofalides; and Fiat owner Gianni Agnelli. Greta Garbo had been invited, but, perhaps sensing disaster, had declined.

It did not take Tina long to realize that she and the distinguished group had been invited along to witness and provide background color for Onassis's courtship of Callas. She played along, however, out of a mixture of curiosity about how far the humiliating drama would be carried and to await an opportune and dignified moment to quit the field. In the late 1950s, divorce among the Greek shipping families was still rare and highly scandalous. That, coupled with Onassis's belief in Tina's fundamental weakness, may have led him to assume that she would tolerate the Callas spectacle. And then too, hadn't she done the same to him with Herrera? Tina was in no mood for such tit-for-tat game playing or, indeed, for prolonging a marriage that brought her nothing but pain. In order to have ample and unequivocal justification for divorce, she decided to suffer through the seagoing nightmare.

Given the starry-eyed oblivion of both Callas and Onassis, who had already become lovers in clandestine meetings ashore, Tina did not have to wait long for grounds. The world's two most famous Greeks would disappear from the group for prolonged strolls around the yacht's deck, often hand in hand; would disappear together in port cities for many hours; and finally one night, after lights out, Tina caught them in the act on the floor of the yacht's main saloon. Unlike Tina, Meneghini could not contain his outrage and began throwing on-deck tantrums over the flagrant spectacle his wife and Onassis were making. His histrionics were threatening the tranquillity of Sir Winston's Mediterranean idyll, and it was decided to cut short the cruise before Meneghini strangled Onassis. The illustrious passengers, in agitated disarray, disembarked in Monte Carlo.

Christina and Alexander were among the passengers on this trip, probably the most notorious cruise since Antony and Cleopatra sailed down the Nile together. Both children were aware of what was happening, having already become familiar with such adult antics through their mother's romance with Herrera. One female guest described Christina as a watchful, slightly ominous presence. "You wouldn't be aware she was there," the older woman said, "then you would notice her sitting off to the side, taking in everything that was happening."

For Christina and her brother, the clamorous entrance of Callas into their father's life was far more serious than their mother's dalliance with Herrera. Heretofore, they knew that no matter what bad things happened in their family, their father could set things right. Now their father was the perpetrator of the bad things, so they could see little hope. Also, their mother's misery was obvious to them, and that sort of pain spreads quickly to children, although Alexander demonstrated a childlike ability to shut out the unpleasantness and fasten onto a positive interest.

Of all the illustrious guests on board, Alexander had curiosity about one only, Gianni Agnelli, for the simple reason that Agnelli owned an automobile company. While his parents' marriage was going up in smoke, his father was forging a liaison between international café society and the world of opera, and Winston Churchill sat on the deck available for conversation, the ten-year-old Alexander appeared to ignore it all, instead bombarding Agnelli with questions about his automobiles.

After her guests' scramble onto safe ground at Monte Carlo, where Onassis had also disembarked, pleading a business emergency, Tina, with Christina and Alexander, took the yacht on to Venice, where the cruise was supposed to have ended. She had promised Elsa Maxwell, as had Onassis, they would be in Venice for her large annual party. Onassis assured Tina he would join her in Venice in time for the party. But as soon as the *Christina* had cleared the Monte Carlo harbor, Onassis boarded his Piaggio seaplane and flew to Milan, where Maria was waiting for him in her town house, having sent the obstructive Meneghini on to their villa on Lake Sirmione.

Not content with at last having Maria to himself to pursue their passion behind closed doors, Onassis trotted her to every conspicuous restaurant and nightclub in Milan. Word of the tumultuous cruise and its romantic developments had gotten out as soon as the shaken passengers could get to telephones, and news photographers were overjoyed at the generous opportunities Onassis was giving them to document the sensational love affair for a curious world. Newspapers around the globe splashed on front pages photographs of Onassis and Maria—dancing cheek to cheek (which required her to bend down considerably), cooing at nightclub tables, and most tellingly, entering her house together late at night.

Tina could not fail to see the photos and was infuriated. In a year and a half, Onassis had managed to convert her from a disaffected wife who passionately wanted her freedom to the butt of an international front-page humiliation. Only a relatively few insiders knew of Tina's infidelities; Onassis had made sure that the whole world knew of his. Now, in the eyes of most people, Tina was the victim, the betrayed, the loser. But Tina was not interested in his cruel games—or, indeed, in how she appeared to the public. She saw in his grandstand play the opportunity for escape she had been awaiting. By the evening of Elsa Maxwell's ball, which Onassis predictably skipped, Tina had made her plan.

The next night, she told Christina and Alexander's governess to pack their things. Waiting until the *paparazzi* had decided the *Christina*'s passengers were aboard for the night, Tina spirited Christina and Alexander into a motor launch, which ferried the trio up the Grand Canal and across the lagoon to the airport, where Stavros Niarchos's plane waited to take them to Paris. The destination was her parents' apartment, but this was no angry flight to her parents until apologies were made and relations returned to normal. Tina had no doubt she was journeying out of Onassis's life for good.

Christina later told a friend, "I didn't know what was happening that night, but I had a strong sense we were losing something important, something we would never get again, but I didn't know what."

About two years later, as a student in the Headington School in Oxfordshire, Christina and her classmates were given an assignment to write an essay describing their most memorable vacation. Christina wrote about being at her aunt's villa in Glyfada outside Athens and of a walk she took alone in her aunt's garden. She described the beauty of the plants and flowers, the fruit trees and the blue sea in the background. Most of all she remembered the seclusion and peace of the lovely spot. Her teacher, Rosemary Gawthorne, was struck by Christina's choice. "I knew that young girl had had many thrilling vacations—cruises on her father's yacht in the company of famous people, exciting escapades few other children could match in New York, Paris, and the south of France. But she did not choose to write about any of these experiences. Instead, her favorite recollection was a quiet garden at her aunt's. I thought that was most interesting."

On another occasion years later, Christina told a friend that her dream when she was young was to live in a peaceful house by the sea and play board games with other children her own age. The remark and the school essay revealed the toll taken on her by the *Sturm und Drang* of her parents' marriage, and the small amount of pleasure she had derived from her privileged childhood. The princely pastimes and costly treats were associated in her mind with her parents, and that meant with fighting, hypocrisy, and deceit—painful recollections that more than outweighed the unique experiences and expensive diversions.

When the strain had grown too onerous in the Onassis household, or when, for any number of reasons, Onassis wanted his children out of the way, Christina was sent off to her aunt's house in Glyfada. The villa became her childhood refuge, and Artemis Garofalides, although devoted to her brother, Aristotle, was one of the few close relatives who felt sympathy for Christina, who knew what she was enduring, and who strived to give her the love and understanding missing from aboard the *Christina* or at the Château de la Croe.

Artemis was an intelligent woman who had both sophistication and good sense. For Christina, her visits to her aunt were a blessed relief and a chance to regain her strength, so that she could return to the Onassis wars and renew her efforts to snatch small amounts of parental love and attention. Throughout Christina's life, Artemis Garofalides remained for her a haven of compassion and sympathy to which she would retreat in difficult periods. During Christina's childhood, however, as hard as Artemis tried, she could not replace the love

Christina so badly needed from her parents and which came in random, insufficient spurts.

Once settled in Paris, Tina invited her New York lawyer, Sol Rosenblatt, to fly over to consult with her about a divorce. He advised her to establish New York residency. His theory was that the threat of a divorce in New York, where adultery was the only grounds, would induce Onassis to make a quiet settlement of differences. In her vindictive frame of mind, Tina liked the idea of the scandal a New York divorce would guarantee. As for her requirements, she wanted no money, but she did want the children, and she wanted to assure that Onassis provide handsomely for their future.

While showing no inclination to lessen his involvement with Callas, Onassis was adamantly opposed to a divorce. His attitude was curious. Very few women on any level of society would have tolerated as long as Tina did the brutal way in which he flouted their marriage before such a broad audience. Her flight and refusal to discuss a reconciliation surprised him. He considered her position as his wife a ceremonial role of state, a post for which she was well compensated in jewels, furs, houses, and yachts. And even though, until Callas, they still made love (which Tina said made her feel "dirty"), and in spite of the friction between them, her primary function, in his eyes, had long ceased to have anything to do with his love life. He clearly expected Tina to stand aside while he indulged to the fullest his passion for Callas, then be waiting to resume her role as wife and mother when the affair had run its course.

Tina was having none of it. With Christina and Alexander at her side, she sailed to New York and settled into the Sutton Place house. Christina was enrolled in Miss Hewitt's Classes on East Seventy-fifth Street and Alexander was placed in Buckley on East Seventy-third Street. Tina attempted to set up a meeting with Onassis, but he, stunned by her decisiveness and still determined to block a divorce, refused to meet with her. Thoroughly exasperated, Tina invited reporters to her house and issued a formal statement:

It is almost thirteen years since Mr. Onassis and I were married in New York City. Since then he has become one of the world's richest men, but his great wealth has not brought me happiness with him nor, as the world knows, has it brought him happiness with me. After we parted this summer in Venice, I had hoped that Mr. Onassis loved our children enough and respected our privacy sufficiently to meet with me—or, through lawyers, with my lawyers—to straighten out our problems. But that was not to be.

Mr. Onassis knows positively that I want none of his wealth and that I am solely concerned for the welfare of our children.

I deeply regret that Mr. Onassis leaves me no alternative other than a New York suit for divorce.

For my part I will always wish Mr. Onassis well, and I expect that after this action is concluded he will continue to enjoy the kind of life which he apparently desires to live, but in which I have played no real part. I have nothing more to say and I hope that I will be left with my children in peace.

Christina's classmates at Miss Hewitt's recall her as abnormally quiet, rarely speaking. She would respond to what others said or did, civilly answer a direct question or laugh when someone clowned, but she never volunteered a remark or a comment. She developed no friendships. In those pre-uniform days at Hewitt's, Christina dressed simply and was distinguished by her very dark coloring and her sad and unusually large eyes. One teacher recalled her as "a sweet girl, very nice, but an average student, nothing special." In languages, she was far ahead of her classmates, but way behind them in other subjects, particularly math. Her math was so bad, in fact, that she had to be tutored. Curious to discover how the math deficiency had occurred, the tutor asked a few questions and quickly learned that her father had often bullied previous headmistresses into releasing Christina for a cruise or a visit to some exotic part of the world he suddenly wanted her to see. He had had little concern for what these interruptions might do to Christina's education.

None of the people who knew Christina at that moment in her life appeared to have any idea of what was troubling her and driving her back into a modified version of her five-year-old mutism. Divorce was not an uncommon experience among students at Miss Hewitt's, but Christina had become adept at concealing her feelings. Although she gave no outward signs, she was in a state of seething turmoil. A long time later she told a friend that, for the first year after her parents' divorce, she cried every night when she went to bed.

On one occasion Christina made her feelings about parental neglect clear, not just to some classmates, but to the entire school. At a Christmas program to which parents had been invited, Christina, being one of the tallest girls, led the procession into the assembly hall singing, along with everyone else, "Adeste Fideles." Once in her seat on stage, she later explained to a classmate, she scanned the audience and saw that no one from her family had come to watch her sing, not even her governess. Others in the audience were perplexed to see the ungainly dark girl go through the entire program of Christmas songs with her mouth resolutely shut. Only later did they learn why the Onassis girl had staged her conspicuous boycott.

In filing for her New York divorce, Tina surprised everyone by naming as corespondent, not Callas as the world expected, but Jeanne Rhinelander, the school friend whom she had caught in bed with Onassis at the Château de la Croe. Tina had several reasons for dredging up, and proclaiming so publicly, this two-year-old betrayal: she wanted to deny Callas the satisfaction of being the cause of her marriage's breakup, to establish that the operatic escapade was far from Onassis's first, and to repay her school friend for sleeping with her husband. But while Tina displayed healthy impulses for revenge, they rarely lasted. After a few months had passed, her anger with Onassis subsided and she was dissuaded from the idea of a New York divorce, which could easily degenerate into an ugly circus, in which her own infidelities would be paraded alongside his. Christina and Alexander would have to endure more pain and no one would win except the press. Tina agreed and, after a brief meeting between her lawyers and Onassis's to establish her modest requirements, she obtained a quick Alabama divorce on the grounds of mental cruelty.

Eager to return to Europe, but not wanting to snatch Christina from yet another school, Tina resolved to make the Sutton Place house her base for the time being. Once the school term ended, however, she grabbed Christina and headed for Europe, stopping for a week of shooting at a friend's estate in England, then moving south to Monte Carlo, where she threw a large dinner party at the Hôtel de Paris and, still harboring some spite, announced she had not been as happy in thirteen years. Knowing of Onassis's difficult schedule, now complicated by his new romance, Tina was happy to agree to let him have the children when he wished, but was soon surprised by the ever-increasing frequency of those requests. Also surprised but very pleased, the two children, now nine and eleven, fell into a pattern of frequent journeys from one parent to the other.

Whatever Onassis's motives for his affair with Callas, it was soon complicated by a genuine passion for her. He had become ensnared in his own net. But if the relationship between Onassis, Tina, and Callas was complex and multileveled, it was clarity itself to Christina and Alexander. Their parents' marriage had, quite simply, been broken up by a conniving, marauding Maria Callas, and their hatred of her was implacable. Whenever they visited their father, she was invariably present, which for them all but spoiled the visits.

From her point of view, Callas was basking in the glow of her first genuine love affair. Not only had she fallen deeply in love with Onassis, she was thrilled by the lavish settings, mostly the yacht *Christina*, where the crew had been instructed to treat her as their mistress. Within weeks of the collapse of their first cruise together, the yacht set to sea again, this time with Callas and Onassis the only passengers and a stripped-down crew of forty. Such idyllic isolation was not to last, and back on land, Callas was nonplussed to discover her lover seemed to want his two children to share with him his new happiness. Already uncomfortable, the situation was made considerably worse by the palpable hostility of Christina and Alexander.

Charm and tact were never the great diva's strong points, and her stilted upbringing had left her hopelessly inept at negotiating human relationships. Still, she made heroic efforts to befriend Christina and Alexander, both of whom were not interested. Convinced that her parents would still be married if only this *opera singer* hadn't ruthlessly vamped her always-innocent father, Christina sought to punish Callas in whatever way she could. In their few conversations, she forced Callas to repeat every remark, and when there was a more specific opportunity to show her hatred, she snatched at it. Arriving at the *Christina* one time from Milan, Callas brought both Alexander and Christina expensive cashmere sweaters. Sullenly, they accepted the gift-wrapped boxes, then left them in the yacht's main lounge, conspicuously unopened.

To endear herself to these particular children, Callas could not have chosen a worse means than expensive presents. Apart from owning everything the most grasping child could want, Onassis's children, at the ages of nine and eleven, were already sharply cynical about Greeks bearing gifts. They witnessed the jewels their father gave their mother after a terrifying fight, the gifts he gave valued employees after humiliating dressing-downs. They themselves had closets full of presents brought them to compensate for stretches of neglect—the longer the absence the larger the gift. They had come to see presents as cover-ups, mollifiers, bribes. Opulent gift boxes were, for them, the language of betrayal and treachery.

With the new disaster in their lives, the treachery, from both children's point of view, was entirely Callas's; they in no way blamed their father. Christina made extra efforts to comfort him and endear herself. For his birthday, she gave him an odd straight-backed chair inscribed "With love and many kisses from Christina." The uncomfortable chair remained in Onassis's private quarters on the *Christina*'s front bridge until his death. Onassis did his share of fence mending as well. He gave Christina a pearl necklace and presented Alexander with a Chris-Craft, with which the small boy immediately terrorized harbors from St. Tropez to Beaulieu. Alexander's recklessness behind the wheels of boats, and later cars, was seriously alarming, and he had a number of accidents. Miraculously, however, he avoided seriously injuring himself or anyone else. Once, when he took his father out for a ride, Onassis screamed for him to slow down, not from adult concern about harbor rules, but from his own terror.

Alexander was as hostile to Callas as Christina—he would later sneeringly dub her "The Singer"—and he soon found a satisfying way to use his new boat against her. Having been told by Onassis to keep quiet in the afternoons when Callas took her naps, Alexander and Christina would gun the noisy boat in circles around the yacht during Callas's nap period. When in outrage she complained to Onassis, he surprisingly advised her to ignore the affront. If she pretended that she had not heard them, he told her, they would stop.

It was a curious solution for a man with a reputation for toughness and ferocity, but then he may not have wanted, once again, to lose all his shoes. It was also symptomatic of his idiosyncratic approach to their discipline: if they bothered or displeased him, punishment was swift; their transgressions against others made him smile. Alexander and Christina waged independent campaigns to unsettle Callas and win their father's attention. Occasionally their strategies would align—as with the speedboat caper—but more often they would retreat into their individual repertoires of protest and dislike. At one point later in the affair, Callas confronted Christina and accused her of trying to destroy her relationship with Onassis. With disappointing hypocrisy, Christina vigorously denied doing anything of the kind.

During the first summer after the divorce, Tina took the children to visit their Aunt Eugenie on Spetsopoula, Niarchos's five-thousand-acre private island south of Athens. Tina was close to Eugenie, but because of Onassis's hatred of Niarchos had found it necessary to see her sister in secret. Now liberated from Onassis's rigid rules, Tina could see as much of Eugenie as she wished, finally giving Christina and Alexander the opportunity to become acquainted with their four Niarchos first cousins. Christina would later become quite close to her Niarchos-Livanos contemporaries, with whom she shared Greekness, family blood, and great wealth, but at their first meeting she regarded them as crashing irrelevances in her private torment.

For their part, they recall Christina's entrance into their lives as strained and difficult. In the summer of 1960, they were playing on the Spetsopoula beach when Christina was brought down from the main house. This was their cousin, they were told by their mother, and they were to be nice to her. Christina was wearing a red bikini bottom and no top. Her playful attire contrasted sharply with her mood. As they splashed and tossed a ball in the shallow water, she stood off to the side glowering at them and resisted their efforts to get her to join them. She pretty much refused to speak to them at all. As Spetsopoula became a frequent and prolonged stop in Tina's good-times circuit, Christina quickly loosened up with her cousins, and they came to like one another. Her unbending standoffishness on the first visit, however, was a good indication of the inner pain she was nurturing about her disrupted life.

Unlike Christina, Alexander did not internalize his anger and pain but channeled them into ever more defiant acts. At age fourteen, he capped a history of bad school grades and truancy by staying away from Onassis's Avenue Foch apartment for an entire weekend without telling anyone where he was. This so angered Onassis that he banished his son from the palatial apartment, where Alexander had been living alone except for servants, and sent him to live in the Livanos apartment.

Onassis also sent his close friend Professor Yanni Georgakis, one of the few academics he respected (and whom he would put in charge of Olympic Airways), to talk with Alexander to discover the reason behind his many problems at school. In the course of the conversation, Georgakis was struck by the shrewd reading the sixteen-year-old had of his complex father. Among many insights, Alexander remarked that he and his sister learned long ago never to apprise their father of their feelings or vulnerabilities. If they confided such things to him, Alexander said, sooner or later Onassis "would hit us over the head with them."

For whatever reason, Onassis began telling Christina and Alexander that he and their mother would eventually get back together. He may once have wanted a reconciliation, but as time went by he appeared to want it less and less, although he continued to hold it out to his children as a likely possibility. Perhaps his feelings about Tina were no clearer in his own mind than his contradictory actions would indicate. Regardless of the actual chances of a reconciliation, the hope for it that he instilled in his children merely fueled their dislike of Callas. If she was marked for dismissal, they asked themselves, why didn't she leave now?

In his dealings with Callas, Onassis used his children's unabated resistance to her as an excuse for not marrying her, as she so fervently desired. Callas's motives were not financial although she herself was not rich; she never sought money from Onassis and she never got any. She simply wanted to legalize the most important involvement in her life. But to Onassis marriage was a trump card only played in the most desperate circumstances. Alexander and Christina had been badly shaken up by the divorce, he would argue; they must be given time to adjust to the new situation.

As usual, he was using any trick to hang on to his options and maintain his escape routes. Had Callas insisted, Onassis probably would have agreed to marriage. He was very much in love with her and she had many formidable assets in his eyes: she was a fellow Greek, a self-made success, and as world famous as he was. In addition, he was strongly attracted to her physically, as she was to him. Onassis was perpetually excited by his altogether accurate notion of her as a full-blown but untapped woman. To close friends he confided he was in the euphoric state of being totally in love at an age he thought put him past such intense feelings.

Still, all his business instincts told him to treat their relationship like any other "deal," paying no more than absolutely necessary in whatever currency was being called into play. When Callas became pregnant, he talked her into an abortion, although she very much wanted a child and felt that, at the age of thirty-seven, she would probably not have another chance. As much as he was enthralled, Onassis never for a moment considered relaxing his business obsessions for her, although she was more than willing to give up her operatic career for him. And, as he had done with Tina, he would disappear or otherwise exclude Callas from his life for long stretches. When he took the Churchills on a cruise, for instance, Callas was not invited. Their fondness for Tina, he said, would make the situation uncomfortable. His children, on the other hand, were shown no such consideration. Despite such high-handed manipulations, Onassis would remain Callas's lover for nine years.

To celebrate her freedom, Tina threw herself into an intensified program of high-level socializing and recreation. While skiing in St. Moritz in February of 1961, the accident-prone Tina broke her leg, this time quite seriously. Ever protective, her brother-in-law, Stavros Niarchos, sent his plane to fly an English bone specialist to Tina's Swiss hospital, and the doctor discovered eighteen separate fractures. When she was strong enough, the specialist had her flown to his hospital in Oxford, the Nuffield Clinic, where she was required to undergo a prolonged recuperation. That left Christina with no parent in America, or even an aunt or grandparent, so she was plucked from Miss Hewitt's, enrolled in her old Paris day school, and billeted, along with her brother, in her Livanos grandmother's apartment on the Avenue George V.

During Tina's recovery, her younger brother, George Livanos,

who was living in London, taking over the reins of the Livanos shipping interests, telephoned a friend in the clinic's neighborhood,
Sunny Blandford, and asked him to drop in on his sister to cheer her
up. Blandford was the Marquess of Blandford, son of the tenth Duke
of Marlborough and heir to one of England's most illustrious duke-
doms. Tall and handsome, he lived in Lee Place, a Georgian mansion adjacent to the grounds of Blenheim Palace, the sprawling pile
that had been the birthplace of his cousin, Winston Churchill, and
which Blandford would inherit when he assumed the dukedom. He
and Tina quickly became friends.

Tina had other visitors. Onassis, having already met with her once
in Paris in a try for reconciliation, flew to Oxford for another meeting. Word of his visit reached the press, which speculated in print
that remarriage might be in the air—column items that displeased
Tina and infuriated Callas. Alexander and Christina were flown
across the channel for brief visits. On a day-to-day basis, however,
Blandford had Tina pretty much to himself. For her part, Tina was
grateful for his attentions, which soon became more than kindness
to a friend's crippled sister.

Having already wearied of her gay-divorcée whirlwind, Tina responded enthusiastically to Blandford's interest; when his courtship
intentions became clear, she was intrigued. Anyone meeting Tina
for the first time would have assumed she was British, with her
clipped Mayfair accent that had been honed at a London grammar
school and never altered by her adolescence in New York. She loved
England and felt herself to be, not Greek, not American, but British.
The prospect of one day becoming the Duchess of Marlborough and
mistress of one of the world's grandest houses—the ground floor
alone covered eight-and-a-half acres—was certainly a pleasant rev-
erie while staring from the window of her hospital room.

She wrote a friend that Sunny was "the nicest man I ever met."
Others found him stuffy and boring, probably because he reserved
his store of charm for situations requiring it. Sunny's father, the
Duke of Marlborough, was at first unenthusiastic about the match,
dubbing all the Greek shipping families "common Greeks." When it
was pointed out to him, however, that the common Greek money
she would bring into the family might improve the pheasant shooting
at Blenheim, he warmed considerably to the notion of Tina as a

daughter-in-law and settled into the comforting certainty that he and his son had blue blood enough for any wife.

When Tina was finally released from the Oxford Clinic in April, she returned to Paris and told Christina and Alexander about the new interest in her life. She had more or less decided to accept Blandford's offer of marriage but wanted to allow her children time to adjust to the idea. Finally, on October 23, 1961, in Paris, in a media free-for-all wedding, Tina Livanos Onassis became the Marchioness of Blandford and, in the eyes of everyone present including herself, would be the next Duchess of Marlborough. Christina, who was still nine, called Blandford "uncle" and had come to like him, which was fortunate since she would now be living mostly under his roof. Still, she was not going to acquiesce completely to the further distancing of her mother from her father. She insisted on wearing to the wedding a clumsy fur hat Onassis had brought her from Moscow, which was, she told friends years later, her "silent protest."

# 5

# TO THE MANOR MOVED

*W*hen Tina and Blandford returned from their honeymoon at the end of 1961, Christina was brought over from Paris to Oxford by her governess to take up permanent residence at Lee Place. Arriving at the seventeenth-century stone mansion early one cold and damp evening, she was shown into the library, where her new family was waiting to meet her. She wore a dark-blue traveling suit and a blue hat with a white ribbon, which someone present described as an "upside-down pudding basin." As she usually did when dealing with strange circumstances, she fell into a sullen silence, making barely audible sounds when spoken to. Alien adults were nothing new for her; what held her attention in the group was Blandford's two children by his first wife, James, the six-year-old Earl of Sunderland, and Lady Henrietta, aged three. Both children gawked back at this large, dark girl with sad black eyes. They saw her only as an unwanted and foreign-looking intruder, whom the adults, for some reason, were presenting as their new sister.

Although Christina was accustomed to large, formal houses, this one was dark and gloomy and distressingly full of people she had never seen before. She of course knew her stepfather, who, while courting Tina, had made some inroads in befriending Christina. Then there was her governess, Mademoiselle Lahare, whom she didn't like, and her mother whom, at the moment, she had good reason to mistrust. Since the night in Venice when Christina had been snatched away from her father and her family had been shattered, more than a year had passed—her estimated duration of crying herself to sleep. On her first night at Lee Place she did the same.

Her despair over her wrenching new life was short-lived. Blandford, who basically had little interest in children, bent every effort to make Christina feel welcome and ordered his children to behave similarly. Suddenly Christina, who had grown up starved for companions her own age, found herself with a brother and sister. Although they were both considerably younger, they had the winning attribute of not being adults. She quickly became very fond of both of them. She also found that Lee Place was quite an agreeable spot, not the tomb of her first impression.

It was actually a warm, comfortable house with a stable and extensive grounds. Even better, her mother wasted no time applying her Livanos fortune toward making it more agreeable. She installed a swimming pool, bought Christina a dog and a pony, and later a horse. She ordered that a wing be built onto the house, which would have a large screening room on the ground floor and, above, two bedrooms and two baths. These were to be rooms for Christina and Alexander and may have been Tina's graceful way of avoiding any tension-causing shuffling of sleeping quarters to accommodate the family that came with her. It didn't take Henrietta and James long to realize that their new stepmother brought many treats and other good things into their lives—"After Tina arrived, there was always plenty of everything" was Lady Henrietta's way of putting it—and some of this benefit-induced acceptance probably carried over to Christina.

Alexander remained with his grandparents in Paris, but, at Tina's insistence, would make periodic visits to Lee Place. When he did, the difference between the Blandford rearings and the Onassis lack of any was obvious, and to the starchy Blandford, maddeningly so. As young children go, Henrietta and James were well mannered and well behaved. In contrast, Christina and Alexander were like feral creatures, totally wild and undisciplined. On the holidays when Alexander came to visit and the entire family dined formally together—

with butlers, footmen, many courses—Blandford would boggle in lordly fashion as the Onassis children jumped up, chased around the table, then, seated again, flicked occasional bits of food at one another.

Sometimes angry and pleading with Tina to tame her children, Blandford still managed to convey to his new charges a steady brand of fatherly affection unknown to them. Once having established his paternal affections, however, he tended to avoid them, as he avoided his own children, and retreated into his aristocratic pursuits. "For a good part of the time," recalled Lady Henrietta, "we children simply didn't exist for my father."

On normal days when Alexander was back in Paris, Christina and the Blandford children were served high tea at six and then put to bed. Once the house was quiet, Blandford and Tina dined at eight-fifteen. In a fundamentally untroubled situation, Tina was mildly concerned about her children's bad table manners and other derelictions; although she had never had much authority over them, she worked on smoothing out these wrinkles. Since the mayhem was usually instigated by Alexander, his long absences allowed a reasonable level of decorum to the household.

For her part, Christina quickly responded to the warmth her prefabricated family was showing her, and was as eager as her mother to make a success of the new arrangement. As they all grew familiar with each other and fell into routines of accommodation, Lee Place became as happy a home as Christina had ever known. At age ten, Christina's motherly instincts were triggered by Henrietta and James, both of whom were affectionate and unspoiled, and she lavished affection on them both. She also grew genuinely fond of her stepfather, whom it had been agreed she was to call "Uncle," but whom she soon began calling "Sunbun," a name she continued to use after she became an adult and he became the Duke of Marlborough.

When enrolling Christina in the socially prestigious Headington School for girls nearby in Oxford, Tina met with the headmistress, Peggy Dunne, who remembered being surprised by the interview. "Christina's mother seemed very nice," Miss Dunne recalled, "but I was struck by how shy and unsure of herself she was. She was quite concerned, however, that her daughter fit in comfortably at Headington's. We discussed in detail Christina's previous schooling and her academic weak points."

Once enrolled, Christina was driven to school each morning by a chauffeur and accompanied by her governess. Because walking home from school or riding on a bus was the students' principal opportunity to socialize, Christina was somewhat cut off from her classmates, but she gradually made a few friends. Since the first grim days of her parents' breakup, when Christina, stunned and shattered, was thrown into Miss Hewitt's Classes in Manhattan, she had gradually emerged from her near-catatonic shell.

Christina's bedroom at Lee Place had cheerful wallpaper with a sweet-pea pattern and windows that overlooked a garden. She had a horse named Cobweb, which she spent hours brushing, and a poodle named Jeffrey, about whom she was less enthusiastic. Her Spencer-Churchill stepfamily was struck by her silence about her former life. According to Lady Henrietta, "Christina never said, 'When we lived in New York' or 'on a cruise aboard the *Christina* . . .' It was as though she had no life before Lee Place."

Feeling very much at home with Blandford's family, Christina felt a sense of security that she had never known before. That she was, at last, part of a stable and affectionate family brought a major change in her personality, or rather, permitted the emergence of a personality that, in the unpredictable and peril-ridden ambience of her earlier childhood, she had been wary of revealing. She had grown accustomed to being miserable and living in fear that disaster was imminent. Now, with no disaster on the horizon—it had already happened—Christina felt the relaxation of hardened defense muscles and the release of enormous psychic energy. The result was a fierce exuberance that caused her to rush from one of her pastimes to another. Her governess accused her of being "a butterfly, always flitting from one thing to another and never staying with anything." It was an aspect of her character that would remain with her, to varying degrees, throughout her life.

At bedtime at Lee Place, it was generally the duty of Christina's governess, Mademoiselle Lahare, to put her to bed and tuck her in. One evening as the time approached, however, Christina whispered to James and Henrietta's nanny, "Are you going to come by my room and wish me goodnight, Nan?" Nanny Charoneau said she would, and after Christina was in bed with her lights out, she entered the room.

"Is that you, Nan?" Christina said softly.

Charoneau went to Christina, kissed her on the cheek, and said, "God bless you, dear." She was then surprised to feel Christina's arms come up and give her a tight hug.

Nanny Charoneau was not the only one to experience the new, affectionate Christina. One night the nanny looked in on James and was alarmed to see the small boy's bed empty. Hurrying to Lady Henrietta's room, she found that bed empty as well. Then she went to Christina's room in the new wing. There in Christina's bed the three children were asleep, Christina in the middle, a little aristocrat under each arm.

Looking back on this period, Henrietta thought that Christina, in addition to feeling part of a family for the first time, felt a greater freedom at Lee Place than she had previously known. "If Christina wanted to go down the slide of the swimming pool ten times, there was no one standing over her telling her 'That is enough,' or 'Be careful that you don't hurt yourself.' Her life before she came to us was highly supervised by people paid by her father to look out for her. She seemed very happy to get away from all that."

Christina made a friend at Headington's, Miranda Lane, whose father owned a men's clothing store in Oxford. Many years later, Miranda would remember her first impressions: "Christina was quiet at first and seemed foreign, although she spoke English perfectly but with an American accent. She bit her nails until they disappeared. At school, she worked hard, but was not a brilliant scholar. Still, she tried. In the mornings before school, she would phone me to check her homework against mine. An invitation to Lee Place was always a treat. Christina had so much that none of the rest of us had—swimming pool, a horse, a trampoline.

"She didn't like her governess at all and gave her hell—bossed her around, argued with her about everything. . . . Christina was very status conscious. She'd get upset if someone referred to Mademoiselle Lahare as her nanny. 'I'm too old for a nanny,' she'd snap. 'She's my *governess*.' Christina also resented having to eat apart from the adults. She felt she was old enough to eat with her mother and stepfather. She was really quite spoiled. Her favorite expression was 'It's a bore.' When she was given her horse, she threw herself into riding, but then when it turned out she wasn't very good at it, she pronounced riding 'a bore.' She'd say that about almost any activity after a time. She would lose interest in things very quickly."

For the Easter holiday in 1962, Christina invited Miranda to join her on a Mediterranean cruise aboard the *Christina*. "I had never been out of England before and was thrilled," she recalled. "We went to Christina's Aunt Artemis's house in Athens for a few days, then boarded the yacht. Christina was delighted to find that Callas was not on board, but the Churchills were and the Montague Brownes with their daughter, Jane, who was a little younger than Christina and me, about nine, I think. Christina loved the ship. It was home to her and she ran around excitedly showing me and Jane everything. She and her father got along well. They seemed to enjoy each other, have fun together. But Christina loved defying him. As soon as he declared some part of the ship off limits to us—the engine room, for example—she would take us there. She was constantly naughty, disobedient. He didn't seem to mind very much.

"Sir Winston was very, very old, completely senile, I think. He was also very fat, squat, and couldn't walk. He had two nurses with him all the time. In his efforts to divert him, Mr. Onassis told us girls to go on deck and talk to him. With Christina in the lead we three girls would go to Churchill and try to make conversation. He would just sit there looking at us blankly with this great, ugly cigar hanging out of his mouth, completely oblivious to us. He had no idea who we were, nor did he care. He never responded to anything we said, paid no attention to us at all. Actually, Mr. Onassis paid no attention to me either, except one time. I had my eleventh birthday while we were on board, so that night we were allowed to join the adults in the main drawing room, where we were usually forbidden. On the way back to England, we stopped at the Onassis apartment in Paris. I met Christina's brother there. He seemed quite distant from Christina."

That summer, Blandford and Tina rented a house in Villefranche, where Christina spent most of her holidays, with intermittent cruises aboard the *Christina* with her father and the dreaded Callas. One time, when she was leaving Headington's at the end of the school term to join the yacht in Italy, her classmates expressed their envy and Christina cut them off. "It would be all right," she said, "if I didn't have to go ashore all the time and listen to that woman screech her lungs out." She then did an unkind impersonation of Callas hitting a high note. The Livanos family had also bought their own Greek vacation island, theirs named Coronis, where Tina opted to spend her summers with her mother and brother. Her father, Stavros Livanos, had recently died. The island became the primary summer spot for Tina and Blandford, with Christina joining them much of the time.

Onassis, however, missed his family badly and pestered Tina constantly to send his son and daughter to him, if only for a weekend during the school term. Although Tina usually obliged, she sometimes gave in to Christina's wish to remain in Oxford. For the first time, Christina had a life of her own—school events, parties, guests at Lee Place—and it was no longer convenient to drop whatever she had planned and fly to her father. In later years, this turnabout prompted a bitter remark: "When I needed him," she said, "my father didn't want me around. Then when I didn't need him so much, he wanted me with him all the time."

Not only was Onassis more interested in spending time with his children since the divorce, he took a far greater interest in their development, perhaps fearing that Blandford's family, the Spencer-Churchills, would purge the earthy Greek blood of the Onassises and convert it into the thinned-out blue variety of England's great dynasties. On one of her visits to her father in Paris, Christina had just returned from a hairdressing appointment, and her father asked her what sort of person the hairdresser had been. Christina replied that she didn't know. Well, was it a man or a woman? A woman. Was she married or single? Christina didn't know. Was she born in Paris? Christina had no idea.

"Listen, Christina," Onassis said, launching into one of his admonitory lectures, "you've got to *talk* to people. Find out as much as you can about them. You never know when you might learn something or hear something interesting. It's better than just sitting there."

Since Christina had only recently emerged from a period when she spoke as little as possible even to those closest to her, Onassis was asking a great deal to expect her to draw out strangers with probing personal questions. In an adult life that was densely populated with unfamiliar faces—waiters, servants, salespeople, and functionaries who eased her way—Christina never developed a knack for making small talk with these people, even when her confidence and spirits were high.

On another occasion when Onassis was in England, he took his two children to lunch with the Churchills at Chartwell. On the drive back to London, full of wine and self-approval, he proclaimed, "One lunch with Winston Churchill is as good as three years in a university." Having never finished high school, Onassis probably based his dismissal of higher education on his experience with its products. Few meaningful educational benefits could have been derived from conversation with Churchill at that point in his sad deteriorioration; if there had been, however, it would have been the only higher education Christina and Alexander ever received.

When Onassis purchased his private island, Skorpios, he probably did not do it to keep up with Niarchos. Spetsopoula was five thousand acres, Skorpios an uncompetitive four hundred. When in 1959 Onassis had a falling-out with Prince Rainier and lost control of the Société des Bains de Mer, he lost his taste for Monaco and needed a new summertime port for the *Christina*. A Greek island would give him a base in the country he considered his native land, although he had never lived there until he was a teenager and then only briefly. His ambition had made him abandon Greece, as it had made him abandon everything and everyone he loved, and now his ambition made it possible for him to buy back a piece of it. These sentimental considerations of an aging tycoon were reinforced by the recent vogue for the Greek islands among well-heeled pleasure seekers. Buying a Greek island was not only patriotic, it was now chic.

At the time Onassis bought Skorpios, it had a population of two, a farm couple who raised olives. It would eventually have as many as a hundred employees tending to guests, maintaining and operating elaborate support services, such as a laundry, a dry cleaner, a bakery, and a dairy, as well as effecting such on-going improvements as extending gardens, paving roads, installing drains. Immediately after purchasing the island, he set about building a main house and six-teen guest houses. Within two years, by 1964, the island became as important to him as the *Christina* had been ten years earlier. After a few more years, it would surpass even the yacht's rare echelon of luxury.

In those early years, Skorpios became for Onassis and his two children an exciting adventure, marred, for Christina and Alexander, only by the presence of Maria Callas. Each summer when they ar-rived, a major new embellishment would have appeared—a harbor deep enough for the *Christina*, complete telephone service for all the rooms, a swimming pool—and each new facility would be opened with elaborate fanfare. When the island's electrical power plant was completed, the fifteen-year-old Alexander was selected to throw the switch in a mock-elaborate ceremony.

In the relaxed manner of Lee Place, Christina gradually let down her guard, and a devilish side of her personality emerged. She unnerved the adult members of the household with her imaginative pranks and by goading James and Henrietta to new heights of mischief. One night when taking a bath, Christina found a piece of hose and, with a drainboard, rigged a water slide on which she would send the tiny Henrietta shooting down into the tub. Hearing the screams of de-light, governesses rushed to the scene to find the room awash and naked children flopping on the floor like up-ended goldfish.

"There was a terrible commotion, which of course Christina loved," Henrietta recalled. She also remembered a visit all three children made to her grandfather, the Duke of Marlborough, at Blenheim Palace. Driving across the majestic grounds with Bland-ford at the wheel, Christina leaned from the window and yelled at strolling tourists.

"Hey, you over there! Stay off the lawn! My uncle owns this place."

"My father rather enjoyed it," Lady Henrietta said, "but then he was very fond of both Alexander and Christina. Sometimes when he was driving us somewhere, Christina would suddenly reach across from the back seat and say, 'Let me fix your hair, Sunbun,' then muss his hair, which he hated above anything."

Christina became very fond of Nanny Charoneau. As the adult in charge of her stepbrother and sister, Charoneau had no responsibilities concerning Christina and no direct authority over her, which may have been why Christina was able to develop a friendship. Slender and tall, Charoneau was a warm but no-nonsense Englishwoman in her thirties, who at first found Christina spoiled and willful and who threw her support behind Tina's half-hearted crusade for discipline. Although Christina and Nanny Charoneau became close, Charoneau would see the best and worst of the adolescent Christina.

One day when she was about thirteen, Christina was eager to buy a pair of shoes she had seen advertised in the local newspaper and feared would be quickly sold. She asked Charoneau to drive her into town. The older woman said she would take her to the shoestore as soon as she finished a chore. Christina continued to nag, every ten minutes coming to her with such whines as "Come on, Nan, can't we go now?" Annoyed, Charoneau reminded Christina that she could not go until she had completed a particular task. Finally they set out. Arriving in Oxford, they were unable to find a parking place immediately.

"There's a place, Nan," Christina said. "Park over there."

"I can't. It's illegal."

"Don't worry," said Christina, "I'll pay the ticket."

"Yes, and it will go on *my* record."

Christina grunted her annoyance. Charoneau reached over to open the car door and snapped angrily, "If you're in such a hurry, go into the shop by yourself. I'll park and join you." Christina jumped from the car and slammed the door. About three minutes later, Charoneau walked into the shoestore.

"Oh, hi, Nan. You're here already?" Christina said brightly.

"Yes, and you still have to wait for the saleslady after being so disagreeable to me. You must learn some patience, Christina." She was cold to Christina for a few days and that clearly made an effect.

Christina's breezy offer to pay Charoneau's fine was an early instance of a response that would come to dominate her behavior: wielding her wealth to overcome any obstacles to instant gratification that might litter her path. Those who remembered Christina at Miss Hewitt's said she gave no indication that she had more money than anyone else or that she considered herself in any way special. In regard to cash, neither Onassis or Tina were generous with their children. Onassis, who lavished costly gifts on them, saw cash as allowing too much independence, so withheld it. Tina, who was notoriously tight with money, had loosened up with Christina to soothe the pain of the broken home; so at thirteen she may have had a stash of money and apparently had learned that getting more was not a problem. Whatever the cost of an Oxford parking ticket, Christina was perfectly willing to pay it to get to the shoestore a few moments earlier.

Once settled into her life as a British marchioness, Tina was unhappy with her daughter's emerging raucousness, and increased her efforts to turn Christina into a proper English gentlewoman. Headington's had on its curriculum such suitable subjects as needlepoint and music appreciation, which Tina saw that Christina took, but she also hired a riding instructor for Christina and insisted she study the piano. Christina's enthusiasm for learning to play the piano was minimal; her mind would wander during lessons and she never practiced. Finally, after several months of no progress, her teacher, Rosemary Gawthorne, threatened her. "Christina, if you don't start practicing at home, I will have to drop you as a student."

Christina seemed to take the warning in stride, but at the next lesson she brought a note from Tina, which amused Miss Gawthorne as a poignant glimpse of a committed socialite straining to be a parent.

> We're very sorry Christina has not been practicing for her piano lessons, but the fault is ours. My husband and I have had Princess Margaret staying with us and, during her visit, we have forbidden Christina to go near the piano.

While Tina struggled to be a good mother to Christina, she doted more and more on Alexander as he developed into an attractive young man. She also began to grow restless with her life as an English country gentlewoman. After a few years of marriage to Sunny, her life once again slid into a miasma of boredom and unclear desires. Having years earlier turned to frivolous pleasure to assuage her unhappiness, she had become addicted, like a postoperative patient, to her social painkiller and sought ever-increasing doses.

But pleasure as pursued by the British upper classes began to pall. Although Tina's Lee Place house parties became social pinnacles and she was a shining fixture in the highest circles, she generally found herself moving with these social treasures through muddy bogs surrounded by wet dogs. By birth, shooting was Sunny's main enthusiasm. Not sharing his genetic lineage, Tina's tastes ran more to dressy parties in Monte Carlo and St. Moritz. She wrote plaintive letters to her sister Eugenie of her growing discontent.

Christina, meanwhile, continued to have a fine time. Physically, she was large for her age, but not fat. She had shoulder-length black hair, and although the dark circles under her eyes remained, the overall effect was not terrible. At one point Tina contemplated her daughter's face and said, "Of course, as soon as you mature, we will have to get your nose fixed." While that may have held out hope of one day having a button nose like the one her mother had had surgically sculpted after a skiing accident, it still brought home to Christina that she would have to endure the next few years with a great, unsightly *thing* on her face. As she entered the self-conscious years of puberty, Christina grew concerned about her looks to an obsessive degree. She developed early, but it was testimony to the familial warmth she felt at Lee Place that she went through the difficult maturing process with relative ease.

While Christina was enjoying a taste of stable family life, Alexander was growing up in Paris under the casual and sporadic supervision of his father and his grandmother, Arietta Livanos. Onassis eventually forgave Alexander for his unauthorized weekend sabbatical and decided to allow him to leave his grandparents' home, how occupied only by Arietta, and make other arrangements for his housing. Feeling the time had arrived for Alexander to have a sex life, he gave his son a rousing send-off with an evening at the notorious Paris establishment of Madame Claude. When Alexander passed through his initiation with considerable honor, Onassis rewarded his schoolboy son with his own Paris apartment. Rumors circulated that the gift apartment was supplied with a resident mistress, but that was apocryphal. Alexander proved himself quite capable of finding his own partners. In spite of the new cordiality between father and son, Alexander would surely have assumed any woman his father supplied was a spy.

As usual with Onassis, another motive lurked behind the generosity and leniency of giving his son an apartment. An apartment of his own would encourage Alexander to develop an independent life. In that way Onassis hoped to spare Maria Callas the taunts and other affronts that came with Alexander's holiday appearances aboard the *Christina.* As always, Onassis proved himself willing to spend major money to avoid minor domestic friction. In baiting Callas, Alexander had graduated from such boyish antics as speedboat noise to the more adult hostility of addressing her in the most insolent tone he felt he could get away with. When Christina was present, he particularly enjoyed showing off how skilled he had become at skirting this fine line.

It wasn't long after deflecting Alexander with his own apartment, however, that Onassis joined his son in the Callas baiting. Predictably, he went into the hostile phase of his love affair, the one that had produced black eyes and bruises on Tina and Ingeborg Dedichen. He began to treat Callas with contempt, sometimes speaking rudely to her in front of guests and other times acting as though she were not present. Still, the sexual side of their relationship was as strong as ever and he continued to want her company on a regular basis. For her part, Callas was still deeply in love with Onassis, as she would remain for the rest of her life. To avoid his unprovoked angers, she would retreat to her cabin aboard the *Christina* and endlessly play opera recordings. Her increasingly less happy tenure in the Onassis world did not evoke any sympathy from Christina and Alexander. They never showed her the least pity.

When Onassis gave Alexander his own apartment, it was with the proviso that he do better in school. Instead, he nearly got himself thrown out. His grades, much to the anger of the competitive Onassis, had never been very good. Now he was threatened with expulsion. On top of that, he took an unauthorized leave of absence from the school—a two-day jaunt to Deauville—that got him suspended. Onassis was infuriated and pulled him from school altogether, announcing he would not pay for an education that Alexander clearly did not want.

Baroness Fiona Thyssen, who would later become the principal romantic involvement in Alexander's life, put a harsh reading on Onassis's motives. Having no education himself, she theorized, he feared having an educated son. To be sure, Onassis had repeatedly shown himself to be casual in his approach to the education of both his children—except for the bits of street wisdom he tossed their way or the occasional lunch with Winston Churchill. But, rather than seeing formal education as a threat, he may have been genuinely disdainful of those who had one and felt there were better preparations for life.

Baroness Thyssen also overlooked that on more than one occasion Alexander had refused to continue school and Onassis had been forced to use a variety of strategies and pressures to get him to return. His announced weariness of forcing an education on a son who didn't want one may have been sincere. When he pulled Alexander from school, many assumed Onassis was taking this extreme measure to knock sense into his son's head, and would later relent and resume Alexander's education. He never did. Instead, he put Alexander to work in the offices of Olympic Maritime, which had remained in Monte Carlo, with the announced intention that he should "learn the business."

With his children's futures on his mind, Onassis also decided Christina should attend a French-speaking school and Tina had no objection. They settled on St. George's, a Swiss boarding school for girls in a magnificent mountain setting overlooking Lake Geneva west of Montreux. Once enrolled, Christina was unenthusiastic about the loss of freedom, complaining constantly about the strict rules, but she gradually came to see the boarding-school stint as a tedious inevitability for rich girls. At St. George's she ran into something new to her: a prejudice against Greeks. The school had 150 students, about two-thirds of them boarders, the rest day students. The majority were English or French, and they clearly considered the handful of Greek girls to be a breed somewhat below the salt. As a result, the Greek girls banded together.

A classmate remembered that Christina was very concerned about her looks. For long periods, she would stand in front of the mirror and moan, "Look at my nose, look at those circles around my eyes. I look like my father."

Neither of Christina's parents was particularly attentive to her when she was at St. George's. Many years later, her stepbrother, James, mentioned that when he was away at school he had received a letter from Tina every week.

"Every week!" Christina exclaimed. "I think I got two letters from her in two years."

Students were allowed to leave the school to visit their parents one weekend every month, but on a number of those weekends Christina was forced to remain at school, both of her parents being otherwise engaged. Then, suddenly, Onassis would arrive at school and, making some excuse, take Christina away for a day or two. At first the headmistress permitted these impromptu excursions, even if they meant that Christina missed classes, but she soon lost her patience with the flagrant breech of regulations.

A roommate remembered that Christina once received a message telling her that her father would arrive the next morning to pick her up; she should have her overnight bag packed. Christina was thrilled, but feared that the headmistress would forbid her to leave. The following morning, from the window of her room, Christina watched gleefully as Onassis's limousine swept up to the school entrance and he emerged carrying a huge bunch of red roses and a box of chocolates. "Just watch," Christina told the other girls. "He'll talk that old hag into letting me out of here!" In such a flamboyant fashion Onassis might appear several times in one month, then two more months would pass without so much as a phone call.

In her second year at St. George's, the fifth form or eleventh grade, Christina was moved out of the dormitory and into a small residence called the Châlet. It was a major improvement in her life, as the girls lucky enough to be in the Châlet enjoyed more freedom. Their only supervision was an elderly woman who was easily fooled into thinking her charges were obeying the rules. In the Châlet, Christina shared a two-room suite with two girls, Keti Thandaris of a wealthy Greek merchant family and Susan Handal, who was from Chile. Keti remembered that Christina was very mischievous.

"Nothing serious," she said, "no one had an affair or anything like that, but Christina would organize trips into town and bring back great quantities of candy, potato chips, and other snacks. This was strictly against the rules. She found a way for us to sneak it in a side entrance so no one would find out, then hide it in our rooms."

Among the forbidden delights Christina smuggled into the Châlet were bottles of Coca-Cola, which she consumed in great quantities and which would remain a lifetime addiction. Keti remembers that she got along well with the other girls, rarely indicating that she felt her father's wealth and fame entitled her to special considerations. "Unless she got mad," Keti later said. "I remember her getting into scraps with other girls, growing very haughty and saying something like 'My father's worth such and such and yours is only worth such and such'—you know the kind of things kids say when they get angry or feel put down, but generally she never mentioned her wealth and got along with everyone."

# 6

# ENTER JACKIE

*W*hen Christina was fourteen, her father delegated her to replace him on a trip to Japan for the launching of a new tanker. Onassis disliked both the country and its people, but that did not stop him from doing business with them. The prospect of several days of toasting and bowing repelled him, and he arranged to send Costa Gratsos and other top executives for the ceremonial occasion. He also felt that he, like royalty, should be represented by a blood relative.

Christina, of course, was thrilled at the assignment. Ship launchings were nothing new to her—she had launched her first tanker when she was two—but this would be one of her first journeys without at least one parent at her side. Once in Tokyo, she threw herself into the planned sightseeing and handled the formal occasions with adult aplomb. Her father had told her she could buy herself an expensive gift as a souvenir of the trip, so she got her principal chaperon, Onassis's public-relations man, Nigel Neilson, to take her on a tour of the exclusive shops along the Ginza. In a jewelry store, Christina came running up to him holding out two pearl pins.

"Look, Nigel," she said excitedly, "aren't they fantastic?"

"They certainly are," he agreed.

"My problem is, I prefer this one, but the saleslady says the other is much more beautiful."

"How much are they?" Neilson asked.

"The one I like is $1,500. The other is $4,000."

Neilson had come to know Christina on this trip and found her an astute young woman. He looked at her in amazement, however, when he realized she did not suspect the saleswoman of pushing for the better sale. When he suggested as much, Christina looked dashed, then agreed he was probably right. Classmates of Christina's at St. George's would find themselves equally surprised that Christina had so little idea about money—how much things cost or, more important, how it could motivate people.

"She'd lived in Paris for years," said one girl, "but hadn't the least idea of the price of the Métro or a film ticket. She never rode on the Métro, of course, and if she went to a film, someone else paid."

Onassis, always so keen on imparting practical knowledge to his children, seemed to have the parvenu's desire to keep at least his daughter aloof from shopgirl concerns about money. He seemed to have had the opposite theory with Alexander, who was struggling along on his $12,000-a-year salary—not much, even for a teenager, on which to maintain an international lifestyle. Onassis was eager for Alexander to have the accouterments of a rich man's son and lavished on him gold watches, expensive clothes, sports cars—but no cash. When Alexander turned eighteen, Onassis presented him with a Ferrari, registered in the company's name, of course, but Alexander's to race around the Riviera in, terrorizing the Upper, Middle, and Lower Corniches.

Alexander seemed to take little pleasure in a Riviera bachelor life many his age would consider paradisiacal. He had fallen into a routine of work, water skiing, and tearing around in his Ferrari at night. He had almost no friends and seemed uninterested in acquiring any, although he was guaranteed feverish popularity in a country his father had recently owned. To keep Alexander company, Onassis assigned a young crewman of the *Christina*, Yorgos Zakarias, to take him water skiing and generally look after him during his leisure hours. While the two young Greeks became friends, Zakarias was ill equipped to help Alexander with the problems tormenting him, primarily the normal adolescent urge to break loose from a dictatorial father. His conflict was intensified not only by the fear of losing the perquisites of being the son of Aristotle Onassis—he had already seen how quickly his father could withdraw them—but also by his deep admiration and love for his father, which survived all the fear, anger, and mistrust.

Onassis had brought both Christina and Alexander up to venerate money and to be disdainful of those without it. Although Alexander had proved himself capable of criticizing his father and rejecting his views, he had absorbed this tenet of the Onassis ideology. Once, during the height of his later struggle with Onassis for his independence, he told his lover, Fiona Thyssen, that the two men he most admired were his father and Howard Hughes. But his admiration for moneymaking genius had a negative side: Alexander was thoroughly intimidated by his father's wealth and, like so many children of self-made parents, despaired of ever approaching a similar achievement.

At the moment, Alexander's pessimism had a more elementary focus: he despaired of ever gaining his father's approval. As he performed his tasks at Olympic Maritime, if he made the least mistake, Onassis would rail at him interminably, often in front of others and often over the international phone lines. If he did something well, he never got a word of approbation. Like so many of those closest to Onassis, Alexander had allowed his father to become his entire life, the sole custodian of his ego, then watched powerlessly while he was excoriated and misused by this omnipotent being. His way of dealing with the impasse was to suffer whatever Onassis handed out, then jump into his Ferrari, also handed out by his father, and speed suicidally along the twisting Riviera roads.

While Alexander was undergoing these torments at Onassis's hands, Christina was growing closer to her father than she had ever been before. For Onassis, Tina was a defector and Alex was a problem; that left it to Christina to be his family anchor while he pursued new romances and built new empires. He seemed to want her with him all the time and lavished attention upon her. He admired her forthright manner and found many similarities between her emerging character and his own. On more than one occasion he was quoted as saying that Christina should have been the boy and Alexander the girl, cruel remarks that invariably found their way to Alexander in the gossip-plagued Onassis empire.

These remarks were probably aimed at encouraging the sturdy character Christina was developing, but since they were calculated to reach Alexander's ears, they could also have been made in an effort to goad his son to greater efforts. Intentionally or not, Alexander was well aware that Christina was being pampered, coddled, and spoiled, while he, underpaid and underappreciated, plodded away at his desk in Monte Carlo. Unable to accept his own responsibility for his father's disapproval any more than he could accept Christina's part in her favored status, he chalked it up to his sister's "sucking up" to their parents. As he brooded over the injustice and perfidy of it all, he came to dislike her and, as Callas had learned, Alexander's dislikes were rarely concealed.

If schooling and friendships did not provide Alexander with an escape route from his father's fearful domination, his healthy Onassis sex drive would present one instead. With several casual romances behind him, jet-set flings that had died of their own listless predictability, in the winter of 1967, Alexander, aged nineteen, met a beautiful and wealthy divorcée, the Baroness Fiona Thyssen-Bornemisza, and fell resoundingly in love with her as she did with him.

A Scotswoman, Fiona Thyssen was born Fiona Campbell, the daughter of a rear admiral in the Royal Navy. After school, she pursued a modeling career, and, with her remarkable looks, wasted no time in becoming a top London model. She was married for nine years to one of the world's richest men, Baron Heinrich Thyssen, by whom she had two children. Divorced in 1964, she was, when she met Alexander, a chic and exotic (she walked a panther on a leash) luminary in the upper social precincts of London, Paris, and Switzerland.

Had Alexander brought home an African pygmy for his father's approval, he could not have provoked a worse reaction. Onassis hated everything about Fiona—her social prowess, her glamour, her worldliness, her lack of Greekness, her lack of virginity, her lack of a fortune; but most of all he hated, as other fathers might, her age. She was thirty-five, which made her sixteen years older than Alexander and a year younger than Alexander's mother. Then, too, there was the suspicious coincidence of her having been married to a man of legendary wealth and now taking up with a boy of comparable expectations. When Alexander tried to soften his father toward Fiona by insisting his feeling was not casual but deep and long-lasting, the announcement only hardened Onassis's conviction that the match was disastrous. Having already cut funds to Alexander to a sub-sistence minimum, Onassis could only threaten disinheritance. That, he assured his son, would be the immediate result if he married Fiona.

For the moment, Alexander contented himself with being allowed the freedom to pursue the affair. Naturally, the match had Europe's rich and social agog with excitement, and the press was equally in-trigued. Each time a photograph of Alexander and Fiona appeared in the papers, Onassis would call him—usually at Fiona's house—and behaving as though he had just learned of the romance, rant endlessly about the stupidity of it. One quote that reached Fiona upset her more than the others she had heard: "You can have any-thing you want in the world," Onassis was reported to have said, "except Fiona."

Onassis did not confine his telephone rantings to Alexander's liai-son; he complained about his work in the offices, his lack of under-standing of the shipping business, his recklessness with cars. On occasion, the phone calls would start out in a friendly way but cre-scendo into apoplectic tirades. Onassis would often call up drunk, talk about the weather—he once sang "Singing in the Rain" for five minutes over a transatlantic line—his bowel movements, go to the bathroom, then return to blast his son's affair with "that old woman."

So Fiona could understand what he was up against, Alexander began taping the phone conversations. Her verdict was that Onassis was deranged and that he was deliberately keeping his son in a de-structive emotional turmoil. Thrown against her will into a battle with Onassis—and with Tina, who in a less flamboyant manner was even more opposed to the match—Thyssen began to see herself as Alexander's deliverance from a cruel and crippling parental oppres-sion. Whatever her strengths and weaknesses in the contest, she was not afraid of Onassis, and that, more than anything else, may have been what pitted him so resolutely against her.

If Alexander's love affair with Fiona Thyssen managed to flourish despite Onassis's opposition, it may have been because Onassis him-self was in the throes of an epic new infatuation. Ever since the assassination of John F. Kennedy, Onassis had been in rather constant, although highly discreet, attendance on Jackie. Callas, who seemed to have an intelligence network to rival Onassis's own, learned about the super-secret but blossoming friendship and drew a conclusion that was still unthinkable to the rest of the world.

Callas knew, however, as the rest of the world did not, of a dinner for one guest Onassis had given at his Avenue Foch apartment, for which he instructed his most trusted live-in servants, Jorge and Eleni (who later worked for Christina), to keep to their quarters while he personally served the food. The rest of the staff was to remain out of the apartment for the evening. Familiar with both his ambition and his treachery, Callas learned of this mystery dinner guest and arrived at her own guess of who it had been.

Callas spent a good part of the summer of 1967 with Onassis on Skorpios, but she would depart occasionally for a business meeting in Paris or to deal with personal matters in Milan. When Fiat owner Gianni Agnelli dropped anchor at Onassis's island on an impromptu visit, he and his guests were stunned to see Jackie Kennedy shoot by on water skis. During their visit, she showed up for meals, quiet and withdrawn, then disappeared as soon as manners permitted. Jackie's visit, however, was brief; Callas still considered the island her summer home. But she knew she was being phased out, if she was not out already. Aware that she had yielded all her cards to her lover, she retreated to her new Paris apartment on the Avenue Georges-Mandel, and waited in torment to see how the game played out.

Callas never forgot the teen-aged Christina's spitefulness toward her. "Not a nice girl," she was once quoted as saying. "Hard. She treated me as if I were Ari's mistress." Years later, when Christina was an adult living much of the time in Paris, where Callas also lived, the two women never encountered each other. Callas had become a recluse after Onassis's death in 1975. And in 1977, when, at the age of fifty-three, she was found dead in her apartment on the Avenue Georges-Mandel, it was given out that she had died of a heart attack, but a contributory cause was that she, like the Onassis women, had become an abuser of mood-altering pills. As with Eugenie and Tina, the possibility of a deliberate overdose was never completely ruled out.

As an adult Christina grew uneasy about her behavior toward Callas. A few days after her death, Christina was at a Paris dinner with a group that included Prince Michael and Princess Marina of Greece. Christina fell on them. "I know you were great friends of Maria's," she said. "What was she like? Tell me, what kind of person was she?" Christina brought up the subject a few days later with Hélène Rochas. "You knew my father and Maria well, Hélène. Do you think Maria loved my father?" Hélène Rochas assured Christina that Callas had loved Onassis deeply, adding, "He was her great love."

"It's a pity they did not make their life together," Christina said from the vantage point of one who was beginning to realize how great an obstacle to a solid relationship money could be. "They spoke the same language."

Christina, knowing of her father's lack of enthusiasm for formal education, prevailed on him to allow her to leave St. George's one year shy of graduating. Onassis now had additional reasons for wanting his daughter to be constantly available: to serve as chaperon or beard on his outings with Jackie Kennedy. As for Tina, she was too lost in her own dissatisfactions to care about her daughter's truncated education. For some time, Tina had owned a small house in Reeves Mews in London's ultra-fashionable Mayfair. A small apartment was found in the mews for Christina, but when her mother was away, she moved into the larger house. The plan was for her to take courses at London's Queen's College, which she had enough credits to enter.

Christina did not take to college; she was having too much fun going to parties and flying off to Switzerland to ski. A friend remembered her as beng an extremely half-hearted student, and obsessed by her looks. She also was remembered as being obsessively neat about her dress. If a garment she was wearing got wrinkled or in any way soiled, instead of making a repair trip to a washroom, Christina would insist on changing immediately, even if it meant going home.

Through her father, she met a personable young Greek, Peter Goulandris, who was an heir to one of the largest Greek shipping fortunes. Peter was tall, slender, two years older than Christina, and, like her, handsome in a heavily Levantine way. His father had died when he was an infant and he was brought up by his mother, Maria Goulandris, who had been born a Lemos, perhaps the richest of the Greek shipping families. As soon as he had finished school, Peter had

*Christina, age three, aboard the yacht that her shipping-tycoon father named after her. Unwanted by both her parents, she was brought up in numbing luxury by a succession of servants.*

2

Neither Tina nor Aristotle Onassis
gave much time to their parental
roles. Whenever Tina's attention
was won, however, it invariably
went to her son, Alexander.

A pudgy child with a prominent
nose and dark circles under her eyes,
Christina looked more like her
father than her beautiful
and stylish mother.

*In the last years of their tempestuous marriage, both Tina and Ari had affairs, maintaining appearances only at public functions, like this 1957 charity gala they attended with Greek actress Katina Paxinou.*

*Onassis flaunted his liaison with the world-famous diva Maria Callas. Christina and Alexander, blaming her for the breakup of their parents' marriage, despised and tormented Callas.*

5

6

When Tina married the Marquess of Blandford,
Christina was enrolled in the Headington School in
Oxford, where her dark, Levantine looks set her apart
from her British classmates.

7

8

*At the reception following their father's marriage to Jacqueline Kennedy in 1968, Christina and Alexander, suspecting their new stepmother's motives, were less happy about the event than the bride.*

*Christina adored her father and he had a special affection for her, but it was on Alexander that he focused his hopes for the future of the Onassis empire.*

*When Christina started seeing shipping heir Peter Goulandris, Onassis became obsessed with the idea of merging his fortune with one even larger.*

*Incensed at being pushed into marrying Goulandris, Christina ran off with a young American, Danny Marentette. Family pressure finally persuaded her to give him up.*

11a

*At nineteen, Christina, here at St.
Moritz's exclusive Corviglia Club,
was rich, attractive, and eager for
whatever excitement her rare
position brought her.*

11b

gone to work for the family business and was applying himself with a diligence and seriousness that impressed everyone. Although the meeting of Peter and Christina appeared casual, Onassis undoubtedly had more in mind than simply expanding his daughter's circle of friends.

At first Christina liked Peter in a big-brother way, but when he indicated he was falling in love with her, she responded and began thinking of him as a boyfriend. She was fascinated to have someone smitten with her. She was also fascinated with Peter's wealth and bored her friends with the Goulandris statistics: 137 ships with a value in the neighborhood of $1.5 billion. Peter's branch of the family controlled sixty ships. If all of that excited Christina, it made her father ecstatic.

A short time earlier, Onassis had told Costa Gratsos and other confidants that he would marry Christina to a son of a Greek shipping family "when the time came." He clearly viewed his daughter as one of his untapped assets, the raw material with which to forge one more brilliant deal at the most propitious moment. She was not just a girl, but a girl who would bring with her an enormous fortune, his fortune, and he felt that circumstance justified his wielding total control over Christina's future. It was still early to push for a wedding, but he knew that a marriage with the Goulandrises would be far and away the best business deal he ever made.

Peter's mother, Maria Goulandris, was a ferocious Greek matriarch, who made Arietta Livanos seem weak willed. She viewed an Onassis-Goulandris match quite differently. A marriage with Christina, she told her son, would be a disaster for him and for the family. Looking down on Onassis, as few could, from a superior financial position, she still held the earlier perception of him—one that had been largely expunged by his colossal wealth—that he was an unsavory upstart whose flamboyance and slick deals had brought discredit to Greek shipowners. She also thought Christina was too spoiled and flighty. But because of her son's infatuation, Maria agreed to let him see Christina provided he did not get serious about her.

With Christina floundering in London with her half-hearted stab at higher education, her father pushed her to come to New York and go to work for Olympic Airlines, the company he had founded in 1957. Naturally, Christina's career was not his reason. Onassis had quietly moved his base to Manhattan, and wanted his daughter nearby. He had decided to promote her from chaperon to full co-conspirator in his top-secret courtship of the widow Kennedy. He may have felt a grown daughter provided a cover of respectability for his romantic campaign, or he may have been prompted merely by the loneliness of the world-class lothario.

Either way, Christina was one of the few human beings whose silence he felt he could count on with such an inflammatory bit of gossip. As expected, Christina was discreet, but mainly because she hoped the affair would burn itself out before anyone learned of it. A man living on the scale of Onassis, however, could have few secrets from his legions of attendants, and he would soon be dashed to learn that he was able to keep his romance quiet as long as he did for the unflattering reason that most of the world's population found the idea of a love affair between him and Jackie unthinkable.

The insistence on secrecy, of course, came from Jackie, who had imposed a Cupid-and-Psyche rule that their romance would end the minute word of it got out. Onassis, who would have liked to announce his conquest on the NBC Evening News, understood her desire for secrecy, which primarily resulted from the urgings of her favorite brother-in-law, Robert Kennedy, who was then running for President. Jackie was also aware of the furor that would erupt when she indicated she was unwilling to dedicate the remainder of her life to the memory of John F. Kennedy. For a prize of this magnitude, Onassis was willing to wait for his moment on the Evening News.

Between Christina's departure from London and her arrival in New York, there were four or five missing months, even allowing for summer visits to Skorpios and Coronis. People involved with the Onassis family—friends, servants, schoolteachers—had come to expect sudden disappearances followed by equally sudden surfacings weeks or months later. Christina's friends would not think it strange, even after day-by-day contact, to be informed by a butler that Miss Onassis was out of the country and was not expected back until the following year.

It was most probably in the late summer of 1967 that Christina had her face altered surgically—her nosed trimmed and the dark circles smoothed away from her eyes. Whenever she had the operation, it was a great success. The transformation was remarkable, but she was slow to adjust to her improved good looks. Years later, when she had gotten over her embarrassment about the drastic step and could talk openly about it, she told a friend, "It takes you about three years to realize you no longer look the way you always did."

An apartment was taken for Christina in New York in the East Fifties, which happened to be across the street from the apartment of her St. George's roommate , Keti Thandaris, who had no brothers or sisters and lived with her mother and her father. Keti's parents liked Christina, felt sorry for her, and were happy to have her for dinner whenever she wished, which was often. Christina was, of course, lonely, but she also idealized the Thandaris family—a father, a mother, and one daughter all living happily under one roof.

"Sometimes at night," Keti recalled, "we would go into my mother's room and sit on her bed talking with her. Christina would say that all she ever wanted was to have a normal family like ours, a family that lived together." But then Keti added, as if contradicting herself, "I'm sure Christina meant it, but she had grown so used to one kind of life, flying here and there, houses in different cities . . ."

During evenings with the Thandaris family, Christina began to show a remarkable appetite for unearthing memories of the past. Not only did she love evoking pleasant experiences, she would savor them slowly, then, when the last morsel of pleasure had been extracted, she would urge Keti to join her in a quest for fresh recollections.

"When we had run out of shared experiences," Keti recalled years later, "she would ask us to tell stories about our family, episodes unrelated to her. Not only did she love listening to these family tales, the silly kind every family has, she would urge us to retell ones she particularly liked each time she came over. She never got tired of hearing some of them, and would sometimes break in and try to tell the story herself."

Keti also kept photo albums, and Christina loved to spend hours looking at the photographs of their life together at St. George's. On many afternoons at five-thirty, the time Christina arrived home from her father's offices, she phoned Keti to ask if she might drop by to look at the scrapbooks. Most days Keti said yes, but some days she would beg off—she had to go out, her mother had guests—but Christina persisted.

"Let me send my maid over for the albums," Christina would

plead. "You know I'll take good care of them and get them back to you later tonight."

It became a pattern. One or two nights a week, Christina would phone, the maid would arrive and collect the heavy books, and Christina, a sixteen-year-old girl, in her own Manhattan apartment with plenty of money and many friends nearby, passing up the films, theaters, nightclubs, and restaurants that might have enlivened her free hours, would spend the evening alone foraging for scraps of happiness in a childhood that had contained little. Christina would retain her fondness for delving into the past. Countess Aline de Romanones recalled attending a dinner party years later at Stavros Niarchos's villa in St. Moritz. She found Christina, away from the other guests, absorbed in photo albums and crying softly. She was looking at pictures of her family, most of whom she had now lost.

In New York in the spring of 1967, Onassis and Jackie made one of their first public appearances together, at a dinner party he gave at the Greek restaurant Mykonos. Among the other guests were Rudolf Nureyev and Dame Margot Fonteyn. For Onassis, who rarely had much interest in artists unless he was sleeping with them, the guest list appeared to be an effort to please the cultural-minded Jackie. This subtlety was not lost on Maria Callas, who read about the party in the Paris newspapers. Christina was also present at the dinner and, like everyone else in the world at that time, was still in awe of the world's most famous widow.

Shortly after dinner, Onassis organized a Caribbean cruise on the *Christina*, in the midst of which all of the other passengers except Christina disembarked to make way for the arrival of a mystery guest, who was, of course, Jackie. For Christina, the period of forced togetherness did considerable damage to her regard for her father's new enthusiasm. She found Jackie vapid, dull, and most of all, far too exhilarated by her father's luxurious living style. Also clear to Christina was the incongruity of the match—something to which her father was blind. Apart from the most obvious difference, their ages, Jackie was reserved, affected, and stultifyingly ladylike, while Onassis was volatile, earthy, and unabashedly vulgar. Christina knew what Jackie saw in him. What could he see in her?

As Christina began to realize that his preoccupation with Jackie wasn't simply his usual celebrity chasing or womanizing but a serious matrimonial campaign, she was dismayed. Word of their frequent meetings had seeped into the press, so Christina no longer felt the need for total secrecy. She told a few close friends that her father was "hopelessly in love" with Jackie and began referring to her disdainfully as "my father's unfortunate obsession." Never having abandoned the hope of her parents' reconciling, she hated the idea of his remarrying, but she always assumed that, if he ever did, it would be to the despised Callas, who still figured prominently in Onassis's appointment book.

When Christina learned that not only was her father hoping to marry Jackie but that Jackie was all in favor of the idea, she didn't know which of them disgusted her more. With this ghastly possibility looming, she abruptly stopped talking to others about the romance, perhaps at his insistence. Christina could be wildly outspoken and indiscreet about herself and those close to her, but if she was convinced secrecy was necessary, she was better than most at filing something under "top secret" and forgetting about it. She would also learn that, to keep something out of the papers, she could tell no one. To curry favor with the gossip columnists, even her closest friends would phone in Christina's latest confidence.

When Jackie's mother, Janet Auchincloss, had bearded Onassis in his London hotel suite in 1964, her concern was for her second daughter's good name, since it was rumored that he was having an affair with Princess Lee Radziwill. A brief four years later, she was forced to receive the same Mr. Onassis at her Newport estate, Hammersmith Farm, as the one person her number-one daughter wanted with her to ease the shock of Robert Kennedy's assassination. But even with this evidence of intimacy, Janet Auchincloss and her family did not suspect Jackie was sleeping with the rough sixty-eight-year-old man, who Mrs. Auchincloss thought looked like a toad. If anyone had suggested matrimony was in the air, he would have been hooted off the grounds. The only one present that June weekend who knew matrimony was precisely what the visit portended was Christina, whom Onassis brought with him—perhaps to show that he, too, had a family.

If he hoped Christina would help charm the Auchinclosses, he miscalculated badly. Christina was in no mood to cooperate in her father's marital plans, although she was growing resigned to their inevitability. She had been somewhat mollified to know that the dreaded wedding could not occur any time soon. According to her father, Jackie had promised Bobby Kennedy she would wait until after the presidential elections before even so much as announcing her intentions.

To Christina, this was a gift of precious months in which her father's ardor for Jackie might cool as it had for Callas. But now, with Kennedy's assassination, that obstacle had been suddenly removed and Christina knew that her father was thrown into his legendary high gear and charging toward the finish line. At first Onassis had thought that the second Kennedy assassination would so shock Jackie his plans would be indefinitely delayed, but when he saw her reaction was quite the opposite—she wanted to speed up their plans —he took full advantage of her panicky and confused state to push to a conclusion his ultimate and "crowning" ambition.

Jackie, who had impressed the world with her strength and self-possession following her husband's assassination, fell completely apart after her brother-in-law's. It may have been simply that she could handle one violent death among those she loved, but not two. To the people around her at the time, she seemed completely disoriented, referring to Bobby as her husband and issuing instructions as if she were still First Lady. A few days after the shooting, during the weekend she spent at Hammersmith Farm, she had pulled herself together to a degree, but in the eyes of her family, Jackie's having forced the notorious Mr. Onassis on them when they were all still in shock over Bobby's death was every bit as deranged as her other symptoms.

Christina, suffocating with the secret she hated, entered into the Newport visit with all the enthusiasm of a hostage. Having finally won her father back from Callas, she was now about to lose him to someone worse. Christina never doubted Callas's feelings for her father, only Callas's right to have such feelings for her *mother's husband*. With Jackie, Christina did not believe there was any feeling at all. Her anger and hostility extended to the others present at Hammersmith Farm. That they were Jackie's people, her support group, was enough to make them Christina's enemies. But she also considered them upper-class fools, too vapid and blind to see the disaster about to befall them all.

Jackie's half-brother Jamie Auchincloss, Janet's son by Hugh Auchincloss and her youngest child, was closest to Christina's age and was given the job of looking after the Onassis girl during the weekend. An outgoing, good-looking young man, Jamie sailed into his task with well-honed charm and was clobbered for his efforts. All of his ploys to jolly up Christina were met with either sullen grunts or downright rudeness. On the few occasions when she talked at all, it was to deliver such winning opinions as that Americans were boring and drank too much, or the Newport mansions were ugly and pretentious. After two days of this, Jamie decided she was the most disagreeable girl he had ever met and summed it up years later by saying he wanted to shake Christina and say, "What is your problem?" Although Auchincloss did not know it at the time, she had a very real problem and so, in her eyes, did he. Since she was forbidden to tell him what it was, her sullen performance at Hammersmith Farm appeared to him and the rest of the Auchinclosses as nothing more than gratuitous bad manners.

When Christina finally made the vehemence of her disapproval known to her father, tension grew between them and they began to fight constantly, not just about Jackie, but about everything. Onassis felt betrayed. He had made Christina his confidante and fellow conspirator and now, when he had at last made clear what exactly it was they were conspiring for, she was defecting. Like other rich parents, receiving nothing but grief from their offspring over a proposed remarriage, Onassis began to suspect Christina's motives. Did she give a damn about his happiness or was she merely concerned for her inheritance? When he voiced this suspicion to Christina, it only increased her anger with him. Finally the feelings between father and daughter grew so tense that Christina quit her job in the Onassis New York offices and returned to England. She was glad to be out of the whole sorry affair, and he was glad to be rid of a daughter who was becoming an increasingly sour note in his carefully orchestrated amorous plans.

Eager as both Onassis and Jackie were to wed, there were still a number of arrangements to be made and a prenuptial agreement to be worked out. When Jackie finally made her matrimonial intentions known to her mother and to the Kennedys, they were aghast. A few feeble family efforts were made to talk her out of it. A delegation of Kennedy women led by Ethel and Joan told Jackie of the damage such a marriage would do to the Kennedy name. But Jackie felt that she had done enough for the Kennedy name and was now in a mood to please herself. Soon the Kennedy forces learned, as the Auchin-closes had, how determined she was to marry Onassis. All of her grief and self-pity over the violent deaths of first her husband then her brother-in-law seemed to be channeled into a viselike resolve to do as she wished in this one matter. The universal disapproval seemed only to have the effect of making her even more eager than Onassis for an early wedding. Once she was married, she figured, the arguing would end.

About six weeks after the Hammersmith Farm weekend, Christina had her Skorpios vacation interrupted by the arrival of Senator Ted Kennedy, who disgusted her with his heavy drinking and girl-grab-bing revels. Again, Christina was one of the few on Skorpios at the time who was aware that Kennedy had come to work out the financial arrangements of the marriage, which Christina simply saw as the purchase price for her father's famous bride. Such a fiscal approach to marriage, repugnant to most people but more so to a teen-aged girl, only intensified her repugnance for the entire Jackie *Anschluss*. And Teddy's boorish behavior on the island gave a grotesque clown-ishness to what Christina saw as a snowballing calamity for her family.

If she knew more than others about how far things had progressed, Christina was also privy to an aspect of the relationship between her father and Jackie that few others knew about. That was the degree to which they doted on each other and seemed to be in love. Even so, she may have had more reason to suspect Jackie of mercenary motives than mere intuition or her customary condemnation of women close to her father. Even at seventeen, Christina viewed Jackie's love-struck effusions with the skeptical eye of a fellow woman.

On October 15, 1968, when the Boston *Herald-Traveler* astounded the world with the news that Jackie Kennedy would shortly marry Aristotle Onassis, a family council of war was convened at Artemis's villa in Glyfada for the purpose of holding the wedding immediately. With the news out, they could all look forward to a media nightmare until Jackie and Onassis were married. Speed would cut short the horror. A posse of reporters bearded Onassis in the cocktail lounge of Athens's Grande-Bretagne Hotel, and he confirmed that he would be marrying "tomorrow or within a few days" depending on his next conversation with Jackie. With blushing-bridegroom geniality, he then excused himself from further comment, saying, "I have so many family problems in my head to settle, please leave me alone now and give me your blessing."

The truth was that Onassis had *two* family problems—Christina and Alexander—who were then waiting for him at his sister Artemis's villa, where Jackie was also staying. As soon as the marriage plans had leaked out, he had summoned his children to tell them formally of his intentions. Onassis had voiced a few second thoughts to Christina in the weeks before, and she clung to the hope that he would not go through with the wedding. That hope was squashed and Onassis was resigned to their taking it badly. He had allowed them to believe that not marrying Callas had been an accommodation to their feelings. He now had to explain why, in this instance, he was flouting their feelings entirely.

Taking them into the library at Artemis's villa and closing the door, he told them of his decision to marry right away and they reacted forcefully, but with disappointing predictability. Alexander jumped into his Ferrari and drove into the night at death-courting speed, and Christina had an ear-splitting, vase-smashing tantrum that drove Onassis and his bride-to-be out into the night in search of dinner and tranquillity.

Busy with his own controversial love life, Alexander had never met Jackie until the council at Glyfada, and was too angered at having been left out of the intrigue to worry much about the appropriateness of the match. He was more than willing, however, to accept Christina's fortune-hunter verdict and shortly delivered one of his famous epigrams: "It's a perfect match. My father likes names and Jackie likes money." Feeling less strongly about the marriage than Christina did, he was still eagerly in favor of insurrectionist moves, and promptly fell in with his sister's intention to boycott the wedding.

When he learned of their plans, Onassis delegated Artemis to change Christina's mind, while emissaries from the Onassis high command prevailed on the despised Fiona to change Alexander's.

Outraged that his father would attempt to use a woman he had treated so shabbily for his own disgraceful purposes, Alexander phoned his father and, with an Onassian instinct for a deal, agreed to come to the wedding if all criticism of his relationship with Fiona would cease. Onassis, who never felt bound by promises to his children, agreed.

The wedding day, October 20, 1968, was cool and rainy. Only family members and a few close friends jammed the tiny Skorpios chapel, while three hundred journalists, all but a small delegation forbidden on the island, bobbed in boats offshore. Alexander and Christina, both grim and silent, arrived for the ceremony, which they considered no more than a marriage between Jackie's greed and their father's ego. They knew their mother's marriage to Blandford was finished, and old hopes had revived of their parents' remarrying. They were, however, adult enough to live with their disappointment over this demolished dream.

Nor were they concerned about their inheritance. By the terms of the prenuptial agreement that had been worked out with the help of Jackie's great friend and confidant the financier André Meyer—Teddy's effort having been scrapped—she had waived her right under Greek law to 12.5 percent of her husband's estate on his death in exchange for an up-front cash gift of $3 million. Alexander and Christina had no reason to fear that the marriage would cost them a single percentage point of their inheritance. Even in his love-struck state, Onassis's entire thrust in the negotiations had been to protect the hundreds of millions marked for his children.

With no concern about money, Christina and Alexander had an overriding fear that their father was allowing a transparent fortune hunter to make a fool of him. They predicted he would be hurt and humiliated—viewed by the world as an aging Don Pasquale hoodwinked and tormented by a grasping young wife. Because of their strong feelings against Jackie, they foresaw that they would be cut off from their father, that the family would be even more divided than it had been during his affair with Callas. Throughout the service, Christina cried quietly, not altogether inappropriate at a wedding, and Alexander worked on facial expressions that would leave no doubt how contemptuous he was of the proceedings.

Christina expected and, for her father's sake, dreaded the world-wide cry of dismay that greeted the Skorpios nuptials, but Onassis was surprised and stunned by it. Having been seduced into seeing himself through Jackie's moonstruck eyes as an altogether worthy suitor, he was now forced to see himself through the unclouded eyes of the rest of the world. From every corner of the globe headlines told him he was an ugly old man despoiling a lovely young woman; he was a social climber trading on tragedy-induced celebrity; he was a shady character cleansing his act with a venerated icon. If he had hoped his marriage would call attention to his merits, it had a thunderously reverse effect. It was painful, even for one as tough-skinned as Onassis, to learn that the fulfillment of his dreams did such damage to everyone else's.

# 7

# ALL THIS AND LOVERS TOO

$O$nassis never let his children's feelings affect his major personal decisions, regardless of how strong those feelings were or how much the decisions affected their lives. Once having acted on his decisions, however, he would usually turn his attention to repairing the damage done to family relations. Since Alexander now had two reasons for avoiding his father as often as possible—his liaison and his father's— he was almost always absent, so was harder to placate.

Christina, on the other hand, was less willing to yield the field to Jackie and dutifully turned up when her father requested her presence. His appreciation was Onassian. He set Christina up with a $4,000-a-month allowance and gave her freedom to travel wherever she wished. He also lavished on her a number of gifts, the most spectacular, her eighteenth-birthday present, was a Greek shawl in which he had wrapped $50,000 worth of jewelry, handsome pieces Jackie had helped select.

While still struggling along on his miserable $12,000 a year, Alexander was at first angered by the rewards showered on his sister and more convinced than ever that she was "sucking up." Far from emulating her efforts to get along, which he considered honor-destroying hypocrisy, Alexander merely shifted to his new step-mother the insolence he had honed on Callas. On one occasion, sitting with his father and Jackie in a Paris nightclub, he listened to their gossiping about a well-known woman who had recently married a very rich man. The usual speculations were made about whether or not the woman's motive had been her new husband's wealth. Alexander was suddenly overwhelmed by a double injustice: his father had made similar slanders against Fiona only to have married a woman who was, to say the least, vulnerable to the same gold-digger accusation. Fixing Jackie with his gaze, Alexander said, "Surely you don't find anything wrong with a woman marrying for money, do you, Jackie?"

Such moments of unveiled hostility, which Onassis privately felt were the way the upper classes sparred, were usually followed by angry repercussions from him but were quickly forgotten. Before long, Alexander was also benefiting from Onassis's marital happiness, or so he thought. Arriving at Fiona's house in London, he excitedly told his mistress his father had bought him a beautiful seaside villa at Lagonissi, a fashionable seaside resort not far from Athens. Alexander was thrilled at this sudden spurt of generosity, but Fiona was wary.

"Good," she said, "and I'll take a house nearby."

"What do you mean?" Alexander replied perplexed. "You'll live with me."

She closed her eyes and shook her head "no." "Don't you see?" she said. "That's exactly what your father wants. It's a trick to compromise me. If I move in, he can say I am living off the Onassis money. I've been around too long to fall into that sort of trap."

Alexander, who thought he had been sufficiently cynical to view the $300,000 villa as a bribe for his acceptance of the marriage to Jackie, was impressed with Fiona's canny insight at perceiving a further motive and quickly agreed with her. He was coming to admit what she had been saying for some time, that everything in his future —happiness, an unharassed love life, growing up—depended on wresting independence from his controlling father.

He telephoned Onassis in Paris to say he didn't want the villa, "but thanks anyway." In spite of such moments of bravado, Alexander now knew he would never have a tolerable life unless he could break the final and perhaps strongest tie, the economic one. Fiona, who had become adept at the resonating remark, admonished him,

"Being afraid of your father is not a career." In order to be free, she argued, he had to find a way of making a living outside of the Onassis empire. They agreed that, without so much as a high-school diploma, his prospects were not bright.

One of Onassis's justifications for forcing on his children a marriage they loathed was his belief that Jackie would bring cultivation and refinement into their lives. There was no doubt they needed both. Despite a succession of governesses and good schools, as well as a mother who had been reasonably well brought up, Alexander and Christina had remained remarkably ignorant of the fundamentals of moneyed-class style. It was probably because they keyed off their father, a man who flaunted his vulgarity, and all other influences seemed to them the phony posturings of inferior beings, in most cases beings who lived off their father. Also, since they were given a choice, which most children were not, they opted for wildness.

Whatever the reason, both Alexander and Christina were entering adulthood lacking the countless behavioral niceties that informed the style and polish of the people among whom they would be spending their lives. Christina in particular was plagued with some unattractive personal habits, such as twisting a strand of hair around a finger, laughing too loud, or accumulating saliva in the corner of her mouth as she talked—flaws that easily could have been purged in childhood, but no one had bothered or dared. Tina's efforts at gentrifying her daughter had suffered from the same lack of resolve as her marriage to Blandford; in both she seemed to have little more than a mild curiosity about where it would all lead. And most of the improvements in Christina that occurred at Lee Place were abandoned as the marriage lost momentum.

Fiona Thyssen was astounded by Alexander's lack of such rudimentary social equipment as table manners. It was not that he flouted the rules; he didn't know them. Many people in Fiona's world of international society applauded her success in domesticating Alexander, and word of her accomplishment reached Onassis. Although his indifference to his children's bad breeding was its primary cause, he was still pleased to hear of his son's renovation and requested that Jackie do a similar overhaul on Christina.

In the early months of 1969, when both women were in New York, Jackie made the effort. She took Christina shopping, to museums and the theater, and gave dinners with the aim of introducing her stepdaughter to people of taste and cultivation. At her father's insistence, Christina went along with the program. Always civil to Jackie but careful never to cross the line to a hypocritical friendliness, in front of others she called her stepmother "*kyria,*" the Greek word for "madam," which was a sly ruse to conceal from outsiders her stiff formality. After a few weeks, the Christina-burnishing project was abandoned. Both women hated the enforced togetherness, and occasional transatlantic diatribes from Onassis were not enough to keep it alive.

There was an unfortunate and lasting result of Onassis's scheme to turn his daughter into a little Jackie. Whatever inclinations Christina may have had for the finer things, which were probably not great, were permanently extinguished by having them forced on her by the person she most disliked in the world. If Jackie was to have become a role model for Christina, the plan had the opposite effect. Instead of adopting Jackie's cultivation and refined tastes, Christina rejected such embellishments *because* they were Jackie's. Her stepmother's hateful superiority in most areas of human deportment worked powerfully to strengthen Christina's feelings of inadequacy. Jackie's slender figure was a particular sore point to the weight-prone Christina.

"I always feel like a cow next to her," she told a friend. She also felt devoid of style, grace, manners, education, culture, intellect. But if Jackie was the embodiment of those assets, Christina, at a crucial point in her development, wanted no part of them.

For all her dislike of Jackie, Christina managed to find a positive aspect to her father's foolish marriage: her new siblings. Thrown together with John and Caroline Kennedy on the *Christina* and on Skorpios, she grew genuinely fond of both children. She particularly liked Caroline, whom she dubbed "a terrific girl." Considerably younger, they triggered her motherly instincts, as had Blandford's children, and she enjoyed taking them on outings—sightseeing trips from the yacht or tours of islands near Skorpios. She would often be mistaken for their governess, which amused and pleased her. Christina probably never learned that Caroline had been as violently opposed to their parents' marrying as she was. According to a close friend of Jackie's who had been in the Fifth Avenue apartment at the time and overheard it, Caroline, on being told of the wedding plans, had thrown a tantrum comparable to the one Christina had thrown at Glyfada.

In July of 1969, Christina attended a combined celebration of Jackie's fortieth birthday and the nine-month wedding anniversary at her Aunt Artemis's house. During the evening Jackie remarked she had never been to an Athens nightclub. Immediately, Onassis herded the party into a fleet of limousines and took them to his favorite local haunt, the restaurant Neraida in Piraeus, where he became a casebook study of a joyous Greek—dancing, singing, shouting toasts in Greek. He saw to it that champagne flowed for everyone in the house, and he paid the orchestra to play all night.

Christina, who made an effort to enter into the spirit of the marathon exuberance, outlasted some of the guests, but finally gave up around five in the morning. Jackie held the course, something she would shortly cease to do on such outings, and remained at her husband's side until the last guest had left at 9 A.M. According to later reports, it was estimated that Onassis spent close to $20 million between October 1968 and October 1969 on gifts for Jackie and on indulging her whims for decorating, construction, travel, and clothes. Still in love, he clung to the conceit, which he would shortly revise, that he could afford the extravagance of any woman. Christina saw what was happening, as did everyone close to Onassis. For her father's sake, she made an effort to get along with her stepmother, but she was sickened by the buying orgy and felt her worst fears about Jackie were being quickly confirmed.

In the fall of 1969, Onassis, still feeling euphoric about his own love life, turned his attention to Christina's. Negotiations were reopened with Peter Goulandris, and once again help was enlisted from Tina in bringing off the match. Tina, who had inherited her mother Artemis's relish for pairing shipping fortunes, was as enthusiastic about marrying Christina to Goulandris as Onassis. To him, the objections of Goulandris's mother, Maria Goulandris, were a minor detail that could easily be overcome.

Over the past year, Christina's warm feelings for Goulandris had cooled considerably. On a number of occasions, he had disappointed her on plans they had made, often pleading an obligation to his mother that he had to fulfill. Eventually, he admitted to Christina that his mother was strongly opposed to a marriage. That made Christina angry—her father was a good man, and Maria, not knowing her, had no right to pass judgment. But even beyond his mother's disapproval, Christina was bothered by the degree to which Goulandris allowed it to influence him. He was an adult and was supporting himself, even if it was by working for a Goulandris company. Christina complained to a friend, "Why doesn't he tell her to go screw herself the way my brother told my father when he tried to get him to give up Fiona? Like Peter, Alexander works for the family business and is the same age." Except for the occasional tantrum, Christina had yet to demonstrate her headstrong, defiant side, but it was stirring within her and she hated the lack of it in Peter.

While trying to decide how to get her father to abandon his marriage plans for her, Christina went to stay with her uncle George Livanos in St. Moritz for Christmas of 1969. At the super-exclusive Corviglia Club high up on the ski slopes, she met a young American, Danny Marentette, who was having lunch with Livanos. When she joined their table, Livanos, by way of aiding conversation with the stranger, told Christina that Marentette had just come from a month of shooting big game in Kenya. With the forthrightness that was increasingly marking her style, Christina announced her disapproval of killing animals. Marentette defended himself with theories about hunting's being a way to control population explosions among species, but, in battles with her father over his whaling fleet, Christina had heard that justification many times and rejected it. They flailed away heatedly for a while until Livanos eased them onto a new subject. Although she was unimpressed with Marentette's arguments, she was intrigued by him. Not only did he stand up to her, he didn't drink too much and he wasn't boring.

Raised and schooled among the rich in America, Marentette was a bright, easygoing young man with a ready sense of humor and a good amount of charm. He was on the short side—only about two inches taller than Christina, who was five feet five inches tall—but he had curly brown hair, a prankster's twinkle in his eyes, and a calm, unhurried manner, which Christina particularly liked. She noticed he walked with a slight limp she later learned was caused by a malformation of his hip. Marentette came from Detroit's poshest suburb, Grosse Pointe, where his father owned a manufacturing company. His mother, Margaret, had inherited considerable wealth that sprang from newspapers and television stations. Her great-grandfather was James Scripps, founder of the Detroit *News*, whose half-brother, E. W. Scripps, had started the Scripps-Howard chain of newspapers. The family, however, was not as rich as it had once been, and while Marentette had sufficient money to travel among the wealthy and indulge himself in pleasure-related enterprises—at the time he was working as a blood agent, rather a marriage broker for horses, and owned two racehorses himself—he was not rich at all by Onassis and Corviglia standards.

Perhaps because he often found himself surrounded by people who outranked him financially, Marentette, while being friendly to all comers, had perfected the pose, so common among those who once had a lot of money, of an almost snide indifference to wealth, but particularly wealth of more recent origins than his family's. From the vehemence of his defense of shooting animals, Christina could see Marentette was not intimidated by her and he certainly wasn't trying to charm her. That interested her. She was beginning to recognize the symptoms of money awe in those she met when they heard the Onassis name—increasingly the reaction would both please and disgust her—and she was struck by Marentette's lack of it.

She invited him to her Uncle George's for dinner, and they began skiing together and going out in the evenings. His hip problem, she was pleased to discover, in no way affected his skiing. If anything he was a better skier than she was, and her skiing was something on which she prided herself. About four days after they met, Christina decided she was wild about Marentette and they went to bed together. The love-making was a success and Christina was ecstatic. As always when she was excited about something or someone, Christina would take to the telephone. From St. Moritz, she placed endless calls to Europe and America in search of a friend who knew Marentette and who might express an opinion about him. She was delighted when she found a New York schoolmate who knew him well.

"Isn't he wonderful?" Christina prompted. "What do you think?"

"Danny is great," the girl replied. "I mean, he's cute and very amusing, but . . ."

"But what?"

"Well, he's not someone I would think about getting serious with."

Christina was so upset with this negative note that the friend backed down and said that Marentette simply wasn't the man she, personally, would want to go through life with. Christina was only slightly mollified, but it would have taken far more than a mild demur to dissuade her. Far more appeared when her father learned of the romance. Although Onassis hated St. Moritz and was happy to leave it to the Livanoses and the Niarchoses, he kept close watch on Christina's activities there. Within a day or two of her being seen with Marentette, he had a complete check run on him. Because of Marentette's blood ties with a publishing dynasty, his gentlemanly upbringing, his keenness on skiing, riding some animals and shooting others, he would have seemed an ideal catch for England's Princess Anne. He was not, however, good enough for Onassis.

Ever since becoming a very rich man, Onassis had been dodging the sons of once-rich families who populated the fanciest resorts—well-bred losers, in his eyes—and he decided Danny Marentette fit the mold. Onassis did not stop to consider that, by comparison with Peter Goulandris and his family's $1.5 billion fortune, almost anyone would come off a loser. Oblivious of Christina's diminishing enthusiasm for Peter Goulandris, Onassis was progressing on details of an Onassis-Goulandris merger, and he was not prepared to have his plans upset by a boarding-school lounge lizard who owned one or two racehorses.

In the overall context of Onassis's life, his position was understandable. All of his struggle and accomplishment had brought the Onassis family into the matrimonial big leagues. He could not allow his daughter to abandon this hard-won beachhead because of a schoolgirl crush. Having always placed his indefatigable libido at the service of his greater goals, he expected his daughter to behave in a similar fashion and to adopt without question not only his style but his goals. Forcefully, he let Christina know he did not consider Marentette a suitable person for her to become involved with, let alone think of marrying.

Dismissing her father's disapproval as a knee-jerk exercise in control, Christina saw Marentette regularly in New York but stopped short of moving into his apartment. To keep from causing too much alarm on Avenue Foch, she stayed in the suite her father kept at the Hotel Pierre (her own apartment in New York had been let go). Having made this one concession to appearances, she threw herself into the affair. Her days with Marentette were idyllic. In the mornings they would drive out to Belmont Race Track on Long Island to watch his horses train, then return to Manhattan in time for lunch at one of the restaurants, like P. J. Clarke's, where they were sure to see friends. They would often split up in the afternoon while Christina shopped or did errands, then meet in the evening for dinner, a party, or a play.

One night they went to the races at Aqueduct on Long Island with Marentette's trainer. On their way back, they found that they were all too famished to wait until they reached Manhattan to eat. The trainer knew of a restaurant near the track owned by an Italian-American with the connection-evoking name of Tony the Sheik.

"I think it was called Vesuvio or maybe House of Garlic," Marentette recalled. "Anyhow, it was one of these big, noisy family-style places that bring you huge platters heaped with Italian food. They served a homemade wine, a guinea red that arrived in unlabeled bottles and which the other customers mixed with cream soda. We tried it, and I think the soda helped. Christina was fascinated by the place, had never seen anything like it.

"Christina loved the restaurant, so she was full of adventure. After dinner, on our way back to Manhattan, we were driving along a seedy part of Woodhaven Boulevard. Christina spotted a topless bar and said she wanted to go in. She'd been to nightclubs with naked women before—her father used to take her to the Crazy Horse in Paris—but this place was lowdown and raunchy, a complete sleaze palace, and Christina loved it."

Keeping tabs on Christina's flourishing idyll in New York, Onassis was growing more and more exasperated. For a man who had no problem combatting governments and powerful international cartels, he seemed strangely at a loss when it came to confrontations with his daughter. He decided the best way to deal with Christina's romantic obstinacy was to ignore it and push ahead with the Goulandris match; Marentette could be dealt with when the time came. He would let her have her fun, then, when he was ready, tell her what she had to do. Onassis was happy to learn that Peter Goulandris had now decided to go against his mother's wishes and marry Christina. Onassis met with him and they concluded details of the merger, having agreed on the most important point, that both shipping companies would be kept separate. They then set plans for announcing the engagement. Neither Goulandris nor Onassis felt it necessary to include Christina in the negotiations. They simply informed her everything was decided.

For handling Christina, no course could have been worse. Questions of family loyalty, money, her fondness for Goulandris were all swept aside when she realized she was being bartered like a tankerful of crude. Over the phone, Christina told her father she would not marry Goulandris, now or ever. In a controlled fury, Onassis ordered her to come immediately to Skorpios for a serious talk. Saying goodbye to Marentette, she flew to Athens, where Onassis's seaplane took her to Skorpios.

With her captive on his island, Onassis berated her for hours. He stressed her ingratitude, her lack of family feeling, her willingness to accept the benefits of great wealth but her unwillingness to assist in strengthening the fortune. Over and over he came back to Marentette's main drawback: no money. Christina, still angry about her father's marriage to Jackie, was unreceptive to lectures from him on the uses of matrimony. Making her big speech on their opposing views of the institution, she climaxed it by proclaiming, "Love is not a business deal." She was perhaps talking, at that moment in her father's love life, to the wrong man. Tempers flared on both sides. Christina finally stormed off Skorpios and flew back to New York.

She resumed her life with Marentette and avoided her father's phone calls. In furious desperation, Onassis sent Jackie to New York to reason with Christina. Happy for an excuse to return to civilization, Jackie hurried off to present her stepdaughter with fresh arguments for complying with her father's wishes. When the two women met, Christina stunned Jackie and cut off all discussion with the announcement that she was pregnant.

While Jackie gaped, Christina went on to say she was going to marry Marentette and have his child. So flummoxed was Jackie by this new development—which was a lot more family drama than she (or Ted Kennedy or André Meyer) had bargained for—she promptly resigned from mothering Christina after her first assignment and retired in confusion to her Fifth Avenue apartment. Lacking the courage to pass the news on to her husband, she asked Costa Gratsos to do it, then lay low as she waited for the explosion from Skorpios.

When Christina phoned her mother with her family news, Tina took it with more aplomb, but asked Christina and Marentette to fly to London immediately at her expense to discuss the situation. Responding to this more reasonable parental tone, they accepted the invitation and arrived to find Tina sympathetic but unsparing in spelling out the grief they could expect from Onassis.

Tactfully avoiding Marentette's finances, Tina said the objections sprang from his not being Greek. Christina and Marentette didn't care what Onassis's objections were based on, she told her mother; their minds were made up. They were going to fly back to New York, then drive to Elkton, Maryland, where they could get married immediately, without parental permission, blood tests, cooling-off period, and other unromantic formalities. They would prefer having Tina's blessing, but even without it, they would proceed with their plans.

Before they had a chance to carry them out, a bombshell fell into the Onassis and Livanos families, one whose repercussions would last for years. On May 3, 1970, Tina's sister, Eugenie Niarchos, was found dead on her husband's island of Spetsapoula. Onassis, who always boasted of his luck in extraneous events coming to the aid of his strategies, now turned this shocking death into the wedge that would separate Christina from Marentette.

While the various dramas of the Onassis family had until now been the routine fights, affairs, divorces, sorrows, and triumphs other families have—leavened, perhaps, by the antic personality of Onassis, by a Byzantine Greekness to the plots, and by an enormous amount of money, with Eugenie's death the saga veered sharply from prime-time soap opera and moved toward Greek tragedy. Christina and

Alexander had come to love their aunt, whom they had visited every summer since the prohibition against the world of Stavros Niarchos had been lifted by their mother's divorce from Onassis. They were devastated by her death, as was everyone who knew her. She was known to be a weak woman and chronically unhappy, but was greatly admired for her intelligence, her dignity in the face of repeated humiliations from her husband, and her kindness.

Of even greater significance for Christina, Eugenie's death marked the first in a series of calamitous events in the lives of her family—sudden deaths, suicides, suspected murders—some connected, some seemingly random. Onassis singled out one of these tragedies, the one that hit him the hardest—the death of his son—and said it was punishment for his hubris in marrying Jackie. Until his own death in 1975, a series of unlikely and wrenching tragedies suggested that not just Onassis but his entire family was being punished.

The circumstances of Eugenie's death were murky, and a great deal of money and influence was used that rendered them murkier. She had apparently entered a room when her husband was on the phone to America making plans with his former wife, automobile heiress Charlotte Ford, to bring their daughter to the island for a visit. Charlotte was to stay ten days and her daughter would remain for a month. In 1965, Niarchos had divorced Eugenie and married Ford, whom he had made pregnant, when a shotgun had been held to his head not only by her father, Henry Ford II, but by Ford's friend President Lyndon Johnson, a Texan who knew about shotguns.

Within weeks of his marriage to Ford in Mexico, Niarchos rejoined Eugenie, and, after he was divorced by Ford in 1967, resumed his earlier marriage, having never been legally divorced from Eugenie in the eyes of the Greek church. If any woman would appear to have been the winner in that marital triangle, it was Eugenie, but apparently life was better not being married to Niarchos than married to him. She was known to be miserably unhappy and, like her sister Tina, a heavy user of sedatives.

The night of her death, Niarchos claimed he was preparing for bed then changed his mind and went to his wife's room to continue the angry discussion they had had following his phone conversation with his ex-wife. Entering his wife's bedroom, he found Eugenie lying next to her bed, unconscious from an apparent overdose. Nearby was a note, written in red pencil and in English: "For the first time in all our life together I have begged you to help me. I have implored you. The error is mine. But sometimes one must forgive and forget." Then, in a wildly erratic scrawl, she had added with a ballpoint pen, "26 is an unlucky number. It is the double of 12.10b of whiskey."

The meaning of the note, especially the postscript, has never been discovered.

Niarchos said he vigorously struggled to revive his wife. He called his valet and together they forced hot coffee into her. After a surprising delay of a half hour, a doctor was called, not one from the nearest town but a doctor from Athens who was associated with a Niarchos company. Ninety minutes elapsed between the time when Niarchos stated he found his wife and the doctor's arrival. The doctor, finding Eugenie's body covered with bruises, with a particularly severe one on her neck, refused to issue a death certificate, and the body was flown to Athens for an autopsy.

The list of injuries to Eugenie's body was extensive—small cuts and internal bleeding in her neck area; bruises on her left arm, ankle, and leg; a large bruise on her stomach with internal bleeding behind, internal bleeding in her lower back, a two-inch bruise with swelling above her left eye. There were other, smaller signs of violence. Although the bruises went from her ankles to her forehead, the examining doctors concluded that they were consistent with resuscitation efforts and that her death had been caused by an overdose of barbiturates.

Like most people, Onassis did not believe this and led the clamor for further investigation. His efforts succeeded, and a second autopsy was ordered by the Piraeus public prosecutor. It arrived at totally different conclusions. The level of barbiturates in Eugenie's blood was not high enough to cause death, he asserted, and she had died instead from the injuries to her body. A third inquiry raised the possibility that Eugenie had not voluntarily ingested the twenty-five Seconals; rather they might have been forced down her throat.

Considerations other than a desire for truth and justice—including, in Onassis's case, revenge—intruded into the skirmishing of different sets of authority. Because of major business developments, Niarchos had recently joined forces with the military junta that had seized control of Greece in 1967 and this government was just as eager as he to dispose of the scandal. Since he had those in power on his side, it was a tribute to Greek justice that the factions opposing him, led by Onassis, were able to prevent the mysterious death from being quickly hushed up.

After the third inquiry, the investigating magistrate decided sufficient evidence had been collected to charge Niarchos with killing his wife and ordered his arrest. After frantic maneuvers by Niarchos's lawyers, the Piraeus high court suddenly and preemptively overruled the magistrate's decision and the case was dropped. This unexplained action, suspicious to many, did little to counter the widespread belief that Niarchos had killed his wife in a violent rage.

The case was the number-one topic of gossip on the international circuit for months. The manner in which outsiders judged the Spetsapoula tableau—a dead woman in her early forties, a known pill taker, covered with bruises; a tyrannical husband with a legendary temper; an unexplained delay in calls for help—depended more on the innocence or cynicism of the observers than on the evidence turned up by the investigations. There was, however, another element in the guilt-innocence equation that was known to only a few at the time of Eugenie's death: Niarchos had been seriously interested in another woman—her sister, Tina.

One who fell without hesitation into the cynical camp was Christina. Trained by her father from infancy to hate her uncle, she was outspoken in her belief that he had murdered her beloved aunt. Word of her suspicions reached Niarchos. He took no action at the time, but marked Christina clearly in his book as an enemy to be watched. Onassis, who was then engaged in an all-out battle with his ex-brother-in-law for a Greek refinery concession, remained convinced of his guilt and hired his own experts to continue investigating.

When the investigations dragged on with no promise of arriving at fresh incriminating evidence, Christina came to feel strongly that her father should drop the matter. She knew that part of his motive in keeping the scandal alive was to delay if not torpedo Niarchos's huge deal with the Greek generals. With the sudden reversal of his indictment by the high court, Niarchos had this side of his problem under control and his deal was not in jeopardy.

With little hope of new information to reopen legal proceedings, only the whispering campaign was left, which was doing no harm to her thick-skinned uncle, Christina felt, but considerable harm to her cousins, the Niarchos children, who had lost their mother. With the marriage to Jackie, Christina had swallowed a repugnant development in the interest of family harmony; it was now her father's turn to do the same. Alexander, who had become friendly with his Niarchos cousins, agreed, and so, eventually, did Onassis. Privately, however, Christina never abandoned the conviction that her uncle had murdered her aunt.

As grim and startling as Eugenie's death was, and as greatly as it would affect the lives of Christina and her family for years to come, the most immediate result was the use of the tragedy to persuade Christina to drop Danny Marentette. Too distraught for further dissembling to handle her daughter, Tina now abandoned her pose as a sympathetic ally and came out flatly against Christina's marrying Marentette. Arietta Livanos joined the chorus and said Christina should "postpone" her plans. Christina, too, had deeply loved her aunt, and her strong family feelings were strengthened by the grief they all shared. It all combined to jar her from her defiant and self-absorbed pursuit of her own happiness. Early in June of 1970, with her mother's experienced guidance, Christina checked into a London clinic and, at a cost of forty pounds, had an abortion.

If Onassis and his two children were convinced of Niarchos's guilt, two people even closer to Eugenie were convinced he was blameless, her mother and sister. Not only did Arietta Livanos defend her son-in-law and denounce his accusers as evil mischief makers, she immediately began campaigning for Tina to replace her sister, not just as the mother of Eugenie's children, but as the wife of Niarchos. A woman who knew Arietta well said, "I can just hear her: 'Eugenie wants you to look after her children, dear. And look after our darling Stavros, too.'"

Many people concluded that Arietta's machinations were merely old-fashioned empire building so common among the Greek shipping families. If she could persuade Tina to replace Eugenie as Mrs. Niarchos, she could save the alliance between the Niarchos and Livanos fortunes that might otherwise be lost. Since Arietta now had four Niarchos grandchildren, it made outsiders wonder how strong an alliance she needed. Arietta viewed as fortune-hunting beggars men who did not own fleets of ships—including marquesses and dukes—so part of her motivation was undoubtedly a desire to strengthen her daughter's fortune rather than to watch it disappear in overhauling the plumbing of Blenheim Palace.

At the core of Arietta's indefatigable machinations, however, was her obsessive fondness for Niarchos himself. Whether or not the rumors were true that she had had an affair with him before he became her son-in-law—and most insiders considered it "common knowledge" that she had—there was little doubt she doted on him. In adoration of Niarchos she had always stood out in strong contrast to the large numbers of people who detested him. But now, when most of European society was whispering that Niarchos had caused his wife's death, her mother was busy trying to persuade her remaining daughter to marry him.

With or without Arietta's prodding, Tina had strong feelings of responsibility toward her sister's children. Immediately after the tragedy, she took the two youngest to live with her in London. She also had strong feelings for Niarchos and was rumored to have been in love with him even before she had been stampeded into marriage by Onassis. Niarchos never made much effort to hide his feelings for Tina. It had been his plane, in fact, that had delivered Tina from her marriage to Onassis, flying her from Venice to Paris. He had arranged for the bone specialist to rescue Tina when she broke her leg in St. Moritz, and he had often put his ski villa at her disposal. He, and his possessions, were always there when she needed them. His feelings for Tina clearly went beyond those for a sister-in-law. And the origins of the Onassis-Niarchos feud—so self-evident in one sense, so unexplained in another—were hidden somewhere in those early days when Onassis won Tina's hand and then realized his brother-in-law was a strong rival for his bride's affections.

Although Christina and Alexander knew their mother was partial to Niarchos, they had little reason to fear she would do anything as lunatic as marry him. Perhaps they were still reeling from their father's marriage and their aunt's death and couldn't worry too much about their mother's intentions. After several months, however, when Tina began to be seen with Niarchos, Alexander told his mother bluntly, "If you ever marry that man, you will never see me alive again." Tina assured him she had no such plan. Even that wasn't good enough for Alexander. Together with Christina, they made her promise, solemnly and formally, that she would not marry Niarchos. Without hesitation, she promised.

Later in the summer of 1970, Christina invited her St. George's friend Susan Handal to spend most of the summer with her in Greece. Susan flew from New York and met Christina in London. They went first for a week's visit at Lee Place, where Tina, for appearances, arrived just in time to receive them. The two girls then went to Monte Carlo for a few days because, according to Christina, "It was on the way to Greece." She still felt herself to be in love with Danny Marentette and regretted having broken with him. According to friends who saw her on the trip, she at first phoned him five and six times a day, but gradually was forced to admit that the always-polite Marentette had had his fill of the action-packed Onassis spectacle.

Christina and her guest proceeded to Athens to stay for a few days with Christina's surrogate mother, her Aunt Artemis, before going to the Livanos island, Coronis. Christina had her own apartment on the upper floors of Artemis's villa in Glyfada. Onassis, who owned a villa next door, spent so little time in it that he usually stayed with Artemis when he was in town rather than opening and staffing his own house.

"Christina was very close to her aunt," an Athens friend recalled, "and her aunt was a wonderful woman. She adored Christina but could be firm with her. Christina would be in one of her excited states, running around, talking constantly, laughing, and her aunt would say, 'Now, Christina, settle down.'"

Shortly after the girls arrived, Onassis showed up for lunch. Having won the Marentette wars, he was in a generous, fatherly mood. "The *Christina*'s not doing anything right now," he said to his daughter. "Why don't you kids take it for a few days' cruise?"

She and Susan exchanged glances.

"Just us?" Christina said. "I mean, aren't you and Jackie . . . . ?"

"I've got to go to Paris and Jackie's going to New York. The *Christina* is just sitting there. Get some friends together and have some fun."

Christina was stunned. Aware that her father never lent his yacht to anyone, she had trouble believing he would give her the use of it for a party of her young friends. She quickly set about finding friends to join them. Christina had a new friend, Marina Tchomlekdjoglou, a young woman about Christina's age who lived in Buenos Aires, where her Greek family was in the textile business. Marina was in Athens visiting relatives with her brother Jorge (who twenty years later would be Christina's last romantic involvement). They could come. And they could invite Nickie Zoullas, a Greek friend also about Christina's age, and another young Greek, Plato Lambrinos.

A few days later, the group set off on the luxurious ship. They were all bursting with excitement, but none was more excited than Christina, who was having her first taste of being a hostess on a grand scale. It was from her that the crew and staff asked instructions. "Would you like to stop for a swim? What port would you like to visit? How long would you like to stay? What do you want for dinner tonight? What time do you want it? Do you prefer it be served in the dining saloon or on the rear deck?"

"We all couldn't believe how lucky we were," Lambrinos recalled. "But the interesting thing was that Christina felt the same way. Even though she knew she was very wealthy and could do what she wanted, she could see this trip as we saw it. We would sit down to dinner on the yacht's rear deck and say, 'Here we are, a bunch of twenty-year-olds, and we have this huge yacht with a crew of thirty waiting on us,' and Christina would join in our astonishment. She could see how rare it was."

On Christina's orders, the yacht headed for Skorpios, which was still in a relatively primitive state. Christina showed her friends the entire island, ending up at a small house that, at Jackie's request, had been done over. "Jackie stayed here!" Christina exclaimed as though proud of her link with recent American history.

With Christina in the lead, the young people then proceeded to search Jackie's small house like detectives looking for clues. Excitement was highest when they entered Jackie's bedroom, and Christina wasted no time in rummaging through her stepmother's closets and drawers. "Look at this," Christina would say, triumphantly holding up an innocuous piece of clothing as though it were Frederick's of Hollywood lingerie. Then, her eye spotting a piece of paper, she yelled, "What's that over there?"

"Christina found a note in Jackie's handwriting taped to the vanity-table mirror," Lambrinos said. "She got very excited—'Look everyone, look what I found!' We read it, but it turned out to be nothing, a reminder to do an errand in New York, something like that, but Christina acted as though she had found a proof that Jackie had arranged the assassination."

Christina's gratitude to her father for the use of the *Christina* diminished as she came to see the gesture as just another bribe to accept her new stepmother. As the cruise progressed , she grew careless about taking good care of the yacht. Woodwork was scratched, upholstery took a beating, and during some boisterous roughhousing, a trayful of expensive Baccarat wine glasses were smashed. Captain Costas, an easygoing and diplomatic Onassis loyalist, urged Christina to be more careful. He was accustomed to the fastidiousness of his employer, who would trail behind his new wife, picking up discarded items of clothing from the floor, folding them neatly and placing them on nearby chairs for servants to carry away. In the matter of tidiness, Christina resembled her stepmother, and the yacht began to look like a fraternity house after a spring weekend. By the end of the trip she and her guests, according to one of them, "had made a total mess of that boat."

Tina, Marchioness of Blandford, finally decided her marriage was over. She had had her fill of traipsing around the north of England in the rain with soggy, odoriferous dogs ("The aristocracy is all wet," she had once written her sister Eugenie). She did not, however, flee from Lee Place as she had from the *Christina*, but simply began spending less and less time there. That fact seemed to have escaped the notice of her husband, who professed astonishment when he received word from a Paris lawyer that the marchioness was suing him for divorce. If Blandford was surprised, no one else was. His son James, then in his midteens, had been chatting with Tina as she dressed for dinner several weeks earlier in St. Moritz. Sitting beside her at a dressing table, he asked his stepmother when she was returning to Lee Place. "I'm not," she said casually as she applied lipstick.

8

# THE WILY
# POLO PLAYER

••••••••••••••••••••••••••••••••••••••••••••••••••••••••••••••••••••••••••••••••••••••••

*O*n a day shortly before Christmas in 1970 when Christina had just turned twenty, she spent the morning skiing alone on the slopes above St. Moritz, then stopped at the Corviglia Club, where she planned to join her mother and some others for lunch. At a large table in a sun-flooded corner of the dining room, Christina found most of those closest to her: her mother, her aunt and uncle Lita and George Livanos, her uncle Stavros Niarchos, and Gianni Agnelli. As Christina made her way around the table greeting each with a kiss, she came to the only person she did not know, a handsome, lean, somewhat swarthy young man with wavy dark hair. His most arresting features were his eyes, which were large and black with much of the sad, plaintive look of Christina's own.

Agnelli said, "Christina, I'd like you to meet Luis Basualdo. He's from Argentina and he plays very good polo."

Christina found the newcomer attractive, which for her was an added stimulus to the high spirits she always felt after a good session on the ski slopes. Emboldened by her billionaire support group, she felt cocky. Holding out her hand, she said, "Oh, you're the one who sold those crappy ponies to Amanda Haynes." Everyone laughed.

Basualdo, who was twenty-two, came from a respectable but not rich Argentinean family. His father had also been a polo player and, through that aristocratic sport, knew men of great prominence in

America and England. When Luis decided to drop out of school and make a career of polo, his father sent him to his friend Mike Phipps in New York. Phipps, in turn, passed him along to a Honeywell heir who was recruiting players for a team he was forming in Minneapolis. Luis was taken on.

After a match in Atlanta, Basualdo met and fell in love with a nineteen-year-old girl whose parents had died, leaving her a generous income and a large plantation. He quit the Minneapolis team and settled down to a life of love and southern comfort. The episode drove home an important lesson: by doing what he liked best, making love to a pretty girl, the right girl, Basualdo could also enjoy a life of affluence and luxury.

Growing bored after a few months, he left the girl and accepted an offer from the Anheuser-Busch family to play polo in St. Louis. As usual, a blue-chip social life went with the game and Basualdo met many wealthy and prominent people. While playing at the Butler family's estate outside Chicago he became acquainted with Viscount Cowdray, the English multimillionaire whose enthusiasm for polo made him one of the top men in the sport. Cowdray invited Basualdo to join his team in England.

Playing at Cowdray Park, Basualdo fell into the same round of polo and top-level socializing, and had his pick of the good-looking and aristocratic women who followed, so to speak, the sport. After every match one of Cowdray's daughters, Lucy Pearson, who was then about fifteen, would rush up with other admirers and give him a congratulatory hug. One time she startled Basualdo with a kiss on the mouth. After a time he began sleeping with her—sporadically, because of the difficulty of finding a safe trysting place. Ever resourceful, Basualdo rented a Cowdray Park tenant farmer's house on an hourly basis.

During the winters when there was no polo, Basualdo, following the migration of other unemployed young blades in the haut-café set he was now a part of, went to St. Moritz. In that ultra-stylish ski resort, the less well-heeled of them were given small rooms in the eaves of the legendary Palace Hotel, plus their meals, for about $22 a night. The owner of the Palace, Andrea Badrutt, offered this generous deal to the young men in order to supply his big-money, much-married clientele with some attractive young bachelors.

Despite the negligible price of their food and board, the in-house

Romeos had to pay for their own drinks as well as any meals they took in restaurants outside the hotel, which was a common dining practice with the top crowd. That was all very expensive and almost assured that Badrutt's protégés would attach themselves to the wealthy guests on the floors below. The arrangement, rather like a hustlers' training camp, offered titillation to the wives and daughters, but very little to the men who were paying the bills except the gratification of seeing their women happy and the privilege of wining and dining the attic regiment.

Basualdo, who had just inherited a little money and was not, for the moment, quite as rapacious as the others, was still delighted to be taken up by men of the financial caliber of Agnelli, Niarchos, and Livanos, who admired his polo skills and found him amusing. Now, sitting with all of them at the Corviglia Club, a social pinnacle that would have been the envy of the Palace top floor, he was being ridiculed and humiliated by a rich Greek bitch who had never had to hustle a drink in her life.

If Christina had needled him about his bed hopping or his lack of funds, he would have laughed it off, but the accusation of financial dishonesty was, Basualdo knew, the most damaging slur possible with these men, who, even in the best company, kept one hand on their wallets. That the ponies had, as Amanda Haynes later confirmed, been perfectly all right—one had suffered a leg injury after the sale —merely added injustice to the wrong Christina had done to him.

Basualdo's mortification converted quickly to anger. He knew, as did everyone else in international café society, of Christina's recent abortion. He knew as well that the putative father, Danny Marentette, was a touchy subject with her.

"Who gave you that information," he said, glaring at Christina, "Danny Marentette?"

The others at the table laughed slightly, then studied their drinks. Christina was in too good a mood to be fazed by this clumsy attempt to wound. On first meetings with eligible men she was accustomed to flattery and efforts to impress, so she looked at Basualdo with greater interest. Saying nothing, she flashed him a parody smile, then took her seat at the other end of the table.

This barbed encounter marked the start of a major relationship for Christina, one that was intimate, twisted, eventually decadent, and even a bit sinister. For better or worse, it was her longest significant involvement with any man, longer than any of her four marriages. For thirteen years, until shortly before her death, Basualdo was close to Christina—first as a lover, then as a friend, and finally as an extremely well-paid employee who lived with her. He amused Christina and she felt they understood each other. Tired of the wholesale hypocrisy that surrounded her, she found his candid and unabashed corruptibility refreshing.

For his part, Basualdo gave her much psychological support and on at least one occasion he saved her life—or so he claimed. Others would testify that he weathered demands and moods few would have put up with for any amount of money, performing commissions too personal for a regular employee yet too unreasonable to ask of a friend. At the same time he exploited Christina without scruple.

Because of Basualdo's expectations, their unique relationship required the kind of staggering wealth that Christina would soon have. It would also need, from both, odd psychological sets and quirks that interfaced neatly. Although most of her friends and family came to think of Basualdo as a negative influence in her life—the degree of influence alone was enough to cause concern—the relationship, on balance, probably benefited Christina more than it harmed her. Ironically, it would end as it started, with an accusation of financial dishonesty.

Late in the afternoon after his lunch with the gods on Valhalla, Basualdo was lounging around the Palace Hotel indoor swimming pool crowing to two of his top-floor cronies about his success with the Greek tycoons. He did not mention the crooked-horse-trader slur, which still rankled. Conveniently corroborating his tale of social triumph, an attendant brought him a telephone and told him Miss Onassis wanted to speak with him.

Warm and friendly, Christina asked if Basualdo would join her for dinner that evening at her uncle's house. In addition to herself, there would be her mother, her Uncle George and Aunt Lita, Stavros Niarchos, and her grandmother Arietta Livanos—strictly *en famille*. The in-house fortune hunters sitting with Basualdo by the pool were stunned by the invitation, which he accepted.

Dinner in the Livanos house, the famous Villa Bambi, was a stately affair. Soft candlelight permitted views of the surrounding snow-covered mountains, a movie-musical blue in the Alpine moonlight. Inside, discreet lamps pulled attention back to the Cézannes and Monets that ennobled the walls. Subdued conversation played against the muted scrape of serving spoons on silver platters and the ring of crystal. After dinner a just-released film was shown in a screening room on a lower level, where the family members sat in rows of large armchairs. Christina placed herself next to Basualdo as she had at dinner. In the dark, she somehow managed to maneuver her heavy chair closer to Basualdo's so that she could touch her knee to his.

Later they went to the King's Club, the disco in the basement of the Palace and the most popular nightclub in St. Moritz. On the dance floor, Christina ignored the tempo of the music and clung to Basualdo in slow, seductive dancing. At the end of the evening, she told him she would pick him up in her Uncle George's helicopter at ten the next morning to take him skiing. Not nearly as good a skier as Christina, Basualdo managed to keep up with her and they had lunch again at the Corviglia Club, this time just the two of them. When she dropped him at the hotel that afternoon, she said she was going to the Villa Bambi to change her clothes and, having decided they were now a couple, added she would see him later for dinner.

In a corridor of the Palace, Basualdo ran into Gianni Agnelli. "Listen, Luis," the Italian tycoon said, taking Basualdo's arm as they continued to walk, "Christina is keen on you. Why don't you do something about it? This could be very good for you." Basualdo replied that he liked Christina too, but he wasn't in a position to fall in love with her. He was involved with another woman, Justine Cushing, whom he was meeting in a few days in St. Anton, across the border in Austria. Later that night at the King's Club, the manager, Peppo Vanini, took advantage of Christina's momentary absence from their table to whisper the same sort of go-get-her pep talk in Basualdo's ear. When Basualdo mentioned he was leaving for St. Anton, Vanini said, "Don't do that. She's really excited about you. She'll be distraught."

After a few more days of constant companionship, Basualdo told Christina he had to leave the disco early that night. He was taking the train the next day to St. Anton. He had to pack. Christina said, "You're not really going to leave?" When he assured her he was, she asked if she could come to his room to help him pack. They left the club and, by a series of back stairs, sneaked up to Basualdo's room.

As Basualdo packed, Christina lay on his bed and chattered without stop. Her theme was the joys of St. Moritz, the many dazzling parties coming up over the New Year's holiday, the planeloads of exciting, amusing people who would be arriving in town, the good skiing the weather assured. The unspoken text, of course, was that Basualdo was a fool to leave. Finished packing, Basualdo told Christina it was late, it was time to take her home. She flung herself on her back and stretched her arms out to either side. She began moaning and pretended to be having an immobilizing seizure. He went to the bed, lay down on top of her and started kissing her. She responded and they made love.

Getting dressed later, Christina expressed dismay at what had occurred. "If my father knew about this, he'd kill me and probably you too. I was a virgin. That's very important to Greek men."

"How did you get pregnant then?" Basualdo taunted her. "Immaculate conception?"

Changing direction, Christina admitted that Danny Marentette had been her lover—her first, she insisted. She had "fooled around" with Peter Goulandris, but not actually made love. Since Marentette, there had been no one. Basualdo was the second.

Much as he had enjoyed his romp with Christina, Basualdo held to his plan to leave St. Moritz. The following evening in a plush St. Anton ski lodge, after he had enjoyed a prolonged amorous reunion with Justine Cushing, the bedside telephone rang. Answering, he was surprised to hear Christina's voice; he had not told her where he would be staying.

"Angel," she said, "when are you coming back?"

"I never said I was coming back," he replied.

"But you must. You'll miss the best parties of the year. St. Anton is a farm village. Everything is happening in St. Moritz. Besides I miss you."

Basualdo said he would think about it. The next afternoon, Christina called again with the same persuasions. He was flattered by her persistence and impressed by the strength that seemed to energize her determination. Still he refused, but after another day, with the newness of Justine wearing off, Basualdo began to feel that more fun, excitement, and above all, opportunity lay in the Swiss rather than the Austrian Alps.

When he announced he was returning to St. Moritz, Justine broke down in tears. Basualdo pleaded important social commitments. But when that explanation did not seem to jibe with the daily *après-ski* phone calls he had been receiving, he admitted that Christina Onassis was in love with him. Experience with other women had taught him that, to cool Christina's ardor and assure that she wouldn't bother him further, he would have to deal with her in person. The next day Basualdo bid farewell to a teary and disillusioned Justine and boarded a train to start his journey back to St. Moritz.

Christina, always prone to sentimentalizing past experiences, would refer in later years to her reunion with Basualdo at the St. Moritz station as one of her greatest romantic moments. "It was," she would sigh, "just like that scene in the Moscow train station when Lara ran into the arms of Dr. Zhivago," forgetting, or more likely ignorant of, the main-chance calculations that brought about her reunion with Basualdo. But whatever the motive that drew him back to St. Moritz, the more usual boy-girl mechanisms soon took hold. Christina was not overweight in those days. Although she had large thighs, her arms were slender and her breasts superb. For a time, he began to think himself in love with her.

They went skiing together every day, made love in the afternoon, had dinner with friends, socialized and danced all evening, then sneaked up to Basualdo's room and made love again until three or four in the morning, when Christina left Basualdo's room and returned to her family at the Villa Bambi. Since he no longer felt the need to escort her the short distance, she would pick up a taxi in front of the hotel, first getting twenty-five francs from Basualdo for the fare.

When they were alone chatting, Christina often rambled on about her family's wealth, perhaps by way of holding Basualdo's interest. She talked about the fortune her father had amassed, her mother's millions, how rich she was going to be. To Basualdo, who had money worries, Christina's stock taking did not excite him as she hoped and began to rankle. One early morning when she asked for the cab fare home he snapped, "If you own so many fucking tankers, you can pay your own way home!" Stunned, Christina left without a word and slammed the door. The next evening she presented him with an expensive cashmere sweater, the only gift from her, he said, during the period they were lovers.

On other occasions when they talked alone, Christina was reflective about the great wealth that would one day be hers. She never showed any anxiety about the awesome responsibility, Basualdo recalled, the unwanted burden, or any of the negative aspects that, inexplicably to the rest of the world, sometimes oppressed those slated for sizable fortunes. Christina relished the idea that she would one day be very rich; she was excited by the prospect and looked forward eagerly to a time when she would have independence and financial power.

Basualdo and Christina spent the next two months together in St. Moritz, following the same routine of skiing by day, nightclubbing and love-making by night. After one particularly late hotel-room session, she was in a hurry to leave. Rather than dressing completely, only to get undressed a few minutes later when she arrived back at the Villa Bambi, she stuffed her panty hose into her handbag and rushed out the door. The next morning, while Christina was still asleep in her room at the Villa Bambi, the panty hose were discovered by her grandmother, Arietta, who took the incriminating evidence directly to Tina.

It was testimony to the indelible Greekness of those very rich, cosmopolitan shipping families that George Livanos and his elderly mother lived together in his St. Moritz pleasure palace. For principal members of powerful families, all in possession of fortunes, it would be more customary for each to have his or her own residence and make their bows to family solidarity by locating in the same cities and resorts. In the Livanos household, Arietta was not only always present, she was, in the family nexus, a dominant force.

Arietta had not been born to the shipping fraternity but was the daughter of a prosperous Greek merchant, which perhaps made her more of a tribal infighter than those of maritime blood. Putting her aggressive maternal nature in its best light, David d'Ambrumenil, an Englishman who was a close Livanos friend, would say she cared about nothing but her family, that she would go to any lengths to protect it and further its interests. He thought her terrific.

Others found her terrifying. Her family-protection program involved knowing everything that went on under her roof and as much as possible about the activities under the roofs of friends and relatives. Rummaging through her granddaughter's handbag was completely in character for a woman who was also known for browsing through the luggage of her son and daughters' house guests when they were out of their rooms. Victims of her police-state curiosity considered her a ruthless meddler and tireless busybody. To her admirers she was a woman of style and sophistication. But she brought to her family's luxurious, art-filled mansions the wiles and strategies of the black-dressed matrons of a Greek fishing village.

Now Arietta urged Tina to take action. Reluctantly, Tina, with Arietta at her side, confronted Christina with the handbag discovery; they knew, she said, of her affair with Basualdo.

"We know *that*," said Arietta slyly, then added as perhaps an admonitory wild card in case she had overlooked something in her investigations, "and many other things as well."

Tina was not in the best position to exert moral authority over her daughter. Having recently divorced Sunny Blandford, she was now engaged in an all-out affair with Stavros Niarchos, her first husband's most hated enemy and a man many still believed had murdered her sister Eugenie. Since she and Niarchos were all but inseparable in St. Moritz, the affair was known to everyone. Even without such stains on her honor, Tina was rarely comfortable in the mothering role, least of all when it involved sexual propriety.

Further sullying the judicial purity of the family tribunal was the strong possibility that Arietta had *also* had an affair with Niarchos. In other words, Onassis's hated rival had enjoyed the favors of his sister-in-law, his mother-in-law, and now his former wife. The private histories of the Greek shipping families more often than not revealed similarly crisscrossed relationships and alarming entanglements, but none more than the Livanos-Niarchos-Onassis complex.

Fortunately, Christina did not challenge her mother's and her grandmother's credentials, perhaps feeling no such confrontation was necessary in view of the mild sentence they had passed: it was all right for her to continue seeing Basualdo, indeed to sleep with him, but she must under no circumstances consider marrying him. His lack of money and a career—along with the inevitable suspicions of fortune hunting—were cited as the principal reasons. Christina could be assured of the anger and harsh reprisals of her father if she did anything rash.

Later that day, Christina gleefully reported the conversation to Basualdo, stressing for dramatic effect the persecutions she was suffering on his account. But the family's prohibitions did nothing to dampen her infatuation or diminish her round-the-clock involvement. Tina made good her claim to harbor no ill feeling toward Basualdo; she gave him skiing lessons and favored him with other friendly attentions. Even the formidable Arietta seemed to warm to him, but only with Christina's pledge that marriage was not in her plans. There seemed little doubt, however, that if marriage had been necessary to keep Basualdo in her life, she would have defied them all.

One night at the King's Club, Basualdo was sitting at a table with Christina and some friends when he was startled to be greeted effusively by Lucy Pearson, who was visiting St. Moritz with classmates from the Swiss school she attended. Since her father, Viscount Cowdray, was a friend of Christina's stepfather, Sunny Blandford, the two young women knew each other slightly. They greeted one another pleasantly, then Christina turned to talk to others at the table. Lucy asked Basualdo when she could see him alone.

"Come by my room tomorrow morning at ten," he whispered, knowing that Christina never arrived before eleven.

At ten-thirty the next morning, there was a loud knock at Basualdo's door. In the best tradition of French farce, Christina had arrived early. Given Lucy and Basualdo's compromising situation, letting her in was out of the question. The only hope was to remain quiet until Christina decided he was not in his room and departed. That was made difficult by Lucy's insistent questions to Luis about who was knocking so boldly at his door at this hour and why he could not respond. When Christina finally went away, Basualdo spirited the schoolgirl down the much-trafficked back stairs.

After about a month of her St. Moritz love affair, Christina grew even more obsessed with Basualdo. She stopped seeing friends, preferring to dine alone with him and to avoid the nightclubs. Eventually, she insisted they ski alone, even by-passing the ritual of lunch at the Corviglia Club. When a skiing accident put Basualdo in the hospital, Christina stayed at his bedside every day for the week he was there. As Christina would demonstrate many times in the future, her loves, even those that were short-lived, were intense and all-consuming.

When the time came for Christina to return to her London apartment, Basualdo accompanied her but soon missed the glamour and excitement of St. Moritz and grew restless. Adding to his ill ease in his relationship, ominous signals of displeasure were emanating from the Onassis and Livanos clans as they registered their dismay that Christina's affair was surviving the ski season. Christina enjoyed needling Basualdo about his growing unpopularity in the Greek shipping community. Basualdo began to fear that the disapproval might translate into some sort of strong-arm discouragement. Even without bodily harm, he could not see a future in his relationship with Christina and announced that he had to go to Argentina to conclude another pony sale. After that, he would return to Europe and accept an offer to play polo in Hamburg.

Christina was first dismayed, then incensed at his plan, which clearly excluded her. If he left, she said, she would start seeing other men. He told her to go ahead. When he was back in Argentina, she phoned every day full of reports on her new beaus, young men like Mick Flick, the handsome and dashing Mercedes Benz heir, with whom Christina was becoming increasingly infatuated, and other bachelor luminaries on the international party circuit. But whatever show of resilience Christina succeeded in making with her talk about romantic diversions was usually undermined by a sign-off plea that Luis return to her.

Free of Christina and casting about for more hopeful prospects, Basualdo reestablished contact with Lucy Pearson in England and Justine Cushing in New York. Having lived down her St. Anton abandonment, Justine invited Basualdo to come stay with her and he accepted. When he arrived in Manhattan, he heard that Christina was in town staying at the Regency. He phoned her and got a warm reception.

"Angel! You're here in New York! Come over immediately." They made enthusiastic love, once again putting Justine on hold, but this time only for a few hours. Basualdo decided it would be a mistake to renew his intense involvement with Christina; he liked her very much, but she was too erratic, too unstable. He announced his intention of following through on his plan to return to Europe and play polo in Hamburg. Again Christina grew angry and said she never wanted to see him again. In Europe, Basualdo worked on developing his affair with Lucy Pearson. He heard Christina was seeing an American named Joseph Bolker and was relieved.

Given his policy of never letting tastes and emotions interfere with financial strategies, it was surprising that Basualdo did not marry Christina when he had the chance. But as he summed up his decision years later, "It was all too much for me," meaning Christina's willfulness, the complex family, the power that added menace to their enmity. He also knew that his only income was what he could earn playing polo, hardly enough to support Christina, who was used to living extremely well and reveled in doing so. In the matter-of-fact tone of one stating the obvious he added, "At the time Christina only had an allowance of $4,000 a month. Her parents were both in good health. Lucy, on the other hand, did not have to wait for anyone to die to inherit. When she turned eighteen, she took control of an income of $800,000 a year."

# 9

# BEVERLY HILLS HOUSEWIFE

*I*f the Onassis family spent a great deal of time and energy condemning each other's choice of lovers, it was because all of them seemed uncannily deft at selecting partners who guaranteed outraged reactions. It perhaps began with Callas, whose major accomplishment and world fame could be seen as Onassis's snide comment on Tina's aimless frivolity. Tina's retaliation with Blandford could have been an equally harsh comment on Onassis's modest origins and lack of refinement. Alexander jumped in clumsily but effectively with the thoroughly unsuitable Fiona. Onassis topped them all with his dizzyingly askew marriage to Jackie.

Christina had entered the family recreation timorously with Marentette and Basualdo, but even these modestly offensive choices caused enough commotion to alert her to the game's possibilities, and she would soon become as adept as any of them at choosing the jarring lover as a means of family communication. Tina would shortly make the most telling shot, but Christina would prove herself the most persistent player and continue slogging away on the field well after her mother and brother were dead. Even with the death of her chief adversary, her father, she was a long way from having made all her points.

Christina had powerful feelings for her first two lovers, feelings unconnected with her family turmoil. She genuinely liked them and was strongly attracted to them. But that did not explain the reckless way in which she jeopardized her family's respect and love, as well as risking her inheritance, for infatuations which she had learned, even at that age, were not once-in-a-lifetime occurrences. With the first two men in her life she had also learned something that linked up with her childhood behavior mechanisms: the more distressed her family was by her romantic choice, the more attention she received. She was evolving her own form of the game: falling in love as a tantrum.

At age twenty, Christina seemed happy, almost exhilarated, by her new freedom from school and job, with ample means to move about in quest of pleasure. Privately—and from childhood she had become skilled at concealing her inner feelings when she chose to—she was in a good deal of pain. Although she loved her mother, Tina was an emotional write-off because of her own erratic quest for happiness and because of her obvious preference for Alexander, a cruelty to Christina she did little to conceal.

Even before her mother's preference became obvious, Christina had focused on her father—as did most people around him. As an adult, she had just begun to develop the closeness with Onassis that had been absent from her childhood when she lost him again to the ludicrously unworthy and extraneous Jackie. And on top of that betrayal, Christina had to deal with her father's opposition to her own attempts to make a satisfying life and his plans to sell that life off as a shipping asset.

At the end of 1970 and early 1971, Christina found herself careening around the world's pleasure capitals in a quest the complexity of which she little understood. She was looking for a man, to be sure, but he had to fulfill all kinds of needs beyond the usual ones of pleasing her and making her happy, requirements in themselves difficult enough to find. Christina needed a man who would also serve as an expression of outrage and an instrument of revenge and who could draw all attention to her.

These other needs, although unrecognized, were so pressing that they seemed to preclude the more fundamental qualities most young

women her age would seek in a life partner—the stability, compatibility, and persistent love that would augur well for creating a family
and sharing a life. It seemed that Christina could not or would not
divert and channel her score-settling drive into creating a family of
her own—a course that might have been—and almost was—her
salvation. She still had too much to work out with the family she
had.

The overriding importance Christina gave to her snarled relations
with her family was reinforced by the world-wide attention given
their every action, particularly those of her father and his famous
wife. While other unhappy children emerging into adulthood might
have put behind them the failures of their family relationships, evoking the residual pain for an occasional drunk or cry, Christina was
being told constantly of the importance of these people, her people,
and how worthy they were of her ongoing struggle with them. In
some strange way, the relentless clamor of the world's press over the
drama's principals seemed to aggravate and keep alive the routine
domestic problems that in other families would have been shrugged
off or would have faded with time. But for the Onassis family, the
magazines, TV shows, and newspapers that covered their activities
became an ever-present Greek chorus, there to cheer on or condemn
the central figures, and in Christina's case, to remind her that this
was the drama to which she had been assigned, and with which she
must remain.

It took Christina a while to recover from Basualdo's defection and
she never lost an opportunity to denounce polo players as "untrust-
worthy." She amused herself by going out with the young men in the
Paris circles she preferred, the rich and social pleasure seekers with
whom she had grown up. Her dates were usually with men she had
known for years, heirs like herself, only less rich. But when she began
seeing these more appropriate bachelors, she noticed a marked loss
of interest in her activities from her family. Nothing would come of
these flings to threaten the plans that were now firm: she would be
married off to Peter Goulandris and forgotten.

To add to that anxiety, Christina found that she was getting fat. In
April of 1971, she checked into a weight-reducing spa in Germany

and slimmed down to a man-catching size, then went to Monte Carlo to divert herself for a few days and show off her new figure in a bathing suit before returning to London. Early May was a slow time of year on the Riviera, but at the indoor pool of the Hôtel de Paris she ran into Rodney Solomon, a Londoner who was a good friend of her mother's and also a staunch member of the group George Livanos had drawn around him.

With the large pool to themselves, Christina and Solomon were chatting quietly when a middle-aged man in a bathing suit entered and took a chaise not far from theirs. He had a thick head of wavy gray hair, sharp features, and a trim, athletic body. In appearance, he could have been a younger version of Onassis. Large, dark-rimmed glasses gave him a serious look, an Onassis power look. He also possessed, as Christina soon discovered, a good measure of her father's outgoing charm.

The pool room was too vast and sepulchral for two of its three occupants to ignore the other, so Christina incorporated the newcomer into the conversation. Seeing she was intent on befriending the man, Solomon instigated introductions. The man's name was Joseph Bolker and he was from Los Angeles. Traveling around Europe, he had dropped by Monte Carlo, which he often visited, to look in on the convention of the Young Presidents Organization, to which he belonged.

"You look too young to be a president," Christina said in her flirtiest tone. "How old are you?"

"Forty-eight," he replied.

"You don't look it," she said with her now customary directness. "What are you president of?"

"I have my own construction company in L.A."

Christina's looks were at their best, the German spa having done its work. In a tight black bathing suit, her body was sleek and supple. Her naturally dark hair was growing back to cover the blond she had affected in her desperation to win Mick Flick, who told Christina he only liked blondes. The variegated result was dramatic and oddly attractive. Bolker responded to her flirting with some of his own, and they had a pleasant and titillating hour together.

Bolker told Christina that he had been born in Nebraska, had a paper route as a boy, had done well in business. He now sat on the boards of many cultural and philanthropic organizations. He had been recently divorced from a wife by whom he had four daughters —one of them exactly Christina's age. As he talked, Christina sensed a youthful innocence and an amiability that contrasted appealingly with his worldliness and Hollywood suavity. Eventually Bolker announced he had to go to his room to pack. He was leaving Monte Carlo in the morning.

"Where do you go from here?" Christina asked.

"I'm going up to Germany then over to London."

"I live in London and I'll be back in a few days. You should give me a call."

When he said he would be delighted, Christina scrawled her number in a loose-leaf notebook she usually had with her, ripped out the page, and handed it to him. In later retellings of this original encounter with Christina, Bolker would stress that he was not aware she was Christina *Onassis* until he saw the last name on the scribbled note. Looking at it he said, "Oh, that Christina."

"Yeah," she replied, pleased as she always was to be recognized, "*that* Christina."

While it was understandable that Bolker would hope to deflect suspicions that he was inflamed by Christina's money, it strained credulity that, when they were introduced, he would not pick up on the hard-to-garble last name Onassis, especially in Monte Carlo, a resort he visited frequently and where the name was ear-catching, to say the least. Although he had his own money, Bolker would have had reason to be defensive about his marital record in his reminiscences about Christina. His first wife was the daughter of the extremely rich developer and philanthropist Mark Taper, and after Bolker's involvement with Christina he married Dene Hoffheinz, whose father was the well-known Texas millionaire Judge Roy Hoffheinz, a one-time mayor of Houston and the prime mover behind the Astrodome.

As for Bolker's own money, it was no great shakes by Onassis standards; even when she was infatuated with him, Christina referred to him as "a dinky millionaire in real estate and building." But Bolker had other reasons for finding a newsworthy match tempting. His divorce from Janice Taper had been acrimonious and he had made a formidable enemy in her influential father, who closed a number of doors to him in Los Angeles power circles. For a man who may have been wondering if he was over the hill socially as well as sexually, the flattery of attracting a young woman of legendary wealth must have been intoxicating.

Back in London, Christina was delighted when Bolker phoned her from Germany. He told her he would be coming to London in two days and would like Christina to dine with him and a married couple who were old friends of his. After a successful dinner and the departure of the other guests, Bolker took Christina to a quiet place for a nightcap, where she poured out to him all her frustrations and problems with her overbearing father and her distracted mother.

While Bolker was closer to Onassis's age than Christina's and may have resembled him, he was definitely one thing Onassis was not: a good listener. Christina's efforts to talk to her father about her own concerns were either dismissed autocratically or ignored as he jumped to some subject of his choosing. Alexander had become so unnerved by the difficulty of speaking to his father that he had taken to writing scripts to be used when the dreaded phone calls arrived. With his father ranting either about his inadequacies or about irrelevances, Alexander would resolve not to hang up until he had waited out the digressions and diversionary tactics and made his points.

For Christina, to have a kind, intelligent man, one who had made his own way in the world, show her such sympathy and understanding was a sorely needed balm. After two hours of purging herself of her concerns, she felt better than she had felt for some time. Returning to her Reeves Mews apartment, they went to bed and made love. After a few idyllic days together in London, Bolker told her he had to tend to his business in Los Angeles. He would return, however, the minute he could get free.

Unknown to Christina, her father had learned of the fledgling romance, in all probability from Rodney Solomon, who may have jumped at the opportunity to be useful to his good friend Tina's first husband. However he obtained his information, Onassis knew of the encounter early enough to have Christina's London phone tapped before Bolker arrived in England.

Onassis, without indicating to Christina he knew of her involvement, stepped up his campaign for her to marry in a manner useful to Onassis interests. Mick Flick had replaced Peter Goulandris as Onassis's number-one choice, which exasperated Christina enormously since she too would like it if Flick wanted to marry her. But he did not, and rather than sympathizing, Onassis managed to convert her rejection into further proof of her obstinacy. No matter what Christina told him, Onassis was convinced no man in his right mind would turn down a chance to marry his fortune, so the fault must be Christina's.

Onassis did not personally eavesdrop on Christina's conversations with Bolker. He had his people in London do it, which was fortunate since her lengthy transatlantic conversations with Bolker were taken up mostly with complaints about her father's hatefulness toward her. Onassis gave orders that he be informed only of developments in the relationship. He soon learned, for example, that Bolker and Christina planned a weekend together, not in her London apartment but in a hotel in Brighton, where neither was likely to run into friends who might, heaven forbid, take word of the assignation back to Onassis. Doing nothing to thwart the tryst, Onassis instead had investigators dig into Bolker's past in the hope of finding shady business dealings or other hurtful information. The results were disappointing, but Onassis persevered.

Ignorant of her father's sleuthing, Christina noticed that he was being more horrid to her than usual, picking arguments over the most inconsequential matters, but had no idea why. In the midst of their one-sided battling, she came down with a severe case of the flu and was forced to stay in bed for over a week. To pass the lonely hours, she ordered a television set for her bedroom and sent the bill to Olympic Maritime. Spotting the bill, Onassis was infuriated and refused to pay it. In her next conversation with Bolker, she bemoaned his arbitrary stinginess.

"Only a short time ago," she moaned, "he gave me a matching emerald necklace and bracelet, which I was told was worth $250,000, yet he won't cough up for a lousy television. Why, Joe, why?"

Bolker suggested that it was because outsiders would not see the television set, while the entire world would see the jewelry and know what a rich and generous father Onassis was. Christina thought Bolker was the wisest man she had ever met. Onassis's stinginess may also have been a manifestation of the anger he felt about her affair, but was not yet willing to reveal. Ironically, with each piece of unprovoked nastiness, in Christina's eyes, from her father, he was driving her closer to Bolker. Onassis had set in motion a ludicrous vicious circle that was pushing Christina to the conclusion he wanted least.

Within a few weeks of the Brighton weekend, Bolker and Christina made a date to meet in a small inn in France. After their third tryst in Europe, Bolker began to realize that the affair was not just a dalliance for Christina; she was becoming dependent on him. When they were on different sides of the Atlantic, she would wake him at 8 A.M. with her first call of the day and usually follow that with four or five more calls. The time had come, Bolker decided, to tone down the romance. But he quickly came to realize that neither the difficulty of meeting nor the twenty-eight-year age difference, two obstacles he repeatedly stressed, was going to cool her ardor. He took the coward's way out by making himself unavailable to her. Pleading business problems, he canceled their next tryst, then had his secretary field her calls.

Early in July of 1971, Bolker was dumfounded and dismayed when Christina arrived unannounced at the door of his Century City apartment in Beverly Hills. If he had first seen her as an intriguing and ego-invigorating romance, he now saw her as a messed-up teenager. Did her parents know where she was? No. In that case he was going to telephone Tina immediately to let her know her daughter's whereabouts. Since Tina was then in a rented villa in the south of France, Bolker could not have located her without Christina's help. She could have stonewalled his efforts to call her mother, but she docilely gave him the phone number. Whatever other reasons Christina had for flying to Bolker, she did not appear to want her audacious action to be overlooked by her parents.

Bolker told Christina to go into his bedroom so he could talk frankly with her mother. Tina, who was seven years younger than Bolker, quickly took in the situation, but adopted a surprising line. Instead of demanding that Bolker send her daughter immediately back to Europe, she said she did not want her to stay with him *unless they were married*. Tina's sudden insistence on propriety was uncharacteristic. She had flaunted her own lover, Reinaldo Herrera, under the noses of her husband and children and she had voiced no objections when Christina was sleeping with Marentette or Basualdo. Now with her daughter approaching twenty-one, Tina insisted she marry or come home. It was possible she knew how much Christina cared for Bolker and was simply trying to assist her daughter in her matrimonial hopes. But in light of even more surprising subsequent actions, it seemed that Tina, whose divorce from Blandford was now final, may have been using Christina's crisis to aid an agenda of her own.

Bolker knew that Christina was listening to the conversation from the bedroom extension, so began addressing his lament as much to her as to Tina. He did not want to get married. He was too old for Christina. He was too set in his ways. He had four grown daughters, one exactly Christina's age. Tina, clearly irked at this litany of her daughter's undesirability, cut him short. He should, in that case, send Christina back to Europe immediately.

Bolker went into the bedroom to find Christina near hysterics. Why wouldn't he marry her? What was wrong with her? Why was she good enough to sleep with, but not to marry? She was in such a state he left her alone to calm down. Bolker had no reason to suspect all that was coming together for Christina at that moment. Her father had elbowed her out of his life to spend more time with a scheming fortune hunter, and despite her efforts to smooth over their differences and resume the relationship they had had before his marriage, he was being horrible to her. And now that she had found a replacement for Onassis in her life, one who was kinder, steadier, unattached—and who had the added benefit of enjoying sex with her—he, too, was pushing her aside.

Not hearing any sound from the bedroom for a time, Bolker reentered to find Christina sprawled on the bed moaning softly. There were several open bottles of pills on the bedside table. He rushed to get a doctor who lived across the hall, and together they walked Christina around the room, poured liquids into her, then made her throw up. According to Bolker, when Christina revived she told him she was going to continue trying to take her life until he married her.

Onassis was on Skorpios celebrating Jackie's forty-second birthday when he heard that Christina had married Joseph Bolker in Las Vegas on July 27, 1971. He went into a violent rage that lasted throughout the day. His frenzy so alarmed Jackie that, rather than trying to offer wifely support and comfort, she took a book and hid on a remote beach. Also present at the time was Onassis's general factotum, Johnny Meyer, who had weathered many Onassis tantrums, but who said later that it was the worst day in his stormy years with Onassis, one that he would not go through again for all the money in the world. That Bolker had previously been married to an heiress was all Onassis needed to convict his new son-in-law of being the crassest kind of fortune hunter. Christina's new husband immediately replaced Niarchos as number one on Onassis's most-hated list. He saw Bolker as nothing more than a fellow business buccaneer, of a much lower order, of course, but one who had dared invade with intent to plunder the innermost reaches of his domain. He immediately formulated a strategy for destroying him and bringing Christina to heel.

Contemptible as Bolker was in Onassis's eyes, it was what he indicated about Christina that drove Onassis mad. Marentette could be looked on as a minor mistake of her youth, Basualdo as a rich kid's sophisticated dalliance. With Bolker, Christina had drastically escalated her malfeasance. Matters were aggravated by Onassis's dawning fear that he himself might have made a stupid marriage. The devastation he felt went even deeper. From his earliest youth, Onassis had viewed love relationships as means to advance his ambitions. Since ambition was so much a part of him—in a sense it was all he was— choosing advantageous lovers or wives did not preclude real feeling, even full-blown love.

Because of Onassis's own success at combining love and ambition, he was less able to comprehend anyone, particularly his daughter, marrying for love exclusively. And in his daughter's case, it was not just a marriage with no advantage, she was actually throwing away a great deal—he would see to it. A love affair with Bolker was bad enough; marriage was a disaster. Regarding this institution, Onassis's views had grown even more idiosyncratic than they had been in his youth. Although he was at first very much in love with Callas, he had not married her. Marriage was a major trump card only to be played when the stakes were enormous. If you had emotional needs, you saw a psychiatrist, you didn't jeopardize millions with a marriage based on *emotion*.

Even when Onassis had calmed to a degree, he was no less determined to crush the marriage. He summarized his angry feelings with a blanket pronouncement: he could no longer trust Christina. While he secretly admired her defiance (he once said, "Obedience without the stuff to break loose once in a while isn't worth a shit"), he saw her as being totally unmindful of the rare position he had given her, and guilty of making erratic, nonsensical decisions that casually put at risk the fortune he had fought so hard to create. That anyone's amatory or psychological needs could be so overriding earned only his contempt.

He was shaken in other ways. For a man who routinely operated on a high level of paranoia, he now saw himself and his empire exposed and made highly vulnerable by one of those closest to him. Her marriage to Bolker changed forever the way he thought of her. For years he had increasingly rejoiced in their many similarities of character. Now he had harsh, irrefutable evidence that he and his daughter were profoundly, dangerously *different*.

After Bolker and Christina returned to Beverly Hills from Las Vegas, a good friend of Bolker's, Erica Bruson, gave a party for the newlyweds that served as their wedding reception. Christina found herself in a receiving line having her hand pumped by a large number of her husband's friends, well-dressed, well-off Los Angelinos, most of them over twice her age. She stopped one woman. "I know your face," Christina said. "I've seen your picture in the newspapers. You look very nice. Will you be my friend?"

She was talking to Muriel Slatkin, then owner of the Beverly Hills Hotel, whose sister was married to the flamboyant financier Ivan Boesky. Slatkin, who was twice Christina's age, was stunned, but, as forthright as Christina, she smiled at her and said, "Sure I'll be your friend, honey."

"After I get out of this receiving line," Christina said. "Let's find a place where we can talk."

When the last guests had arrived and the receiving line dispersed, Christina immediately tracked Muriel down and dragged her into a bedroom. They sat on facing twin beds and chatted—the newness of Los Angeles, what a wonderful fellow Bolker was, her father's anger with her.

As they talked, Muriel came to realize how cut off Christina was from the life she had known until now and how badly in need of a friend she was. Even so, as Slatkin listened, she developed a concern of her own, which she finally blurted out. "Look, Christina," she said, "I like you. You are a nice person and very bright and I'm happy to be your friend here in Los Angeles, but I'm old enough to be your mother. I know plenty of nice girls your age. I could introduce you to them."

"I have friends my own age, but I like older women. I like you."

"O.K.," Muriel said, "you're on."

Once the excitement of the surprise marriage had subsided, Bolker settled back into his regular life with almost no deviations, except that he now shared his bachelor digs with a twenty-year-old Greek heiress. He went to the office every day, jogged, and worked out at his gym. In the evenings he often had committee meetings of one of the many civic and cultural organizations in which he was active. Left on her own much of the time, Christina threw herself into homemaking. She learned to shop, to cook, and to keep household accounts.

Bolker's life was strange to her. His apartment building had a flashing marquee around the entrance, giving it the look of an amusement arcade a long way from the Avenue Foch. Luxurious as his apartment was, it was small by Onassis standards and was furnished for a trendy Hollywood bachelor: leather furniture, shag rugs, endless potted plants, and, in the bedroom, mirrored walls. Occasionally Christina would meet Muriel for a gossipy lunch at Le Bistro, during which Muriel would counsel her on shops, restaurants, excursions from the city, people she would enjoy meeting.

Christina loved Muriel's house and proclaimed it the prettiest in Southern California. When friends from Europe passed through Los Angeles, Christina often called to ask if she could bring them over to see it. Impressed with Muriel's establishment as well as her record as a businesswoman, Christina pumped her about personal financial matters—how much she paid her servants, how much she spent on food, how much on running her house. If Slatkin knew the answer, she usually told Christina. If, in return, Muriel asked a similar question that touched on Christina's finances, she refused to answer. In later years, when Christina was running her own houses in different parts of the world, she would telephone Muriel with questions about how much she should spend on one budget item or another.

Both women discovered they loved the barbecued chickens sold at Gelson's, the posh supermarket close by Christina's apartment. Some days they would buy one and take it back to Christina's for a chicken feast. Because of this shared pleasure, Christina nicknamed her new friend Chicky-Wicky. While she was learning the ropes of running an American household, Christina was fascinated with her new life. After a time, a Greek maid was found for her and she was given the name of a Greek cook in Los Angeles she could hire to prepare special dinners.

On Sundays, Bolker took Christina to Hollywood's Greek Ortho-dox church, something she requested more from homesickness than religious fervor. As she hoped, they ran into people who knew her father—members of the Skouras family, the film moguls who had built the church, and others who remembered Onassis from the 1940s. After the services, Christina chatted happily with these distant acquaintances, then returned to the flashing marquee of Century Plaza feeling a little less as though she had moved to the moon. In an attempt to live up to her role as the wife of an established busi-nessman, Christina gave a few small dinners, for friends of Bolker's mostly, but also including people she had known in Europe, like Zsa Zsa Gabor and Marisa Berenson.

For a time, Christina heard nothing from her father. She knew he was furious at her marriage, but felt confident that he would even-tually forgive her, perhaps understand, and come to accept Bolker. The first intimation she had that this was not to be was the arrival in Los Angeles of Johnny Meyer, who had come on her father's behalf "to talk things over" with her and Bolker. Meyer, who had once worked for Howard Hughes, invited them to a lunch at the Polo Lounge of the Beverly Hills Hotel. Christina had known the gregari-ous Meyer since she was a child; they were fond of each other and she naïvely assumed he could, when she told her side of things, be made an ally.

Meyer listened sympathetically to all they had to say—that they were in love, they wanted nothing from her father, they wanted to be left alone. Then, slowly starting his counterattack, he pointed out that a good part of the Onassis business was with the Saudi Arabians, who would take a dim view of a Jewish son-in-law so close to the Onassis throne. In fact, they would probably not renew their transport contracts. Such a pullout would alarm the banks, which might then call in their loans. As Mr. and Mrs. Bolker dug into their eggs benedict, Meyer nonchalantly painted a picture of the vast Onassis empire collapsing because of one thoughtless interfaith marriage. Although he stated his suppositions in calm, measured tones, Meyer seemed to feel no marriage since Henry the Eighth's to Anne Boleyn threatened, on a religious point, such widespread havoc.

Bolker was unconvinced that he represented a threat to Onassis-Saudi relations. He told Meyer he had "many Saudi friends" whose government had "no quarrel with American Jews." Meyer then tried a different approach. He told Christina of her father's deep hurt that she had not informed him of the wedding until after it had taken place, so hurt, he added casually, that Onassis intended to withhold the trust fund of approximately $75 million that was to have come to Christina when she turned twenty-one in a few months.

Rather than telling Meyer that she didn't care, that she would sacrifice anything to be with her husband, Christina angrily denounced her father for withholding "what was rightfully hers." Bolker murmured something gallant about being capable of supporting his wife, but this went unheard as Meyer and Christina wrangled over her $75 million. The money, Meyer said with finality, would be hers the minute she divorced Bolker. Her father felt, Meyer added, that if she chose to act against his wishes, she should not expect him to pay for it. He did not relay Onassis's pithier way of expressing this sentiment: "I'll be damned if she thinks she can run her fucking act on me."

While Onassis's ultimatum, however civilly delivered, cast a pall over the lunch's conviviality—Bolker sipping coffee as he learned he was sufficiently odious to block Christina from her inheritance—both he and Christina persisted in thinking of Meyer as their friend, who would smooth over Onassis's vengeful wrath. They were therefore stunned, after Meyer made his report on his lunch with the newlyweds, that Onassis went further into vindictive orbit. He had not expected Christina to tough it out, but felt confident his inspired idea to withhold her trust would bring her quickly to heel. Meyer may have exacerbated matters further by delivering a strongly negative appraisal of Bolker. Whatever the cause, the situation worsened and Onassis's anti-Bolker strategy switched to a brand of hardball that he knew well.

Unknown to Christina and Bolker, their friend Meyer remained in Los Angeles to launch a vicious campaign to damage and discredit Bolker. Having always been valuable to Onassis because of his wily resourcefulness, Meyer had contacts all over the world, but because of his years with Howard Hughes, nowhere were these contacts more extensive than in Los Angeles. He hired a detective agency to uncover damaging information about Bolker but didn't wait for their reports, which turned up nothing. He immediately began spreading stories that Christina's husband was a shady character with strong Mafia connections. Coming from Meyer, who was in a position to know, these allegations were particularly hurtful.

From his Skorpios command post, Onassis leaned on his vast network of friends—and some of Christina's whom he felt he could trust—to telephone her with these rumors and similar slanders. On hearing the tales, Christina, who knew her father's tactics, had little doubt as to their origins. Still, they unnerved her, if only for what they revealed about the despicable lengths to which her father would stoop in order to wreck her marriage and, in the process, Bolker's career. She felt certain that her father was behind the stories, but she had no way of knowing if there was perhaps some truth in them.

In addition to the whispering campaign Onassis had others launch, he himself phoned people he knew Christina was seeing in Los Angeles and tried to enlist their aid in persuading her to abandon the marriage. Muriel Slatkin received such a call. Christina became increasingly upset by the calls she was now getting regularly. As soon as Bolker left for the office in the morning, a time when most brides would be thinking of a surprise dish for dinner or new curtains for the bedroom, the calls would begin—friends telling her they had been upset by phone calls from Ari, strangers saying her husband was a crook, relatives like Artemis Garofalides telling her she had betrayed the family—and finally calls from Bolker complaining about similar calls he was getting at his office. As he later said, "When a billion dollars leans on you, you feel it."

Christina had known her marriage would cause problems, but secretly had hoped to impress her father and the others with her show of independence. She was dumfounded by the barrage of hostility. She had known her father would not like her choice, but she had never realized the choice was not hers to make. Over lunch with Muriel Slatkin, she poured out her confusion. "Why is he so down on Bolker? Why is he so angry?"

"Come on, Christina," Muriel replied. "I'd be angry too. Look, the guy is thirty years older than you, he's got four grown daughters—one of them your age—and he's Jewish. I'm Jewish too, but Onassis is your father and he seems to have strong feelings along those lines."

"Believe me, Muriel," Christina said earnestly, "I never had any idea he was anti-Semitic."

"I believe you," Muriel replied and changed the subject.

Muriel would do what she could to help her new friend rise above her father's anger and make a life for herself in California. She had grown genuinely fond of Christina and found her highly intelligent and very big-hearted. "She was so kind and generous," Muriel recalled, then as an afterthought added, "—with everyone but me. I was once in her bedroom and saw all the eye brushes she had, there must have been twenty-five of them. I asked her if she'd give me one. 'No!' Christina snapped. 'Why not?' I said, 'You've got twice as many as anyone could possibly need.' 'No,' she said again and that was that. A few weeks later, I was at a party with Christina and she raved over a pin I had on. It was a fake diamond, but it was good-looking and I had just bought it. 'Would you like it?' I asked. She told me she'd love it. I unclasped it and she put it on. 'O.K., Christina,' I said, 'now can I have one of your brushes?' 'NO!' she shouted and roared laughing.

"God, did she have a loud laugh. She was always swinging from one mood to another completely different—truly mercurial—and sometimes she could be very abrupt. I'd disagree with her about something when we were standing talking at a party, and she'd look at me, then turn and walk away, not mad, but not saying a word either. But most of the time she was a lot of fun, even with all that she was going through. I loved her."

As Onassis's badgering campaign continued, Christina and Bolker both tried to rise above the fracas, hoping it would soon subside. Christina found consolation in taking long walks on the beach, telling friends, "To a Greek, the sea is life." Bolker took her to La Jolla for a weekend and she quickly came to love that corner of California, spending hours pitting her strength against the surf. Although Christina and Bolker were having a good time together, making love and genuinely enjoying each other's company, Onassis's battering campaign was wearing them both down, and the strain ultimately affected their relationship.

At lunch one day, Muriel told Christina that she and her husband were going to Mexico for a few days, first to Acapulco and then to Puerto Vallarta, where they had never been before.

"It sounds great," said Christina. "Can Joe and I come too?"

"No," Muriel said. "We want to get away from everything and everybody, even you."

At first, Christina's interest in the trip had been mild, but now that it was denied her, she wanted desperately to go along. Muriel was adamant. She and her husband had been working hard and they both needed a quiet break. They went to Acapulco, and after a few days there, they proceeded up the coast to Puerto Vallarta. Arriving at their bungalow and waiting for the bell boy to open the door, they were flummoxed to see Christina jump out of the bushes, a sheepish Bolker behind her. "Hi, Chicky-Wicky!" Christina bellowed. Muriel Slatkin recalled spending a very pleasant few days with Christina, but said that she and Bolker did not seem to be getting along. "She spent most of her time with us," she said. "I don't know where he was."

At the beginning of October, Tina phoned her daughter to say she was in New York for a few days and suggested Christina fly in to talk over the situation. Later the same afternoon, Christina caught a plane to Kennedy Airport and went directly to Tina's suite at the St. Regis. She implored her mother to explain to her why Onassis was being so destructive and asked her advice on what she should do. To Christina's surprise, Tina urged her to stand up to him, hypothesizing that the furor he raised was nothing more than a game of wills; he would give in when he realized Christina was determined. "You have only been married two months," Tina reminded her daughter. "If you stick it out, your father will come around."

"But what about the money?" Christina said. "I was counting on my trust funds to buy a house for me and Joe. If I had a house on the beach out there, I'm sure I would come to like living in California."

Tina thought about this for a minute. Despite her Livanos millions, she was notorious for never spending a penny unless absolutely necessary, so Christina was stunned when her mother announced she would provide the money to buy a house. Christina returned to Los Angeles with two things she never expected: her mother's wholehearted moral support in her marriage and a check for $200,000. If her father's angry opposition to her marriage had taken her by surprise, her mother's all-out endorsement of it surprised her almost as much.

Back in Los Angeles, Christina promptly acted on a cautionary bit of advice from her mother. She and Bolker went to a lawyer's office and signed a marital agreement in which they each renounced any claim on the other's money. Seeing it as a way to lessen the furor, Bolker was happy to sign the agreement, but aware that such formalities usually preceded a marriage, he suspected that in this case they were prelude to a divorce.

A few weeks later, a bombshell struck Christina, an event so shattering for her she at first failed to see a possible connection between it and her mother's surprising assistance. On October 22, three weeks after the trip to New York, she received a telephone message from the Century City switchboard operator with the news that her mother had married Stavros Niarchos in Paris.

Already feeling cut off and forlorn, Christina was totally devastated and felt that the little sanity that remained in her world had been demolished by the worst possible catastrophe. If revenge and hate can be reasons for marriage, this pairing was inspired. Both parties knew it would send a knife through Onassis, who still loathed Niarchos and still considered Tina his wife. In fact, Onassis could be viewed as an absolutely essential component of the match.

But Christina cared little for the psychological underpinning of her mother's grotesque action. A number of considerations made the marriage an abomination to her as well as to members of both families. Tina's sister, the mother of Niarchos's children, had been dead only a little over a year. If that didn't put a break on Tina's plans, Christina felt, the most minimal sensitivity to the feelings of Onassis would have kept her from making such a step. Tina knew how strongly Christina and Alexander felt about Niarchos, indeed had promised them that she would never marry him. In fact, Alexander had told Tina that if she ever broke that promise he would never speak to her again. Tina also knew that many people in her world believed without question that Niarchos had strangled her sister Eugenie in a fit of rage.

Aside from the affront Tina's marriage constituted to countless people, most especially her own family, Christina had additional reasons for being driven almost over the edge by the news. She, more than anyone else, believed Niarchos had murdered Eugenie and that he was a dangerously sick man who would now murder her mother. Buckling under the devastation her own marriage had brought to family relationships, Christina could not comprehend the careering ramifications of this fresh calamity.

When she realized that only weeks before she and her mother had had long talks, during which Tina never so much as hinted at marital plans of her own, Christina felt foolish that she had believed her mother to be an unexpected bastion of support. She now saw Tina as a confused schemer, whose assistance in Christina's marriage to Bolker had probably been a ploy to keep the "Christina crisis" boiling as a diversion from her own outrageous plans. She was furious at her mother's duplicity and she was equally tormented by fears for her mother's safety. Two days after learning of the marriage, Christina, overwhelmed by the conviction that she and her family were doomed, once again took an overdose of pills. And once again, she was rescued in time.

As Bolker did what he could to be helpful in the ongoing Greek tragedy that had landed in his life, Christina more and more came to view him as a nice man but an irrelevance to all that was troubling her. If she had married him to make a statement, that particular point had now been made, yet she was stuck with him although the dialogue had moved on to different areas. Sympathetic as Bolker tried to be, he could, Christina knew, have no idea of the torments she was suffering.

One person who would surely understand was her brother, who Christina knew hated Niarchos even more than she did. When she phoned him at Fiona Thyssen's house in London, she started out by discussing the Niarchos horror, but quickly switched to her own marital problems. Fiona sensed the depth of Christina's turmoil and shrewdly saw in it an opportunity for a rapprochement between brother and sister. She urged Christina to fly to London to discuss both problems. Happy to be offered a plan of action of any sort, Christina promptly accepted and boarded a plane to London.

When brother and sister were face to face in Fiona's drawing room, both knew they had patching-up of their own to do before they could forge a united front against their parents. The meeting's first minutes were tense. In Fiona Thyssen's recollection, the reconciliation threatened to collapse into acrimony when Alexander blurted out the things about his sister that had rankled for years. "Why should you be free to run around and do what you want," he taunted, "while I have to work at the shipping offices?"

Christina answered limply, "I'm only twenty. Why shouldn't I have fun if I can?"

"You don't care about anything but clothes and hair styles."

"That's not true. But what do you want me to do? Cure cancer?" Then Christina made her own accusations. "I heard you called me 'Queen of the Maze.' "

"Well, weren't you?"

Fiona, who had had to talk Alexander into the meeting, later said she had to "beat heads together." She let them discharge their rancor for each other for a time, then called a halt to their bickering with the clear-sighted observation: "With a father like yours, you can't afford to be enemies." After a few more increasingly half-hearted recriminations, brother and sister came to see that they really had very little quarrel with one another. They then got down to a serious discussion of Christina's most immediate problem: her marriage.

"Are you in love with Joe?" Fiona asked.

"We shouldn't be married," Christina said sadly. "It's my fault. I forced Joe into it. He's a terrific guy and I'm screwing up his life." As she described the persecutions she and her husband had suffered at Onassis's hands, Alexander and Fiona were amazed. Christina added that, apart from the harassment, she had discovered that life in Southern California was not for her. She missed Europe. She felt herself at an impasse and didn't know what to do about it.

"What's the problem?" Alexander jumped in. "You don't want to be married to him and he doesn't want to be married to you. That's what divorce is for."

Christina tried to articulate her inability to act, but succeeded only in getting across the notion that because their father was now so steamed up over the marriage she was afraid to make any move, either for fear of making another mistake or for fear of appearing to give in to his pressure.

"Look," said Alexander, who was happy to admit his sister to his one-man Onassis-defying league, "We don't need Dad winding us up all the time. Act on your own. Do what *you* want to do."

Fiona agreed wholeheartedly. "That's right. Bolker's not after money, is he?"

"Not at all," Christina admitted.

"Well, then, it's simple," Fiona said. "Be the first in your family to act with a little dignity. Go back to Los Angeles, tell Mr. Bolker you want a divorce, and in a few weeks the whole thing will be over."

Christina was pathetically grateful for their support and advice and acted as though they had brought her through an insoluble dilemma. She found herself looking at Alexander in a totally different way. He had developed from a snotty, trouble-making brat into an attractive, level-headed adult. Christina envied him his slim figure and his facial features—especially his bright, sympathetic eyes—which overcame the liability of the Onassis nose. Full lips and a head of wavy, dark hair rounded off his maturing looks, which appeared to particular advantage as he sat in the London mansion of his beautiful mistress.

With Christina's immediate dilemma so handily settled, she and Alexander fell to discussing the problem they shared, their mother's marriage to Niarchos. Fiona, who had come to hate Tina more than Onassis himself, struggled to keep silent as Alexander, with a surge of youthful Greek passion, swore that he would stick to his pledge never to speak to his mother again, that, in his eyes, she was dead. Christina told them her main worry was the humiliation for their father the marriage to Niarchos would cause, and, since she considered Niarchos a violent madman, the danger it represented for their mother. Alexander's anger was such that he felt a little Niarchos rough stuff was what their mother deserved. Still struggling along on his $12,000 a year, he exploded when he learned of Tina's $200,000 gift to Christina and was immediately convinced of the motive behind it that Christina had only gradually come to suspect.

"She wanted you out of the way so she could marry that creep," Alexander snapped. "She didn't give a damn whether your marriage was good for you or not. She was keeping Dad on *your* back so he'd stay off *hers*." Christina, who had more or less arrived at this conclusion on her own, sadly agreed.

Turning to their own plans, Alexander and Fiona told Christina of their scheme to get him through college so he could build a career independent of their father. Fiona was renovating a house in Switzerland where Alexander would complete his credits for the baccalaureate so he could enter the university. Christina listened in awe, knowing how their father would react when Alexander announced he was quitting Olympic Maritime so that he could finish his education subsidized by the despised Fiona. With all the lover-related turmoil churning among the Onassises, Ari's marriage to Jackie seemed like very old news.

Christina came away from the meeting impressed with Fiona, but more impressed with her brother. There were many reasons for her approval, not the least of which was his obviously solid love affair with a woman of good sense and maturity. The air now cleared of sibling grievances, Christina was delighted to find warm feelings for her brother returning and felt the same change had occurred in him. That she had infuriated their father was enough to enhance her enormously in his eyes, she was happy to discover, and her insurrection seemed to have exonerated her completely from his main charge, that she sacrificed principles in order to curry favor on Avenue Foch.

For her part, Christina had not realized how much alike she and Alexander were; they shared the same sense of humor and the same talent for analyzing people with a gimlet-eyed lack of mercy for those of wealth and position. He appeared to Christina to have a great deal of common sense and, even better, backbone, two qualities she was trying to develop. When they had reminisced about shared growing-up experiences—gunning his speedboat to wake Callas from her nap or pushing the sass-Jackie gambits as far as they dared—she knew her reconciliation with her brother was complete and she laughed as she had not in months. They had in common so much experience— experience she now realized, after seeing something of more normal worlds, that was extremely rare and unfathomable to outsiders.

· · ·

Christina arrived back in Los Angeles to discover that Bolker had arranged a large twenty-first-birthday celebration for her, a sit-down dinner at Le Bistro for a hundred people. It was a glamorous evening with many celebrities—a sad, Hollywood-at-its-best display from a husband who knew as soon as she arrived home that he and Los Angeles were marked for scrapbook entry. When Christina later told him of her decision, he was understanding and agreed divorce was probably the wisest course. She liked him even more because of the calm resignation with which he met this final test of his patience.

Their disengagement was warm and sentimental. They had silver keys made for each other—one to his Century Plaza apartment, one to her London flat—and quietly got a clean, no-frills divorce. If, in later years, Bolker indulged himself in the white lie that he had no idea who Christina was when he met her, he need not have bothered. He never tried to get a penny of the Onassis millions. He played out his hand with Christina with complete honor, one of the few to do so, and probably derived more grief than benefits from the relationship.

Onassis, from his Avenue Foch command center, was triumphant and took full credit for the marriage's end. In a gesture to soften his victory, he had Olympic Airways fly to Christina an olive branch from Skorpios, complete with ripe olives. Relieved her war was over, Christina said goodbye to Muriel and the few others in Los Angeles she valued and came away feeling she had lost a husband, but gained a brother—and regained a father.

# 10

# THE FLIGHT
# OF ICARUS

*I*n 1972, before heading back to Europe and resuming her pre-Bolker life, Christina decided to review the Luis Basualdo file. As her attraction to Bolker had worn off, she began recalling the delights of her less-troubled affair with Basualdo and was certain it was not over for either of them. She decided to use the same ploy on Basualdo that she had used on Bolker: show up on his doorstep, which was then in Argentina. But before attempting to resume her interrupted romance, she had to lose the pounds she had gained in the final, anguish-filled months in Los Angeles. She would stop off in Rio de Janiero—swim, get healthy, and put herself in fighting trim for another bout with the polo player.

In Rio, at one of a round of parties to which friends took her, she met another polo player with whom she fell into an instant affair. Sympathetic to her desire to lose weight, her new lover urged her to try an all-fruit diet, which would enable her to drop ten pounds in a week. The diet, which was successful, delayed her arrival in Buenos Aires about ten days. The idyll in Rio had two important ancillary benefits: it neatly punctuated the end of her marriage and reestablished in her own eyes her sexual allure.

Grapefruits and nights of passion having restored her self-confidence to a bravura degree, Christina proceeded on to Buenos Aires, where she stayed with her friend Marina Tchomlekdjoglou. After a long evening catching up, Marina said she had to go to bed, but Christina, on the kind of impulse that was becoming emblematic of her style, decided she could not wait until the next day to surprise Basualdo. She took a taxi to his apartment building, arriving at three in the morning.

As luck had it, Basualdo was in bed alone when he was awakened by the house phone. A Mrs. Bolker was in the lobby, the concierge told him, and wished to see him immediately. Drowsy, Basualdo could not place the name. After Christina's marriage, when he had phoned from Germany to wish her happiness, she railed at him, saying that, after the way he had dropped her, she never wanted to hear from him again. It did not occur to him that the woman downstairs was Christina, who he thought had disappeared forever from his life into the mists of Southern California. When he told the operator to ask the woman to phone him in the morning, Christina came on the line and in a loud, unmistakable voice said, "Angel, I'm here. I've flown all this way to see you."

Alone in a hot and steamy Buenos Aires, with most of his friends out of the city, Basualdo was glad to see Christina and to learn that she was once again single. Their reunion was passionate. After a morning in bed, they headed for a restaurant to celebrate the resumption of their affair. Over lunch, he told her he was at the point of leaving Buenos Aires for a week to ten days. He had to drive into the pampas to play polo and to transact some horse business. Why didn't she come with him? She might enjoy seeing some of Argentina. Christina was thrilled at the idea.

For the next few days they were as happy with each other as either had ever been. The weather was warm, the pampas evocative, the nights moonlit. Basualdo later recalled taking siestas with Christina rolled up together in a hammock. Raving over the beauty of Argentina, Christina said she would like to buy a house there, marry Luis, and raise a family. They talked idly about this but Basualdo doubted if Christina's settling-down mood would last. As he predicted, after five days she began getting restless and suggested they return to Buenos Aires, where they could go to a disco she particularly liked. So much, thought Basualdo, for settling down forever in the pampas.

Basualdo was set to return to Europe, where he was still involved in an affair with Lucy Pearson. After visiting Lucy in England, he planned to resume his polo-playing job in Hamburg. He once again pointed out to Christina that he was in no financial position to support the kind of life she was accustomed to, and once again she got angry. When they arrived back in Buenos Aires, they found a clutch of reporters and photographers waiting outside the door of Basualdo's building.

"What the hell are they doing here?" she asked Basualdo. "No one knows I'm in Argentina."

The reporters quickly told them why they were there. When Christina and Basualdo had had lunch in the local restaurant the day they had left Buenos Aires, she had left behind her purse with $22,000 in cash. The purse had been discovered by a waiter, who had turned it in. Unknown to Christina and Basualdo, the Buenos Aires newspapers had been full of the story, and reporters had learned from Basualdo's concierge when they were expected back in town. In the pampas, what few expenses they had had were paid by Basualdo; Christina, perhaps as a measure of her happy state, was unaware she had lost her pocketbook. She gave the honest waiter a generous reward and posed for pictures with him.

The bizarre incident distracted Basualdo and Christina from the unsatisfactory conclusion of their romantic reunion, and both flew back to Europe with vague plans to meet again. Although Basualdo had not mentioned this to Christina, he had already asked the Hamburg team's owner if Lucy Pearson could come with him for the new season and had been told he could not bring a woman unless they were married. Basualdo and Lucy had discussed the matter and decided that they would get married, not because they wanted to be married, but because they wanted to be together in Germany. Only eighteen, Lucy knew that her parents' consent was unlikely, so they decided to marry secretly. Before he settled in Hamburg, where she would join him, Basualdo had to fly to Munich to conduct some team business with the owner. He and Lucy got married in London the morning of his departure.

On the plane to Munich, Basualdo was seated next to an attractive Englishwoman in her mid-twenties with whom he struck up a conversation. She was Prunella Vance or Lady Marbly, the daughter of Sir Ronald Marbly, and had just separated from her husband. Pick-

166 ··· CHAPTER TEN

ing up on the theme of matrimony, Basualdo mentioned that he had
been married that day. Understandably, Lady Marbly remarked that
he appeared to lack a bride. When he explained, she expanded on
the sorrows of a solitary honeymoon.

In an effort to cheer up the lonely bridegroom, Lady Marbly called
for champagne, and by the end of the flight she had sportingly agreed
to fill the nuptial gap. After collecting their luggage, Basualdo and
his stand-in bride proceeded to Der Königshof, the hotel where he
was to stay with the owner of the Hamburg team. Knowing of the
marriage to Lucy Pearson earlier in the day, the German sportsman
was nonplussed to greet Basualdo with another lady on his arm, but
he adjusted quickly. For the next three days, the three shared a suite
and enjoyed a jolly celebratory stay in Munich.

Some months later a friend of Basualdo's was introduced to Lady
Marbly at a party in London and he blurted out, "Oh yes, you're
the one who stood in for Lucy Pearson on her honeymoon with
Basualdo." Her ladyship, having reassumed her London moral code,
was outraged. If Christina had known this story, it might have softened the pain of having, once again, let Basualdo slip through her
fingers. Slipping through fingers was what he did best.

The reconciliation of Alexander and Christina was an important
change in the delicate equation between Aristotle Onassis and his
children. But neither Christina nor Alexander was deluded that their
new-formed alliance might prove an effective counterbalance to
their father's power over them. They knew too well that, as forces
against their father strengthened, so did his determination to prevail.
Still, their new friendship gave each the comforting awareness that
they had an ally within the small family, one whose sympathies were
informed by rare and painful experience. For Christina, being able
to take her Ari problems to an understanding veteran of the same
wars was a sizable addition to her meager store of emotional-support
resources.

At the moment, however, Christina had less need than usual of
such support. Having put behind her an impulsive marriage and the
wrath from her father that it had produced, she threw herself into
the heady business of being a young and sexually viable heiress.

Many of Europe's more desirable bachelors lined up to pay court, and, as if to attone for Bolker's inappropriateness, she gave all comers a fair hearing, if not a tumble.

Once Christina had knuckled under to her father's wishes and divorced Bolker, he made good on his promise to release her $75 million trust fund, which she now was of age to receive, and she found herself a very rich twenty-two-year-old divorcée. Her breathtaking marriageability had Europe's society press again rapacious to discover by any means possible her romantic inclinations. If, as Oscar Wilde said, a bachelor is a public temptation, a youthful, attractive multimillionairess is a public incitement.

If a male happened to be in her line of vision, the merest glimmer in Christina's eye was considered news and was routinely spread across the glossy magazines in ten countries. Among the young men touted as romantic interests—and it required no more than one public appearance together—were Baron Arnaud de Rosnay, who was a childhood friend; Patrick Gillis, who had established himself in the amatory big leagues with a turn as Brigitte Bardot's lover; and various others best viewed under strobe lighting. Christina still continued to see the marriage-resisting Mick Flick. All were suitable enough, but as serious marital candidates they were exaggerated—the first two by the press, the last by Christina herself.

Now that Alexander and Christina were friends again, they began meeting for dinner when they were in the same city. With their new cordiality, his jealous irritation with her behavior changed into affectionate amusement. The bravado of her Ari-defying Beverly Hills escapade gave her new stature in his eyes, while its outlandishness made him think her future exploits might be worth watching. His life remained one of commuting from his job in Monte Carlo to his mistress in London, and, shortly, in Switzerland, when Fiona moved there as the first step in the scheme to liberate Alexander.

Now he occasionally stopped off in Paris to see Christina. As soon as her divorce from Bolker was final, they met for a celebration dinner at Maxim's, Christina's treat. When they were settled at their table, he looked at her quizzically and then, smiling, said, "Well, the Prodigal Daughter has returned to the fold." Christina replied that she may have only broken loose for a short time, but at least she had broken loose. Did that mean she was going to be a good girl from then on? Hardly, Christina told him. More seriously, he asked her what *was* on her agenda.

"I have no idea," Christina replied happily. "Isn't it exciting?"

In fact, she had a pretty good idea as the next few months would indicate: a great many parties and nightclubs followed by journeys to other cities, where she would indulge herself with more parties and more nightclubs. Without apologies to anyone, she threw herself into a dogged quest for fun. If she found a replacement for Bolker, that would be fine, but that was secondary. Her main goal was to enjoy being young, attractive, and rich. She would explore the most pleasure-bent corners of Europe, New York, and South America, to exploit to the fullest the highly privileged youth she had almost thrown away to become a lower-echelon Hollywood wife. Bolker had been middle-aged and middle-rich. She was very young and very rich. She knew she hadn't loved him that much. How serious could her problems have been?

All her father had asked of her was a modicum of sanity, but then all she had asked of him was to be permitted to do one thing she wanted, however much he did not want it. She had defied her father and was still alive to tell about it. He had won, but just coming out of the fracas without serious injury was a major victory for Christina. Having now felt her father's fullest wrath, she was no longer terrified of it. Since Onassis believed his victory over her insurrection had been entirely his own doing, he eased up considerably on his criticisms and hectoring vigilance. He also indicated he wanted to end his marriage to Jackie, which was the best possible news to both Christina and her brother.

Within just a few months, Christina's life had changed from a rancorous snarl in which everyone was mad at her to an exciting lark in which she was everyone's friend. She was free, had all the money in the world, a green light from her father to cut loose, and sweetest of all, less anxiety about what he thought. Everything now came together to permit Christina to do what she was coming to believe was her sole duty, the object of her life, in fact—simply to enjoy herself.

· · ·

In pursuit of this program, in late January 1973, Christina returned to Rio, where she joined her friend Marina and some others to attend a round of parties and kick up her heels far from the relentless curiosity of Europe's tabloid press. She had a wonderful time as she always did in South America and as she always did with Marina, who invariably located and infiltrated the most attractive and amusing young crowd. On the day of January 22, driving in a hired car to go shopping, Christina deciphered from what for her was the gibberish of a Portuguese news broadcast some words that sounded like her brother's name. She asked the driver to turn up the volume and tell her what was being said.

There had been a plane crash in Athens, she was told. Alexander Onassis was seriously hurt. In a daze, Christina rushed back to the hotel to prepare to leave for Greece and found two messages, one from her father's bodyguard in New York, George Tzaferos, another from her Aunt Artemis in Athens. Reaching her aunt first, Christina went numb as she learned Alexander's head had been crushed and he was not expected to live.

"If Alexander had been killed in an automobile accident," Fiona Thyssen said many years later, "no one would have thought it the least surprising, but a plane—that was something different."

To everyone who knew Alexander, his death-defying recklessness behind the wheel of a Ferrari or Maserati was widely known. And he had terrorized many people, including his father, driving a motorboat. Piloting an airplane, however, he was altogether different—scrupulously careful and cautious, leaving the daredevil in him behind on the ground. He had been flying since obtaining his license at eighteen, and his enthusiasm for planes had increased with age. One of his greatest thrills had been when, shopping with his father for commercial jets for Olympic Airlines, he was permitted to take the controls of a Boeing 707. He knew, however, that his father was doggedly against his flying. They argued about it constantly, and Alexander's caution as a pilot may have stemmed from a fear that even a minor mishap would result in his being permanently grounded.

One of Onassis's basic themes in the running argument between father and son on the subject was that flying was too risky a pastime for his only son and heir. Onassis would cite disasters to support his belief, finding one close at hand. Late in 1972 his private jet had crashed into the Mediterranean off Antibes; no trace of the plane or of the two pilots aboard at the time was ever found. They were experienced, skilled pilots, Onassis said. They were now dead and no one knew why. Alexander would counter such examples with his strong belief that, if proper attention was given to details, flying was not dangerous. He would hold forth at length on his theory that most airplane crashes resulted from an accumulation of small human errors rather than massive equipment failures.

Because Alexander's tragic accident in Athens led to such a prolonged period of fault seeking, accusations, and bitterness—and would dominate the lives of every member of the family for many months—the circumstances leading up to it took on considerable significance. A Piaggio seaplane had been one of Aristotle Onassis's first accouterments of wealth. Since it was kept aboard the *Christina* and could, on a moment's notice, whisk him to the nearest airport, where a commercial jet could then take him to any part of the globe, it became a symbol of his restless nature and his impulsive, bravura business style.

With the Piaggio, Onassis could leave a yacht party in mid-Mediterranean, fly to London for a meeting, and be back in time for dinner with his guests. Perhaps sentiment was involved in his reluctance to part with the plane, but Alexander and others had pleaded with him for several years to replace it with a helicopter. Alexander argued the greater maneuverability of the helicopter, the additional uses to which it could be put, but his principal argument was that the Piaggio was no longer safe. It broke down constantly, needed frequent repairs and, most recently, a thorough overhaul ordered by Onassis, which was started the previous fall, in November 1972, and would be finished by mid-January 1973.

Since the decision to renovate yet another time had seemed to indicate a prolonged life for the old plane, Alexander was delighted when his father told him, as they dined together in Paris on January 4, 1973, of his intention to get rid of the Piaggio and buy a helicopter. The changeover would take time, however. Meanwhile, he would use the refurbished Piaggio once more, for a Caribbean cruise with the *Christina* that Onassis was planning for late January.

After the cruise, he would drop the plane in Miami, where it would be sold. Alexander had been overjoyed that his father had finally listened to reason, and even more that his father had finally listened to *him*.

As the time drew nearer for the cruise, delivery of the Piaggio was delayed and Onassis began pressuring everyone to make sure it was ready. Then, with delivery only a few days off, Onassis's pilot, Donald McGregor, developed an eye infection and was grounded by Greek aviation officials. This unexpected problem sent Onassis into a frenzy. Being trapped on his yacht among frivolous social types whom he sometimes enjoyed but other times couldn't abide ("Those people I socialize with," he once was quoted as saying, "they're all shits"), was to him the highest form of claustrophobia. Not only did he fear being incarcerated with bores, but he quaked even more at the dreadful thought of being trapped at sea while others were snaring juicy business deals on land. This was more than enough to give delivery of the Piaggio top priority on his agenda and send him shouting into his do-it-or-else mode.

An urgent call went out for a replacement pilot, which should not have been a problem for a man who owned an airline. But because the man in this case had a reputation for imposing on his personal pilots long and erratic hours, even longer idle waits in outlandish places, and occasional temper tantrums, no one would volunteer. Finally, a pilot responded to an ad that had been placed in an American aviation magazine. He was interviewed at length by telephone and invited to Athens to undergo the only remaining obstacle to his employment, a round of trial flights in the Piaggio. He was Donald McCusker, a World War II Navy pilot who had also test-piloted for North American Rockwell and other American aircraft manufacturers. In addition, McCusker had had considerable experience with amphibians.

The earliest McCusker could arrive in Greece was on the morning of January 22nd, a Monday. On Saturday the 20th, Onassis phoned his son at Fiona's house in Switzerland and pressured him to fly to Athens to take the new man through his trials, since the grounded McGregor was no longer qualified to do it. Alexander and Fiona had plans to fly to London that day to attend her brother's wedding, but since public appearances where press photos of them together might be taken had been the major cause for a recent split—he hating the problems the publicity caused him with his family, she hating the guilty slinking-around—Alexander may well have seized on the excuse to skip the wedding, oblige his father's urgent request, then join Fiona a few days later in London. He told his father he would be in Athens for McCusker's arrival on the 22nd.

Alexander and Fiona spent a particularly pleasant weekend together in the place she had rented in Morges, Switzerland, while her new house that would be the base for Alexander to complete his education was being readied. Destructive problems in their relationship had been resolved and even greater problems between Alexander and his father were vastly improved. Prospects were brighter for the pair than at any time in their five years together. They made their plans to meet in London two days later and parted warmly. Because of their planned rendezvous, when Alexander arrived in Athens on Sunday evening he was as eager as his father, but for different reasons, to complete the pilot chore as quickly as possible.

On Monday morning, January 22, McCusker, who had sat up all night on an Olympic flight from New York, was startled to learn he would not be allowed a day to recover from his journey, but would be put through his trial flight that very afternoon. He, Alexander, and McGregor boarded the plane shortly after 3 P.M., McCusker at the controls, Alexander as co-pilot, and McGregor in the seat behind. When they were all in place, Alexander realized they had forgotten to pick up a preflight check list, but decided that, because he had done the checks so many times, he could go through them from memory, which he proceeded to do. The plane had been checked out on the ground following its overhaul, but had not yet been flown, so in the interest of speed they were combining the plane's test flight with the pilot's trials. It was a brilliant day in Athens, cold and sunny, with an unusually low pollution level.

Cleared for takeoff, the plane started down the runway and McGregor noticed that Alexander had neglected to fasten his seat belt. He would tell him when they got into the air. Reaching about one hundred miles per hour, the Piaggio rose from the ground and almost immediately veered to the right. McCusker pulled on the controls to correct the turn and, to his horror, the plane veered further to the right. The right-wing pontoon struck the ground, then the wing itself hit, causing the plane to cartwheel 450 feet along the tarmac before it crashed to a stop. From takeoff to crash had been, in McGregor's later estimate, approximately fifteen seconds. McCusker and McGregor were injured, McCusker quite seriously, but both were expected to recover. Alexander's head was so badly mauled he could be identified only by the monogram on his pocket handkerchief.

Onassis and Jackie were in New York when they heard the news, Tina and Niarchos were in St. Moritz, and Fiona was in London, dressing for her brother's wedding-night dinner. By the next morning all of them were in Athens. Christina had been unable to make connections from Brazil that would get her there any sooner than late afternoon. Jackie had brought with her a top Boston neurosurgeon. Onassis had chartered a British Airways Trident to bring another renowned neurosurgeon from London in addition to having a top heart specialist flown in from Texas. In his desperation, Onassis even dispatched a plane to Skorpios to bring an icon that was alleged to have miraculous curing powers.

Tina was so distraught she had to be heavily sedated and kept in a room near her son. In her shock Fiona could remember erratic thoughts. "When I saw him completely bandaged, I could see that his nose was all right. 'Thank God,' I thought. He had just had it fixed and was very proud of the new shape." Fiona also recalled another bizarre occurrence. "Jackie came up to me. I thought she was going to offer a word of sympathy. Instead she asked me if I knew anything about Alexander's dinner with Ari in Paris at the beginning of January when Ari had told him of his plans to get a divorce. She wanted to know if he had mentioned a settlement figure."

By early Tuesday afternoon, all the doctors agreed that, while Alexander's heart was still beating, his brain had ceased to function and there was no hope. In a daze, Onassis agreed with the decision to remove heroic measures and permit his son to die, but insisted that they wait until Christina arrived from Rio. At six-fifteen she came into Alexander's room—disheveled, sleepless, unbelieving, numb. She was greeted by the hideous sight of her brother, his head completely bandaged except for his nose and his eyes, which were closed. Christina spent a half hour with him, until her sobbing became so uncontrollable she was led from the room and taken to her aunt's villa in Glyfada. Within ten minutes of her leaving the hospital room, the medical team removed the support systems and Alexander died.

The enormous grief felt by Christina, Tina, Fiona, and the Onassis aunts was totally superseded by the overwhelming despair of Onassis himself, and in a sense the others deferred to his anguish. For Onassis, Alexander had gradually become in his disillusionment the only aspect of his life that gave his brilliant accomplishments any meaning. Now in his seventies, locked in a marriage that was a public farce and a private torment, he had nothing to look forward to except more yacht parties, more ordinary mortals dazzled by his wealth, and more affronts from the envious.

An only son has a very special place in any father's emotions. In Greece there is a saying that if a Greek man has a son and a daughter, he has an only child. But for a Greek man who had wrenched so much from his earthly existence, and whose age made inescapable the knowledge that, despite his godlike achievements and attributes, he too would die and be forced to abandon the rare empire he had created, the only son took on a near-religious importance.

The degree to which Onassis had avoided any serious preparation of Alexander for one day assuming direction of his empire sprang from his not uncommon belief that he would continue forever. Given his highly competitive nature, he also may have felt that a well-trained and competent Alexander would be a threat and challenge to his diminishing powers as he grew older. At the time of the accident, Onassis had only recently made the difficult switch from believing he wasn't ever going to die to the only slightly less palatable awareness that he was not going to die any time *soon*. His assumption of ample time relieved any urgency to the grooming of Alexander, but it permitted Onassis to admit his son's importance to him, an importance reinforced by his growing approval of the admirable adult Alexander was becoming. It was at this happy point in the evolution of his complex feelings toward his son that Alexander was so abruptly killed.

Onassis had always been prone to that special paranoia reserved for those who themselves have stooped to tampering surreptitiously with the lives of others. A man who could plant a listening device in his own daughter's apartment could suspect far worse machinations from others. With no evidence except the seemingly inexplicable nature of the crash, Onassis was convinced Alexander's death was not an accident, that the plane had been sabotaged. There was, of course, an official investigation, but in addition Onassis hired crash experts from England and a top French investigative journalist—all to uncover a plot—and offered a $1 million reward for proof that the plane had been sabotaged.

His list of suspects was a good indicator of his overheated mental condition. Niarchos, of course, was high on the list as was the CIA, the rough-stuff arm of a government he felt was out to punish him for nearly pulling off the Jiddah Agreement. He speculated that the family of his two pilots killed in the crash off Antibes had rigged the Piaggio for revenge. But his list continued on into ever more irrational plots. He suspected Tina of having conspired to murder her beloved son in a convoluted scheme to consolidate the Onassis-Livanos and Niarchos fortunes. He also suspected Jackie of somehow having been behind it, for nobody knew what reason. It was surprising, given the breadth of his obsessive search for culprits, that he never suspected Christina, who, as Onassis's remaining heir, was the only one who would directly benefit from Alexander's death.

The official investigation concluded that the aileron controls, the cables that worked the plane's flaps and caused it to turn left or right, had been reversed during the overhaul. This meant that a turn in the pilot's wheel would have an effect opposite to that expected. A large jet takeoff just before the Piaggio's clearance may have caused a backwash that pushed the Piaggio to the right, for which McCuster tried to compensate by a turn to the left. When the plane then veered *further* to the right, he pushed the wheel hard left, causing the plane to turn sharply, disastrously, to the right and crash. Both the official Greek investigation and Onassis's British experts concluded the evidence left no doubt the cables had been reversed. Whether or not making such a repair mistake was difficult or easy was a matter of dispute, but almost everyone agreed that it was possible for it to have been done as an innocent error.

The arguments against its being anything else, that is to say, a plot of some sort, were strong. Alexander had only decided to come to Athens two days before the accident; the work on the aileron shaft had been finished two months before. The chances of someone's effecting unnoticed such a major internal change in the plane in those two days were almost nil. In the preflight safety routine, pilots are supposed to check *visually* to see with their own eyes that the flaps are working correctly. Indeed, Alexander had once reprimanded McGregor for neglecting to do this. Had Alexander, McCusker, or any other pilot done this very routine visual check on that day, he would have seen the controls on the Piaggio were not working as they should, and canceled the flight.

Then too, a cable-switching assassin would have no reason to think Alexander or his father would take the plane for its post-overhaul trial flight; that was almost always done by those who had worked on the overhaul. If the normal procedure had been followed, the *test pilots* would have encountered the steering problem, not Alexander or any of the Onassis family. This change from the usual pattern was another accommodation to Onassis's impatience. Another point undermining a conspiracy scenario was that those on the plane with seat belts fastened got out alive.

To kill someone by reversing aileron cables would then have required two improbable pieces of negligence on the part of the victim and would have been a highly uncertain, in addition to enormously troublesome, method of murder. If it can be granted that errors in plane overhauls occur, a fair conclusion would be that Alexander's two acts of documented negligence, forgetting to make the visual check and to fasten his seat belt, were the main causes of his death —in conjunction, of course, with the reversed cables. The blame for these oversights must go to Alexander rather than McCusker, since he was the pilot in command of the flight even if he was not at the controls.

As unbearable as this conclusion was to Onassis, it was not nearly as unbearable as a further conclusion many drew: that Onassis's hurrying everyone to ready the Piaggio was the root cause of the disaster. He had pressured Alexander to squeeze time from his schedule, thus putting his son in a rush to complete the job; he had demanded that McCusker be tested the day following an all-night Atlantic flight; he had insisted that the plane's test flight be combined with a new-pilot trial. All of these elements had led to a corner-cutting carelessness that was not typical of Alexander. As for the mechanical-error aspect of the accident theory, that was also repugnant to Onassis, since his own Olympic Airline staff had done the repairs.

And hovering over the whole tragic tableau was the memory of Alexander's repeated pleas to get rid of the dangerously old and obsolete airplane. Among Onassis's reasons for not doing so were sentiment for a plane that had served him well and the comfort of a plane to which long use had made him accustomed. More than anything else, however, the reason that one of the world's richest men did not want to replace the Piaggio was *economy*. He didn't want to spend the money. Unable to admit the grotesque possibility that frugality had caused his only son's death, Onassis clung desperately to the idea of foul play: someone else was to blame—not Alexander, not Olympic's maintenance people, and certainly not himself. When he found out who was responsible, he, Onassis, would be totally exonerated.

Obsessed with finding a scapegoat, Onassis relentlessly pressured the Greek authorities, and managed to get McCusker and three mechanics indicted for manslaughter. Eventually all the baseless charges were dropped and McCusker, who had merely answered an ad, only to find himself hounded for years by one of the world's most powerful men for killing his son, countersued and was awarded damages of $800,000 by Olympic Airlines three years after Onassis's death.

Christina and the others in the family at first humored Onassis's plot obsessions—they would have supported any theory he had about anything in their desperate attempts to assuage his terrible grief—but as his obsessions grew to worrying proportions, they made tentative attempts to lure him from the suspicions that were becoming increasingly preposterous with each new finding. Everything supported the theory of innocent mechanical error. When they tried to point this out to Onassis, however, they quickly learned that the mildest attempts to dissuade him were met by near-violent explosions and cries of betrayal, if not of collusion. Perhaps his consolers had not yet deduced the even worse furies for Onassis—his own guilt—that lay behind the protective screen of his plot theories.

His obsession with finding some other culprit than himself was not the only symptom of his deranged state. There was considerable indecision about where Alexander should be buried, but Onassis at first refused to have Alexander buried at all. He wanted to have the body frozen until medical science was able to reassemble shattered skulls, and for this purpose he contacted the Life Extension Society in Washington, D.C., which had done extensive research in the field of cryogenics. He would have adhered to this program if his philosophical sparring partner, Professor Yanni Georgakis, had not persuaded Onassis that he "had no right to impede the journey of Alexander's soul."

Then Onassis agreed to have Alexander buried in Athens as an accommodation to those who pleaded for a grave accessible to all who had loved him, especially Fiona, who had not been welcome on Skorpios when Alexander was alive and doubted she would be now. Onassis then changed his mind and decided to bury Alexander on Skorpios, not only because he intended to be buried there himself, but because, in those grim days after the accident, he planned to spend as much time as possible by his son's grave. In the few years remaining to Onassis, he would sometimes disappear suddenly from jolly dinner parties on Skorpios. Most guests knew where he had gone.

Even with the grave's location decided upon, Onassis remained erratic about his son's burial. He wanted Alexander buried inside the island's chapel, but was reminded that this would constitute a sacrilege, in that only Greek Orthodox saints may be buried inside chapels. Able to find a loophole even in church law, Onassis had Alexander buried just outside the chapel, but then, having obtained the priests' blessings, extended the chapel to cover the grave. A few weeks after the tragedy, Onassis had a poignant meeting with Fiona, in which he assured his old adversary that any time she wished to visit Alexander's grave she was most welcome on Skorpios.

So worried was Christina about her father's unstable condition it served to distract her from the terrible pain that she herself felt at the loss of her brother. In the months just before his death, she had projected a prominent role for Alexander in her future. She knew that her father would eventually die, but by then Alexander would be a mature, experienced adult and a worthy replacement as the solid male influence in her life. She looked forward to that very special relationship that only a father or brother can serve: a man with whom she was extremely close, whose background paralleled hers, who cared deeply about her, but who, being equally well off and romantically neutral, had no ulterior motives for his affection. Actually, Alexander, she knew, would be a better friend than her father. He was more of an equal and did not have his father's mania for control.

For different reasons, she and her father were in the same wrenching predicament: they had both just recently "found" Alexander—partially through opening psychically jammed doors and partially through Alexander's development from a willful brat into a sensitive and intelligent young man—only to lose him as soon as they realized how much he meant to both of them. For Onassis, it was a brutal punishment for his cavalier handling of his most important love relationships.

When his children had been young, his love for them had been only sporadically made manifest, and only if nothing more important was afoot. Although he had humiliated Tina on a global level, he was surprised and dismayed when she chose to withdraw altogether from his game. He never stopped loving Callas but marrying Jackie satisfied more of his ambitions, so Callas, who fervently returned his love as no one else ever had, was blithely and cruelly abandoned. Although he had come to love and respect Alexander and had begun to view him as something more than a flawed manifestation of his own ego, Onassis knew he hadn't loved him *enough*. Harshly but with justification, one of Alexander's friends summed up this belated love, "Onassis started being a good father the day Alexander died."

Onassis himself began to see a connection between his tragedies and his own actions, not, of course, his human foibles like penny-pinching and childish impatience, but rather his most grandiose deeds, for which he had received retribution. If he was to be forced to admit to faults, they would be on a lofty, cosmic level. When he had pulled himself together enough to travel, he appeared late one night at the door of Callas's Paris apartment, threw himself sobbing at her feet, and said that Alexander's death had been punishment for his *hubris*, his god-defying arrogance in marrying Jackie. Callas believed that his treatment of her was cause enough for punishment, without worrying about what it did to the gods. But she was long past showing him such resentment and did what she could to comfort him.

Christina also dedicated herself to her father's grief, having lost her stomach for rich-girl escapades. When her mother came up with a matrimonial plan for her, one that had the usual Livanos fortune-merging stamp but was also aimed at gratifying and distracting Onassis, Christina was happy to cooperate. Tina's idea, which she thought quite brilliant, was that Christina should marry Philippe Niarchos, the oldest son of Stavros and Eugenie. Christina had always liked Philippe. That they were first cousins was a minor blemish on a plan that promised to shower benefits on both dynasties. Tina was confident Onassis's aversion to Niarchos would be overruled by the prospect of having his daughter, and eventually his fortune, in the hands of a Greek male who knew ships and owned a good many himself.

While eager to be helpful, Christina warned her mother that she had no romantic feelings for Philippe; she had known him too long as almost a brother. Tina, who had demonstrated how she disdained family relationships standing in the way of advantageous marriages, urged Christina to give her plan a try. If she and Philippe lived together for a while they might be delightfully surprised by what developed. It is not every girl whose mother sets up a romantic interlude for her daughter, so Christina agreed to give Philippe an audition. Like good Greek soldiers, the cousins planned a weekend together, but, to Tina's annoyance, the conjugal experiment collapsed in a giggling shambles.

Christina turned to more customary ways of helping a father through his grief and was gratified to find that Onassis wanted her with him frequently. In the summer of 1973 she went to Monte Carlo to clear Alexander's belongings from his apartment, then flew to Skorpios with the packing cases, which included the set of Samsonite luggage that Fiona had said were, "except for his clothes, his only possessions."

Even after five months, Onassis's grief was still intense, and he would wander off from his own lunch and dinner parties and sit for hours by Alexander's grave, crying. The tanker business was booming, and he could make as much as $4 million profit on one ten-day run with a very large or ultra-large crude carrier from Kuwait to northern Europe; he ordered new ships to capitalize on the oil demand. But it was clear to all of his lieutenants that his heart was no longer in making vast amounts of money.

Christina did what she could to distract him from his agony, but the shared mourning, rather than bringing them closer together, developed into a particularly difficult and painful time in their relationship. When she was with him on Skorpios, he would often ignore her and devote himself to other people. He also made no mention of training her to assume control of the companies, nor did he for many months. When Onassis did take notice of Christina, it was to find fault. His son's death, rather than causing Onassis to value more highly his remaining child, instead made him more critical of Christina than he had ever been. He didn't like the way she dressed, she was too fat, she was too frivolous, her friends were society bubbleheads. The approbation she had won by divorcing Bolker was forgotten. She was no longer the cherished prodigal but now, more than ever, she was the in-all-ways-inadequate daughter.

Although Christina did not need strong analytical powers to discern what lay behind his dissatisfaction with her, Onassis was unwilling to risk her missing the point. When in his cups, as he now frequently was, he would blurt out the unspeakable. Staring morosely into his fifth Johnny Walker Black Label, he would say, "Why couldn't it have been my daughter rather than my son?" He uttered similar cruelties on several occasions, once within Christina's hearing. She listened, watched, and suffered, clinging to the consolation she was hearing from her aunts and others: this would pass. He had to love her. He had no choice.

# 11

# THE UNRELENTING CURSE

$\mathcal{L}$ater in the summer of 1973, Onassis began to emerge sufficiently from his grief to realize that he must begin educating Christina in running his huge shipping enterprise. After months of silence on the subject, he finally began talking with her about the role for which she now had to prepare herself. This pleased her enormously. In his attempts to give her an overview of his unwieldy operations, however, Onassis succeeded only in establishing their complexity. Intricate corporate structures designed to confuse tax collectors were equally confusing to Christina.

With no pedagogic gift, Onassis managed to get across the principle that Olympic Maritime was not a huge company that owned a fleet of tankers but rather a ship brokerage firm that leased the ships of a long string of shipowning corporations, most of them Panamanian, all of them owned by Onassis. Beyond that loose principle, the organizational chart seemed to exist only in Onassis's brain. He could draw on it for his decisions but could not describe it with coherence to anyone else. He was like a virtuoso pianist attempting to articulate the mental process behind striking specific keys. His stabs at elucidating Christina generally ended in making her fear that it was all hopelessly beyond her. The usual parent-child tensions did not help the educational process; one or the other of them would become angry before much information had been imparted. Finally, Onassis decided to turn her over to his top lieutenants for a crash course in becoming a Greek tycoon.

In hopes of diverting himself from his grief, Onassis had particularly requested youthful guests on Skorpios, so the summer was enlivened by the arrival of a group of fashionable young Parisians, among them Florence and Hubert Michard-Pelissier, the children of one of Onassis's French lawyers. Florence, whose wedding to Jean-Noël Grinda Christina had attended nine years earlier, was now separated from her husband. Another guest was Marie de Luynes, whose brother, the Duc de Chevreuse, had married Christine Roussel of the French pharmaceutical family. Marie had brought along her sister-in-law's younger brother, Thierry Roussel, who had also been at Florence Grinda's wedding, although Christina had barely noticed him among the throng of other schoolboys. Now twenty, tall and handsome with curly blond hair and bright blue eyes, Thierry exuded self-confidence and spirit. On this occasion, Christina noticed him.

Both of them spoiled and brash, Christina and Roussel hit it off immediately and were soon having a heated summer romance, which Onassis emerged from his grief long enough to approve whole-heartedly. He had a good impression of Thierry, felt he had energy and intelligence, and knew that his last name connoted a large fortune. After several talks with the young man, he concluded that he had brains enough to help Christina run the empire. Thierry's father, Henri Roussel, had sold to his brother his share of the family company, Roussel-Uclaf, to devote himself to big-game hunting. To pursue the sport, he owned a ranch in Kenya and a villa in Marbella on Spain's Costa del Sol. Thierry, only recently out of school, had not yet decided on a career and was concentrating on having a good time.

At the end of Thierry's Skorpios visit, he invited Christina to visit him in Marbella in September, and he left her in a euphoric haze. Florence Grinda advised Christina to cross Roussel off as a pleasant summer interlude. From others Christina had learned that he was involved with a beautiful Swedish model, but Florence reinforced the bad news with devastating particulars. Thierry lived with the Swedish woman and was in love with her.

In such a situation at the age of twenty-two, Christina's store of worldly knowledge, most of it supplied by her father, served her badly. She had accepted his wisdom that beautiful women with no fortune don't count for much, are not formidable competition when it comes to matrimony. Men of substance have affairs with them, he told her, they don't marry them. In her insecurity, Christina had been only too eager to believe such cynical wisdom even before she met Thierry, but now she clung to it in lovelorn desperation. Reinforcing such a theoretical hope, she knew what had transpired between Thierry and her and this sweet knowledge helped her throw off Florence's warning.

When Christina arrived in Marbella, she had half assumed she was there to make plans for their wedding. She was dashed to learn that Thierry had reconsidered. He told Christina about his Swedish mistress, Gaby Landhage, and said he had decided he could not give her up, strong as his feelings were for Christina and aware as he was of what he was passing up. Christina was crushed and, as was becoming her pattern, made her heartbreak known to anyone who would listen.

One commiserater suggested that, to speed her recovery, she renew her romance with Peter Goulandris, who was still unmarried. Remembering how she had abandoned him first for Danny Marentette, then for Bolker, Christina doubted Goulandris would be eager to renew their involvement. The friend assured her that he had nothing but warm feelings for Christina. As she mentally rehearsed marriage to Goulandris from the new prospective of one experienced in matrimony, many thoughts came to Christina, most of them agreeable. A major change had occurred in her that made the idea of marriage to Goulandris more appealing than it had been previously. With her Bolker insurrection and her father's grief over Alexander, she was no longer bent on defiance and cutting herself free of her father's control. Now she wanted nothing more than to please him. Marriage to Goulandris would be the perfect atonement for her Joe Bolker misalliance, of course, but so ideal was the match in Onassis's eyes it would also be a small compensation as well for the loss of Alexander.

When Christina had undergone the grim task of packing up her brother's possessions in Monte Carlo, she had become good friends with a young Frenchman who had been Alexander's closest male friend at the time of his death. He was François Mazet, a race-car driver who had an atmospheric hideaway high in the hills above Menton a short drive from Monte Carlo. Mazet had helped Christina through some of the most difficult moments after her brother's death and she was grateful to him. He also understood the lingering effects of her grief, the daily depressions, rarely lasting more than an hour, that could strike at any moment. When it was decided she should go to New York to learn the tanker business in the offices of Olympic Maritime, she asked Mazet, with whom she was not involved romantically, to go with her as a companion and he agreed. As a parting gift to Christina, Onassis gave her a maid he prized, a young Greek woman named Eleni Syros, who worked for him on Skorpios and in Paris. She and Christina would become extremely close.

Once in New York, Christina moved into a suite at the Regency Hotel and began going regularly to the Onassis offices. Tracking down friends, she was delighted to learn that Luis Basualdo, whom she no longer despised as a defecting lover, had moved to New York with his bride, Lucy Pearson, in a ploy to liberate her trust funds from British taxes. They were living in great style in a townhouse next door to David Rockefeller on East Sixty-third Street. The house had been decorated throughout by Basualdo's early girlfriend, Justine Cushing, enabling him to swell his legend by romancing Justine on one floor of the large house while his wife was making phone calls on another. When he took Christina on a tour of the house, she was impressed.

"You've done well, Luis," she said, "far better than you would have with me"—which was rather the way he saw it.

Basualdo would remember that one night he, Lucy, and Christina were leaving to see a film when the phone rang. It was Prunella Vance, Basualdo's surrogate bride in Munich, who was in town and wanted to drop by to say hello—and perhaps to check out the marriage she had helped launch. When they asked Prunella to join them in seeing a film, she accepted. Basualdo, struck by having so many of his lovers in one group, picked up the spirit of the occasion and phoned Justine to suggest she meet them at the theater. As Christina, Lucy, Justine, and Prunella sat on either side of Basualdo, staring up, appropriately, at *The Heartbreak Kid*, none of the women was aware of the experience they all had in common.

While Christina was settling into her New York work routine, Onassis was cruising with Jackie and a group of friends aboard the *Christina*. As they approached the island of Lesbos, a radio message arrived from Niarchos. He and Tina were in the north of Greece about to take his new yacht, the *Atlantis*, on a shakedown cruise. Would Onassis and his guests like to meet them somewhere in the Aegean so they could come for lunch and tour the new ship? The cordial invitation illustrated the way in which personal dislikes, hatreds even, were secondary to the thrill of tycoon rivalries, at least with these two Greeks. Niarchos had, in a sense, built his glorious new yacht as a $15 million put-down of his rival Onassis. What would be the point if Onassis could not see the splendiferous ship and go limp with envy?

Onassis understood this game rule and knew he was obliged, sooner or later, to visit the yacht—a latter-day meeting on the Field of the Cloth of Gold—but implicit in Niarchos's invitation, coming when it did, was a larger ramification—a meeting between Jackie and Tina. Although the two women had met, they had not, since Onassis had married Jackie, been called on to socialize. Shortly after reading the radio message, Onassis summoned one of his guests, Lady Sarah Churchill, to his bridge quarters for a policy consultation. Because Lady Sarah was Sunny Blandford's sister, Onassis wanted assurance that his guest had no objections to seeing Tina. She assured him she did not. Onassis was pleased.

"I want to accept the invitation," he told her. "Tina is the mother of my children. With my son gone, I've only got Christina. I would like to have normal relations with Tina. Jackie is not going to like this, so please back me up if she tries to use you as an excuse."

After dinner that evening, when the guests were distributed in groups around the main saloon sipping coffee, Lady Sarah noted that Onassis and Jackie were sitting alone by the fireplace. He was in an armchair, she sitting on the arm—an affectionate tableau except that Lady Sarah could see they were arguing. Jackie motioned to her to join them. "Help me out, Sarah. Tell Ari the last person you want to see is your ex-sister-in-law, after the way she treated your brother, the divorce, all that."

Lady Sarah attempted to make light of it. "Oh, now, Jackie," she said, "if I had to spend my life not seeing my brothers' ex-wives and they avoiding my ex-husbands, we'd all be reduced to a much smaller group." When Jackie persisted, Sarah added that whatever her host wanted to do was fine with her. As Jackie turned her attention back to Onassis, Sarah fled to the group she had left, keeping an eye on the fireside squabble. Suddenly rising to her feet, Jackie announced to the room that she was going to change into something more comfortable, then added, "I feel like drinking pink champagne. Will you have a bottle ready when I get back please, Telos dear?" Her use of her pet name for Onassis signaled a change in mood, or perhaps strategy.

Everyone sensed that something was afoot, but Sarah was the only one who was certain that something was trouble. Feeling she had become as involved in the domestic squabble as she cared to be, she pleaded fatigue and retired to her cabin. The other guests sat transfixed when Jackie returned in a diaphanous black negligee that swirled over black satin breeches. Again she sat on the arm of her husband's chair, but her manner had changed from whining truculence to kittenish seductiveness. Holding a glass of pink champagne in one hand, she used the other to pet and fondle a grim-jawed and impassive Onassis in a coquette performance that "would have been embarrassing enough behind closed doors," as one guest later put it.

Getting nowhere with Onassis, Jackie then toured the saloon conscripting allies. With discomforting obviousness, factions soon formed along Greek and American lines. Peter Duchin and his wife sided with Jackie, saying with hesitant prissiness they felt it was in poor taste to visit Niarchos and Tina. Onassis's sister Artemis and some young Greek friends of Onassis believed a visit to his former wife was civilized and tension reducing. All sensed the bitter power struggle that was in progress, and the atmosphere became heavy with thinly masked hostility.

Some of the guests awoke the next morning to see through their portholes, anchored a hundred yards from the *Christina*, the most stupendous yacht any of them had ever seen, a sleek and shimmering seaworthy palace that handily fulfilled its main purpose of dwarfing the *Christina*. At breakfast Onassis's guests learned that the lunch invitation had been withdrawn; an exhaust fan had fallen on the head of Niarchos's chef, who was too shaken to cook. Onassis had immediately suggested that he and his guests would come to the *Atlantis* for drinks and to tour the ship, then they would all return to the *Christina* for lunch. Niarchos immediately accepted the suggestion. Jackie, who until this development had had the option of pleading a last-minute indisposition and remaining aboard the *Christina*, was now thoroughly checkmated and was visibly angry. She knew that with the Niarchos group coming to the *Christina* for lunch she was now obliged to join the tour to the Niarchos yacht. Hiding in her cabin when they all returned was unthinkable.

She did not, however, take defeat gracefully. At one point during the morning she stopped a ship's officer and asked what Onassis had ordered for lunch. The man did not know. "Well," she said, "if it's one of those damn spaghetti things with fish, I'm going to cancel and order something else." In similar ways she made her annoyance known to everyone on board.

As the time approached to visit the other yacht, Jackie grew increasingly nervous. She held back as the Onassis group descended the gangplank to the tender that was to transport them, making sure she was the last to leave the *Christina*. As they were bouncing in the small boat with the *Atlantis* looming ever nearer, ever more grand, they could see Niarchos and Tina standing on deck waiting to receive them. Jackie leaned over to Lady Sarah. "Are you going to kiss her?" she whispered.

"I don't know," Sarah replied. "I don't plan those things. They either happen or they don't." When Jackie boarded the *Atlantis*, she and Tina brushed cheeks.

If Jackie was uneasy at the encounter, she was steely stoicism compared to Tina, who greeted her guests at the top of the gangplank, her body trembling and her hands shaking so badly that she grasped those of the new arrivals as if to steady herself rather than in warm welcome. As the group set off on the tour of the ship—which was of an opulence that none of them had ever before seen, for the simple reason no more luxurious yacht existed—Jackie announced she would pass up the tour and would prefer to remain in the saloon and have a drink. Somewhat perplexed by this display of bloody-mindedness, Niarchos gallantly denied himself the pleasure of seeing Onassis boggle at the *Atlantis*'s technological and decorative glories to remain with Jackie. He ordered champagne as Tina took the others around the new ship.

When the Niarchos party—which consisted only of Tina, Stavros, and Madame Dubonnet, the ship's decorator—returned to the *Christina* for lunch, Onassis seated Tina to his right. He indicated Jackie was to sit at the opposite head of the table, with Niarchos on one side, Lady Sarah on the other. Other guests, including Sarah's husband, Theo Rubanis, were relegated to "B" status at a smaller table off to one side. As Jackie was about to take her place at the head of the "A" table, she paused to appraise the seating arrangement, then suddenly announced she thought she would have more fun at the other table. She turned and walked toward it, accepting the place Theo Rubanis offered while a steward brought another chair.

Onassis, as stung as everyone else at his wife's rudeness, said quietly, "Sarah, will you be hostess?" Sarah moved to the head of the table, where she spent a good part of the meal listening to Niarchos tell the group of the heroic efforts he had made to save the life of his former wife, Eugenie, who had been a good friend of all within earshot. This labored self-exoneration did little to lighten the atmosphere and instead reinforced what was emerging as the lunch's theme: crimes past and misdemeanors present. Tina, who seemed bolstered by Jackie's petulant performance, enthused to Onassis about her pleasure at being once again aboard the *Christina*. She told him how silly she thought it was that they didn't see more of each other and burbled similar blandishments of the sort Jackie perhaps had hoped, if not to prevent, at least to avoid hearing. At the "B" table, conversation was muted and strained.

Ever since the first months of his marriage, Onassis had complained that Jackie was never present when he wanted her. He could now add that she was sure to turn up when he would prefer she didn't. He found himself growing physically tired more readily and he felt himself emotionally drained by his wife's caprices. When he poured out his grievances in lengthy phone conversations with Christina, she was gratified that he had come to share her unfavorable opinion of Jackie, but began worrying about the toll being taken on her father by the strains in his marriage. She had always considered him invincible, but it now looked as if he had met his match.

For her crash course in being a shipping tycoon, Christina was put in the hands of Costa Gratsos in the Fifth Avenue offices of Olympic Maritime, where she was delighted to find a childhood friend, Nicholas Papanicolaou, a Greek-American and a Harvard and Columbia Business School graduate, who had been hired the year before by her father in an attempt to infuse the companies with young Americanized blood. After a time, Christina was sent for more specialized training at the Wall Street offices of Frank B. Hall, Inc., ship-insurance brokers for whom Onassis was a highly valued client. Since insurance is one of the most complicated aspects of the shipping business, in addition to being one of the costliest, it was felt Christina should spend several months devoting herself to this one aspect of shipowning. For their part, the Frank Hall people were happy to have a hand in the training of one who might someday replace her father as a large-scale buyer of insurance. Every morning at 9 A.M., Christina's chauffeur would drop her at the Hall offices and she would spend the day learning about deadweight tonnages, the array of coverage needed, and the complex rates.

At first she was given a desk in an anteroom of the large, plush office of Jim Sathakos, a top executive who was a friend of her father's. When during the training she moved about the offices, she looked with longing at the large rooms on lower floors where scores of women sat working in a convivial clatter. After a few days, Christina asked Sathakos if she might be transferred to one of the large rooms; she found it lonely where she was. All of Frank Hall's hundreds of employees knew of Christina's presence, and word of her request spread quickly throughout the offices. When she was given a desk in a room full of workers, she received a warm reception. The women took Christina to lunch and, during off hours, gave her walking tours of the Wall Street area, which Christina found fascinating.

Some of the women, while liking her, were made uneasy by her sharp and unexplained mood swings. They found she could be friendly and outgoing one minute, then suddenly withdraw into herself and glower at anyone who approached. Abrupt changes of mood would always plague Christina, but at this particular time in her life there were many visions that could have plunged her into depressions—a jilting French Adonis; a whispering, free-spending Jackie; a beaten and dying aunt; a brother's crushed skull. She suffered these spells, and perhaps baffled and upset others because of them, but she never used them as an excuse to be let off the work program she had undertaken.

Sathakos, a suave and handsome Greek-American twenty years Christina's senior, would remember her as a remarkably apt student. "She threw herself into the many details," he said, "and would pick up complicated matters in a remarkably short time. I remember one day she was reviewing an Onassis policy. She noticed that a certain aspect of the coverage was absent. She went over it again and again until she was sure she was right. Then she called her father and told him she had found an oversight. He replied that she must be mistaken; his people could not have made such a mistake. But, by God, she was right. One entire aspect of the ship, I forget which, was not insured. She was extremely pleased with herself—and, of course, he was pleased to."

Sathakos would also remember Christina as being punctilious about her working hours. "For weeks she showed up on the dot and worked like the devil. Usually she'd take a half hour for lunch or have a sandwich and a Coke at her desk, then go right back to work. One day she didn't show up at all. I figured she'd gone shopping or something. She called late in the afternoon very apologetic. Her father had wanted her to have lunch with him and the head of Mobil Oil. She hoped it hadn't inconvenienced us, thrown us off our schedule. I was struck by how concerned she was."

Onassis was now moving into high gear on his program to groom Christina. They flew to London together to meet with the directors of British Petroleum, Dutch Shell, and other important clients. On one occasion they had lunch with K. Y. Pao, the renowned Chinese tanker lord, one of the world's major shipowners, who operated his extensive fleet out of Hong Kong. Unlike Alexander, who after years working in the Monaco headquarters had said, "I don't have a clue how it all fits together," Christina felt she was getting a grasp of the overall picture. Costa Gratsos gave her high marks as well and told

Onassis she was arriving at an intuitive sense for the shipping business that he would pit against his own experience or Onassis's wizardry.

In October of 1973, the tanker business collapsed throughout the world as a result of OPEC's oil squeeze. After a period of unprecedented prosperity, the world's shipowners suddenly found themselves with vast tonnages lying idle. This was not the only problem that faced Onassis. Since he had admitted defeat on a major plan to build an oil refinery in Greece, the Omega Project, he had decided to build one instead on New Hampshire's small stretch of Atlantic coast. Although he had the support of a pro-industry governor, which in Onassis's power-oriented mind was all he needed, he shortly discovered establishing an oil refinery on a scenic American coast in the ecology-minded seventies was an ambition on a par with attempting to build a nuclear reactor on Manhattan's Upper West Side.

While charging ahead with this ill-fated scheme, Onassis, with his usual notional approach to global issues, decided the key to the oil crisis was Egypt's Anwar Sadat, and he resolved to become acquainted. Having no introduction to the Egyptian leader, Onassis created his own. In the late fall of 1973, he arranged a cruise on the *Christina* to Egypt and sailed raucously into the Alexandria harbor, horns honking, the yacht festooned in lights, and with the globally significant Jackie at his side. Together the Onassises sent a wedding gift to Sadat's daughter, who just happened to be getting married a few days after the *Christina*'s arrival, and, as expected, Onassis and his guests were invited to the wedding. When he responded by immediately inviting the Sadat wedding party to the *Christina* for a lavish dinner party, they accepted and his quick invasion was complete.

It was put out at the time that the Egyptian cruise was a stratagem cooked up by Jackie and Christina to distract Onassis from his grief over Alexander. In fact, the trip was pure business, a vintage Onassis strategy of conquest. Rather than originating the idea, Jackie, who had lost her zest for world leaders after her first year in the White House, had to be pressured into accompanying her husband. Not so Christina. With her tentative new enthusiasm for the responsibilities that would one day be hers, she loved every minute of the trip, even though it necessitated traveling with her stepmother. Much of that animosity was mollified by her father's insistence that, at the many official functions they attended, Christina be given a place comparable to that given his wife.

As a reward for Jackie's cooperation in conquering Egypt, Onassis promised her a New Year's trip to Acapulco, the Mexican resort where she had spent her honeymoon with John Kennedy. As he boarded his jet to depart for the trip shortly after Christmas 1973, he had an array of problems that almost dislodged Alexander's death in his preoccupations. His new friendship with Sadat had provided no optimistic insights into the duration of the oil crisis, but rather confirmed the analysts who predicted it would drag on for years—even if peace in the Middle East was worked out immediately.

Adding to Onassis's woes, he had just learned that the skyrocketing price of fuel had all but bankrupted the airline he owned outright, Olympic, and it was continuing to lose money at an alarming rate. His ambitious real-estate venture the super-luxurious Olympic Tower on Fifth Avenue, was about to open to a catastrophic slump in the real-estate market. Always proud of his physical stamina, Onassis was now plagued with worries about his health. He was feeling constantly tired, not at all typical of him, and he had trouble throwing himself into the giddy social whirl Jackie had arranged for them in Mexico. The endless parties with empty people of taste and refinement only served to remind him of how incompatible he and his wife were.

On the flight back to New York, Jackie picked the wrong moment to badger Onassis into buying her a house in Acapulco. Had she had any knowledge of her husband's affairs, she might have realized how stupefyingly ill-timed her request was, but, oblivious of tumbling oil prices, idle tankers, combative New Hampshire ecologists, unsalable co-ops, and her husband's grief and deteriorating health, she saw nothing in his refusal but another symptom of his stinginess toward her. She usually made her displeasure manifest by sulking or disappearing. Now, locked on a plane with a boorish old man, the memories of a horrible vacation in a place she liked still festering, she met his anger with some of her own.

Shouted diatribes were nothing unusual for Onassis, but Jackie now broke her characteristic reserve and berated him in return for his vulgarity, his insensitivity to the finer things, and his penny-pinching refusal to give her a winter home. By way of justifying her request, she blurted that she had lost her good name by marrying him and, for a loss of that magnitude, she was entitled to compensation. Leaving his wife stewing in her fury at the bad bargain she had made, Onassis took himself to another part of the plane and rewrote his will, altering the wording to leave her as little as he felt the law would allow. After making provisions for his sisters and a few others, he split the bulk of his estate between Christina and a philanthropic foundation in Alexander's memory.

The flight was a sorry end for Onassis's fabled love life. His lifelong quest for ever more advantageous romantic involvements had started as an adjunct to his primary goal: amassing great wealth. Claudia Muzio, Ingeborg Dedichen, Tina Livanos, and Maria Callas had been way stations on his path to glory. And the culmination of his climb was Jackie Kennedy, who had youth, grace, beauty, and was the most famous woman in the world. In order to marry her and satisfy his addiction to triumph, he had trampled on the sensibilities of his children, his friends, the public, and the one woman who had truly loved him—only to find that his costly prize was a punishing harpy who was gobbling up his fortune and making his last years on the earth he had conquered a private misery and a public embarrassment.

En route to New York, Onassis's jet put down in Palm Beach to refuel. Deciding he was hungry, Onassis, a sullen Jackie at his side, walked to the airport's coffeeshop. Sitting in a vinyl booth, the still angry husband and wife, like seasoned social troopers, ordered food and chatted about inconsequential matters. Smug in the knowledge that he had stripped his wife of many millions of dollars by a few strokes of the pen, Onassis felt a little better. He had not so much gotten back some of his own but taken steps to hang on to it. Just as Onassis was about to bite down on a bacon and tomato sandwich, the fuel attendant appeared and told the man who had just disposed of a billion dollars and had otherwise had a very bad day, that his Sunoco credit card had expired and he would have to pay for the fuel in cash.

· · ·

In January of 1974, Christina flew to Skorpios for a family gathering to mark the first anniversary of Alexander's death and to commemorate the chapel renovated to include his grave. Jackie stayed in New York. No one expected this to be a happy occasion, but for Christina it was made worse by her father's worrying physical condition. Even though he would soon be seventy-four, he had always seemed remarkably fit and energetic for his age. Now he was definitely failing. Christina tried to cheer him with the news that she was again seeing Peter Goulandris, who was also in New York, working out of his company's office there.

Onassis was pleased, but at that moment he was not an easy man to cheer. He was beginning to suspect his days as a business terror were over, his farcical marriage with Jackie was over—he was simply waiting for a return of his energy to get a divorce—and his own life would shortly be over and along with it his hopes for a continuation of the Onassis line. At the time of Alexander's blossoming, the prospects for leaving the world as the founder of a great shipping dynasty looked bright, but now, despite Christina's good showing and her newfound stability, they looked dim indeed.

In the spring of 1974, Onassis was diagnosed as having myasthenia gravis, a degenerative muscular disease, which could be aggravated by alcohol and insufficient sleep, two habits he was highly reluctant to change. With Onassis, the primary effect of the disease was his chronic and extreme fatigue and a slight inability to control his facial muscles, an affliction that accentuated his wasted appearance. Medication could hold the disease at bay for a time, he was told, but basically it was incurable.

Faced with the likelihood of her father's death, Christina suffered inward panic—at the prospect of yet another severe emotional loss, to be sure, but also at her unreadiness to take over the empire. While she was learning, she could relax under the certainty that she had ample time to absorb it all. But now, facing her father's mortality, she could only echo Alexander in thinking what a jumble it all was.

Depressions over her brother's death continued to besiege her, but increasingly she was able to throw them off with her new interest in business and her romance with Peter Goulandris, which was building in what, for Christina, was a mature and measured fashion. Unlike her other involvements, this was not a sudden passion, but rather a gradual ripening of a long friendship into admiration and, she desperately hoped, adult love. She berated herself for her mistreatment of Goulandris in 1969, when she jilted him for Danny Marentette, and her failure to see what a fine husband he would make. When the diagnosis of Onassis's illness forced her to confront the likelihood of her father's death, she took comfort in the stable relationship she was building with Peter—both for the solid happiness for herself that it held out and for the consolation it gave her ailing father.

In August, Nicholas Papanicolaou, sitting at his Olympic Maritime office in New York, received a phone call from Christina, who said brightly, "Guess what I did? I tried to kill myself."

She was in London's Middlesex Hospital, where she had been rushed after Eleni had discovered her unconscious from an overdose of sleeping pills. She and Peter had had a fight, she later explained, during which he had told her he would not marry her then or ever. She had no doubt of the seriousness of his declaration and felt everything coming down on her. Having at last picked men—which she began increasingly to see as her one function in life—who were not lunatic disasters both from her point of view and her father's, the comely Roussel, then Goulandris, they had both rejected her. The ones who wanted her were not good, and the good ones did not want her—even with a half-billion-dollar dowry.

Hearing of Christina's suicide attempt, Tina flew immediately from the south of France in her husband's jet and stayed at her daughter's bedside, sleeping upright in a chair, smothering her with a motherliness that was as uncharacteristic as it was obsessive. Her solicitude was all the more remarkable because of the bad condition Tina herself was in at the time; she had begun to drink heavily and relied increasingly on pills. A Parisian woman who remembered her in these days said that when Tina was simply sitting at a dinner table her hands would shake uncontrollably, and her body would occasionally shudder for no apparent reason.

For a time, Christina's distress distracted Tina from her own. She was beginning to admit that her marriage to Niarchos, which had caused such enormous upset in those she held most dear, had not proved her salvation, but rather had increased her unhappiness. Like Jackie, she felt her marriage had cost her heavily. She had braved the scandal of marrying her sister's husband only to find him now flirting with other women in front of her, probably having affairs, stripping away the one justification for having lost the love of her son and almost having lost that of her daughter as well.

Christina quickly recovered, as she usually did from her emotional overloads. Her cheery, look-at-me phone call to Papanicolaou didn't necessarily prove her suicide attempt was a sham—at the moment of ingesting the pills she may have wanted to die—but it certainly demonstrated the speed with which she was able to pull out of her spasms of desperation. Tina was no longer able to match her daughter's resiliency and remained deeply depressed by what had happened. While she stayed with Christina, they had thoughtful talks, which were not intended by Christina to be accusatory but which confirmed what Tina already knew: her large share of the responsibility in Christina's unhappiness. Emotionally starved herself, Tina had to face that she had contributed heavily to the same crippling plight in her daughter.

Tina returned to her sour marriage badly shaken by her daughter's crisis. She had never recovered from her beloved Alexander's death, and now her sole remaining child had proved herself to be an emotional invalid, wretched and unstable, with little chance of ever being happy. Of the many players in this House of Onassis drama, Tina had always been the most reflective and most adept at viewing them all, herself included, from a clear-eyed distance. But in order to experience one of these contemplative moments, she had to be free from her own self-absorption and that had not occurred for some time.

Christina's crisis shook Tina from the tunnel vision with a mirror at the end, and she once again surveyed the entire stage, horrified by what she saw. Adding to her sense of leaving a wake of havoc behind her was a terror of what lay ahead. For a woman who had always sought solace in her beauty and the lovers it would bring, the arrival of middle age was a disaster for which she had no compensations. She stopped going out and spent more and more time with her mother, who had also begun to use pills. Paris acquaintances who happened to see her on the street in the next few months said she had aged remarkably, that she had seemed to have lost her looks in less than a year.

Christina returned to New York, where she continued to work at the offices of Olympic Maritime. One day at the office, Nicholas Papanicolaou received a phone call from Onassis in the company's Monaco offices. He wanted Papanicolaou, as diplomatically as possible, to get Christina to Paris immediately. Tina had been found dead in Niarchos's Paris house. The cause was apparently an overdose, and this time there were no bruises on the body. Onassis knew of his daughter's recent suicide attempt and also knew how much she loved Tina and hated Niarchos. Fearing what might happen when she learned her mother had died in circumstances similar to those of her aunt's death, Onassis did not want Christina told of Tina's death. Papanicolaou was to invent a pretext to get her to Paris without delay. Onassis felt it would be safer all around if Christina was with him and surrounded by family before she learned the truth.

Papanicolaou went to Christina's office. "You've got to go to Paris immediately, Christina. Your mother's very sick."

Christina became frantic. "What has happened? You've got to tell me, Niko." She hammered at him, immediately sensing he was not telling her the entire truth and unwilling to accept the illness story.

Finally, Christina said, "She's dead, isn't she?"

Unable to keep up the pretense, Papanicolaou admitted it was true. Christina took the blow with the stoicism of one who had expected it. When she learned that Niarchos had been in the house at the time of her death and that he had delayed releasing the news of the death until the following day, Christina's grief quickly hardened into the blackest of suspicions. She had always believed Niarchos would kill her mother just as she felt he had killed her aunt. Now, she believed her worst nightmare had become a reality.

That evening, Christina, with Eleni at her side, was on a plane to Paris. Arriving in the morning, she went immediately to a lawyer and before noon had obtained a magistrate's warrant for a full investigation into the cause of her mother's death. Onassis found himself in the odd role of calming his daughter, urging her to wait for the findings of the investigation. He later told friends he feared that Christina would herself kill Niarchos.

The autopsy conducted by the public prosecutor's office determined that Tina had died of acute edema of the lung. No mention was made of barbiturate levels in her bloodstream, which, for one so widely known to have taken such pills, was a curious omission. The coroner's report had little influence on the widespread belief that Tina had taken her own life—a far more charitable view than Christina's belief that it was murder—but, if evidence of either ever reached the authorities, it was never released. Once again the gossips could have it any way they wished.

Tina was buried beside her sister Eugenie in the Bois de Vaux cemetery in Lausanne. Throughout the ceremony, Niarchos cried audibly. Also in tears was Sunny Blandford, now the Duke of Marlborough. When approaching her former stepfather, Christina, who had held herself together during the service, fell into his arms and broke down in sobs.

"What is happening to us, Sunbun?" she said. "First my aunt, then my brother, and now my mother."

Christina's efforts to prove foul play infuriated Niarchos and precipitated open warfare between niece and uncle that quickly became uglier than any that had marked the decades of Onassis-Niarchos skirmishing. Niarchos had no doubts about who was supplying the press with material for the slurs and innuendos against him—few cared as much as Christina and no one else would dare—so he counterattacked viciously with a statement that told the world for the first time of Christina's August suicide attempt. This had shocked Tina deeply, he said to the press, and had contributed strongly to her death. *He* had not killed Tina, he seemed to be saying, Christina had.

In November of 1974, Onassis's condition worsened and he checked into New York's Lenox Hill Hospital in a desperate attempt to discover a way to arrest his muscular deterioration. Although he had used an assumed name, word of his presence in the hospital got out, and the Olympic Maritime offices issued statements saying Onassis's condition was treatable and that he would soon be well. Everyone close to the situation knew this was not true, including Onassis himself.

Christina was with him constantly, and the two became closer than they had ever been before. He loved reminiscing with her about the past, and Christina was deeply gratified to be the one he relied on to help him through this ordeal. As members of his staff came by to brief Onassis on developments and receive instructions, Christina stood to one side, listening quietly. If she failed to understand something, she would ask him to explain it to her when they were alone. The parts of his body most affected by the disease were his facial muscles, and he was unable to hold his eyes open. Christina devised her own remedy: she cut adhesive from the ends of Band-Aids and used the flesh-colored patches to tape his lids open. Onassis was grateful but hated the procedure, prompting Christina to tell him his miserable condition was punishment for his sins.

With little improvement, Onassis left the hospital, knowing every effort had been made to slow the disease. Christina was interviewed at the time and told a reporter, "My most fervent wishes are that my father get better and that I shall meet a man who loves me for myself and not my money. Happiness does not depend on money. Our family is the best proof of that. . . . Since the death of my mother and my brother, we have learned how short life can be and with what terrible suddenness death strikes."

Onassis left the hospital to dire business news. Olympic Airlines was in deep trouble. In addition to the inflated fuel prices, the Turkish-Cyprus conflict had had a devastating effect on Greek tourism, which was the airline's revenue mainstay. When he had launched the airline, Onassis had turned it over to trusted lieutenants, telling them he wanted no part of running the operation, that as long as they didn't come to him for money, he knew they were doing a good job. This edict almost guaranteed they would not "come to him for money" until it was too late, and that is what happened.

The new Greek Prime Minister, Konstantine Karamanlis, was an old friend, who Onassis first assumed would bail him out with a massive infusion of government money. He was dashed when, instead, Karamanlis, irked by Onassis's dealings with the colonels who preceded him in power, moved to assume control of the airline. Shortly before Christmas in 1974, Onassis flew to Athens to fight, at first to retain ownership of his airline, but when that proved impossible, to win the most advantageous terms possible for converting it to a state-run airline.

The negotiations were a sorry conclusion to a brilliant business career. Onassis would haggle over a point, finally reaching an agreement late at night, only to arrive at the bargaining table the next morning with a shift in his position. Rather than wresting more-favorable terms with these antics, he succeeded only in maddening his adversaries. He refused to recognize that he was no longer operating from a position of strength. The airline was losing money badly and, even worse, the Onassis name no longer struck as much awe in the hearts of fellow Greeks.

The enormous effort he expended amounted to little more than a sad dumb show of a once brilliant negotiator, whose virtuosity belonged to another era and who was, from habit, going through ploys and maneuvers that no longer made sense. The result was a payment to Onassis of $69 million, which sounded favorable, but his responsibility for Olympic's outstanding debts meant he netted about $35 million. The settlement also had the unusual proviso that Christina, should she choose, could buy the airline back after Onassis's death.

At the beginning of February 1975, Christina was skiing in Gstaad with Peter Goulandris. They had reconciled and were again talking of marriage. On February 3, she received a call from her Aunt Artemis in Athens telling her that she must come right away: her father had collapsed with severe stomach pains and was extremely ill. She flew immediately to Athens and Jackie flew in from New York along with a heart specialist, Dr. Isadore Rosenfeld. A liver specialist, Professor Jean Caroli, was flown from Paris. Immediately the doctors disagreed on a course of action. Caroli urged the immediate removal of the gallbladder. Rosenfeld felt Onassis was too weak to undergo surgery and should be flown to a New York hospital to recuperate sufficiently for the operation.

Jackie, who had appeared unperturbed by Onassis's condition, suddenly asserted her rights as the wife by insisting that he be flown to the American Hospital in Paris. Since her casual approach to the crisis already grated on Christina and Artemis, they were disinclined to believe Jackie's reason had anything to do with Onassis's medical treatment and suspected instead she was concerned about her entertainment and social prospects for what might be a long siege. Onassis agreed to Paris, and he was bundled into a limousine, clutching a red cashmere blanket from Hermès that Jackie had given him.

Arriving in Paris, Onassis refused to go directly to the hospital but ordered the car to take him to his Avenue Foch apartment. Despite warnings that the press was waiting for him there, he said he wanted to spend one night in his long-time home. In a mild Paris evening the apartment entrance looked like a film première with television lights set up and batteries of press photographers and crowds of the curious. Onassis told Christina and Jackie he did not want their assistance going into the building, but would manage the few steps on his own. Moved by this costly show of bravado, Christina started crying softly and Jackie reached over and squeezed her arm. Christina shuddered inwardly as though touched by a leper.

Unable to sleep more than a few minutes at a time, Onassis kept the entire household up most of the night. The next morning, as preparations were being made to move him to the American Hospital, Johnny Meyer arrived and cheered Onassis by saying, "Don't worry, Ari. No one ever died of droopy eyelids." Taking Meyer aside, Christina asked him to arrange a suite for her at the Plaza Athénée. She did not want to stay in the apartment with Jackie. Within a few days, Jackie announced she had to look after her children and flew back to New York. Since she said she would be returning to Paris from time to time, Christina remained in her hotel suite. Artemis also left to be with her husband in Athens. Of the family, Christina, who knew it was just a matter of time, was the only one who remained at Onassis's bedside.

Christina also took a room next to her father's at the American Hospital, where she faced an immediate medical decision. The doctors told Onassis that if his gallbladder was not removed immediately, he would be dead within a week. He first tried to wave them away, then said, "Do what you want." They needed authorization for the operation and, since Jackie was in New York, they went to Christina. They told her that with the surgery Onassis had a fifty-fifty chance of recovering. Christina asked the advice of Nicholas Papanicolaou, who, in the short time he had worked for Onassis, had come to love him and had flown in from New York to be of whatever help he could. Papanicolaou argued in favor of the operation and Christina agreed. She instructed the doctors to operate.

The operation was successful in that Onassis did not die, but he was still a very sick man and remained in the hospital. In a show of support for Christina, Peter Goulandris flew to Paris and moved into Christina's hotel suite. Together they went to Onassis's bedside and told him they planned to marry, making the dying man as happy as he had been in months. Some later said it was a charade staged by Christina for no other purpose than to allow her father to die believing his daughter had at last found a happy and auspicious solution to the dilemma in her life. But according to those close to Christina at the time, that was untrue. Peter and Christina were living together as man and wife, were happy, and had every intention of marrying.

It was not only her resolve to marry Goulandris that pleased Onassis. He had finally come to realize how much Christina loved him and that she was the only one left who did. He wanted her with him constantly, talking to her incessantly about how he would soon be joining Alexander. For once his unabashed preference for Alexander didn't bother her. She, not he, was present to ease Onassis's last hours; their battles were behind them and they loved each other as a father and daughter should.

When Onassis died on March 15, 1975, Christina lost control and, grabbing a surgical instrument, attempted to slash her wrists. She was restrained but was seen emerging from the hospital with a conspicuous bandage on one wrist. Jackie, who was notified in New York of her husband's death, returned to Paris with her mother, her children, and her former brother-in-law, Ted Kennedy. The body of Aristotle Onassis was flown to Greece for burial on the island of Skorpios next to his son. As the casket was brought from a launch onto the island, Christina and her father's sisters led the mourners up the hill to the family chapel. Jackie found herself shunted a number of places back in the procession, behind all of Onassis's relatives and close business associates.

# 12

# CHRISTINA TAKES CHARGE

*D*uring the forty days Christina sat by her father's deathbed at the American Hospital in Paris, the loneliness of her vigil provided a bitter taste of the isolation she would face after his death. Her aunts came in from time to time and Jackie made sporadic trips from New York, but of all those who had been close to Onassis—the relatives he supported, the executives he had enriched, the luminaries he entertained, the many women he had loved—Christina alone stayed by his side until he died. Now he was gone and her sense of aloneness was heightened by the numb disbelief she felt at the string of disasters that had befallen her family—first her brother, then her mother, now her father had died of a rare disease. "What else can happen to us?" she asked a friend. Christina knew full well "what else." She had no reason to believe the curse that had felled the others would spare her.

The morbid ruminations on death that had always been part of her psychological bent now became an almost smug certainty that she would not live a long life. That alone would seem to have granted her full license to spend her fortune and what days she believed she had remaining in any self-indulgent manner she chose. Her mood, in fact, was quite different. It was rather one of family obligation and of completing the atonement to her father that his death had interrupted.

Finding ways to show her filial duty was not difficult. If her father had left her the use of half a billion dollars—as she knew he had and as the will would confirm—he also left her a snarl of problems, a corporate mess that would have cowed even him at his peak. His death came at the worst possible time; the turmoil in world business conditions and within his own companies required the grasp and wizardry of an Aristotle Onassis. For Christina, the self-indulgence would have to wait.

Foremost among the crises was the depressed state of world shipping. Always cyclical, the tanker business was in the worst slump of its history, with no improvement expected for years. For the Onassis fleet of fifty-one ships with six more on order scant business did not only mean less revenue, it meant enormous losses. Idle ships cost vast sums daily in insurance premiums, bank payments, crew salaries, and docking fees. Crucial decisions had to be made immediately if the companies were to survive.

As often happens with the death of an absolute monarch, civil war had broken out in the upper ranks of the Onassis hierarchy. On both sides the combatants were men of age and long experience, all holding strong arguments for opposing courses of action. At times the companies could run themselves (although Onassis had never let that happen); at the moment they desperately needed a forceful leader.

Aside from the internal strife, the organization faced an immediate crisis. Before it was clear that the business depression would be prolonged, Onassis had ordered the construction of six supertankers. Tough negotiations for their cancellation had to be launched, but Onassis had been in no condition for such an ordeal. Time was running out on the period in which they could be canceled at all; the decisions could not be put off.

Important aspects of the Olympic Airlines débacle were still to be resolved. The intricate terms for turning the company over to the Greek government could not be worked out until someone was authorized to negotiate the Onassis interests. Olympic Tower, now open in New York, still had many apartments unsold. There were problems with the bank Onassis owned in Switzerland and the Irish shipyard—two holdings Christina was barely aware of, let alone able to comprehend.

The will gave her all her father's personal properties: the Paris apartment, the villa in Athens, the jet, the helicopter, the island of Skorpios, the *Christina*—with Jackie getting a minority share of the last two. Decisions had to be made about which to keep, which to sell. With faulty planes still very much on her mind, she almost immediately got rid of her father's jet and bought a smaller but brand-new Lear. There was, of course, the problem of Jackie's bequest. Prenuptial agreement or no, she would surely not accept the insulting stipend of $250,000 a year her billionaire husband had left her. Christina braced herself for a legal onslaught from the greedy lady of Fifth Avenue.

Christina also faced an immediate problem of her citizenship. Unlike her father, she was a United States citizen, which meant she could be taxed on any income regardless of where in the world it was earned. Since her Los Angeles marriage, she had spent little time in America. She had no doubt that she would have to renounce a citizenship about which she had no strong emotions and which could easily cost her many millions a year.

Before any of these problems could be confronted, however, Christina had to address herself to the biggest problem of all: the will itself. Through a lack of confidence in his daughter's judgment, an opinion confirmed by her marriage to Joe Bolker, Onassis had devised a complicated document that would result in Christina's receiving the income from 47 percent of the estate. Except for a few bequests, the remaining and controlling percentage went into a charitable foundation to be established in memory of his son. Christina's holdings were to be administered by the foundation's board. The will said in effect: "I love you, I want you to have the use of half my fortune, I just don't think you have the sense to run a large company and administer a half billion dollars."

The will would leave Christina no control of the companies and, even worse, no control of her own money. It was a bitter blow for one who had dedicated the last two years of her life to proving her seriousness and capability. In Christina's never-ending dialogue with her dead father, she knew he had justification for his distrust. In spite of her high marks for dedication and quick learning, she had never really shown that she was capable of controlling $500 million; in fact, she had done a number of things to suggest she was not. For Christina, having been made by her father one of the richest women in the world did little to ease the sting from his permanent vote of no confidence. She could see his point, but he was wrong, and she would show him he was wrong.

Aside from the personal wound of being shunted from power, Christina also knew that if word of the will got out, it would be extremely damaging to the business-community view of the Onassis companies' present state of management. Once having been controlled by a solitary owner, a hands-on powerhouse, a world figure, and a word-is-his-bond negotiator, the Onassis interests would now be regarded as an enfeebled echo of past glory if they were run by a faceless foundation board of unknown Greeks. Almost as bad would be the view that things were now being run by an untested young woman whose hands were tied to prevent her from exercising any real power. Many of the Onassis executives agreed and encouraged Christina to take action.

To Christina and her advisers her course was clear: she must break her father's will and win control of her inheritance. The companies needed someone in an unequivocal seat of power, but even more important, *she* needed it. She consulted her father's friend and lawyer, Stelios Papadimitriou, who joined those in agreement with her appraisal of the damage Onassis's provisions were causing and would continue to cause. He also recognized Christina's resolve, and, perhaps, that she was alive and Onassis dead. He came up with an ingenious solution.

With an unusual provision called the *nomimos mira* clause, Greek inheritance law insists that surviving members of the immediate family—spouse and offspring—receive no less than 50 percent of an estate. Jackie had waived her widow's rights with a prenuptial agreement. If it held up—and that was by no means certain—Christina would be the sole survivor and could demand the courts raise her 47 percent to 50 percent, thereby giving her control. The first order of business was to settle with speed and finality any claim Jackie might be considering. Christina had been surprised and disgusted by the speed with which Ted Kennedy, on the day of the funeral, had opened up financial discussions. Now, Jackie's eagerness to make a deal might be made to work greatly to Christina's benefit.

The will could be filed in any country Christina chose, or in no country at all, since her father had offered the option of keeping the entire document a private contract among friends. The Greek courts, however, held out the best prospects for effecting her scheme. They also held a potential pitfall in that they made it virtually impossible to disinherit a wife, who was assured a minimum of 12.5 percent of a deceased husband's estate—even with prenuptial agreements that specifically renounced those rights. This widow's percent of the estimated Onassis fortune of $1 billion would amount to approximately $125 million.

But was the estate really worth a billion dollars? Onassis offices issued statements that set the fleet's value at only $400 million— probably on the supposition that an idle ship was worth nothing while it remained idle—and ignoring that it could be converted into an efficient money-making machine with one phone call. Because of the sad state of the shipping business, this low estimate may have been close to accurate, for the moment, but it was more likely that it was a calculated distortion aimed at cooling Jackie and her lawyers. Aside from the airline and other nonshipping assets, plus the $50 million Onassis generally kept in cash, the value put on the fleet was low. In any long-term appraisal of the estate's assets, $1 billion was far closer to the truth and may have been conservative. The Onassis interests were not famous for forthright disclosures even when they weren't being stalked by a rapacious widow.

In the Greek courts, the will would be further vulnerable to attack from Jackie's lawyers in that it had been written in a moving plane; Greek law stipulates that a will must be written at one sitting and in one *place*. Whether or not an airborne plane constituted a "place" was the sort of thing that lawyers could deliberate, with their meters running, for years. Even so, the neatest and quickest way for Christina to gain the crucial extra 3 percent was to file in Greece, make a deal with Jackie that would preclude any further claims, then invoke the *nomimos mira* clause to break the will and raise her percent from 47 to 50 and liberate her share of the estate from foundation-board control. Even with the pitfalls of Greek law, Christina decided to take the chance. The will was filed in Greece and she flew to London with her lawyers to meet on May 7 with Jackie and her lawyer, Simon Rifkind of New York.

Christina offered her stepmother $8 million. Jackie countered that the minimum amount she would accept was $20 million. They parted to mull over one another's positions. Negotiations received a near-ruinous jolt when it was reported in Jack Anderson's column and the *New York Times* that, shortly before his death, Aristotle Onassis had taken steps to divorce his wife. Jackie appeared to react violently to the reports and her lawyers demanded a denial from Christina, on threat of scuttling the settlement negotiations and going straight to court.

It was curious that a woman who had accepted with a near Zenlike silence the most scathing press slurs about her mercenary motives for the marriage, her extravagance, even that she charged expensive clothes to Onassis then sold them at thrift shops to raise cash, now reacted so vehemently to the mild assertion that her husband had been considering divorce. It was more probable that the hysteria was not Jackie's but her lawyers', who saw their claims on the Onassis fortune undermined by a public perception that their claimant was a lame-duck wife, which of course she was.

Like a hostage speaking at gunpoint, Christina acceded to Jackie's demand and issued a statement that the marriage of her father and Jacqueline Bouvier Kennedy had never been anything but a happy one and that reports of divorce plans were totally false. It was one of the many oddities of the situation that Christina, who had much to gain by the news reports, was the one to attempt to repair the damage done by them to Jackie's claim. But Christina knew that, if she let her enemy win this battle and the $20 million settlement she craved, she would be winning the larger battle: control of her estate. Her father had coached her on the uses of the outright lie in responding to press curiosity about private matters.

Having seemingly played into Jackie's hand with her statement of mutual respect, which was quoted in newspapers around the world, Christina flew to New York and met with Jackie in her Fifth Avenue apartment. For this meeting, which would be their last on this issue, they were alone with no lawyers present. Christina emerged having agreed to Jackie's latest demand of $20 million, plus a new demand for another $6 million for taxes.

In the most puzzling proviso of his will, Onassis left Jackie one-quarter interest in the *Christina* and Skorpios. Even though he was thoroughly fed up with his wife, he apparently sought to keep her involved with his daughter, perhaps as a model of taste and refinement, which Christina had never shown the least interest in emulating. More likely, since he had never cared much for that side of Christina's development, he felt that Jackie was a major celebrity he had bought and paid for, and he didn't want to release her altogether from the family. Whatever his reasons, neither woman wanted any part of from-the-grave manipulation. For additional undisclosed amounts, Jackie relinquished her rights to the island and the yacht.

A final stipulation, one Jackie had far greater reason to desire than Christina, was that neither woman would ever speak publicly about their dealing. With everything agreed, Christina wrote Jackie a check, which she showed contemptuously to a few friends who were with her at the time, for $26 million. Once she received the money, Jackie flew to Greece to pick up personal possessions left on Skorpios and on the *Christina*; from the yacht, she also picked up a jade Buddha inlaid with rubies, the prize of Onassis's spotty art collection and said to be priceless.

Both women abided by their no-comment pact. In fact, Christina let it be known that her former stepmother's name was never to be mentioned in her presence. The rule was not just a way of expressing her dislike; she was serious. Although Christina's feelings about Jackie were more mixed than this edict would indicate, any unexpected mention of Jackie could quickly topple her from the most zesty elation and plunge her into one of her black Greek moods. Shortly before she died, Christina broke her own rule when she told a friend, "Jackie was the most mercenary person I've ever met. She thinks, talks, and dreams of money, nothing but money. The joke is I would have given her fifty times what I gave her for the pleasure of never having to see her again. What amazes me is that she survives while everyone around her drops. She's dangerous, she's deadly."

With Jackie effectively out of the will, Christina could now take the document to the Greek courts and, by invoking *nomimos mira*, claim the sole survivor's 50 percent. The courts agreed, and Christina was at last in control of her fortune. Had Jackie or her lawyers ever been aware of how crucial they were to Christina's scheme for control of a half billion dollars, it is unlikely they would have so gracefully stepped aside for a modest 4 percent share of this amount or a 2 percent share of the entire estate.

Because of the erosion of the foundation's half of the fortune due to minor bequests of her father's, Christina also became the majority owner of the Onassis companies, and the apparatus by which the foundation board managed her assets was nullified. This was a total victory and put her in complete control of her half of the Onassis fortune. Next came the problem of how the assets were to be divided. Should Christina be given half interest in each vessel or should the vessels themselves be parceled out? Both parties preferred the latter course, especially since the men of the foundation board, for the most part the same men who ran the companies, had no more confidence in Christina's ability to manage a shipping company than her father had. If she chose to navigate her tankers into the rocks, their ships would not be affected.

With stock holdings it is an easy matter to parcel out an estate to the nearest penny. With assets such as tankers, which can't be cut in half, the figures must be rounded off to the nearest $5 million. Christina said she wanted to keep Olympic Tower. No one objected, so a dollar equivalent in ships was given to the foundation. She also determined that the Swiss bank and the Irish shipyard should be sold, since she knew nothing about those businesses. With those loose edges trimmed, the Onassis fleet was split between Christina and the foundation by lottery.

In a villa she had rented in St. Moritz, Christina waited by the phone for word from the final meeting in Geneva telling her which ships were now hers. Off the coast of Africa and in the Persian Gulf, deckhands, wipers, fitters, engineers, and officers of twenty-five ships had little awareness that they were now working for a twenty-four-year-old woman they had never seen.

Once having removed the will's crippling provision, which shackled decisive action, Christina breezed into the American consulate in Paris and renounced her American citizenship, thus saving herself many millions each year in taxes. She was now armed to fight the array of battles that awaited her. To friends and business colleagues she insisted that her motives for "reinterpreting" her father's will were purely pragmatic: she needed control of her fortune to save it. But few doubted she was also determined to prove to her father that he had misjudged her; she would run the empire in a way to make him proud.

One of Christina's first administrative actions was to counter the speculations that she was being propped up as a mere figurehead. To show that she was in control, she flew to London and met with the directors of British Petroleum and other clients, making a statement to the press that was, as hoped, quoted in newspapers and business journals around the world: "In the future, if anyone wants to do business with our companies, they will have to speak to me." She flew to Japan to make the same announcement to shipbuilders and refinery owners.

Next came the sticky matter of canceling the construction of the six new tankers. Her lawyers told her it was too late to cancel three, but that they could negotiate their way out of the other three. Christina told them to set up the negotiations. When she and her advisers sat down to discuss the terms of cancellation with a French shipbuilder, a senior negotiator for the company said to her: "Tell us, Miss Onassis, is your preference to negotiate the normal way or do you wish to do it your father's way?"

Christina experienced one of the panics she felt frequently in those days, when she had not the slightest idea what was meant by the question. She asked him to clarify. Completely deadpan, the French negotiator continued. "With your father we would start with a very high figure then spend hours of haggling until we got down to a fair amount. That is the way he liked to do business. Our normal way is to give a fair figure that you can quickly agree on and we can all leave this depressing meeting room in a matter of minutes."

Christina laughed and said she was prepared to give it a try the normal way.

Even though Christina was off to a solid start and had made no missteps on slippery terrain, many of the men who had worked for her father believed that the swashbuckling days of Ari's vision and daring were over. But the less romantic among them knew that his highly individualistic methods, while they might confuse, divert, and mystify his adversaries, were not always the most effective means to an end.

An excellent example of the change of operating style occurred within a few months of Onassis's death. For many years he had wanted to own an oil refinery, first trying to achieve that goal with the ill-fated Omega project and the Byzantine dealings with the military junta that ruled Greece. For all the time and bribe money it cost him, Onassis netted nothing but the stigma of dealing with fascists. The New Hampshire project came to life to replace Omega. After many months of fighting with state legislatures, town councils, and environmental groups, he withdrew in costly defeat. Christina got herself a refinery with no fuss or bother. She bought one, or rather half of one. It was a refinery near San Francisco, which she acquired in partnership with the California-based UCO Oil Company. Her father would not have seen the fun in that.

Because Christina was making an impressive debut in the world of international business, long-time Onassis executives had little idea of the degree to which they intimidated their new boss. There was nothing in the background of these rough-hewn, hard-driving Greek men who had grown wealthy working for one of the most audacious and successful businessmen who ever lived to prepare them to work for an inexperienced young woman, a woman they knew from the tabloids, if not from her father's laments, was given to harebrained romances and late nights at discos. "I feel like a little girl being hauled up in front of the faculty every time I go to the office," she told Florence Grinda.

Christina began taking her problems to Nicholas Papanicolaou, who had proved himself such a friend during the Paris death vigil and who was one of the top executives close to Christina's age. A year earlier, when he was twenty-five, Onassis had offered him Costa Gratsos's job. At the time Papanicolaou had decided he wanted to go off on his own, but when Onassis died, he told Christina he would stay on until she felt her control was secure. In the first days she relied on him heavily.

"Nick, Creon Broun gave me this memo today. What should I tell him?" Or: "Nick, do we have to have so many meetings? Why can't you all deliberate and bring the alternatives to me?"

According to some, Papanicolaou would come to regret his designation as Christina's in-house favorite, if only because she began requesting beyond-the-call-of-duty personal errands and insisted that he be available at all hours for counseling. Fond as he was of Christina and eager to help put the organization on a steady course, he saw himself as a businessman, not an all-purpose factotum, and he decided he would leave the Onassis companies as soon as he felt the youthful new owner could get along without him.

As diligent as she was about business matters, Christina's aversion to the company offices, whether in Monte Carlo or New York, grew so strong that she started taking an amphetamine to bolster her confidence each time there was no way to avoid making an appearance. As soon as it was possible, she would exercise administrative control by phone, but until a number of the more substantial problems were resolved, she knew she had no choice but to appear in person.

A prime cause of her discomfort was the friction that was mounting between Christina and her father's top lieutenant and oldest friend, Costa Gratsos, who kept a large office in Olympic Tower overlooking St. Patrick's Cathedral. This wily and popular Greek had come out of Argentina with Onassis and had been with him throughout his meteoric rise, a rise in which Gratsos had had a substantial hand. Onassis had once asked Gratsos to negotiate the sale of his whaling fleet to the Japanese; he returned with a check for $15 million when Onassis had told him he would accept $3.5 million. Like Onassis, he was not an outstanding day-to-day administrator or a meticulous office manager; he was a visionary businessman, a dreamer of deals. Christina, who needed a meticulous office manager, did not understand this. He, in turn, his head full of memories of infantile tantrums, harebrained romances, and frenzied partying, could not make the adjustment from seeing her as his old friend's troubled daughter to accepting her as his replacement.

A blowup was inevitable. When it came, four years later, Gratsos was more or less asked to leave. It was a sad ending to a long partnership, but almost more than any of her other actions, the cashiering of Gratsos demonstrated Christina's resolve to run her own companies. She hired Louis Anderson away from Exxon, where he was highly regarded as head of its chartering subsidiary, the world's largest chartering company. Recruiting Anderson was Christina's attempt to bring modern American business techniques to her father's feudal companies. But Anderson encountered considerable resistance from the old guard, who preferred progress in their own way and at their own pace. Anderson was Greek-American, which he found was not the same as being Greek. Eventually he left to join an English firm.

Very shortly into her reign, Christina was confronted by the kind of calamity that would try the mettle of the most seasoned ship operator. One of the three new supertankers, the *Olympic Bravery*, was on its way from the shipyard in France to be mothballed in Norway when it ran aground and sank. The ship had cost $35 million. There was an investigation and the insurers, satisfied the timely disaster had been an accident, paid off a cool $50 million.

Many would have congratulated Christina on her good fortune—shippers were desperate to get rid of ships and lay hands on cash. But instead of banking her windfall, a course her father would have disdained, Christina bought another new supertanker, which the reclusive American shipping tycoon, Daniel Ludwig, was selling at the distressed price of $27 million, at least $10 million less than it was worth. This brought her out of her nautical disaster with a bigger ship and a profit of $23 million. Buying a ship at any price in 1976 was taking a sizable gamble. Christina banked on the shipping depression's ending before her new supertanker became a loss. Her hunch proved correct.

In addition to all of the business problems confronting the empire she had inherited, there was a major family battle going on that had to be resolved. Since the death of Christina's mother in 1974, Stavros Niarchos had been highly reluctant to relinquish any of his wife's fortune, despite the opinion of most lawyers that it should pass to Christina both by right and according to Tina's wishes. The disputed fortune was $77 million, far less than the $250 million the press reported, but too much to shrug off to a man Christina detested. The entire business infuriated her.

After many months of legal wrangling, the matter was finally settled in Christina's favor. Niarchos agreed to turn over to her assets in the amount of $64 million. He would keep $9 million in cash and one ship, whether for out-of-pocket costs in maintaining Tina or sentiment wasn't known. Christina decided not to contest this imperious decision, and peace, on the surface at least, was declared between the two warring houses after twenty-three years.

For all Christina's successes and display of business acumen in a very difficult time for shipping and for her personally, those closest to her were doubtful that her administrative winning streak or her interest would last. Her attention span, in the past, had proven short. In addition, there was fear that the business sharks that circled tanker fleets might have been holding themselves at bay while Christina was protected by world sympathy and admiration. Even her impressive performance did little to reduce insiders' anxieties about Christina's ability to command the empire. Neither family nor business associates could accept the idea of a woman at the helm—it was unprecedented among Greek shipowners—and particularly this woman who was so young, so inexperienced, and so capricious. The shipping slump merely aggravated what they considered a highly perilous situation, but one that could be saved quite quickly and simply: Christina should marry immediately, not just any man but a successful Greek businessman.

The planners and schemers could not maneuver Christina, with no overseeing parent and a half billion dollars behind her, into any course, major or minor, she didn't want. In this instance, she wanted precisely the same thing. She was coming to dread the momentous decisions constantly demanded of her. With every one of her father's top men—whose loyalty was to him, not to her—pushing his own agenda and schemes, there was no one she felt she could completely trust. Such were Christina's reasons for wanting what everyone else wanted for her, a husband who could share the burden of running her empire. And overriding either Christina's wishes or those of her counselors were, as always, the wishes of Aristotle Onassis. Obliging him in this matter would be the final act of her atonement and vindication.

# 13

# A PROPER GREEK MARRIAGE

As an inducement to matrimony, family arm twisting had always assured a strong negative reaction from Christina. But her marriage to Bolker had shaken her confidence in her own romantic decisions. Her traumatic year in Los Angeles as the Onassis-defying maverick had left her frightened and exhausted. Now her father had died without seeing her settled in a sound marriage, and she needed help in running her empire. She was in a mood to listen to the advice of those who loved her.

Something else had happened shortly after the death of Onassis that explained Christina's openness to matrimonial suggestions. Having drifted along for many months with the growing certainty that she would eventually marry Peter Goulandris, Christina was strengthened in that decision by Peter's unstinting support throughout her Paris death vigil, and by the closeness they had developed during those bleak months. He had been her security during a difficult time, and she looked forward to making that security a permanent part of her life. The reassuring inevitability of their course hit a snag when Christina became pregnant, but to her this simply meant that they would marry sooner than they had planned. According to Christina she was thrown, however, when Goulandris insisted she have an abortion before they got married. She obliged him in this chronological nicety, feeling that, for the moment, the important objective was that they marry.

Immediately following the funeral on Skorpios, Christina had gone to Monte Carlo to meet with her executives at Olympic Maritime. Goulandris had flown to his mother's house on Lyford Cay in the Bahamas to make his intentions known. Christina was to join him there as soon as she could get away and they would work out the details of their marriage. But when Christina arrived on Lyford Cay, the plan foundered. Maria Goulandris, who had overcome her distaste for Christina's family enough to fly to Greece for Onassis's funeral, was far from convinced that the marriage of her son to Christina was a good idea. During talks with Christina, Maria made a disparaging remark about Onassis or, according to some of Christina's friends, about Christina herself.

Whatever the triggering remark, it infuriated Christina. Heated words were exchanged, a form of discourse at which both women excelled. Christina was ordered to leave the island, and told never to bother Peter in the future. Seeing that her lover's support evaporated when his mother was in a rage, Christina had some harsh words for Peter as well—remarks that ruled out, not just marriage but a continuation of their involvement.

With that emotional support snatched from her, and buckling under the weight of her unsolved business problems, Christina blanched at the prospect of setting out again on a husband search. She was, therefore, particularly receptive when her trusted confidante, her much-loved Aunt Artemis, urged on her a marriage candidate who could match Goulandris in three important categories: he was young, rich, and Greek. Artemis's choice was the second son of Stratis Andreadis, a self-made Greek tycoon in the buccaneer vein of Onassis. Andreadis owned a fleet of merchant ships, several banks, some insurance companies, a fertilizer factory, and the Athens Hilton. He was also a director of seventeen other corporations.

In the eyes of many, his son Alexander was a spoiled, rich lollabout, even though he had a degree from a maritime college in Zürich and had done graduate work in economics. Titularly, he was in charge of the family shipyards, but was thought to be more interested in his collection of antique Rolls-Royces, in sleeping until eleven, and eating spaghetti. As a sacrificial lamb to demonstrate that the new Greek government did not coddle the rich, Alexander had been drafted into military service and became a minor media celebrity as "the richest private in the Greek army." He still had six months to serve.

Christina's second cousin Costa Konialidis, who had run Olympic Airlines and had excellent connections in the Athens business community, had heard rumors of problems in the Andreadis empire. He cautioned Artemis and Christina that the marriage to Alexander could be a mistake. Investigations were under way that might land Stratis Andreadis in serious trouble. As it turned out, Cousin Costa was right, but since he could not at that time substantiate his gloomy disparagements, they had no effect on the women's matrimonial momentum.

Behind the rumors Konialidis had heard was very real trouble. The ouster of Papadopoulos as premier in 1973 had been accompanied by popular outcries for reforms and retribution against those who had grown rich under the military dictators. Andreadis was one of the first to come under judicial scrutiny, and investigators had little difficulty in turning up enough evidence of questionable practices to charge him. He was accused of selling shares in his banks to subsidiaries that he owned outright. He was also alleged to have been transferring bank funds to Panamanian companies that all evidence suggested were also owned by him. To keep his empire from collapsing in a barrage of scandals—and perhaps keep himself from jail—he desperately needed $20 million.

Artemis apparently did not know of the Andreadis family's financial problems. To her, Stratis was simply an old friend who owned a fistful of corporations and had a marriageable, if slightly plump, son. Her motive in pushing the match may have been nothing more than a desire to see her errant niece solidly married, and she seized upon the idea of a merger with such a financially prominent Greek clan. That Alexander came from a big-business family, and had engaged in administering some of that big business, boded well for the support he could provide Christina in running a similar empire. From the point of view of the elder Andreadis it was also a very desirable match.

Artemis and Stratis worked tirelessly to persuade Christina to give every consideration to young Andreadis as a potential husband.

Christina was intrigued. A meeting was arranged between the two at the Athens Hilton coffeeshop, a nice plain-folks touch with the subtle subtext of the hotel's ownership by the Andreadis family.

Christina and Alexander had known each other slightly but had not seen each other for many years. Andreadis, who was then thirty-two, was a nice-looking young man, but was thirty pounds overweight and sported Elvis Presley sideburns that accentuated the pudginess of his face. Whatever the flaws, the package succeeded with Christina, no doubt helped by the titillation of the meeting's conjugal purpose, and she found herself instantly attracted to him. With the success of the first meeting, Artemis moved to the next phase of her plan. Christina and Alexander should take a short cruise together on the *Christina* to see if they "got along."

At sea in the Mediterranean with the entire yacht to themselves—except for Artemis, who came along as a complaisant, if not invisible, chaperon—they found themselves enjoying the roles they were being assigned. Like two film actors who discover more in their love-making than sheer professionalism, they were happy to discover that their physical encounters turned out as well as the coffeeshop chat. For Christina, to have her romantic urges receive enthusiastic adult encouragement was a refreshing and perhaps exciting novelty, and she began believing herself in love again. Almost as soon as the ship returned to Athens, Christina and Alexander announced their engagement—a little over a week after their first meeting. The wedding was set for July 22, 1975—four months after the death of Onassis.

A small obstacle to the marriage was Andreadis's two-year affair with a stunning Greek-American, Denise Sioros, whose father, an American Foreign Service officer, had been stationed in Athens. While this was a respectable profession, it was insufficiently impressive to protect Denise from being unceremoniously dropped when her lover's allure was enlisted in the cause of higher finance. He was quoted as saying to Denise by way of explanation and goodbye, "There's too much involved. It's like being appointed king for life."

When word got out about the imminent nuptials, the press clamored for details. With becoming self-deprecation, Artemis expressed surprise at the rush to the altar by telling a reporter, "Everything was so sudden. Christina is very happy because, for the first time, she found a man who really loves her"—which might have seemed an unfair dismissal of Bolker, Basualdo, Marentette, and Goulandris. Alexander's father, Stratis Andreadis, joined the duet of disingenuousness by saying that the proposed wedding had taken him by surprise, then further distanced himself from any interest in the matter by adding, "But that's life. It's filled with surprises."

Jackie Onassis, whom Christina had not planned to invite to the wedding until Artemis urged her to reconsider, seized on an opportunity to combat the rumors of strife with her in-laws and arrived in Athens in time to add her voice to the rampant hypocrisy. "I do love that child and I'm happy she has found him," she whispered to a battery of reporters. "At last I can see happy days ahead for her. They are a wonderful couple." Since Jackie and Christina were still locked in their deadly struggle over a financial settlement, the statement, like Christina's invitation to the wedding, was no doubt cynical, but generous nonetheless.

The marriage took place in a Byzantine chapel at the foot of Mount Hymettus in Glyfada. Although only fifty people were invited to the service, the streets outside were thronged with reporters and the curious, many of them in bathing suits, from the beach nearby. Christina was forty-five minutes late, which was fortunate for Jackie, who had arrived only fifteen minutes earlier with her son, John. Christina wore a layered white dress by Saint Laurent with a pale purple sash. Her arms and head were uncovered. There was a gold cross on a chain around her neck and she carried a bouquet of small pink roses. The ceremony was performed by Father Marius Bapergolas, and Christina was given away by her uncle, Artemis's husband Theodore Garofalides. The small, crowded chapel was stiflingly hot and the service long. When it finally ended with the traditional three-time circling of the altar by the bride and groom, sweat-soaked socialites scrambled for fresh air.

Since marriages of this kind are thought to hold the same sort of broad public interest as lottery winners and sunken treasure, the details were reported assiduously by the world's press, which had barely recovered from Onassis's four-alarm funeral. A punctilious *Newsweek* stringer in Athens sent a telex to the New York office correcting a previous dispatch: "CHRISTINA DRESS WHITE, NOT OFF-WHITE AS SAID EARLIER." The *New York Times*, for its news story of Christina's first public wedding, showed a keen sense of rank with a photo, not of the bride and groom, but of Jackie and her son arriving at the church.

It was announced that there would be no honeymoon, as Alexander was obliged to return immediately to his army unit. While this may have seemed heartlessly unromantic of the Greek military, the real reason was considerably less patriotic. Alexander, along with his father, was due to appear in court on a claim, later withdrawn, that they had improperly expropriated land from poor farmers in order to build an oil refinery—the same refinery, ironically, that Onassis had struggled so long to establish. For the bride and groom, it was a small inconvenience, as they had already had their honeymoon aboard the *Christina*, an experience so pleasurable that Christina hoped to replicate it with a Caribbean cruise when Alexander was discharged from the army the following winter.

Before this cruise came about, however, Alexander delivered a bombshell. Because the Andreadises' financial predicament was of an urgency that precluded graceful delays, shortly after the wedding he asked Christina if she would mind depositing $20 million in one of his father's banks. By way of sour coincidence, it was the second time in the six months since her father's death that that amount had been requested of Christina. Even though the estate was not yet settled, her fortune, at that rate, would be gone in five years.

Christina was floored. For weeks she had been hearing how rich the Andreadises were, how bright and experienced Alexander was in the purlieus of high finance, how much manly strength he could lend to his young bride's enormous load of responsibilities. He had also said something about love. Now he stood before her unmasked as simply another opportunist, a standard-issue fortune hunter who had cloaked himself in his father's paper holdings to lower her guard and gain access to her billionaires' fortress, and, once in, to the money itself.

By now, Christina could acknowledge the extent to which Joe Bolker had been a mistake in judgment, but her choice had been far superior to this, the choice of wiser, cooler adult heads, who had pushed her to the altar with him. She felt foolish and badly used. What affection she had for Alexander instantly curdled to contempt. Christina had been flattered to win a rich young spouse who could have had his choice of so many women and, since he didn't need her money, was in a rare category of suitors whose motives were above suspicion. It enabled her to discover all sorts of other attractive qualities in a man she might otherwise have ignored. When he was found not only to desire money, but to need it desperately, he quickly lost his primary appeal and, before her eyes, became just another of the vast army of fortune seekers. Christina, with her chronic insecurities about her allure, was particularly sensitive to the possibility that she could be loved only for her money. On learning of Alexander's acute financial needs, she suddenly noticed that he was fat.

When her husband's tainted devotion was revealed, Christina did not yield to her impulse to end the marriage immediately. Knowing that Alexander and his family were about to undergo an excruciating ordeal in the courts and in the press, she did not want to add to their woes with a major scandal that would underscore their financial problems. She was not without feeling for Alexander. While turning down his request, she acquiesced to his plea that she never speak of it. She knew he was just a loyal foot soldier in his father's big-stakes machinations, a role that her own father had tried to foist onto her. But the revelation finished him as the central involvement in her life.

Just as she was forced to acknowledge that her marriage was a sham and a sad joke, with her the butt, Christina learned she was pregnant. She wasted no time in undergoing an abortion. In addition to the marriage's imperfections, her own state of mind was too unsettled for her to consider having a child. She had not yet recovered from the deaths of all three members of her immediate family— mother, father, and brother—in a two-year period, and she still faced an array of business and legal problems that came with her inheritance. She very much wanted a child, but now was not the time and Alexander was not the man.

Inevitably, her abrupt change in feeling for Alexander put a massive strain on their relationship, and their discord erupted in some rowdy public displays. One much-reported incident occurred in the lobby of the Hôtel de Paris in Monaco, where Christina was enjoying a late-night game of backgammon with a group of friends. Alexander, after many efforts to get his wife to come to bed, picked up the board before the astonished players, threw it across the lobby, then dragged Christina to the elevators.

On another occasion many observed them yelling at each other on a Paris sidewalk. Andreadis was trying to get Christina into a limousine, insisting they were expected for lunch at Maxim's. She wanted to shop. In a voice that could be heard a block away, Christina shouted, "For the last time, I don't feel like eating."

Andreadis grabbed her arm and forced her into the car. At lunch, she excused herself to go to the ladies' room, then bolted from the restaurant. She returned to the table an hour later, smiling broadly, her arms full of purchases.

Andreadis was furious, although he was not innocent of the sort of willfulness he found so hateful in his wife. Christina had recently purchased a glistening new yacht, which she named the *Alexander* after her brother rather than her husband. It was to replace the *Christina*, which she considered too big and too memory-ridden, and which she eventually gave to the Greek government in accordance with her father's will. Because Alexander hated cooking smells, he insisted Christina remove the new boat's galley. It was a costly and destructive renovation that obliged the yacht, whenever anyone on board grew hungry, to head for the nearest port.

Matters reached a climax at a dinner Christina and Alexander gave in the Villa Cristal, in St. Moritz, which she had recently purchased. A terrible fight erupted shortly before the guests arrived and, after they did, Christina refused to come out of her bedroom. When she learned that Nicholas Papanicolaou had arrived, she sent word that she wanted to speak with him. He came into her bedroom and she launched into a catalog of her grievances against Alexander. In all the complaints, Papanicolaou recalled, Christina never mentioned that Alexander had asked her for a large amount of money. Papanicolaou saw this as evidence that the stories of the Andreadises' financial distress were exaggerated. But having promised Alexander she would not speak of that touchy matter, Christina, even in her fury, was keeping her word. In addition, she was beginning to see money requests as business, perhaps routine business. Alexander's boorishness, his excess pounds, and his attempts to boss her around like a Greek housewife of another generation—that was personal. Although she acknowledged his intelligence, she also resented Alexander's laziness. Both of them had positions in the companies their fathers had created. But she grew irritated by a sizable difference in their approach to their jobs. She went to the office most days, while he hung around the house doing nothing. Throughout the evening, Andreadis commuted between the dinner guests, whom he tried to entertain, and his irate wife, whom he tried to placate.

Because of his family's legal and financial difficulties, Andreadis prevailed on Christina to remain in the marriage until the other scandals subsided. For his sake, she agreed to put off moves toward divorce and persevered for a time with the marital charade. Both players, however, were too young and too willful to deceive for very long anyone who spent time around them. For Christina, the terminal annoyance came when Alexander broke his leg in a motor-bike accident on Skorpios. Christina wrote on his cast, "Too bad, Alexander, better luck next time"—and left for Switzerland for a romantic reunion with Peter Goulandris. Her marriage to Andreadis was dissolved in July 1977.

In her ongoing dialogue with her dead father, Christina could now say, "See, Ari, your choices aren't any better than mine." Peter Goulandris had come back into her life, but now in the new guise of an old and dear friend, with whom she occasionally made love. She had abandoned any idea that he would be her salvation, and the Andreadis fiasco made her wonder if salvation was possible with the kind of men she met in her *haut monde* circles. But lacking alternatives or the imagination and volition to produce some, she threw herself into the same round of high-powered partying that amused her and —who could tell?—might produce one man who could make her happy. For Christina, Andreadis had been a narrow escape. Because she had never been truly in love with him, breaking the tie was painless. She would not always be so lucky.

# 14

# THAT RUSSIAN WINTER

While Christina was waiting for an appropriate moment to end her marriage to Andreadis, she resumed without scruple her field-playing single life. Andreadis was stuck in Greece and she had business to attend to in Monaco, Paris, London, and New York—cities where she had many friends, as well as pending boyfriends, for companionship in fun. With the Andreadis involvement, she had switched her business headquarters to Monte Carlo. The Olympic Maritime offices there had a private entrance to the owner's office, and employees who had not seen their boss for weeks would be startled to see her office door open and Christina emerge, glasses hanging on her nose, carrying a sheaf of papers as though she had been working there for weeks.

Clever employees figured out a way to tell if she was in town. Christina had taken over her father's old penthouse on top of the company building. If she was in Monte Carlo, a red bikini could be seen hanging out to dry on the penthouse terrace balustrade, an all-weather, in-residence symbol rather like the Queen of England's ensign flying over Windsor or Balmoral. Once her presence was known, a red rose would be placed on her desk every day, a gesture that might be seen more as a nod to her sex than to her ownership of Olympic Maritime. Of the company's executives, who numbered over a hundred, Christina was the only female.

Some serious business problems were to a degree inhibiting her renewed pursuit of pleasure. Although her tanker fleet was still making money despite the Arab oil embargo—she would show a profit of $22 million in the three years following her father's death—a costly 5 percent of her ships were idle, and forecasts indicated that the percentage would rise. It was clearly a moment for finding a bold new initiative, and Christina, remembering a scheme her father had discussed with her, thought of the Russians.

Although the fact was not generally known, Russia was producing more oil than any other nation, far more than it needed domestically, but lacked the ships to export it. Shippers knew of this potential for business, but avoided dealing with the Russians, who were known to pay less than the going rate. Onassis had explored the Russian possibility when he found himself boycotted by oil producers in the fifties and again after the Mideast crisis of 1973. Remembering her father's interest, Christina decided to investigate the possibility herself. In October of 1976 she had to journey to Tokyo to negotiate the cancellation of two unwanted tankers ordered by her father when business was still booming. She decided that, en route, she would stop off in Moscow to explore the possibilities of leasing some of her idle ships.

Her plan was to set up a relatively small deal by way of a trial—to offer the Russians five of her smaller dry-cargo vessels on five-year leases. In Moscow, she called on the head of the Russian Maritime Department's tanker division, Sovfracht, who turned out to be a personable man in his mid-thirties named Sergei Kausov. Expecting some sort of gruff, monolingual bear, Christina was relieved to find that Kausov spoke excellent English and good French and had a spirited wit. Impishly, he reminded Christina that he had called on her the year before in her Monte Carlo office. She assured him she remembered. Seeing that she didn't, he pushed on. "You were quite rude to me then, you know."

Christina was apprehensive. "Oh, God," she said, "what did I say?"

Unsmiling, Kausov said, "You asked me what a Russian was doing in Monte Carlo—and on whose money. I was quite offended."

She looked to see if he was still offended, fearing that her renowned bluntness had cost her a five-ship deal. To her relief he broke into a broad smile and said, "But I recovered."

The smile brought information, both good and bad. It showed Kausov bore her no grudge and had considerable charm. She didn't mind being played with, as long as the game ended quickly and happily. But on the negative side, the smile revealed two gold teeth that she could have done without, especially as she was starting to find him attractive. He was short, only five feet four inches to Christina's five feet six. Thirty-five years old, he had thinning blond hair and a glass eye, the result of a childhood accident, he said. But even with these flaws, he was still quite handsome and good fun. Although she found herself drawn to him and began to think he might enliven her Moscow stay, Christina resisted propositioning him with her usual rich-girl-wants-you directness. Such an escapade might be frowned on, if not by this Russian, who seemed interested, then by his superiors. They flirted some, but talked business more.

That night she phoned her top executives in Monte Carlo and New York. They all advised against accepting Kausov's terms. Even though he had agreed to the solid five-year charters Christina wanted, the fees that the Russians were willing to pay, she was advised, were too low. Conditions would probably improve and they should not lock themselves into a hard-times deal for such a long period. The consensus was that she should decline the offer and proceed to Tokyo. Christina disagreed. To her, bad deals were better than no deals. Also, despite her advisers' certainty that world tanker conditions had hit bottom and would soon improve, Christina had a hunch they might worsen. Ignoring everyone, she signed the deal and got on a plane to Tokyo. Almost immediately her hunch proved correct as shipping rates fell further. What had one day appeared a slick transaction for the Russians suddenly became a coup for Christina.

Several months later, operating from her Paris apartment, she needed clarification on some points of her Russian contract. Through the French agents for Sovfracht, she set up a lunch with the Russians' two Paris representatives. When one of them turned out to be Kausov, she was surprised and delighted. Beaming with pleasure, he told her he had been transferred to Paris and was now head of the Sovfracht office here. Lunch was like a reunion between old friends and went on for over two hours. When the meal ended, Christina offered to drop the two men at their office. When the other Russian excused himself to do an errand, Christina and Kausov settled into her limousine for the long drive to the Paris suburb of

Neuilly, where the Sovfracht offices were situated between a butcher shop and a café.

During the drive, Kausov launched a discussion about food and expressed dismay that Christina knew so little about Russian food. She was, she assured him, eager to learn. He suggested she let him take her to a fine Russian restaurant he knew in Paris, L'Étoile de Moscou. They met a few days later, stuffed themselves with L'Étoile's blini and red caviar, laughed a great deal, and returned to Christina's Avenue Foch apartment, where they spent the night.

Sex with Kausov, according to several of her close friends, was an epiphany for Christina. He was intensely passionate and could not get his fill of his new Greek lover. They began meeting regularly, but chose their spots carefully to avoid being seen. She was still married and was willing to maintain appearances, if not fidelity, for Andreadis's sake. Even more than that, she knew how the press would react if they learned that the world's most famous heiress was having an affair with a Communist. She was titillated by the shock the news would cause, but she had no stomach for the problems, so went to pains to keep her new love a secret.

Kausov was even more fearful of exposure, telling Christina that the minute word of their affair got out he would be thrown onto the next Moscow-bound plane and would not be heard from again. They met in suburban bistros, little-known Russian restaurants, and, on a few occasions, for intimate dinners in Christina's Avenue Foch apartment. The last was risky since the Parisian press, hungry for celebrity news, often staked out Christina's entrance. By some miracle, they got away with it, at least for a time.

Christina was dashed to learn that Kausov was married and had an eight-year-old daughter. His wife, Natasha, lived in Moscow and was a cellist. These obstacles did little to cool Christina's burgeoning interest. She found Kausov quick and intelligent and felt increasingly comfortable with him. He had a few social defects that needed correction, such as his dinner-table gambit of removing his glass eye, but these blemishes had little effect on her accelerating passion. By way of justifying the affair, Christina repeatedly cited to friends Kausov's lack of interest in her wealth, although some hearing this wondered how in good conscience a Communist could appear too excited about it. A Paris friend who was in on the secret mentioned another aspect to Kausov's allure. "Christina loved the forbidden nature of the whole thing. Here he was a Russian, a Communist, and a married man. She was energized by all the obstacles and was exhilarated by the scandal the affair would cause if word of it got out."

After a time, they decided to risk assignations in Kausov's quarters at the Sovfracht offices in Neuilly, which would have seemed safe enough. Most of Christina's world had never been to Neuilly. It was, however, because of this meeting place that word of their romance finally found its way to the public. The French security organization, Le Service des Renseignements, had Kausov, like most Russian officials, earmarked as an alien to watch, and from time to time agents staked out his quarters. They were stunned to discover that the large Mercedes frequently seen in front of his place at night belonged to the famous Christina Onassis. This unexpected and juicy revelation was quickly passed to the gossip press, which began printing first, insinuations about an exotic new love in Christina's life, but soon full accounts of Kausov and Christina.

In February of 1978, with her divorce from Andreadis behind her, Christina took Kausov to Rio for the carnival. They knew they were straining Kremlin indulgence with the trip, but decided to risk it. Taking a huge suite in the Copacabana Palace overlooking the ocean, Christina had a rapturous time pursuing her three favorite activities: swimming, dancing, and love-making. Her strong feelings for Kausov developed more slowly than they had with any of her previous lovers or husbands, all of whom were instant infatuations, but by the end of the ten days in Brazil, she was more in love than she had ever been before and told Kausov she wanted to marry him.

Back in Paris, calamity struck without warning. Kausov was recalled to Moscow with a suddenness that left little doubt the reason was his affair with Christina, and perhaps their Rio trip. He did not tell her he was leaving and left no message for her. He simply vanished. Sovfracht and its English agents confirmed that he had returned to Russia but they could give Christina no reason why. Even more frustrating, she had no idea how to reach him in Moscow, since the Russians considered telephone books and directory assistance as wanton divulgence of important information. Anyone would be upset to have his or her lover snatched away, but for Christina, who was less skilled than most at patience and self-denial, the sudden loss of Kausov to forces unknown drove her mad.

All of her heiress resources were brought to bear on the crisis. She offered one of her tanker captains $250,000 if he would sail to Leningrad on a pretext then smuggle Kausov out aboard his ship. The captain, not wishing to take early retirement in a *gulag*, refused the offer. Hoping to find an unemployed James Bond, she met with private detectives and self-styled soldiers of fortune. The word spread in those manly circles that Christina Onassis was willing to pay $500,000 to whoever could find her lover and bring him out of Russia. All candidates balked when they learned Christina had no idea where in Russia he was, or if indeed he was in Russia—even if he was alive.

Dosing herself with tranquilizers, Christina phoned or visited anyone she thought might help. Her frenzy made apparent to her friends and executives her seriousness about the Russian, and they grew alarmed. Officials of Olympic Maritime spoke darkly about the valuable strategic information that could fall into Russian hands through Christina's relationship. With knowledge of the Onassis ships' routes, they argued, a picture could be drawn of Western energy needs, which proved to be panicky nonsense, since everyone, Russians included, could obtain this information for a small fee from a London firm. Others worried about the divulgence of the company's future plans. As with all shipowners, that was extremely valuable competitive information—Onassis often did not divulge future intentions even to his most trusted aides until contracts were signed—and anyone in the business quickly learned to guard such information carefully.

Some even believed the Onassis ships would slip into Russian hands, or that company offices would be moved to Moscow. Later, as marriage seemed imminent, the Greek government joined the hysteria by wailing that the island of Skorpios would become a Cuba-style enemy base a few yards off its shores. Most of the fears were absurd and must have given the Russians considerable pleasure. The tortured scenarios served to cover up the fact that no one had the slightest idea what the ramifications of Christina's relationship to Kausov might be. On reflection, however, most acknowledged that they depended pretty much on Christina herself, and here, as usual, she received a unanimous vote of no confidence.

Refusing to give up her efforts to find Kausov, Christina flew to

New York and went directly to see her old friend Nicholas Papa-nicolaou. On entering his office, she closed the door, started to speak, then burst into tears.

"Oh, Nicki," she sobbed. "I'm so miserable. I haven't heard from Sergei since he left for Moscow. It's been weeks. He could be dead. I will be too if I don't hear something soon."

A little more conversation convinced Papanicolaou that Christina was sincerely in love with the Russian and wanted nothing more than to marry him. She also relieved Papanicolaou about the effect this development in her private life might have on the operation of the business. It was a purely personal matter, she assured him, and would change nothing in the way she ran the Onassis interests. Papanicolaou had an idea. A friend of his, Keith Baird, was a top executive for Armand Hammer, the legendary American oil man with strong Kremlin connections. Baird might persuade Hammer to intercede with the Russian authorities and convince them they had nothing to lose and much to gain if one of their citizens married Christina Onassis. To Christina's delight, Hammer agreed to do what he could.

Shortly after arriving back in Europe, Christina received word that Kausov had been located and would contact her. She was ecstatic. When he called, he told her he had been removed from his job at Sovfracht and sent to teach English in a small Siberian town. Brushing aside his government's obvious role in their separation, Kausov said he had at first decided it would be better to end their affair, that he should return to his wife. After a month away from Christina, however, he found he missed her too much and was prepared to divorce his wife so they could marry. It was exactly what Christina had been praying to hear. There was a stipulation, however. They would have to live in Russia. Having been driven almost insane with fear that harm had come to Kausov but even more by the fear that she had lost him, Christina probably would have agreed to live in a trailer in Vladivostok.

The locking mechanism that leads to permanent love bonds was quickly activated in Christina—both by the nature of her personality and, in this case, by the bizarre circumstances surrounding the Kausov romance. The willfulness that had been the product of both the coddling and the deprivations of her childhood joined forces with her adult feelings of having experienced more than her share of hard knocks to make this bonding mechanism snap shut the minute she saw an opportunity for happiness, no matter how slim or outlandish. So many of the disasters in her life were caused by hair-trigger infatuations that locked her into relationships before she had had time to weigh the consequences or before the passion could cool enough to allow a clear view of where a particular involvement might lead. While the recent tragedies that had so devastated her might have immobilized another person into a paralyzing self-pity, they instead reinforced Christina's grasping impulsiveness to a near desperate level.

Another very important factor in Christina's determination to marry Kausov was sex. Her psychological quirks and emotional gaps combined to produce a strongly sensual nature. When she was trying hard to get Mick Flick to take her to bed, Christina would amuse her friends with the line "Why won't he do it? Rich girls need it too." It appeared that Christina needed it more than most. A strong mutual attraction was her fondest dream. If she had sexual feelings for a man, she was irritated when they weren't returned, yet considered it a miracle when they were. Miracles didn't come along every day. When they did, Christina seized them with the mindless desperation of a starving person who comes upon some questionable food.

Ever since she was a little girl with a big nose and dark pockets under her eyes, Christina had always had wrenching doubts about her attractiveness. So indelible was this negative self-view that a fortune in plastic surgery and Paris's finest beautification strategies could not put it to rest. While the ugly duckling had not emerged a swan, the end results were better than she thought. She felt little confidence in her ability to excite men and often suspected ulterior motives when she succeeded.

But there could be no such suspicions about Kausov. No one had ever lusted after her so passionately or satisfied her so well. His many other attributes—his humor, his charm, his air of mystery, his allure of forbidden fruit—were mere bonuses to the fundamental sexual needs he fulfilled. His disadvantages—his wife, his gold teeth, his height, but above all his nationality—were by comparison minor problems Christina had no trouble sweeping aside. She would bolster her sexually determined course by rationalizations: she was tired of luxury, she wanted to live the simple life, she wanted to live where no one noticed her or cared who she was. While it was true that the Russians would pay no attention to her in public, her love for Kausov was bringing her more attention than she had ever had before. And no marriage would so stun and shock the world since her father married Jackie—a comparison that in itself suggested a supporting motive in Christina's odd Russian escapade.

As it became known that the stalled romance had sprung back to life with renewed vigor, Christina's friends and business associates began a campaign to dissuade her from making what they insisted was a huge mistake. Aside from pointing out the obvious problems in a cross-ideology marriage, they threw in discouraging things about Kausov himself. The rumor she began hearing over and over was that he was a KGB agent. Although Christina had had recent experience with slanders against her first choice in a husband, the evidence in this case could not be so easily shrugged off.

For no apparent reason, Kausov clearly enjoyed privileges granted few Russians. While claiming to be on a small salary, he seemed to have plenty of money. He had moved about freely in France, even leading gastronomic tours of the French countryside. Far from making these excursions on the sly, he wrote them up for the Paris newspaper aimed at ex-patriate Russians. Such public enjoyment of Western pleasures often earned other Russians a quick return trip to Moscow, but it caused no problems for Kausov. Arguing against his KGB status was the sudden recall just when the romance with Christina was about to escalate to matrimony. Suspicions that he had been placed in her path as an elaborate setup were dismissed by knowledgeable KGB watchers, if for no other reason than that the Russians, for a seduction assignment, could surely have found an agent with two eyes and a full set of teeth.

The most likely scenario was that when on her first trip to Moscow Christina had made apparent her interest in Kausov—dissembling in this area was unknown to her—he went to the KGB and asked permission to pursue an involvement. An opportunity was recognized—

for a propaganda coup, if nothing else—and his transfer to Paris was the result. But if such KGB connivance took place, the recall became difficult to explain. One possibility was that the KGB felt that matters were slipping from its control, that Kausov might defect. His trip to Brazil, a hospitable country for fugitives, may have alarmed them about this likelihood.

It was also possible that the Russians failed to see the advantages to them in a Onassis-Kausov marriage—the notion may have been as boggling to the Kremlin as it was to the executives of Olympic Maritime. In hopes of netting some shipping information, they may have played along solely with the idea of a romance. When marriage loomed, the Russians may have called time out so they could regroup —rather in the same spirit as recalling arms negotiators when new proposals hit the table. From Kausov's removal to a Siberian cooling-off tank, it appeared he may have overstepped whatever plan the KGB had authorized. Armand Hammer's intercession may have brought pressure on the KGB from above to permit the comedy to play out. The result may have been a rebriefing of Kausov—this time for bridegroom duty.

Among those who were alarmed at what they feared Christina was about to do were her ex-husband Alexander Andreadis and her despised uncle, Stavros Niarchos. Andreadis had recovered from the scathing things Christina had said publicly about him at the time of their divorce and had remained in her life as a caring older brother. Alarmed by the Russian peril, he telephoned Niarchos and asked him to dissuade Christina from such lunacy.

"Why would she listen to me?" Niarchos was said to have replied. "She didn't listen when I told her not to marry you."

When Kausov resurfaced, he gave Christina his home phone number, a routine move in most affairs but a sizable risk for a married Russian. He and his wife had separated and steps had been taken to get a divorce, a relatively easy matter in Russia if both parties agree. He boasted later to reporters that he had "tricked" his wife by telling her he did not love Christina but had been asked to seduce her by the KGB. He needed a divorce, he told her, in order to hold on to a car and other expensive presents Christina had given and which the government could confiscate. If, however, he got a divorce and put the booty in his wife's name, the government could not touch it.

Since in Russia the government has never had any hesitancy about touching whatever it wishes, Kausov's story of trickery was probably a rather clumsy attempt to throw off the track those suspecting his motives in marrying Christina and to deflect allegations made by his understandably bitter wife that he had, indeed, gone after Christina at the insistence of the KGB.

Kausov told Christina he needed several weeks to make all necessary arrangements for them to marry. Now that word of the romance had leaked to the Western press, which was rabid to learn the details, the need for secrecy became greater on Christina's end than on Kausov's, where the press ignores such frivolous matters. Because in France phone calls to Russia must go through an operator but can be dialed directly in England, Christina flew to London three times a week for no other reason than to talk privately to Kausov. Since Kausov's superiors had come down on the side of true love, the eavesdroppers Christina feared were Parisian telephone operators, who could pick up a few extra francs by selling tidbits to the gossip press.

In late May, Christina got the long-awaited word: she could come to Moscow in about five weeks. On June 24, she boarded a train in Paris, first giving her maid Eleni, who was not permitted to accompany her, $200,000 in cash. As the women wept in each other's arms, Christina said she might never see Eleni again and she wanted to leave knowing that she was provided for. When Christina arrived in Moscow the next day, Kausov met her train and took her to the Intourist Hotel, where he had arranged a twelfth-floor suite overlooking Red Square. Without interference, they spent several hours taking up where they had left off in Rio. Their heroic love-making marked the climax of their relationship, but it was also a turning point. From this moment, everything started, almost imperceptibly, going downhill. Believing only days before she would give up everything if she could just have Sergei, Christina now found that, reunited with him, she hadn't meant quite *everything*.

Except for the brief visit in 1976, Christina had never spent any time in Russia and she was not prepared for the bad food. Like most Westerners, she had assumed good food is always available if you are willing to pay for it. She was horrified to discover that in Moscow's best restaurants the food was rarely good and often worryingly bad. As were her accommodations. Having always stayed in the fanciest suites in the best hotels and grown up in and around one of the very finest, Monte Carlo's Hôtel de Paris, which for many years her father owned, she found herself in shock at the low level of comfort in Intourist's best. But these were minor irritations compared to discomforts to come. Among other shocks, Christina had yet to experience a Russian winter.

As the excitement subsided from her dramatic plunge into forbidden Russia, Christina looked at her new home with mounting dismay and realized that the only reason she had been forced to abandon her own sumptuous world was a bureaucratic prohibition against Kausov's leaving Russia. A simple exit visa, a piece of paper, would allow her to retain both her own lavish life and the man she loved. If it weren't for this cruel and arbitrary obstinacy, she and Kausov could be living like rajahs anywhere in the world they chose. When Christina loudly protested their forced residency, the Russian officials hinted that possibly sometime in the future Kausov would be granted an exit visa, perhaps as soon as six months. The only reason Christina could figure that they wanted to hold Kausov captive for that insignificant amount of time was to reap the propaganda benefits of having the world's richest young woman appear to elect Moscow as the place to build true happiness.

Another harsh blow was that Kausov had not yet found them an apartment, although the authorities had indicated that Christina would be placed at the head of a lengthy list of Russians, many of whom had been waiting for as long as ten years. Until granted an apartment, they would have to live with Kausov's mother, Mariya, in her cramped, two-bedroom, one-bath flat in the Lenin Hills across from the Moscow Film Studios, where she worked as an assistant to a film director.

The wedding was set for August 1 but, perhaps in hopes of lessening the press coverage, Christina denied vehemently any such plans to the many journalists who were being drawn to Moscow by the rumors that a wedding was imminent. When her Aunt Artemis heard Christina was definitely marrying Kausov, she said publicly that her niece should be examined by a psychiatrist and maybe declared incompetent. This word, when used by Christina's closest Onassis relative, was not just a nasty epithet but had a far more ominous ring; it could be the legal device for stripping Christina of her millions.

Few people in Christina's life were thinking of anything so drastic, but all hated the prospect of her marriage. In a last-ditch effort to avert calamity, Costa Gratsos, who still worked for Christina but who, at seventy-six, was unenthusiastic about such intrigue, flew to Washington to confer with the State Department about the geopolitical ramifications of the marriage and to learn whatever he could about Kausov's KGB connections. On the latter score, he came away empty-handed, although he was assured Kausov could not do what he had been doing without the KGB's blessing. Armed with this information, Gratsos then flew to Moscow to plead with Christina to abandon her plan.

Feeling she had sacrificed a great deal in the past three years for her father's companies, Christina was stung by her executives' sending Gratsos to thwart her in an action she saw as a purely personal bid for happiness. Her marriage, she told Gratsos, would in no way affect the operation of her tanker business and she had no plans to make her husband privy to those operations. She had not confided in Andreadis, a fellow Greek, about such things, why would she now do so with a Russian? "Do you think we're going to discuss oil shipments in bed?" was one remark that found its way into the press, perhaps revealing how she still saw the relationship. Defeated, Gratsos had no stomach for hanging around for the wedding a few days later.

At the end of July, Christina told the now-frenzied media people she would hold a press conference on August 1, the location to be announced. The day of the wedding, she let out the word that "the conference" would be held in the Youssopof Palace of Weddings, indicating clearly to the patient reporters that the moment had arrived. The Russian press continued to ignore the entire circus, failing to mention even that Christina was in Moscow. If their editors were indifferent, however, the photographers of Tass and the Novosti Press were doing a thriving business in selling pictures on the side to foreign publications.

Moscow's principal Palace of Marriages was on Griboyedov Street and had been a residence of the famous Prince Youssopof who had murdered the troublesome monk Rasputin in one of his family's two St. Petersburg palaces. In 1978 it was a people's marriage factory, where bewildered couples were hustled in and out, about seven minutes per couple, with all the romance of registering an automobile.

At nine forty-five in the morning, with an army of journalists, photographers, and television cameramen crowding the street outside the building, Kausov arrived in his grayish-brown Volga, which Christina had bought for him. After removing the car's windshield wipers to avoid theft, he pushed through the crowds and entered the building. A few minutes later, Christina pulled up in a battered yellow Chevy Nova that belonged to John Fotopoulos of the Greek Embassy. She was wearing a pale violet dress with a print of yellow and brown flowers, the top cut in the loose style of a peasant blouse, which provided a deft hint of solidarity with the Russian masses.

Weddings cost a little over $2, but for a few more dollars couples could have an in-house trio play Mendelssohn's march. Christina and Kausov opted for the higher-priced wedding. The ceremony room was oak paneled with crystal chandeliers, but the Youssopof splendor was scuffed, dirty, and politicized by large portraits of Lenin and Brezhnev. The ceremony was performed by a woman official who offered advice and instructions on building a good marriage, then added to Kausov, "Wherever you may go, do not forget your motherland." When she turned to Christina and asked in Russian if she accepted Sergei as her husband, she said, "Da," with audible fluency.

To a reprise of Mendelssohn, Mr. and Mrs. Kausov edged their way past the next couple waiting to be married and emerged together in the street. A recording of churchbells, scratched and rasping, added to the press clamor, which was so vociferous it frightened even Christina, who was used to such energetic attention. They were unable to get to their car and Kausov shattered any nuptial good feeling that may have survived the frenzy by yelling angrily in Russian and English to the reporters to allow him and his wife through.

With effort, they made it to his Volga, where Kausov's mother sat waiting at the wheel to chauffeur the happy pair to the safety of her apartment. In a daze and desperate to escape, Christina smiled and waved limply at the crowd from the car's back seat, but the Volga would not start. Finally Mariya Kausov, badly rattled herself, got the motor to turn over and edged the Volga through the crowd and finally broke free, a carful of photographers in determined pursuit.

· · · ·

It was understandable that the Western press made so much of this marriage. Aside from the movie-script sensationalism of the match, the only news coming from Russia in those days was the grim accounts of dissident trials and agricultural shortfalls. In addition, the country had not had a wedding with such yeasty international implications since Sophia of Anhalt-Zerbst, later Catherine the Great, was brought in to become the bride of Czarevitch Peter of Holstein. Parallels were frequently made between Christina's East-West love story and the enormously popular 1939 Lubitsch film comedy *Ninotchka*, in which Greta Garbo, playing a grim-faced commissar, is wooed and won by a merrily decadent Melvyn Douglas. An aspect of the scenario proved a valid prophecy of Christina's Russian period. The Lubitsch story encompasses the courtship stage of the East-West romance. When Douglas finally lures Garbo out of Russia and marries her, the fun is over and the film ends.

On her wedding night, Christina telephoned a number of her friends. Nicholas Papanicolaou, who no longer worked for her, having gone off on his own, was stunned to get a call in New York. Christina told him she had married Kausov but it was all a terrible mistake. She no longer loved him and she hated Russia. Asking her the logical question of why she had done it, Papanicolaou was told that she did it for Kausov and his mother. They were counting on it and things had "gone too far to stop." Christina was clearly interested in having the word spread among the people most concerned that they should stop worrying, the marriage was a temporary episode.

Christina's relations with Russian authorities had been damaged when, before the wedding, they refused to allow her to bring her Lear jet into Russia so she and Kausov could fly, like civilized people, off on a honeymoon. In fact, she could not bring her plane into Russia at all. The jet had become basic to her mode of operating, and it had never occurred to her it would be forbidden. Now, so far from everyone she knew and loved, she had counted on the jet to lessen her sense of isolation. More of a problem than no jet for the honeymoon, Christina had to confront the problem of no husband; Kausov was not to be allowed to leave the country at that time, since the Russians had no reason to think that, flying into the free-world sunset with his rich wife, he would ever return. Christina was accustomed to doing exactly as she pleased and had difficulty adapting to the rhythms and nuances of Russian paranoia.

Her disappointment and sense of being trapped in Moscow—
which happened to be having its rainiest summer in years—was
heightened by the news that her stand-in father at the wedding,
diplomat John Fotopoulos, and his wife were flying to Athens four
days later. Christina had never yearned so fervently for her family's
country. Suddenly the Russians' consolation honeymoon—ten days
on Siberia's Lake Baikal—appeared horrible to Christina, a cruel
joke. She told Kausov to cancel it and announced she was going to
leave him behind and join the Fotopouloses in flying to Greece. The
marriage had been for his sake; the honeymoon would be for hers.
Kausov, who *was* tuned to the nuances of defection, asked if she was
coming back, reasonably pointing out that he had turned his life on
its ear for Christina. She assured him she would return shortly, probably in a week.

Kausov, like any Russian watching a foreigner breezing across the
closed border, must have wondered why she would come back. He
and Christina had frequently discussed one day leaving together. He
felt sure he could get out, and was more than willing to do so, but
would not emigrate unless his mother could leave as well. That
would take time, perhaps a year, and because of this plan Christina
had always known that, even if her marriage succeeded, her Russian
sojourn would be a temporary one—despite contradictory remarks
she made at the time to the press. She would eventually leave with
Kausov or, if necessary, without him. In the meantime she was telling friends, "When Mariya gets out, I get out."

The Aeroflot flight to Athens on which John Fotopoulos and his
wife were booked had a waiting list of a hundred people, but through
Greek Embassy connections, Christina managed to obtain a window
seat. Although the news of the bizarre Onassis-Kausov marriage was
the main topic of discussion among her fellow passengers, no one on
the plane recognized Christina except one Greek businessman.
When he spoke to her, she pleaded with him to say nothing of her
presence to anyone else. She felt the world's press had been on her
back for many months, and she couldn't face having to explain why
she was leaving the country without her husband four days after her
wedding. During the flight, as she sat alone looking from the window
at the vast emptiness of Russia, Christina fell asleep to nearby voices
of strangers marveling that the famous Onassis heiress had decided
to settle in Moscow.

When Christina flew into Athens and was met by a limousine that whisked her to her aunt's luxurious seaside villa, her sense of her own folly was enormous. Relations between aunt and niece had been touchy since Artemis had pushed Christina into the ill-advised Andreadis marriage. By the time Christina learned of her aunt's public speculations about her sanity, Artemis had already softened her tune and was denying to the press that she had ever objected publicly to Christina's marrying Kausov. When asked for an opinion of the marriage, she had issued a formal statement: "If she has found someone who makes her happy, it makes the family even happier."

Believing that the harsh remark had probably been made, Christina shrugged it off. She had learned that, in dealing with close relatives, she didn't have enough of them to brood overlong on slights and misdemeanors. If she could sit down to dinner with Stavros Niarchos after what he had publicly said about her and she about him, she could certainly forgive her aunt for calling her crazy, especially when she now tended to agree with her.

Despite her public show of family solidarity, Artemis had found a new tune. She greeted Christina with "How could you love a godless man?" Her question may have taken Christina by surprise, as it had never been established that any of her previous lovers and husbands had been particularly devout. Christina avoided the quick and easy answer to Artemis's question—that she no longer *did* love a godless man. She knew how angry that madcap turnabout would make Artemis. Peace, however, was quickly restored and Christina luxuriated in her aunt's hospitality—good Greek food, soft beds, swimming pool, Diet Coke—while they planned an immediate party on Skorpios to celebrate Christina's temporary freedom. The idle Lear jet was pressed into service to round up twenty of her old friends for an austerity-purging weekend of Olympian dining and the most flagrant capitalist luxury.

Alexander Andreadis paid a visit to Christina at the Glyfada villa and, after a long talk alone together, she proclaimed him "her best friend in the world." On August 10 he went along for company when she made a one-day trip to London for a lunch she had arranged with the executives of British Petroleum. The meeting was a gesture aimed at mollifying the world shipping community, to assure her clients that her marriage would not affect her businesses, but the English oil men seized the opportunity to convince Christina of the opposite and alarm her over the risks she was taking. They had invited a high-ranking diplomat from the British Foreign Office to substantiate their conviction that the Saudis, who represented over three-quarters of Christina's business, were deeply concerned that her ships would soon fall under the influence of a member of the KGB. They warned her that, regardless of her own actions and whether or not she kept Kausov ignorant of Olympic Maritime's affairs, the mere fact of her marriage was risking the loss of the major portion of her business.

This was the jolt Christina needed. She sent word to the Saudis that she "would do whatever was necessary to relieve their concern." She resolved to end her marriage but would maintain it until Kausov and his mother were safely out of Russia. It was a selfless and potentially costly action, since she had no idea how long the Saudis would tolerate the marriage. Reinforcing her decision to delay making a break was her awareness of how absurd it would appear if she announced plans for a divorce so quickly. She had no doubt, however, that her marriage was over. She had not resolved her feelings for Kausov and would not tell him yet. But all that was personal. The marriage, she finally admitted, was business.

Her first days out of Russia, Christina spoke to Kausov by phone every morning and evening, but after a time found that he was not home at any hour of day or night. Mariya hinted that he had returned to his wife. When Christina finally reached him, she angrily asked if he still loved his wife. "Yes, I do," he replied with his usual suavity, "and I want to know when she is coming back to Moscow." When Christina returned on August 14, after an absence of ten days, Kausov was not at the airport to meet her. She collared a journalist who had spotted her and was pummeling her with questions, and promised to give him an interview in exchange for a lift home.

As fall approached in Moscow, Christina resolved to make the best of her mistake and settled in until her opportunity for escape arrived. The pre-*perestroika* Russia of 1978 was not a good time for a Westerner to live in Moscow. Leonid Brezhnev was cracking down on dissidents, exit visas were harder to get than ever, and foreign journalists were increasingly harassed for writing disagreeable reports. Christina's living arrangements were atonement for all the luxury she had enjoyed in her life. Aside from the usual strains between wife and mother-in-law, Christina had to share three small rooms with her. With one tiny bathroom, finding space for twenty-five eye brushes would be just one of many problems.

When Christina first arrived in Moscow, Mariya had made an effort to befriend her and had presented her with a garnet bracelet. Because Christina did not like the bracelet yet imagined it was precious to Mariya, she told her she had a terrible superstition about presents and could not accept it. This may have stung Mariya, and behind her mask of warmth was a more unfriendly judgment: Mariya blamed Christina for the destruction of her son's marriage and felt that she was playing with her son—all of which made her far less tolerant of Christina's ineptitude as a housewife.

Tension was building and probably would have erupted, but mercifully Christina's prestige with the Russians bumped them, as promised, to the head of a long list and the newlyweds were granted a seven-room apartment on Tyopoly Stan near the city's botanical gardens. To decorate it, Christina flew in her old friend Atalanta Politis, who was a joyous boon to her cut-off, friendless existence. Not only was Atalanta a much-loved friend, she was Greek to boot.

Christina had been pleasantly surprised by the relative ease with which she had slipped over to Finland, bought a Mercedes, and had it delivered in short order to Moscow. In the first days of her Russian residency she complained mainly about her failure to get hold of the New York *Daily News*. She generally managed to lay hands on recent copies of the *New York Times* and the Paris *Herald Tribune*, but the *News* proved unavailable. She told friends that life without her daily fix of gossip from Liz Smith and Suzy was empty and flat.

Still, when she set out to furnish her apartment, she was unprepared for the difficulty and red tape. Finding the simplest items was next to impossible. In order to buy paint or wood, requisition forms had to be filled out and various offices visited. When she went to buy a refrigerator, her patience was exhausted. Finding a model she liked, she told the clerk she would take it. The startled man assured her that was impossible. It was his only floor model and was not for sale. When told that refrigerator deliveries took six months, Christina had had enough. She offered double the price. When he shook his head *nyet*, she raised it to triple. His eyes darting from side to side, he agreed. As a storeful of Muscovites watched agog, a triumphant Christina had the refrigerator carried out and strapped to the top of her new Mercedes.

After a long period of unemployment, Kausov was given a job teaching English in a Moscow high school, an occupation that did little to increase the excitement of Christina's social life. Her attention was taken up with efforts to wrest a level of comfort from the consumer-unfriendly economy. Life improved considerably when she managed to hire a maid and a chauffeur. Another form of salvation came from the foreigners-only *berioska* stores, particularly the Gastronom on Gorky Street, where for hard currency she could buy edible cuts of meat and other rare treats. As winter came on, Christina was slammed by weather that would be the coldest in the city's history. Early one evening in the *berioska* shop, a reporter encountered Christina all but hidden under a huge fur hat and a fur-lined parka. She had come to do her shopping by subway, she said. Her Mercedes would not start in the minus-45-degree weather.

Even in her exile, Christina managed to do a little shipping business—and pulled off a smart deal. Through Kausov's connections in shipping, she learned that the Russians, despite their shortage of ships, were quietly selling three freighters, two of them almost new, one of them brand new. The prices were excellent. Even though the shipping business was still depressed—she now had 12 percent of her fleet idle—she knew these prices were too good to pass up. To the daughter of Aristotle Onassis, ships were wealth, regardless of the conditions of the moment. She bought the ships. At the same time, for Kausov's birthday she gave him a used tanker worth somewhere between $3 and $4 million. He immediately set up his own company, hiring a Greek associate of Christina's to be his agent. Before their marriage ended, she gave him another ship, bringing his net worth to about $8 million.

As always when she found herself in a difficult situation, Christina gained a lot of weight, fourteen pounds since arriving in Moscow. She blamed this on the only available Western soft drink, sugar-rich

Pepsi-Cola, which she drank in the same vast amounts she drank of her beloved Diet Coke when she was outside Russia. The new pounds did not seem to bother Kausov, but they bothered Christina considerably. Happily, most Russians hadn't the least idea of what she looked like, fat or thin, so she felt free to wander the streets with stringy hair, unabashedly fat, and wearing her horn-rimmed glasses, something she never did when photographers were nearby. People like Atalanta who knew her before she came to Russia said she never looked worse.

For Christina, the historic cold was symbolic of the punishing rigors of her life in Moscow. She had come to dislike living there intensely. Even the scant social life available to her, mostly the foreign diplomatic and press corps, offered little pleasure. The people were nice enough, but they were of different worlds. Her interest in Russian culture had improved little since, returning from her Rio trip in the early days of her romance with Kausov, she had asked a friend, "Who is Dostoyevsky?"

In the few scraps of gossip she managed to find in Moscow—a tattered copy of Newsweek or Paris Match—she read longingly about glittering European events like the wedding of her friends Princess Caroline of Monaco and Philippe Junot; everyone she knew would be there. When she became pregnant, she used her condition as an excuse to make frequent trips "to see her doctors" in Switzerland, where she eventually had an abortion.

When in November she told Kausov she wanted a divorce, the announcement came as no great shock to him. He asked only that she adhere to her promise to wait until he and his mother were safely out of Russia. Out of compassion she agreed, but, feeling she had fulfilled her obligations to him by staying in Russia as long as she had —and by making him one of the richest of his countrymen—she told him she would do her waiting on the cheerful side of the Iron Curtain. She kissed Kausov, said goodbye to Russia forever, and flew off to St. Moritz for the always dazzling Christmas season.

# 15

# RETURN TO
# DECADENCE

*H*appy to be back in her own world, Christina felt deeply foolish about her Russian fiasco and tried to put it behind her and out of her mind. Having dinner with an old friend in New York, she summed up the whole episode with a self-condemning expression. "I blew it," she said airily. "I thought I was in love with Kausov, that nothing else mattered, but when all the obstacles were gone—I was allowed to go to him in Russia, his wife out of the picture—I knew it was all a mistake, but I thought it was too late to back down. I could have gotten out then, but I blew it."

To kick the dust of Moscow from her Givenchy pumps and celebrate her comeback as a rich playgirl, Christina spent $800,000 redecorating her house in St. Moritz, the beautiful Villa Cristal, close by the center of town and on the same road as George Livanos and Gianni Agnelli. She also bought a helicopter so she wouldn't have to rely on her Uncle George for airlifts to the surrounding mountaintops. Back in Paris, she took over Maxim's for a large dinner party to announce her return from Russia. She enjoyed herself so much that she decided to make it an annual, season-opening event.

Arriving for lunch one day at Le Relais in the Plaza Athénée in Paris, Christina was delighted to run into Luis Basualdo, who was lunching with his new girlfriend, a willowy eighteen-year-old English beauty named Clare Lawman. Since an acrimonious divorce from Lucy Pearson, Basualdo had fallen into the kind of unbelievable situation that was becoming his specialty. An enormously rich Argentinean banker who aspired to the world of polo and international society saw Basualdo as a key to this ambition and set him up in a London house with servants, two cars, and a generous living allowance. Caught up in frenzied deal making in Buenos Aires, the banker almost never visited London, but Basualdo made good use of the setup with relentless party giving for the young and aristocratic flotsam who venerated those with remarkably lucky deals. The dream ended abruptly when the banker went to jail.

With a bit of money stashed away but no prospects, Basualdo had moved to Paris with Clare and was hanging around the city's most fashionable nightclubs and restaurants awaiting his next unbelievable situation. Arriving on schedule, Christina told Basualdo she wanted to see a lot of him and that he should visit her at her new villa in St. Moritz. When they spoke alone later and she repeated the invitation, Basualdo said he would love to come to St. Moritz. He would, of course, bring Clare. Christina was unenthusiastic.

"Oh," she said slowly, then, unable to think of anything else to say, asked, "Will she ski with us?"

"Of course," Basualdo replied. "She'll do everything with us. You'll like her."

Basualdo was right. From a good family, Clare had manners as well as brains and a quiet good humor that played nicely against Christina's noisy exuberance. "Christina took to me quickly," Clare recalled. "I don't know why. I was very young and hadn't been around much. She'd been married three times, lived all over the world. But then she was always like that—instant likes or dislikes."

The three became inseparable and Christina dubbed her new friend "Little Clare" perhaps as a slightly bitter reference to Clare's excellent figure, which remained exasperatingly slender in spite of a healthy appetite. As the three made the rounds of Paris couturier shops, a favored afternoon pastime for Christina as she got back into the capitalistic swim, she would often see a dress that she thought would look well on Clare and insist on buying it for her. Working on her own appearance, Christina spent long hours at beauty parlors and managed to lose some weight despite the temptations of Fauchon and Godiva.

When Basualdo and Clare arrived in St. Moritz, Christina put them up in a $300-a-day suite at the Palace Hotel. They spent their time helicopter skiing with her every day and dining and touring the clubs with her at night. Somewhat stunned by the opulent world in which she found herself, Clare, who liked Christina, had difficulty adjusting to her moods. "Sometimes she would go into the most frightful tantrums—screaming, throwing things—but they were often not directed at anyone in particular and Eleni was good at calming her down."

Ever since inheriting her fortune, Christina at times became a child frozen into her fourth birthday party. The presents, the houses, the material world that surrounded her, as well as all the adults—her family, the servants, the guests—everything, everyone was *for her*. It all existed for her pleasure. The function of those around her was to assure her amusement and happiness. Any disruption of this flow of pure pleasure from the animate and inanimate objects in her field of vision—invariably objects she had bought and paid for—was a monstrous outrage and brought down a four-year-old's wrath from a grown woman who knew this was not the way the real world operated, but also knew she was not obliged to live in the real world.

Like other newcomers to Christina's rarefied milieu, Clare boggled at the lengths to which Christina would go to indulge a whim. When she skied, she invariably wore a Sony Walkman, playing popular tapes at a volume that forced others to yell if they wanted to say anything to her, and causing Christina to yell in return. One day when they had taken the helicopter across the border into Austria in search of fresh snow, Christina arrived at the chosen mountaintop and realized she had forgotten to bring her favorite cassette of the moment, a new David Bowie recording. She went into a rage and ordered her helicopter pilot to fly back to the St. Moritz airport, drive to the Villa Cristal, then fly the tape to her at the bottom of the mountain that she was about to descend. Others in the group, even those accustomed to Christina's self-indulgent caprices, were impressed with the sizable expenditure of fuel and manpower for a few minutes' pleasure, or rather to avoid a minor frustration.

Perhaps it was the deprivations of Russia, but Christina now denied herself nothing and didn't hesitate to upset long-standing plans if a contrary mood should strike her. Her staffs in Paris, St. Moritz, and Skorpios were informed of this when they were hired, and Chris-

tina was willing to pay double and triple the going rate for servants
who would question none of her requests, no matter how unreasonable. A dinner for twenty would be ordered for midnight with an
elaborate main course of escalloped veal in a truffle and cream sauce.
Finally assembling her guests at the table around 1 A.M., Christina
would announce, "I don't feel like veal tonight. Why don't we have
liver Veneziana?" The dinner would be scrapped and the freezers
ransacked to produce, forty-five minutes later, an elaborate liver Veneziana for twenty. Some domestic workers were not cut out for this
sort of thing and soon left. Others responded to the challenge and
welcomed the generous hardship pay.

Since returning to the lands of limitless Coca-Cola, Christina
stopped at nothing to assure a constant supply—not just her favorite
beverage, but the right sort. A first-time dinner guest at the Avenue
Foch, far down the table from Christina, watched as her hostess
sipped her Diet Coke and remarked to the man next to her how
strange it was for Christina to drink Coke when the rest of them were
treated to an exquisite and rare Meursault.

"Christina's Coke probably cost a lot more than this wine," remarked the man to her right, a regular guest.

"How is that?"

"You still can't get Diet Coke here in Europe, so Christina sends
her jet to America once a month for about ten cases direct from the
factory."

"But that must cost the earth."

"With fuel and pilots' salaries, about $30,000, I believe. Or $3,000
per case."

"But surely her plane will carry more than ten cases? Why doesn't
she get a year's supply and save all those trips?"

"Christina believes she can tell the difference if the Coke is more
than a month in the can. Before Diet Coke, when she drank Coke
with sugar, she told me that with just one sip she could tell which
bottling plant in Europe her drink came from. She's a true connois-
seur."

Deep in thought, the woman took a sip of her less costly local
product, the 1976 Meursault.

After a few months Kausov was able to get out of Russia, perhaps having pleaded with the KGB for a chance to salvage his marriage. He was assured his mother would be granted permission to emigrate in due time. Eventually he found his own quarters, but for his first month he stayed with Christina on the Avenue Foch while they waited for their Swiss divorce to become final. As a gesture of both gratitude and his undiminished affection, he presented her with an auburn cocker spaniel that they named Yuri. Christina adored the dog, took him everywhere with her, but, at home in Paris, left him for Kausov to look after. For a time, a regular spectacle on the Avenue Foch was Kausov and Yuri on their daily stroll. On his way to being a mini-tycoon, Kausov worked diligently at his new role as a shipowner and stayed behind when Christina went to St. Moritz.

During her Russian sojourn, Christina missed sunny beaches and swimming in the sea more than anything else. Unwilling to await the summer in Skorpios, she arranged to take a group of friends to one of her favorite cold-weather escapes, the Beach and Tennis Club at La Jolla in Southern California. Marina and Alberto Dodero would fly up from Buenos Aires, Kausov would fly from Paris, and she, Basualdo, and Clare would fly from St. Moritz. She would get Muriel Slatkin to come down from Los Angeles for a night or two.

On the plane crossing the Atlantic, Christina was thumbing through a magazine when she spotted an interview with Kausov in which he paid Christina many tributes but mentioned that he was attracted to fat women. She was incensed. The cruel and tactless remark had the effect of wiping out the small residue of happy memories she had carried from her third marriage. Feeling as though she had won a virile man in spite of her imperfections, she now learned that she had won him *because* of them. Instead of feeling attractive and desirable as a woman should who had been as well loved as she had been by Kausov, she now felt the instrument of an unsavory aberration.

When they arrived at the La Jolla club that evening, the manager told Christina that her husband was already there and was settled in her room in the large guest house reserved for her. So humiliated was Christina at the magazine remark that she had uncharacteristically kept her pain to herself, and her companions were therefore stunned when she announced in a loud voice, "I don't want him there! I don't want him in the house with me. Put him in a room in the club."

Without ceremony and with no explanation, Kausov was moved to a room in the clubhouse, a considerable distance from the rest of Christina's guests, and didn't learn his transgression until the following day. She partially forgave him enough to save the party, but occasionally the pain would return and she would mutter a sour remark like one she made to Clare: "I think I'll get on a plane to Tahiti and just leave all of you here." Another time she and Muriel Slatkin were sitting on a terrace over the beach and they saw Kausov strolling along in an outlandish gaucho's hat he had bought the night before in Tijuana, a bathing suit, shoes, and white socks, his arms and legs bare and slathered white with sun-blocking zinc oxide, as was his face.

"Oh, my God," Christina groaned. "Will you look at that, Chicky-Wicky? He looks like Jason in *Friday the Thirteenth*. It's too embarrassing. I can't be seen with him."

Cheered by the sea and seeing her old friends the Doderos, Christina eventually forgot her hurt and resumed the customary warm relations with Kausov. Clare knew that the crisis was over when Kausov, in front of the entire group, jokingly broached the subject that had started the trouble. Sitting on the beach, he appraised Clare's lovely bikini-clad body and screwed up his face in consternation.

"Look at you, Clare," he said with mock seriousness. "How can any man like you? You're so *thin*."

Eventually Mariya Kausov emerged from Russia and Christina obtained a Swiss divorce early in 1980. Kausov and his mother settled in England, where he prospered as a small-scale shipping magnate. He and Christina remained close as friends and, occasionally, sentimental lovers. Had any other Western woman fallen in love with a Russian, the romance, whether it succeeded or failed, would have attracted little attention. Because this particular East-West romance involved Christina Onassis, it became a *cause célèbre* and, for Christina, a painful lesson. She had always believed that her special position increased her chances of having her way; in this case it had lessened them. That Kausov was a Russian and a Communist had seemed to eliminate her biggest problem: being quarry for fortune hunters. But in exchange for a man whose motives she could trust, she had all but sacrificed the benefits of extreme wealth. She emerged from Russia determined to keep those benefits, revel in them, in fact, and find a man to revel with her.

In 1981, Christina fell in love again. Carousing one night with a group of friends at her favorite man-stalking preserve, the King's Club in St. Moritz, she was transfixed by a tall, slender young man with curly dark hair and a very handsome face. With her usual directness, she asked him to dance. He was Nicky Mavroleon, whose mother was Mexican and whose father was a wealthy Greek shipper; he lived in London in the winter and Greece in the summer. Educated in Switzerland and at Eton, he had graduated only a few years earlier. He was twenty-one to Christina's thirty.

Although his family was rich, Mavroleon's father was notoriously tight-fisted and his son had just enough money to place himself among the rich, but little to spend. He returned Christina's interest and they were soon, quite literally, wrapped up in each other. Young, uninvolved, and in a mood for adventure, Mavroleon was intrigued to see appear before him, in the disco's flashing lights and smoky murk, the world's most famous heiress. The obvious electricity between the two was the club's main item of gossip for the evening —not so much a matter of "have you heard?" as of "have you seen?" as chums nodded toward the latest Greek-shipping merger, the sensuously entwined bodies of Onassis and Mavroleon. At dawn, Christina took her new discovery back to the Villa Cristal, where, throughout the following morning, the Doderos, Basualdo, and other house guests calculated the ramifications of the whoops and squeals of pleasure coming from behind the doors of the main-floor master bedroom suite.

Some of Christina's friends were wary of the development for her sake—Mavroleon was too young and too good-looking. Basualdo, who had rapidly ensconced himself as Christina's chief aide-de-camp and wielded considerable power over her complex program for fun and sport, was fearful of being usurped and contrived to stay close by Christina's side at all times, even on the ski slopes, despite a painful back problem. It was not in Christina's nature to phase anyone out, especially when she was happy, and with Mavroleon she was ecstatic.

The affair raged throughout the St. Moritz season, but when they moved to Paris in the early spring, Mavroleon began to have misgivings, much as he relished the benefits of being Christina's favorite—not only the Cartier watches, Hermès jackets, and other fripperies she loved showering on those she liked, but more substantial things like a salary from Olympic Maritime, a sizable loan to pay off his debts, and the use of her jet to run errands around Europe and pay duty calls on his father.

It was on one of these calls to his father that the elder Mavroleon, playing a variation on the Germont role in *La Traviata*, berated his son for becoming the wastrel plaything of a rich *older* woman. Mavroleon was destroying himself and would have no future. Chastened and a bit frightened, Mavroleon returned to Christina and told her he wanted to move out and tone down their involvement. She reminded him of the loan. He said he would repay it when he had a job. Even during the affair's happy period, Christina had not been in the best shape emotionally—she had been plagued by depressions and had been seeing a psychiatrist three times a week. Now her spirits took a plunge and she spoke to friends of suicide, something she had not done before her previous attempts.

Her psychiatrist referred her to another doctor in New York, a specialist in depression. Christina flew there and was immediately diagnosed as having acute depression and placed in Lenox Hill Hospital. Basualdo, who found himself expendable in Christina's life with the advent of Mavroleon, had gone to New York and taken an apartment not far, as it turned out, from Lenox Hill. He now saw her arrival in his lap—shattered, vulnerable, immobilized—as a sign that fate intended for him to remain under the protection of the Onassis millions. Christina, who was delighted to have her good friend nearby, may well have come to the same conclusion. Visiting her every day, Basualdo worked hard to cheer her up with hard-edged gossip and picaresque versions of his own exploits among New York's stylish sybarites. Although cheering up Christina was something Basualdo did better than anyone else, his successes were short-lived and she quickly fell back into her near-catatonic gloom.

While in this nervous and emotional state, Christina received another visitor in her hospital room, Marina Dodero. A good friend since their teen-age cruise on the *Christina*, Marina had gradually become Christina's closest woman friend. She had not, however, flown from Buenos Aires to help with Christina's crisis, but rather to seek massive help in solving one of her own. Her father, she tearfully told Christina, was nearly bankrupt and unless Christina loaned her $4 million immediately, the family would lose their textile business. Christina told Marina she was too sick to think about anything so serious, to please wait until she had her strength back. Marina replied that she couldn't, there was no time. Christina pleaded to be left alone. Marina said if she didn't get the money she would kill herself. Finally, Christina relented and gave her friend a check for $4 million.

"Now, please, Marina," Christina said, "go back to Buenos Aires and leave me alone."

In the course of their discussions about the loan, Christina had asked that Marina and Alberto, to help her recover from her collapse, come stay with her in Paris after she was discharged from the hospital. Totally absorbed with her family's financial distress, Marina had been noncommittal, so Christina gave her the money with a string attached. She would make the loan interest free if Marina and Alberto would stay with her whenever she wished. Marina, Christina later insisted, agreed.

Aside from Marina and Basualdo, practically no one knew of Christina's presence at Lenox Hill, although she remained there for over three weeks. Certainly none of her executives at Olympic Maritime, whose offices were twenty blocks away, knew of either her proximity or her emotional collapse.

Back in Europe and feeling her strength had returned, Christina made a strenuous effort to restore her liaison with Mavroleon to the intensity of the first three months of their affair. He held firm to his resolve to be his own person, not hers, and told her he would not be coming to Skorpios for the summer as they had once discussed. Crushed, Christina invited Basualdo to fill the gap and spend the entire summer with her on the private island. On the condition that he could bring Clare, to which Christina readily agreed, he accepted.

Because of the island's considerable capacity for entertaining—it

could with Christina's renovations comfortably house forty guests—
she intended to make it her primary pleasure base and busily lined
up planeloads of guests to keep the island full of friendly and amusing
faces at all times. While this ambitious social undertaking succeeded
to a degree in distracting her from her heartbreak over Mavroleon, it
was far from a total cure. She telephoned him constantly and she
would indulge herself in such billionairess pranks as sending her jet
repeatedly to buzz his father's summer villa at Porto Heli south of
Athens when she learned Mavroleon was visiting there.

One evening on Skorpios early in the summer, Christina was
wrapped in after-dinner conversation with some older French guests,
leaving Basualdo and Clare sitting alone by themselves to one side of
the large living room in the island's main building. Basualdo, who
was a championship polo player, who had been married to the
daughter of a lord, and who had achieved further status as a formidable London party giver, was outraged at the slight. When later
alone with Christina, he told her that he and Clare were leaving.
Christina was stunned and asked what he was thinking of.

"You ignored us all evening. You can't treat us that way. We are
your friends. Your guests. You should treat us like equals."

Taken totally by surprise, Christina stammered, "What do you
mean, Luis? I treat you very well. You know that I do."

Basualdo acknowledged her generosity but said it didn't give her
the right to treat them shabbily. Tearfully, Christina made apologies.
When she assured him she would never again ignore him and Clare,
he agreed not to leave. Several days later when Basualdo thought the
incident forgotten, Christina said she wanted to talk seriously to him.

"Listen, Luis," she began earnestly. "About what you said the
other night, I spoke to my psychiatrist and he said I mustn't have
that sort of confrontation. It is very bad for me. I'll end up back in
Lenox Hill. So we figured out a way to see that it doesn't happen
again. I'll pay you a salary to stay with me."

As Basualdo remembered this conversation later, he said, "Come
on, Christina, I can't take money from a friend."

"You must," she replied. "It's necessary for my health and peace
of mind."

"Well . . . if it's for your health. How much were you thinking of?"

"I don't know. Somewhere around twenty or thirty thousand a
month?"

*When Christina met Luis Basualdo, an Argentinean polo player, in St. Moritz, they had a brief love affair. He would later become a fixture in her life and eventually a highly paid companion.*

In 1970, Christina invited several friends on a cruise aboard the Christina, acting as hostess for the first time. Many years later, Jorge Tchomlekdjoglou (left) would become her last romantic interest; his sister Marina (far right) was a close friend throughout her life. [13]

Christina turned herself into a blonde in a futile attempt to snare a frequent escort, Mercedes-Benz heir Mick Flick.

15

*Alexander's tragic death in a plane crash at the age of twenty-four shattered the Onassis family. His mistress, Baroness Fiona Thyssen-Bornemisza, whom Alexander had been forbidden to marry, attended his funeral in Athens.*

*In 1971, Christina eloped with Joseph Bolker, a Los Angeles real-estate man who was twenty-eight years older than she. Onassis was enraged by the marriage and marshaled his massive resources to crush it.*

16

*Within the space of two years, Christina lost a beloved aunt, her brother, her mother, and, finally in 1975, her father. At his funeral in Greece, she struggled to conceal her dislike for her stepmother.*

Soon after her father's death, Christina married Alexander Andreadis, the son of another Greek tycoon and a choice she mistakenly believed her father would have approved. The marriage lasted less than a year.

18

In 1978, with the cold war still intense, Christina stunned the world by marrying Sergei Kausov, a Russian shipping official, and moving to Moscow.

19

20 *Christina loved to dance, especially in Greece, where she lost all inhibitions. Here she is dancing exuberantly with husband Sergei Kausov even as she planned to end the marriage.*

21

*Single again, Christina spent her summers on her private island of Skorpios. Her spaniel, Yuri, was a gift from Kausov.*

22

*Often entertaining as many as forty guests on Skorpios, Christina insisted on being photographed with each of them. Here she is with her stepsister Lady Henrietta Gelber and her husband, Nathan.*

*A typical group on Skorpios, including three of Christina's closest friends: Claude Roland (right, foreground), Florence Grinda (left) and her brother, Hubert Michard-Pellisier (left foreground).*

23

Eleni Syros, who had worked for her father, was Christina's devoted personal maid from the 1960s and was with her when she died.

Christina's constant struggle to lose weight was a central fact of her life and may have contributed to her death.

*Christina loved to surround herself with Europe's beautiful people. At a nightclub she gazed at Philippe Junot, former husband of Monaco's Princess Caroline—and probably later picked up the bill.*

*Christina formed quick and intense friendships with women, as she did with Dominique Rizzo, here at one of Christina's large dinner parties at Maxim's, her favorite Paris restaurant.*

28a

*Christina's passion for her fourth husband, Thierry Roussel, was so intense that she was blind to his faults as well as his motives.*

28b

28c

*When Christina gave birth to a daughter, whom she named Athina after her mother, she felt Roussel had made her life complete.*

30

*While married to Christina, Roussel fathered two children by his long-time mistress, model Gaby Landhage. Forgetting her pride, Christina spent vast sums trying desperately to hang on to Roussel and even befriended Gaby, shown here with one of her children.*

*After Christina and Roussel separated, she rented a house outside Paris for weekends and devoted herself to being a mother, seeing only friends with children Athina's age.*

31

*Christina spent most of Athina's waking hours with her, lavishing on her daughter the affection that had been absent from her own childhood.*

*In 1988, Christina was planning a new life in Buenos Aires with the help of her old friends Alberto and Marina Dodero (far right). She threw herself into a romance with Jorge Tchomlekdjoglou, Marina's brother (left), whom she intended to marry.*

34

Christina's funeral in Athens, after her sudden death in Buenos Aires, was attended by Thierry Roussel, Marina Dodero, and friends and business associates from around the world. It marked the end of the flamboyant Onassis dynasty.

When in 1990 Thierry Roussel married Gaby Landhage as expected, Christina's daughter became part of their family. Heir to the Onassis fortune, Athina (in the foreground) will eventually become, like her mother, one of the world's richest women.

"To really help your health, let's make it thirty."

Within two days, Basualdo said, Christina had deposited $30,000 in his Paris account. Sitting in his Manhattan office, the psychiatrist who had treated Christina's depression was probably unaware that he had brought about one of the most fantastic sinecures in the history of human employment—one that was to incense Onassis executives in Monte Carlo and New York, few of whom made as much as Basualdo. For the next three years he and Clare shared every moment of Christina's lavish life, all of their expenses paid, flying on Christina's jet to Paris, St. Moritz, Greece, Monte Carlo, or for longer flights like New York, first class on commercial airlines. Every bill in a restaurant or nightclub was picked up by Christina, who seemed to feel that the large sum she gave Basualdo each month was to assure his constant presence, but it was to be the presence of a pampered guest. Any living expenses he might incur were something apart and were also her responsibility. All that was expected of him in return was to be available at all times for whatever recreation suited Christina—and not to complain if he and Clare were neglected for a few minutes.

On occasion Christina even gave him a bonus for a brief absence. When they were all living in the Avenue Foch apartment, Christina liked to eat lunch most days several floors below with Madame Michard-Pellisier, a wise and witty older woman whom she had appointed a surrogate mother and who was the real mother of her childhood friends Florence and Hubert Michard-Pellisier. Feeling she was abandoning Basualdo and Clare, Christina would give Basualdo sometimes $200, sometimes $300, and tell him to take Clare to lunch at Le Relais.

Strolling to the Plaza Athénée, he and Clare would take a table and order one apéritif. Assured that they had been seen there in case they needed a witness and checking the crowd in order to report to Christina who was lunching there that day, they would then return to the Avenue Foch and raid the refrigerators for lunch, often finding such interesting leftovers as truffled veal for twenty.

While waiting for Mavroleon to return to her life, Christina saw a number of different men. Some were merely old friends like Hubert Michard-Pellisier or Baron Arnaud de Rosnay; others were fledgling romances like Yvon Coty of the perfume family. After they went to St. Moritz out of season on a trial honeymoon, Christina pronounced Coty "sexually selfish" ("All he wants is to get blown") and ended the affair. Visiting Muriel Slatkin in Southern California, Christina had a brief fling with actor Jack Nicholson. Although they went to bed together more than once, the affair seems to have been based more on mutual curiosity than mutual attraction.

After this interlude Christina found herself rushed by one of Hollywood's most famous womanizers, actor Warren Beatty, whom she had met in New York through Princess Diane von Furstenberg. Resolved to play harder to get than she had with Nicholson, she saw Beatty a number of times, bringing him to Muriel's house for secrecy, but refused to go to bed with him on their first few dates. On about the fourth evening together, Beatty seemed so desperate, or perhaps so mortified at the threat to his batting average, that Christina gave in. Thinking her compassion had won her a friend for life, she was stunned when she never heard from him again.

Sometime later, Christina told this story to her friend Aileen Mehle, the columnist Suzy, who was visiting her in St. Moritz. "I never heard another word from him," she said, "no call, no postcard, nothing! Why are men so terrible, Suzy?" Mehle could offer little by way of consolation. (After Christina's death, Mehle wrote a poignant tribute to her friend and mentioned this exchange, without naming the actor.)

Christina was not always the victim in her sexual encounters. When her stepbrother and sister, John and Caroline Kennedy, arrived in St. Moritz as guests of Gianni Agnelli, she was delighted and spent a number of jolly evenings with them dining and nightclubbing. On one of these evenings, Basualdo noticed that Christina and John Kennedy, who had always liked each other, were enjoying each other's company enormously, laughing uproariously and spending long stretches on the dance floor together. Late in the evening, with Kennedy well in his cups, the two ended up at the Villa Cristal, where, Basualdo was careful to ascertain, Kennedy spent the night. When asked if they had made love, Basualdo replied, "I have no way of knowing for sure. Christina never said anything about it, but I know one thing, she was particularly happy the next day."

When she was in her Paris apartment, Christina's days fell into a predictable routine. She generally awoke in the late morning and had coffee and a light breakfast in bed, after which she would take a very hot bath. When she was dressed, she would meet Basualdo and Clare in the library to rehash the previous evening and discuss the day's plans. After her regular lunch with Madame Michard-Pellisier, Christina would take a rest, then order her car and, with Basualdo and Clare, make a chauffeured tour of the city's fanciest shops— Dior, Chanel, Saint Laurent, Givenchy. She would usually buy something at each shop, if not clothes for herself, then gifts for her friends. Finally, they would invariably stop at W. H. Smith, the foreign-language newsstand on the Rue de Rivoli, where Christina bought all the daily papers that had gossip columns and any new picture magazines that had arrived. They would then return to the apartment, where Christina curled up with her magazines and papers, avidly searching for shocking news of her fellow celebrities.

After the quiet period, Christina would dress and meet Basualdo and Clare in the library for a predinner Coke and decide if they wanted to attend any of the cocktail parties to which she had been invited. Most evenings she preferred to eat at home, perhaps with one or two other close friends, then after dinner to watch videos. A friend in New York flew tapes of *Dallas* episodes to her, and she was particularly fond of Sylvester Stallone's *Rocky*, a film she watched many times. On a number of occasions, Clare Lawman recalled, Christina suggested going out to see a film, but then, remembering the *paparazzi* waiting downstairs for her emergence, changed her mind on the grounds that she looked terrible or simply didn't feel up to being photographed. If, however, she had taken her strongest amphetamines, the *mavro mavros* (Greek for "black black"), she would insist, sometimes after midnight, that they all go to a disco.

Other times she would have an impulse to do something on her own minus her entourage. A close friend like lawyer and politician Claude Roland might get a call from Christina saying she was coming over and bringing her own dinner. She would then arrive at his apartment off the Champs-Élysées carrying a bag containing a huge broiled steak and a container of salad. The two would spend a happy evening together, Roland eating whatever dinner his cook had prepared, Christina her streak and salad, and then gossip and watch television until she returned to the Avenue Foch. Regardless of where she spent the evening or how late she returned to her apartment, Christina would usually want to talk with Basualdo and Clare and perhaps watch another video for an hour or two before finally going to bed.

Christina's appetite for the glossy magazines and gossip columnists was ironic. Her marriage to Kausov had undoubtedly netted countless millions for these publications, and they were counting on her for more material. As the reporters doggedly wrote up the routine marriages they were forced to cover—heiresses marrying heirs, counts marrying countesses, stars sleeping with starlets—they stifled their yawns and screamed inwardly, "Where is Christina now that we need her!" She never really believed in herself as a tabloid star, and when she was sprawled on her bed slapping over the pages of these magazines, she was just another of their millions of readers, perhaps more eager than most to gloat over the foibles and faux pas of the rich and celebrated.

When she did come across something about herself, she was thrilled. If she felt a picture was deliberately unflattering or something written about her was unfair, she would get furious, yet she rarely took any action, unless she knew the writer. Then she might pick up the phone, as she did with one financial writer who said her fortune was nowhere near as large as generally supposed, and treat the villain to ten minutes of screamed invectives, then hang up without waiting for his reply. She considered it bad form even to talk of suing.

That rule was put to the test when a scurrilous novel was published in France entitled *La Grecque*, which was about a Greek shipping heiress who lived a life of monumental lasciviousness and self-indulgence in Paris and on the Riviera. Many of the colorful details fit Christina precisely, suggesting strongly that the author had access to someone in her household, but much of the most sensational stuff was pure fiction. On this occasion, Christina talked about suing, but was persuaded that a suit would boost the book's sales.

Christina's tolerance for the liberties the press took with the facts of her life ran out when the popular Italian glossy magazine *Oggi* published a series of articles purporting to be the diaries of Christina Onassis. Never worrying that their readers might wonder why the famous heiress would choose to publish her innermost secrets, or not get an injunction if the diaries were stolen, the magazine went blithely ahead in the face of several public disavowals from Christina. Most of the material was innocuous and banal, based on loose suppositions derived from the well-known facts about Christina's life, such as "I often surprised my mother drinking and taking tranquilizers. For a child this is a terrible spectacle."

But the entries also contained a number of whopping impossibilities, like "The greatest desire of my father was that I marry Alexander Andreadis." Had Andreadis been a candidate while Onassis was still alive, Onassis would either have known of the family's financial trouble or learned of it with one phone call. And taking a particularly dim view of other tycoons' seeking to pull their chestnuts from the fire with his millions, he would have placed Alexander high on his list of suitors to swat. Having publicly denied authorship, Christina tried to ignore the series for a few issues, then, perhaps exasperated by some particularly hurtful piece of idiocy, she instructed her lawyer to warn *Oggi* if it continued publication she would sue. The next installment, which was to have been the last, was dropped.

For all the fuss the celebrity-starved European press made over Christina, she did not think of herself as a celebrity, certainly not when she was in the face of one she considered a *true* celebrity. She was returning to Paris from a party in New York with Claude Roland, who recalled that she was thrilled to learn that Elizabeth Taylor was aboard the Concorde with her. She had met Taylor a few times, Roland recalled, but doubted that Taylor would remember her, so was reluctant to speak to her. At Roland's urging Christina walked back the two rows to Taylor's seat.

"Excuse me, Miss Taylor, I'm Christina Onassis. We met once through my father at . . ."

"Christina!" Taylor cried and pulled her down to embrace her. For the next hour they sat together and chatted merrily.

"Christina was thrilled," Roland said. "But she never would have spoken to her if I hadn't pushed her."

By the fall of 1981 it had become apparent that Nicky Mavroleon was playing truant not just from Skorpios, but from Christina's life in general. She could not even get him to fly over from England, where he was living, to visit her in Paris. Finally concluding that he was breaking with her completely, Christina evolved a desperate plan. Her father had instilled in her a hard-nosed attitude toward press intrusions into their private affairs. "If they want to exploit us with lies in their papers," he would say, "that gives us the right to exploit them with a lie or two if it is useful to us." Christina announced first to Mavroleon, then to a columnist, that she was pregnant and he was the father. She didn't stop with that testimony, but besieged him with letters from doctors attesting to her condition, testimonials from friends that she had slept with no one else, and anything else she could think of to substantiate her story.

Mavroleon was furious and in October manfully flew to Paris to confront Christina with what he had little doubt was a complete fabrication. Never good at lying, Christina broke down immediately and admitted she had invented the story to win him back. Still angry, he left feeling that at least part of his debt to her had been paid. He was still angry when he was interviewed a short time later by the London *Daily Mail* and bitchily said that, while Christina's weight might cause people to assume she was pregnant, she was not. If she had been, he might have been responsible, but she was not pregnant and that was the end of that.

With this final and public break in their friendship, Christina went into a sharp decline, not the crisis of depression that landed her in Lenox Hill Hospital, but a messy stumbling through her days, woozy from barbiturates and mumbling about the life she might have had as Mavroleon's wife. She would sometimes sit and stare straight ahead for hours. Not only was she distraught at losing such a shining catch, she was deeply humiliated by the broad press exposure of the trite and shabby trick she had used in an attempt to block Mavroleon's escape.

For many nights Basualdo, Clare, and Eleni had to all but carry Christina to bed and undress her. Some mornings she was found to have soiled the sheets. Her self-esteem was at its lowest point. Her weight had climbed to 180 pounds, and she did nothing to help her appearance, not even combing her hair or brushing her teeth. When she would emerge from her apartment on the Avenue Foch, it was only after dark when she would insist on dancing at a disco if she had taken the stronger of her two mood-elevating pills, the *mavro mavros;*

with the weaker, the *mavro aspros*, she would have Basualdo take her to scruffy bars in Montparnasse or in working-class neighborhoods rarely seen by members of her circle.

Despite the double pain of having alienated Mavroleon and making a fool of herself in the process, Christina little by little put the episode behind her and soon recovered enough to refer breezily to the affair as "my Mavroleon madness." Unlike some of her fellow heiresses, who came to believe the importance the tabloid press gave their psychic ups and downs, Christina never lost her sense of humor about her foibles for very long, which undoubtedly contributed to her admirable resilience. Another commendable quality was her inability to hold a grudge—to forgive, forget, and move on to other things. Both Jackie and Niarchos had benefited from this facet of her character, which was strongest with men who had loved her and made her happy. In time, the good memories won out over the bad, the original attraction obliterated the final rejection, and former lovers like Basualdo, Kausov, and Andreadis invariably came to hold special places in her affections.

Predictably, she eventually resumed friendly relations with Mavroleon, even though her recovery was rocked by his falling in love with the beautiful Hollywood actress Barbara Carrera, whom he shortly married. Christina's forgiving nature was put to a hard test. When he came to her and asked her to help him out of another financial tight spot, she gave him the money, part of which he used to take Barbara Carrera skiing.

# 16

# EUROPE ON $100,000 A DAY

*W*hen Christina was living in her Paris apartment, her jet would fly once a week to Monte Carlo and bring back whatever documents she had to read and sign. It would also deliver back a large amount of cash for paying the week's bills. The amount varied according to her needs, but it was generally in the neighborhood of $40,000, a good portion of which would be given to her major-domo, Jorge, to dispense to the household staff and merchants. She also kept $100,000 in cash in a safe on Avenue Foch for any sudden expenses that might arise.

Larger bills, such as upkeep of her aircraft, were paid directly from the Monte Carlo office, as were the bills from the expensive Paris shops she visited almost daily. Even with such widespread credit, she always kept $1 million in her Paris checking account; when the balance fell below $700,000 the bank would automatically notify the Monte Carlo office, which would restore the balance to $1 million. Basualdo estimated that Christina spent in the neighborhood of $6 million a year, which would include the cost of running her establishments on Skorpios and in St. Moritz and Paris, outlays for clothing and jewelry, her travels, her bills at restaurants and nightclubs, and her "loans" to friends. Still, she was living well below her income, which was, even during the slump, at least six or seven times that amount.

Because one-half of the Onassis fortune had gone into a charitable trust, Christina was relieved of an obligation to make sizable donations to worthy causes. Each year some $50 million of the family fortune was already going to philanthropic projects. Had this not been the case, Christina would probably not have pursued an important philanthropic course on her own. Her generosity toward her friends was widely known; it was rare for her to turn down a request for money from someone she knew. But her compassion did not often extend to strangers. Also, her father had trained her to mistrust organized charities, insisting they all stole.

Whether a feeling of futility in the face of the world's pandemic ills contributed to her lack of philanthropy was not known by her friends, none of whom were overburdened with concern for the less privileged and never discussed the subject with her. In the world of Europe's rich in which Christina chose to live, there was little tradition of obligation toward the poor, or for that matter, toward the arts, education, or any other worthy causes. Unlike America, where private philanthropy has had a long and honorable history, charity in Europe has always been considered the responsibility of the crown, the landed aristocracy, or the church. The European millionaires who have proliferated since the Industrial Revolution, so rabid to acquire the styles and postures of the privileged classes, seemed to have had a blind spot when it came to a sense of obligation. The few who had charitable impulses upon which they acted were not the sort Christina was likely to encounter lunching at Le Relais or dancing at The Palace.

For all Christina's emotional debilitation in the period following her divorce from Kausov and her difficulties finding a stable relationship with a man, now her top priority, she never lost interest in the administration of her business empire. In 1982 she was elected to the Union of Greek Shipowners, the same group that had blocked her father from buying surplus tankers after World War II. She was the first woman to be honored in this way, which was appropriate since she was the first Greek woman actively to run a shipping company.

Like many of her shipowning colleagues, she was intent on scrapping or selling her less profitable ships and moving more and more of her wealth into cash. By the beginning of 1983, her fleet had shrunk from the fifty-six ships she inherited in 1975 from the even split of her father's fleet, down to thirty-eight ships, fourteen of which were laid up. Even with this deliberate reduction of her shipping operation, Christina was still ranked by *Fortune* magazine as the world's eighth-largest independent tanker owner, larger than any other Greek owner including Livanos and Niarchos.

When interviewed by a business reporter, a spokesman, identified only as one of her father's "oldest associates," was asked if Christina would join the large number of shipowners who were abandoning shipping and putting their money into other fields. "She'll stay in shipping" was the reply. The writer substantiated his source's flat-footed assertion by pointing out that Christina had recently named two of her newest and most splendid vessels after her dead father and dead brother and added, "She would probably sell her islands, her yacht, even her Saint Laurents and Givenchys before sending such ships to the beaches of Pakistan."

The first years of the 1980s were one of Christina's worst periods in terms of self-indulgence and emotional floundering. Still, she was by no means totally consumed by her own business and romantic problems. If she was uninterested in charity in the abstract, she would sometimes go to extraordinary lengths to help a friend in trouble. On a trip to London she received word that her former stepfather, Sunny Blandford, now the Duke of Marlborough, wished to speak with her on a serious matter. When they met, he expressed concern about his son James, who had succeeded him as the Marquess of Blandford. James had become a heroin addict and was, Marlborough feared, going to destroy himself. Ignorant about drugs and addiction, he understandably, if somewhat tactlessly, turned to Christina for advice.

Christina had been extremely fond of James ever since, as children together at Lee Place, she had sent him down her rigged waterslide into her bathtub. They had run into each other socially in subsequent years in London and St. Moritz and she had maintained without effort a feeling of family warmth toward the personable if volatile adult James. Christina told her former stepfather she had an idea. There was a drug clinic just outside Paris, the Château Gage, that was said to be having great success treating addiction. They would send James there. Sadly the Duke shook his head. James would never do it. He refused to have any part of such places.

In that case, Christina said brightly, we will trick him into it. Her plan was that she would invite James to have lunch with her in Paris, sending her plane to pick him up and take him home. Then when he arrived at the Paris airport, she would have an ambulance waiting with attendants who would take James to the clinic, whether he liked it or not. The desperate father agreed. When Christina phoned James, said it had been too long since they had seen one another, and proffered her invitation, he was delighted. To fly to Paris in a private jet, have lunch at Maxim's with good old Christina, and be home for dinner—not a bad way to spend a day.

When the day arrived, as the jet hit the runway at Orly and was starting to brake, James looked from the window and saw that an ambulance was speeding alongside the plane. Thinking that perhaps something had happened to one of the pilots, he was dumfounded when, as soon as the plane stopped, four burly attendants in medical jackets came on board, went directly for him, and roughly conveyed him off the plane and into the ambulance, telling him it was Christina's ruse to get him quickly through Paris traffic. When he discovered what was actually afoot, that he was being hijacked to a drug clinic, he was neither amused nor understanding, but went into a lordly rage.

Locked in a room at the clinic, he managed, with a teaspoon, to unscrew a grill covering his second-story window, jumped to the ground, climbed a wall, stole a motor bike and raced to a Métro stop. His wallet having been removed at the clinic, he cadged twenty francs from a pedestrian and got a train into the center of Paris, then another to the airport, where he used a credit card that was loose in his pocket to buy a ticket back to London. Adding to his urgency was his need for a fix. He had not had any heroin since that morning in London and was starting to feel signs of withdrawal. Once home and injected, he telephoned first Christina, then his father to lambaste them for their treachery and betrayal, sanctimoniously saying that, if they intended to help him, that was not the way to do it.

On numerous other occasions, Christina was able to divert her attention from the emotional void in her own life and focus on the problems of others. In the early 1980s, the sister of a good Parisian friend contracted cancer. Although Christina knew the woman, who was about her own age, she was not one of her intimates. Yet Christina flew into action as though the sick woman were a favorite sister. She visited the hospital almost daily, bringing expensive gifts from her new favorite couturier, Christian Dior. She paid for supplementary consultations with additional specialists, some of whom she flew in from abroad. She kept her friend's hospital room full of flowers. When the woman finally died, Christina fell apart emotionally and telephoned the bereaved family to ask if she might come to them to help them in their grief. Touched and somewhat surprised, the family agreed but found it was more a case of them consoling Christina than the other way around.

But Christina's sick bed siege soon brought her attention back to her own problem, the emotional void in her life. She fell in love with the doctor who had treated her friend. He was an attractive middle-aged man who for many years had been deeply in love with, and lived with, a well-known actress. Christina knew, and was repeatedly told, her feelings were hopeless, but it did not stop her. She did everything she could to be around him, and took to doing volunteer work in the hospital with which he was affiliated.

On the pretext of acknowledging his efforts to save her friend, Christina went to a Faubourg St. Honoré gallery and bought a Pissarro oil for $420,000, which she presented to him as a token of her gratitude. Basualdo recalled that on his drives through Paris with Christina in the afternoon or evening, she would insist that they park in front of the doctor's apartment building, where she would sit, staring up at his windows. Reveling in the pain of it all, Christina would say, "What do you suppose they're doing?" Picking up on the masochistic mood, Basualdo would reply, "They're probably making love," at which Christina would let out an agonized scream.

Not all of Christina's romantic impulses in the post-Kausov years were so fruitless. She began a flirtation with an exceptionally handsome young Italian gadabout, Gianfranco Cicogna, who seemed to be genuinely fond of Christina. But while fascinated by her exotic world of luxury and privilege, and relishing the adventure of running

EUROPE ON $100,000 A DAY · · · 269

around with a rich celebrity, he was not interested, according to Clare Lawman and others who saw him in action, in winning a permanent stake in her fortune. If not in love with Cicogna, Christina was very smitten and was thrilled to have him in her life. She even went so far as to lose substantial weight and got herself into very attractive shape for him. But when Christina began to feel the magnitude of the ten-year difference in their ages, the infatuation proved short-lived, as did the slimmed-down figure. Before long, she had slipped back into her depressed and self-indulgent ways.

So desperate was Christina for some sort of emotional anchor in the early 1980s that she seriously considered Basualdo's suggestion that she marry a friend of his, the Marquess of Bristol, who was well known to be homosexual. Christina liked Bristol, was amused by him, and was intrigued by the idea of expunging her Communist phase with a marriage into the English aristocracy. Tacitly giving up on the idea of a normally happy marriage, she would become a marchioness and the chatelaine of Ickworth, Bristol's magnificent eight-thousand-acre estate in Suffolk. Christina may also have been drawn to the idea of following in her mother's desultory footsteps in acquiring a title.

Basualdo arranged a few meetings in Paris and congratulated Bristol on the auspicious progress of his suit. But the scheme ran abruptly aground when Basualdo learned, through his network of spies, that on returning to London Bristol had said to a group of friends, "The first thing I'm going to do when I marry Christina is to get rid of Basualdo."

Almost immediately after hearing this report, Basualdo was alone in the apartment when a delivery truck arrived at 88 Avenue Foch with twelve-dozen long-stemmed roses, a token of intent Bristol had sent to Christina at Basualdo's suggestion. Tearing up the note, he dumped the flowers in the tub of an unused maid's bathroom. Bristol, having no reason to suspect interference, especially since his marriage broker was ensconced in the household of his intended bride, was stung to receive no acknowledgment of his marquess-like gesture and concluded Christina had decided against him as a suitor.

The episode with the Marquess of Bristol alerted Basualdo to the perils to his position should Christina develop a satisfactory relationship. Mavroleon, in fact, had almost ended his key position in Christina's life, as Bristol would have if Basualdo had not discovered his plan. At the same time, the Bristol episode brought home to him what a strong position he was in to repel usurpers. His presence in Christina's household began to take on a sinister hue. Although an employee, Basualdo had the proprietary instincts of a husband or a lover in keeping "rivals" at bay.

Basualdo became increasingly proprietary about Christina, especially in matters involving money. One January afternoon she had gone shopping in St. Moritz with Basualdo, a handsome young London socialite named Benjamin Clutterbuck, and two other house guests. They decided to stop for tea. After a pleasant hour of tea, cakes, and a few drinks, they called for the check and, when it arrived, Christina handed a one-hundred-franc note to Clutterbuck, who happened to be sitting next to her. Jumping up from the other side of the table, Basualdo grabbed the money and said, "I handle all financial transactions."

Rather than feeling menaced by Basualdo's zealousness in pursuing his role as number-one companion, Christina was amused by it, and she would sometimes add to her amusement by playing on his weaknesses. Once on a slow afternoon in the Avenue Foch apartment, Christina asked Basualdo to run down to the concierge to borrow her cat; she thought it would be fun to let the cat play with her cocker spaniel, Yuri. Basualdo was aghast.

"No way, Christina," he said as forcefully as he could. "I hate cats, and that cat is particularly nasty. I won't do it."

Christina was intrigued. "You're afraid!"

"So what if I am?"

"If I gave you a hundred dollars would you do it?"

"No."

"Two hundred?"

"No."

When she got to $500, Basualdo abruptly left the room. He returned in his heaviest overcoat and gloves, with a muffler covering his face. Christina roared with delight. At the street level, he rang the concierge's bell and informed her that Miss Onassis wanted to borrow the cat for a short while. The concierge declined firmly, saying, "That cat stays here."

Faced with the prospect of losing his fee, Basualdo offered the concierge 100 francs ($20). She agreed. Holding the puzzled cat at arm's length, Basualdo returned to Christina's apartment, where the dog scampered around the cat and got a few hisses for his pains. Christina enjoyed watching the animals cope with each other, but for her the fun had shifted to Basualdo. For the next few days, she told him to get the cat, which he would do, again paying the concierge 100 francs, and again receiving $500 from Christina. On the fourth afternoon, the cat had had enough and took a swipe at Yuri's nose, producing blood. Seeing what had happened, Christina screamed at Basualdo, "Look what that hateful cat has done! Yuri's been badly hurt. Get that horrible animal out of here. I don't ever want to see it again!"

As Basualdo carried the cat down in the elevator, he admonished it through the muffler covering his face. "We had a nice deal going —for the concierge, for me, and you got to see some of the world. Now it's finished. You've blown it." Basualdo hardened his credo that had been developing over some time: in the perilous world of Christina, it was every man for himself.

In February of 1982, the Greek government came after Christina with a $50 million bill for unpaid inheritance taxes. When the Socialists had come to power, they had vowed to go after the many rich Greeks who avoided taxes, and Christina, perhaps paying for the international notoriety her father had sought, was one of the first targeted. When she had presented the *Christina* to the former government in 1978, she had done it as a conciliatory gesture aimed at avoiding this sort of assault on her fortune, even though she believed she was not liable to Greek taxes. On the grounds that her wealth derived from a network of companies, most Panamanian but all of them foreign, she did not feel that she owed the Greek government anything. Leaving her lawyers to thrash out the matter, Christina paid little attention to the negotiations and assumed they would either tell her that her position had been accepted as valid or that it had been rejected and a settlement would be worked out.

She was, therefore, stunned and furious to be arrested at the Athens airport in August of 1983 when she was transferring from her private jet to a commercial airliner. She was wanted, she was told, in

connection with unpaid taxes. In a dingy room in the airport administration building, she was held under guard while her lawyers in
both Athens and Paris made frantic phone calls, only to discover
they had very little influence with the new government. Finally
Christina remembered a friend who was related to one of the new
ministers. The call was made and she was released. The government,
however, continued to press its claim and told Christina's lawyers
they were sending investigators to Panama to look into the Onassis
setup for possible tax fraud.

That information conveniently enabled Christina to cover whatever tracks she felt needed covering, but she countered the government offensive in more aggressive ways, primarily by letting it be
known that she was considering scuttling plans for the $30 million
Alexander Onassis Cardiac Surgery Center that the foundation,
which she in effect controlled, was planning to build in Greece.
Eventually Christina settled the claim for $6 million, but for her the
real shock of the matter, one that she had many hours to contem-
plate while being held prisoner in the Athens airport, was that in
Greece the Onassis name had lost its magic. If the Greeks seemed to
have run out of enthusiasm for the Onassis spectacle, however, the
family's sole survivor had not lost her enthusiasm for Greece.

# 17

# THE QUEEN
# OF SKORPIOS

*D*uring the summers of the late seventies and early eighties, Christina was in residence on Skorpios. Her Lear jet was kept busy ferrying guests from various cities—London, Paris, Geneva—to the Greek army airport at Aktion, where her helicopter was waiting to whisk them away on the fifteen-minute hop to the island. A car was sent to pick up the most favored at their homes, making possible a journey to the island without experiencing a public conveyance or waiting room. Baggage disappeared on contact with the Onassis forces and was not seen again until the contents were found neatly stashed in the closets and dressers of a Skorpios guest room. Once the plane was aloft, drinks and a sumptuous lunch were served.

Christina's guest list was broad. Close friends of her own age were the predominant strain—Atalanta Politis, the Doderos, Florence Grinda and her brother Hubert Michard-Pellisier. She also invited wealthy people who had entertained her lavishly as well as casual friends from the Paris and London party circuits. There would occasionally be relatives, like George Livanos, the young Niarchoses, the Duke of Marlborough and his children of various ages, old friends of her parents, new friends of any age. She tended to favor people with money, who maintained a high style of living, yet who were not terribly stuffy. Most were accustomed to luxury, but most were stunned by the level of it offered by Christina.

Because she was fond of children and enjoyed having them around, an effort was made to include children throughout the summer. A friend who helped with the guest lists saïd that Christina would often invite couples for whom she felt no particular fondness simply because they had appealing children. The island summers with endless streams of guests were for her a great joy, but they presented enormous logistical and social problems, for which she needed the kind of assistance that only a spouse or close friend can give. That was why she had to put friends like Basualdo on the payroll or lend the Doderos a large sum of money on the condition they stay with her—on Skorpios, or in Paris or St. Moritz—as long as she wished.

Intimates were invited for the whole summer, although few were willing or able to stay that long. Other friends were invited for a month and some for stays of one or two weeks. Many of those closest to her grew accustomed to spending their entire summer holidays with Christina on Skorpios. It made for a tidy abatement from anyone's budget, but especially from the budgets of those with a taste for private villas on the sea, round-the-clock service, a fashionable social life, unlimited recreational facilities, and a skilled kitchen staff, who placed before them three gourmet feasts a day.

Christina was a highly solicitous hostess and would not yield to her staff responsibility for her guests' comfort. Before each planeload of new arrivals, she ran from room to room checking beds, reading lights, ice buckets, making sure everyone had been provided with enough towels, fresh flowers, mineral water, cosmetics, notepaper, anything they might want. If guests ran out of an item not in the island storerooms, they had only to inform the majordomo, Jorge, and he would purchase whatever was needed on one of his frequent buying trips to the mainland. Guests were free to use the room phones as they pleased. Here generosity seemed to have no limits, although once, when Christina loaned one of her Paris flats to the Doderos, she was annoyed when they ran up a $15,000 phone bill in less than a month. She gibed them about it for a while but never asked for the money.

Guests were served whatever breakfasts they wanted in their rooms at any hour. In case the other two enormous meals scheduled for each day were not enough, Christina installed a food pavilion next to her private villa, which was accessible to everyone. Large illuminated refrigerator cases were kept full of cold meats, fowl, pâté, salads, cheese, fruit, every manner of fruit juice and cold drink. A cook was on call there twenty-four hours a day to whip up off-hours omelets or plates of pasta. A guest once opened a regular refrigerator and was astounded to see a stack of at least forty Lindt chocolate bars, the large size, stashed so temptingly near the perpetually dieting owner who loved chocolate second only to Coca-Cola.

Christina was constantly on the alert for ways to improve the quality of life on her island. One time she and her good friend Claude Roland were rhapsodizing about the pastries at the fancy food store in Paris, Fauchon. "But, Christina," Roland said, "your plane is going to Paris all the time to pick up guests. Why don't you have the pilot bring down pastries from Fauchon?"

Christina thought this an excellent idea, and from then on the refrigerated cases featured the most decadent and delicious fresh-from-Paris pastry. Roland nicknamed the food pavilion Fauchon and the name stuck.

Rather than quietly applauding Christina's concern for their comfort, some of her guests saw it as a signal to take grievances immediately to the top. The helicopter had kept them waiting, there were flies in the room, jet skiers woke them up. . . . Invariably, Christina would correct whatever had inspired the complaint. Publicly or privately, she rarely indicated she might be doing her guests a favor by inviting them into her charmed kingdom. In fact, she knew from unpleasant experience how difficult the most unassuming could become when catered to in so princely a fashion.

Christina, like many of the very rich, realized that those who accepted her hospitality often felt edgy and somewhat demeaned, whether consciously or not, about such a heady assault on their psychological balance. She was expected to see to her charges' every want, but guests pampered in this fashion were stripped of their ability to take care of themselves. They were economically neutered, reduced to a state of financial nothingness. The expensive house presents from Hermès and Dior brought to Christina were trifling in the face of $1,000-a-day's worth of hospitality per guest—assuming such hospitality was available for money.

Some of her guests delivered their complaints to Christina simply to announce they were used to the finest in all things, and they were not about to accept less from one of the world's richest women. With others it was a more generalized attempt to regain some of the self-possession their excursion into the precincts of great wealth had cost them. Christina was aware of this odd psychology to a degree and accepted the carping lack of gratitude as just another penalty of her good fortune. To keep problems to a minimum, however, she checked the rooms carefully.

Christina generally greeted arriving guests at the heliport, then turned them over to servants, who took them to their rooms, briefed them on meal hours and locations, and told them that gentlemen, because of the hot nights, were not expected to wear jackets. The new visitor would sit down for the first evening's meal thinking that he had arrived for a special-event dinner party with additional guests from neighboring islands and passing yachts. He would soon learn that three to five tables of eight people included no day trippers; thirty to forty was the normal contingent of house guests.

On Skorpios, Christina always awoke at one in the afternoon. Wrapping herself in a bathrobe, her hair uncombed, she would shuffle out onto the veranda of her private villa and throw herself into a deep sofa without glancing at the magnificent panorama of sea and distant hills. On a typical day, sitting waiting for her were Basualdo and Clare, who put down the newspapers they were reading and greeted her warmly.

Clare and Basualdo occupied the one other bedroom of Christina's villa, which was the island's room of honor. Christina would put only her most intimate friends there. If it was not someone in a paid-companion status like Basualdo, it might be awarded to an ex-husband like Sergei Kausov, a sporadic lover like Peter Goulandris, or a long-time girlfriend like Atalanta Politis. She hated sleeping with no one nearby, and if no one was on the island who merited such intimacy with the owner, she put her maid Eleni in this adjoining room.

As her day began, Christina reached for a white coffeepot that had been placed on the coffee table in front of her shortly before by a servant who knew his mistress's schedule. A tray also held a bowl of fresh fruit, sliced and artistically arranged, and a plate of toasted bagels covered by an embroidered napkin. Nearby were pots of cream cheese and apricot jam. Christina poured herself a cup of coffee and started spreading cheese on a bagel.

"Anything interesting in the papers?" she said to her companions.

Scattered about were newspapers from Paris, Geneva, and London. Each day they were picked up by helicopter from the Aktion airfield, but, even so, were a day old. Part of the hour-long wake-up ritual was to skim them for gossip with a relevance to life on Skorpios —which generally ruled out the papers' first ten pages.

"Binki Dupris got married again," Basualdo said in a bored tone.

"Good God," said Christina. "That makes her one ahead of me. I better get busy."

The main activity of this first hour of Christina's day was to rehash the previous evening: who was most amusing, who looked best, who was flirting with whom, who if anyone was on his or her way to having sex when they retired for the night. This last area of gossip was not altogether idle. Christina had an oddly puritanical aversion to sex on her premises, even among husbands and wives. She found it distasteful if any of her guests were too obviously enjoying each other's bodies after lights out. It didn't bother her enough to do anything about it—or perhaps she realized her authority did not reach that far—but she wanted to know what was going on and was not above checking sheets to learn if the privacy she offered her guests was being used for anything unduly physical.

Years later Basualdo was asked about her aversion to love-making among the guests. "It irritated her," he said with the indifferent tone of one who had long ago given up wasting thought on his employer's quirks.

Jorge appeared from the garden path that led down from the main villa. "Good morning, madame," he said in Greek. "Mr. Broun is on line four from New York."

"Oh, shit," groaned Christina. "He knows I don't like to do business when I'm on Skorpios."

"He says it's urgent."

Christina glanced at the white phone that was within easy reach. "Tell him I'll call him in an hour." Jorge departed.

Occasionally, a tanker crisis or a tempting acquisition prospect might wrench Christina into her business mode. If this happened, she would shut herself in her bedroom and talk on the phone for hours, ignoring her guests completely. For the most part, however, her executives knew that when she was on Skorpios she was on vacation; a matter had to be pressing indeed to justify interrupting the island's hedonistic preoccupations.

Not only did Christina shut out business when on the island, she avoided all personal contacts with the outside world. So focused would she become on extracting the maximum pleasure from her vast amusement complex she would wave off phone calls from even her closest friends—unless they were calling about plans to visit the island. When she was on Skorpios, there was no other world.

On this morning the gossiping was sluggish. The guests at the time were almost entirely old friends of Christina's about whom she knew everything, people who had been gossiped dry. Or they were solid, ultra-social types too cautious to provide grist for the morning-coffee rehash. At the moment there was almost no opportunity for ferreting out the kind of romantic cross-currents Christina relished.

After about an hour of chat and newspaper browsing, Christina went to her room to phone Creon Broun in New York, emerging five minutes later, now changed into a thin smock of white cotton, which she wore open over a pale green bikini. The costume did little to hide her enormous thighs and bulging tummy.

With Basualdo and Clare just behind her, she walked down the flower-lined path of inlaid stone to the main beach and swimming pool, where all of her guests were assembled, awaiting her arrival. Dark blue beach umbrellas and chaise longues upholstered in the same color made a sharp contrast against the white stones of the terraces and the azure pool water. Pink oleanders and magenta bougainvillaeas provided splashes of color.

Seeing Christina, the guests waved and greeted her with "Bonjour," "Ciao, bella"; some tried to wish her "good day" in mangled Greek. Those nearest her spot of entry jumped up and kissed her. The guests, since having been served breakfast in their rooms, had spent the morning chatting, flipping through magazines, applying suntan lotion—all knowing that at two o'clock Christina would appear on the beach and their day could begin.

Christina moved from group to group, exchanging kisses and

greetings, then settled for a chat with Hubert Michard-Pellisier and his sister, Florence Grinda, two old friends who had not been seated at her table the night before. They discussed the wedding announcement that was in the newspapers. After a time, Christina asked Michard-Pellisier to join her for a swim. As she made moves to rise, all of those in the group—whether nearby on the beach or further away by the pool—turned their eyes to Christina to learn her pleasure.

When she passed by her guests on her walk to the water, all of them had some winning remark at the ready. She laughed and joked with some of her guests along the way, touched hands with others. From the attention she was receiving, an outside observer might have thought this corpulent young woman was about to swim to Athens. All the guests and a few of the servants standing unobtrusively in the shade of the pool house noted her choice of swimming companion and calculated the ramifications—social, political, or sexual. Since Michard-Pellisier was not known as a troublemaker, the mood was one of relief.

Christina was an enthusiastic swimmer; even when her weight was high, she stayed in the water for long periods of time, often swimming distances few thinner people would attempt. On other occasions when she felt less energetic, she would select one guest, swim out with him or her to an overhead depth, then, treading water, gossip about all the other guests. Today, in a gossiping mood, she and Michard-Pellisier stayed out in the water chatting for nearly a half hour.

For the most part, the start-of-the-day beach scene appeared relaxed and casual—good friends congregating on their own beach with no threat of unwanted intrusions. Anyone familiar with life on Skorpios saw more in the tableau. It was the beginning of the grim-jawed maneuvers to edge closer to Christina, to rise in her affections or merely to maintain one's good standing. During the day, guests on the island pursued different activities, laughed and joked with each other, and, indeed, had fun, but at the same time every one of them kept an eye on Christina and awaited an opportunity to flatter and cajole.

One guest might ambush Christina with a bit of gossip gleaned from the pages of *Paris Match* or *Holà*, a story she would embellish with a bit of firsthand information that would win her an invitation to join Christina for her swim or at her chosen spot on the beach. If the gossip was entertaining enough, it might win a more favored dinner placement the coming evening. With similiar motivations of self-advancement, others would come forward with schemes for some recreational innovations for the afternoon, news of amusing doings at a nearby island, or word of a friend of Christina's in the vicinity who could be invited for dinner—although that was risky if Christina liked the transient enough to divert attention from the established guests. Given the isolation and the clear-cut power lines, Christina's Skorpios would have made a workable laboratory for studying human nature, or at least the nature of the café society subgenus she favored, when confronted with absolute authority— one whimsical, mercurial individual with total power over them all and from whom flowed such highly desirable blessings.

On this day, the guests assembled on the beach knew that Christina would soon emerge from the water and announce an activity— jet skiing, parachuting by motorboat, a beach game, a visit by Jeep to see the animals at the island's farm. Christina was quick to enthuse over any new form of athletic recreation. When she discovered jet-skis, the motorized water skis with a handlebar in place of a towline, she was enchanted by them. Even though they required considerable strength and skill to operate, she immediately bought twelve of the machines for her guests' amusement. Another year, the enthusiasm was motorboat parachuting, a sport in which the speed of a boat was sufficient to fill a towed parachute with air and send its passenger aloft. When Christina was seen circling the sky above her island, hanging from a bright red parachute, one guest risked being turned in by the others and dubbed her "the flying hippo."

By reminding Christina of their amusing, informative, or useful presences on her island, her guests increased their chances of being swept into the group who would join her for the chosen activity. Even those who preferred lying on a chaise reading a book avoided indicating their preference until they knew Christina's. Once she had made her choice, those not included or brave enough to beg off were free to pursue whatever activities they desired.

Today new guests were arriving and Christina wanted to greet them at the island's heliport. Coming out of the water, she accepted a towel from a beach boy, hurriedly dried herself, then, hearing the rhythmic thwap of her helicopter's motors as it approached the island, half ran up the beach to the road, where an open Jeep waited. Behind the wheel was a young island worker in a white T-shirt, with "SKORPIOS" embroidered in blue. Seeing Christina approach, he started the motor.

The arriving guests were Willy and Dominique Rizzo, a popular couple in Paris society and new friends about whom Christina was keen. Willy Rizzo had been a photographer and now had a fashionable shop of his own furniture designs on the Rue du Faubourg St. Honoré. His reputation as a man of visual taste and acuity had been strengthened by a former marriage to Italian actress Elsa Martinelli and now to the beautiful and vivacious Dominique, a slim, dark woman who could have been Christina's prettier and thinner sister.

A man in his fifties, Rizzo was born in Naples and had lived for many years in Paris. He was at times quite funny and, despite an easygoing nature, would stand up to Christina when she was at her most overbearing. Dominique was considerably younger, about Christina's age, and came from a mixed background that included Belgian, French, Jewish, and Arabic ancestors. Christina had known the Rizzos casually for some time. At a party a few months earlier, however, she and Dominique discovered they had both had their noses bobbed by the same plastic surgeon. They had shrieked with laughter at the coincidence and become fast friends.

As the Rizzos emerged from the helicopter, Christina rushed up and gave them such energetic hugs and kisses that she knocked her sunglasses askew. Willy Rizzo broke away and took some photos of his wife and Christina, laughing and in semi-embrace, standing against the helicopter.

"Was your trip down all right?" Christina asked as they walked toward the Jeep.

"Divine!" Dominique replied. "Your plane is a dream."

"Then, you're not too tired to take a tour of the island before going to your room?"

The Rizzos assured Christina they would like nothing better. Willy Rizzo got into the back seat of the Jeep and Christina told Dominique to sit in the front. To everyone's surprise, she did not enter the vehicle but clambered onto its hood, giving Dominique a view through the windshield of little except giant thighs and rolls of tanned flesh.

"I can point out things better from up here," Christina said as she indicated to the driver she was secure enough for him to start off on the way he knew she usually took on these tours. They went first to the island's small farm, which Onassis had installed for Jackie when she was still keen on horses. Christina kept it up to supply the island's kitchens with produce and dairy products and to serve as a depository for the occasional livestock impulse buying she was given to.

One of these impulses had struck the day before when Christina took her yacht, the *Alexander*, to the neighboring island of Levkas to do some shopping. Walking through the main village with Basualdo, Clare, and some others, she spotted a dwarf cow, no bigger than a German shepherd, in the back of a parked truck. She screamed with delight and ran to look at it. She found the driver, who owned the animal, and told him she wanted to buy it. The little cow was a family pet, he said, and not for sale. She offered him $500. No. How about $600? No. When she got to $1,000, the farmer relented and she turned to Basualdo, who produced the amount in drachmas and gave it to the man. Christina was thrilled with her new purchase and immediately had her boatman lead the animal back to the *Alexander*, where the crew tethered it to await her return trip to Skorpios.

Those who witnessed Christina in the throes of one of these acquisitive obsessions knew that once she decided she must have something her bidding had no limits, as her interest shifted from the coveted object to curiosity about the owner's threshold of temptation. What would start as innocent billionaire fun grew sinister and a bit ugly as the shadow of her father's everyone-can-be-bought credo fell over the negotiations. Her father, however, would surely have admonished her for displaying such open-ended determination, which—in the interest of obtaining reasonable deals—he would have considered a terrible reputation to carry around from island to island. It was bad enough to be known as rich, but this was crazy rich. But Christina's zest for both the item and the sport invariably overruled such practical concerns.

At the farm, Christina and the Rizzos got out of the Jeep to coo over Christina's little cow, then headed back across the island. Along the way Christina pointed out exotic trees—breadfruit, walnut, mahogany—brought there from around the world by her father's tankers. She showed the Rizzos pumping stations, generator plants, and all the support machinery that converted this arid rock pile to a bougainvillaea-splashed, jasmine-scented tropical Eden, a bastion of manicured beauty and luxury in a hard, raw part of the world. She took them to the cutting gardens that supplied the guest quarters with fresh flowers, also the herb garden that Onassis had asked his friend Lady Sarah Churchill to design to oblige another whim of Jackie's. They drove to the main harbor, where the *Alexander* sat sleek and gleaming white in the bright sun. It had nowhere near the splendor of her father's *Christina* but was still impressive enough to win approval in the lavish-yacht beauty contests at St. Tropez or Porto Cervo.

"That was a retreat my father built for Jackie," Christina told the Rizzos, pointing to a modest villa just slightly visible behind trees at the top of a rise. "I use it now for servants," she added contemptuously. As the Jeep negotiated the twisting, flower-banked roads, they arrived at a small, secluded beach that had been Jackie's favorite. "She did everything she could to get away from the life on Skorpios," Christina said. "She would rather have had her own island, if she could have gotten my father to buy her one, then leave her alone there. If I'd had the money then, I sure as hell would have bought it for her."

As they approached the main living complex, Christina told her new guests about the origins and history of the buildings, throwing in anecdotes about the celebrated figures who had stayed in them. At the top of the hill, she said, was the main building, in which were the living rooms, some guest rooms, and the broad terrace, where they would dine that evening. "Just below that," she said, "you can see my house. The small one. Behind that is 'Fauchon,' a kitchen where you can get something to eat any time of day or night you want." The Jeep swung up a drive toward the main house. "Now I'll take you to your room. It's big and breezy and has a terrific view. Let me know what you think. You're right next to Lord Weidenfeld. Tell me if he snores."

While Christina was off showing the Rizzos around Skorpios, a number of the younger guests led by Basualdo decided to go for a jaunt on the jet skis. A group of about seven walked to the harbor where the skis were stored and took off in a noisy exploration of the coves and beaches of the island. Resting briefly at a small cove, they decided to head across the inlet to Levkas.

Their entrance into the fishing port of Levkas was tumultuous and a bit reckless as several of the male guests gunned their skis between small fishing boats and pleasure craft. Everyone in the harbor stopped their activities to watch the Hell's Angels arrival. The Skorpios group pulled the skis up onto a small beach and went to an outdoor café directly on the harbor to have a pre-lunch drink. Spirits were high as the group relished the temporary respite from the nerve-racking Skorpios game of follow the leader. Someone said he was hungry and ordered a platter of fried fish; pretty soon everyone was ordering lunch, although they all knew they were expected for the enormous lunch that would be served on Skorpios at five o'clock.

After an hour, they decided it was time to return and rose to leave. The manager approached. Being in bathing suits, no one had any money, but in this part of the Mediterranean money was not necessary for Onassis guests, even if no Onassis was present. As they swept past the manager Basualdo simply said, "Skorpios," and the manager smiled and bowed them to the entrance, knowing he could bill Christina for twice the number of lunches served. For Onassis guests it made for a handy, one-word American Express card, which everyone abused with guilt-free abandon.

The guests left behind on the beach were delighted to hear that lunch that day would be served at the swimming pool. They had all come to dread Christina's penchants for picnics. These outings occurred frequently and would entail the entire group's boarding the *Alexander* and heading off to a remote and deserted beach on another island, usually one Christina had recently come across while jet skiing or motorboating. Two smaller boats trailed along behind the yacht carrying a many-course lunch and cumbersome support equipment, such as tables, chairs, umbrellas, portable stoves, and coolers.

Once at their destination, guests swam and sunned on beaches that were often rocky and uncomfortable, while ten men in white Skorpios T-shirts would scramble to set up tables and prepare the meal. After swimming, guests were usually urged to join Christina in exploring the rocky coastline; this did not sit well with her Parisian friends, whose idea of adventure was a taxi to the Left Bank, but, gamely, they usually fell in behind.

After as long as two hours they were told to take their places for lunch. Waiters with platters of cold lobsters or smoked-salmon pasta struggled to keep their balance on the slippery pebbles, as guests sipped partially chilled ouzo and forced good-sport gaiety on each other, while wondering why they were being subjected to such discomfort. Why had they left behind one of the most beautiful beaches in the world, complete with swimming pool, paved terraces, chaises longues, stereo speakers, handy showers, and flush toilets? But if complaints about travel arrangements and the island amenities were frequent—they could, after all, be remedied by executive order—few Skorpios guests were brave enough to complain about Christina's idea of fun.

At four-thirty, when the sun was at its hottest, Christina's guests began assembling under the vine-shaded stone terrace by the pool house for cocktails and *tapis*, the elaborate Greek hors d'oeuvres Christina loved and served every day at this time when there was no picnic. Some guests still wore bathing suits with shirts thrown over; others, like the group who had just eaten lunch on Levkas, had showered and changed into lightweight resort outfits. The hors d'oeuvres were followed by a lavish buffet lunch that looked like a tropical resort hotel's display for a *Travel and Leisure* photographer. Christina called to the Rizzos, who had been kept busy greeting friends and meeting others for the first time, to join her at her table. During lunch she announced she wanted to take them with her on an excursion after lunch, a visit to another island by helicopter.

If there was a disadvantage to owning a private island, it was the absence of two resort mainstays: shops and new faces. Christina overcame this lack, and appeased her own restless nature, by routinely setting out with two or three of her guests in her helicopter to one neighboring island or another. There she perused the tourist boutiques and took part in the early-evening *passeggiata* that is the high point of each day in most Mediterranean towns. This ancient tradition was now put to good use by vacationers, who had not come great distances to retreat to their hotel rooms each evening.

Tourists from Athens, Paris, and Berlin, once they had showered off sand and salt water, donned their smartest resort wear and strolled the waterfronts to show off their tans, window-shop, scan the harbor for newly arrived yachts, check the pedestrian traffic for noteworthy outfits, and, with luck, celebrities inside them. But the *passeggiata*'s primary objective, particularly for the unattached, was the same as it had been for centuries: to find, by a chance conversation or meaningful glance, a romantic attachment. This was the hour that Christina customarily chose for lively real-world visitations that kept her island enclave from choking on its own exclusivity.

Today, as Christina rose from the table, she signaled to Basualdo and Clare to get ready. When she made her way from the terrace to return to her villa, exchanging a word here and there, many eyes followed her to see who would be invited to join her for an island hop, which, given the helicopter's limited capacity, was the most exclusive Skorpios invitation. Since she had already asked the Rizzos, the craft was full and no others were included.

Loading Basualdo, Clare, and the Rizzos into one Jeep, Christina drove to the heliport, where the pilot had the aircraft's motors going. Once aboard with her four friends, she told him where she wanted to go. He nodded and, as the helicopter rose straight up from its pad, the view of the island was superb. The Rizzos excitedly pointed out landmarks Christina had shown them a few hours earlier.

"I thought I'd take you to Patimos today," she said. "It's a big place for tourists, not very chic, but it has some good shops."

On these outings to nearby resort islands, Christina loved shopping the overpriced tourist boutiques, where she bought endless presents for her guests, especially those left to amuse themselves on her island. A sweater for one, a necklace for another, sandals for everyone—whatever caught her fancy. She would easily spend a thousand dollars on joke items, a lot more for serious gifts. As they accumulated, shopping bags were handed to the helicopter pilot, who would either trail along carrying them, or if the load got too large, head off to stash them aboard the helicopter, then catch up with Christina before her new purchases got too heavy.

The flight to Patimos took about a half hour. "I love the way our landings freak out the tourists," Christina said to the Rizzos as they approached the island. "Watch their expressions as we glide down into them."

She also relished the stir her identity invariably caused. If her face wasn't enough to proclaim it to those who didn't keep up with the European picture magazines, her thunderous helicopter descent into their midst would alert the crowd that a personage of great note had arrived; the uninformed could quickly learn from others the individual's name. Similarly, onlookers had no difficulty determining which of the group emerging from the helicopter was the owner—not by anything Christina did but by the manner in which the others in her party played to her and awaited her cues.

This was particularly true of the Rizzos when they alit on the Patimos beach and walked toward the quai, not out of any excess of deference, but because this mode of taking an afternoon stroll was as new and strange to them as it was routine to Basualdo and Clare. Christina told the pilot she would be back in an hour, which he knew meant no sooner than one hour but might well be two.

The group examined the waterfront shops and Christina insisted on buying Willy and Dominique matching black sweatshirts in a shop where a woman said she could monogram them in fifteen minutes. Selecting gold thread, Christina asked that one say "RIZZO-1," the other "RIZZO-2." In another shop, she saw silver earrings she thought beautiful and said she would buy a pair for each of her women guests. They counted the women and decided they needed nine pairs.

"I'd better take ten," Christina said, "in case I forgot someone. I can always give the extra pair to one of the maids."

Because the shop only had five pairs of the earrings in stock, the group spent much time finding four other comparable gifts. After a few more shops and a stroll the length of the harbor front, the five friends settled in an outdoor café and ordered drinks. They didn't have Christina's first choice, Diet Coke, so she settled for a regular one. As the sun fell behind a hill and evening settled on the harbor, cafés and restaurants turned on neon signs that reflected cheerfully in the water.

It was eight o'clock and nearly dark when Christina returned to her island. She told the Rizzos she would see them at dinner and retired to her villa with Basualdo and Clare. If ever there was a "free" period on Skorpios, these few hours before dinner were it; even Basualdo and Clare were given off-duty status and could do as they wished without fear of failing in attentions to their benefactress or, worse, having another guest succeed in them.

About eleven o'clock guests began assembling for dinner on the terrace of the main house, where candles flickered between large pots of orchids and geraniums. A dreamlike view spread out below: the unobtrusively illuminated pathways winding through flowers down to the beach, the aquamarine rectangle of the lit pool, the yachts moored in the cove, and the lights from mainland villages, silent reminders of the other world shimmering across the water.

White-jacketed waiters stood ready to take drink orders as guests arrived on the terrace. The men were mostly dressed in the Mediterranean-resort evening uniform of razor-creased white slacks, espadrilles on otherwise bare feet and sport shirts freshly pressed by Skorpios hands. The women, as they did every night, had gone all out with jewels, hair coiffed into stylish shape by a resident hairdresser, and couturier creations that struggled to look both casual and worth their astounding prices. Even among long-time visitors, it was rare to see a woman wear the same dinner outfit more than once.

Each evening before dinner, Christina had an odd ritual of having her picture taken with her guests. A photographer was always on hand in quasi-guest status, but his duties were clear: when Christina emerged in her evening outfit, he would be ready to take her picture, often with a group but just as often with individual couples. Some guests were photographed night after night; since many of them were on the island for weeks at a time with little change in their physiognomy, little more was accomplished than to record the clothes or the progress of suntans, but it was done with a sense of purpose as though Christina were building a bank account of happy moments to be drawn on at some future date.

Another evening oddity was Christina's makeup; she would slather a strange white goo on her face that gave her the look of a Kabuki actor. While she was being photographed, she would stare intently into the camera, taking the whole moment quite seriously while her companions would be chatting or otherwise ignoring the camera. Although it was undoubtedly far from their purpose, these pictures made a sad record of her aloneness.

On this evening Christina, wearing gold earrings and a loose-fitting dress of fiery red cotton, looked particularly well, despite her excess weight. Her makeup was white and bizarre as ever. She grabbed the photographer and called the Rizzos. They went into the living room, where she sat them on a large sofa, then sank to the floor in front of them. Draping one arm casually over Dominique's knee, she looked intently at the camera as the photographer clicked away.

This done, she had her picture taken with other guests until dinner was served just before midnight. Christina, invariably with care and deliberation, seated her own table, allowing the other guests to sit where they wished. She usually rotated the guests from other tables for at least one meal at hers but not always, constantly having to keep in mind which guests spoke which languages. For all her willful ways, she maintained a sense of protocol, awarding places of honor to people whose rank she felt merited them—the Duke of Marlborough, a blood relative, or a close friend of her father's—rather than to those whose company she most enjoyed.

On this evening Christina placed at her table Lord Weidenfeld and the Marcie-Rivières. Rosemarie Marcie-Rivière was a woman of simple origins whose former husband had died leaving her stupefyingly rich. She owned elaborate houses around the world: one in Paris, two in Buenos Aires, one in Greece, and one in Rome. She was a flamboyant if somewhat controversial figure in international society, and Christina, who was half her age, liked her and invited her most summers. Christina's sense of protocol continued after dinner when she settled in the main living room with a group of her most august guests, leaving her favorite playmates—Basualdo, Florence Grinda, Atalanta—to amuse themselves in different corners of the room.

With the older, more distinguished guests, Christina was often subdued and tended to listen respectfully to the views and reflections of elder statesmen and tycoons. When she was relaxed and with people she was not in awe of, she loved to chatter, occasionally making newcomers frantic with her desultory superficialities. One woman was so exasperated she reported her frustration to a French journalist, who wrote that Christina entertained her friends on Skorpios by jabbering incessantly about nothing: lipstick shades, new fashions, a French film, never staying on any subject long enough to allow a conversation. The woman had obviously never before encountered anyone who took amphetamines.

Christina would usually remain for several hours in the living room chatting with her guests. Those not in her group of the evening were free to wander off to bed. Those favored with inclusion in her circle were obliged to remain until she was ready to retire, generally around four o'clock. Then she would rise, kiss her guests goodnight, and with Basualdo and Clare in tow, head down to her villa.

While the usual Skorpios day went from 1 P.M. to 4 A.M., the arrival of certain guests brought a change in this lopsided schedule. Foremost among those for whom Christina would straighten out her day was her uncle George Livanos, whom she loved but feared and respected. While closer to a brother's age than an uncle's, he was still the senior member of her family and the closest thing Christina had to an authority figure—certainly the only one she allowed that role. When he was on Skorpios, dinner would be served at a civilized eight-thirty and Christina would be in bed by one. Similar accommodations were made to a few others because of their age or importance, but not many.

On this evening, from the murmur of quiet conversations in the large room Christina's voice suddenly emerged to announce: "I feel like dancing. Let's go to Levkas!"

Although it was close to one-thirty, Basualdo was sent to the telephone to phone the disco that Christina liked on the nearby island and tell the owner to remain open for Miss Onassis's arrival. Basualdo also knew to instruct the man to provide free champagne for the customers already there to hold them until the Skorpios contingent arrived. This gesture also assured their reception would be warm and spirited.

Basualdo then phoned down to the Skorpios harbor and told the boatmen to ready the *Alexander*. As everyone in the living room rose, some of the older guests begged off the expedition and said their goodnights. Others disappeared to their rooms to change to outfits more suitable to discos. Within fifteen minutes cars and Jeeps were loaded with twelve of Christina's friends and the convoy proceeded to the harbor, where the *Alexander* stood ready, its motors running.

If Christina had not opted for the nightclub, she probably would have rounded off the evening with a video film. When showing one of these, it was not unusual, midway through the film, for her to pronounce in a booming voice that it was boring and order it stopped. Some of those who had experienced this said her reasoning was that if *she* found it boring everyone did. By halting the film, she was exercising her hostess obligation to keep the amusement ball in the air; those who liked the film could arrange to see the rest of it later. Others said that her thinking went no further than her own lack of interest, that she didn't give a damn what others thought.

The evening before, a film had been cut off midway through. When the lights suddenly went on, Lord Weidenfeld, who had been enjoying the film, turned to the woman next to him puzzled. She whispered that, because Christina disliked the film, it was being discontinued. Incensed at such high-handedness, the publishing mogul stormed off to bed without bidding his hostess or anyone else goodnight.

It was shortly after two when Christina's group arrived at the disco on Levkas, a large shed with open sides giving out onto the harbor. On either side of the dance floor were rows of wooden tables flanked by benches. Each was large enough for about two dozen people and generally accommodated several parties, which inevitably merged into one as the evening progressed. Strong smells of ouzo, cheap tobacco, cooking oil, and the sea mingled with the hot breezes stirred by overhead fans.

This night, the place was close to full and, as hoped, bursting with life. Since Basualdo's phone call, word had spread—the manager had seen to it—that the famous Christina Onassis and her island party were coming to dance. Stragglers at other cafés and restaurants all headed to the disco for what they knew would be frenzied good times, free drinks, and, perhaps in the bargain, a spectacle of billionaire decadence.

Christina was greeted as a beloved local figure with shouts and waves. The four-piece band struck up one of her favorite Greek songs as the group established a base at the long table held empty for them. Without sitting down, Christina, grabbing Claude Roland, headed immediately for the dance floor.

Christina loved to dance. She was good at it and, once launched into motion, was all but unstoppable. In Paris, when she abandoned a resolve for a quiet evening at home and headed out to a disco, she would keep the ever-present Basualdo on the floor until he begged a respite, at which point his girlfriend Clare would take over. If Christina exhausted Clare before Basualdo recovered, her maid Eleni would be pressed into dance-floor service.

On the Greek islands, where strangers danced with strangers and

Christina was stranger to no one, relief-partner problems did not exist. After she had exhausted Roland and several other men in her group, she was approached by local youths and continued dancing, sometimes to disco, other times to traditional Greek taverna music, which she loved as her father had.

As the night progressed, Christina remained the center of attention, no longer because of her wealth and renown, but because of her spirit and Dionysian energy, which surpassed everyone else's— all the more remarkable because she was probably the only person in the nightclub who was totally sober. Even the members of her party, who during the day were given to grumbling under their breath about her dictatorial hostessing, now found her breathless exhilaration irresistible and joined everyone else in having an unaffected, uncalculated good time.

The music grew more and more lively. Christina, who had been leading everyone on the floor in a classic Greek dance, now climbed to the top of her table and danced with wild abandon by herself as her friends seated below her and everyone else in the club urged her on with rhythmic clapping. She gave off a wild, animal vitality, stomping in time to the music, flailing her arms, and throwing her head back, a thick strand of black hair over her face and one well-formed breast hanging out of her flame-red dress. To everyone present she appeared fat and sloppy and extremely happy.

# 18

# AN ISLAND
# ABDUCTION

*L*ife on Skorpios was not always idyllic and a number of things could bring down the wrath of Christina upon a guest. Drugs were completely forbidden. She told her closest friends, "If I ever catch you or anyone else taking drugs, I'll ask you to leave the island and it will be your last visit." By drugs she meant those used generally for recreational purposes: marijuana, hash, cocaine. She never considered the barbiturates and amphetamines that she took, and that killed her mother, to be in the same evil category. On one occasion, island gossip and her own observations made it impossible for Christina to ignore the serious drug problem of a guest, a close woman friend and a prominent member of Paris society. Christina decided to let it go —provided the woman's behavior did not alarm the more staid guests.

Another potential misdemeanor was a display of sexual avidity—if a guest pursued other guests or, worse, the staff. She felt such carnal enthusiasms should be kept out of sight—off Skorpios, in fact—and as far as the staff was concerned, not done at all. More innocuous but just as dangerous was for a guest to decline Christina's invitations for picnics or to skip other group activities. If they did it more than once, they were risking Christina's displeasure.

The majority of things that would turn Christina against a guest would have rankled most hosts. Others wouldn't have. A guest who seemed to be having too much fun outside of Christina's immediate vicinity was courting trouble. Repeated hilarity at another dinner table, or at another group on the beach, or reports of the rollicking good time a left-behind guest enjoyed when Christina went off in her helicopter—any of those innocent happenings could trigger rejection fantasies and sour Christina on the perpetrator. Although she worked hard and spent vast sums to assure that her guests had fun, she insisted that the fun include *her*. To have fun without her was treacherous, even seditious, behavior.

When any transgression proved too much for Christina's tolerance, the offending guest soon found himself or herself being edged, quite literally, from the center of the Skorpios action. The first sign of disfavor was when Christina, making an excuse, would move the culprit to a less favorable bedroom. If the guest failed to take the hint and Christina's anger persisted, he or she was moved again, with a further weak excuse (there were bedrooms for forty), not from Christina herself this time, but from Jorge, to a bunk on the *Alexander*. This was Outer Siberia. The yacht sat in the main harbor, a long, difficult trek late at night; it was also hot and uncomfortable. When guests on Skorpios ceased to be comfortable, they ceased, whether or not they realized, to be on Skorpios. But the exiled could usually stay on the yacht until they decided to depart; her anger had to be fierce for her to order a guest to leave.

One summer on Skorpios some valuable jewelry of Christina's was stolen; she was convinced it had been taken by the lover of one of her oldest friends, perhaps with her friend's collusion. Christina did not confront the couple or ask them to leave. She did, however, make her suspicions obvious by not inviting either of these regulars to Skorpios for three years.

The jockeying for closeness to Christina, which started on the beach at the day's beginning, would continue to one degree or another until around four in the morning, when she indicated she was ready for bed. With so much maneuvering, it might have seemed impossible for her pampered guests to enjoy the good food, the sleek company, the gorgeous, flower-perfumed island, or the sparkling, blue-black sea. But all happiness emanated from Christina's favor. Without it, they were living on an ash heap.

There was a sinister motive for conniving one's way to Christina's side. Whoever had her ear was able to affect, to a remarkable degree, developments on the island. It might mean little more than a change in the day's plans, but it might also mean removing a fellow guest from favor, rescuing another guest from disgrace, wangling an invitation for an outsider, quashing one of Christina's recreational schemes. Christina's susceptibility to suggestion gave the social conniving of the island parties the refined menace of a Renaissance court.

And in this court, Luis Basualdo was its Machiavelli; no one understood better the strange setup or was more artful in manipulating his employer's quirks. One morning he answered the phone and found Christina's former stepsister and daughter of the Duke of Marlborough, Henrietta Gelber, on the line asking for Christina. Basualdo greeted her warmly and informed her that Christina was still asleep, but he would give her a message. Henrietta and her husband were nearby on Corfu, she said, and wanted to come by and see Christina.

Basualdo knew that, when Tina Onassis was married to Sunny Blandford, Christina and Henrietta were thrown together as stepsisters and developed a warm, loving relationship. He also knew that, if word got out to the other island guests that Henrietta was in the neighborhood and wanted to come to the island, instantly there would be lobbying and plotting to keep her off, not because anyone had anything against her—she was indeed quite popular—but because she would be an interloper who might upset the island's fragile social balance.

Had guests learned that the helicopter was being sent to Corfu to pick her up, Basualdo knew from long experience an immediate outcry would go up:

"Oh, Christina, we are too many already. Why invite more?"

"But, dearest, you told us *we* could take the helicopter this afternoon."

Enough displeasure and confusion would be thrown into the air so that Christina, in the interest of island tranquillity and her own peace of mind, would fabricate an excuse to deflect Henrietta, then make a mental note to call her for lunch in London.

To get Henrietta onto the island, Basualdo knew he had to plot carefully. Before hanging up he told her to be at the Corfu airport with her husband at four that afternoon; he would arrive by helicopter to pick them up. Then he casually mentioned to Christina over her wake-up coffee that Henrietta had called from Corfu.

"Henrietta?" said Christina with excitement. "How wonderful. Did you ask her to come over?"

"No," Basualdo lied, "but I have her hotel number. Why don't I take the helicopter and collect them this afternoon?"

"Terrific," said Christina. "I haven't seen her for ages. I can't wait."

Basualdo knew that obtaining Christina's O.K. was the easy part of his plan. That, in fact, was the trouble—any guest could persuade Christina to agree to anything; they had only to get her ear with no others nearby who might argue against the suggestion. For Basualdo's plan, the difficult part was keeping Henrietta's arrival secret from everyone on the island until he and the helicopter were airborne and beyond the reach of intrigue.

He suggested to Christina that they keep Henrietta's arrival secret to make it a surprise for dinner that night. Knowing how well liked she was, Christina thought it was a fine idea. Basualdo chased down the pilot, told him of Christina's wishes, of the errand's secret nature, and said to meet him at the heliport at 3 P.M.

That afternoon, as the helicopter blades thwapped into motion and Basualdo ascended triumphantly into the air above Skorpios, he could see the consternation his ascent was causing below. Guests on the beach and by the pool jumped up, shielded their eyes against the sun, frantic to see who was aboard the helicopter and where it was headed. Why hadn't they been told? Where was Basualdo going? What was going on?

Henrietta had a delightful visit on Skorpios. Both she and Christina were thrilled to revive the closeness that had come to a natural end with their parents' divorce. Seeing the pleasure her arrival gave Christina, the other guests were charming to Henrietta. She never knew the difficulties Basualdo later boasted had to be overcome to get her onto the island. He didn't do it entirely for Henrietta, he would later admit; he had always "rather fancied her." Had the call been from some friend or former sister Basualdo did not fancy, perhaps he would not have bothered to scheme so assiduously or, indeed, to report the call to Christina at all.

Christina was not oblivious of Basualdo's machinations. She cornered him one day and said, "Listen, Luis, my friends all tell me you are terrible for me, especially as far as men are concerned. You won't let anyone get close to me for fear you'll lose your job. If that's your worry, let me tell you right now, if I get involved with someone, whether or not through you or on my own, I will pay you ten times the $30,000 a month I give now." As usual when confronting a flaw in one of her costly schemes, her remedy was *more money*.

Basualdo knew that the offer was not hyperbole, that Christina would have happily given him $300,000 if she landed in a satisfactory relationship. Recounting her offer after her death, he said almost as an afterthought, "But of course I still kept them away."

If a man was being too attentive to Christina or she appeared too interested, Basualdo would start a quiet campaign of destruction: "He's funny looking." "He's a fortune hunter." "He has a criminal record." He would put in her ear whatever was needed to curdle her enthusiasm, and it rarely took much, perhaps in the belief that, as with various diseases, love can be arrested if caught early. Basualdo later felt guilty about fending off Christina's prospects, but at the time, he said, he thought only of protecting his stupendous deal.

For the most part, Skorpios was free of such high-level romantic manipulations. Christina's guest list, since most of her friends were married or involved, was made up largely of couples. The single males were either old friends or former lovers with whom there was little chance of conflagration. By carefully considered invitations, she could have used the island as a man trap, issuing casual invitations to every eligible man she encountered during the winter, then, once they were in her kingdom, sorting them out for the play-offs. But she seemed to go to pains to avoid such schemes. It was as though, on Skorpios, she wanted a vacation from *all that*.

It was mostly for less sinister reasons that on the island Basualdo rarely let Christina from his sight. Aside from the fear that someone would talk Christina into a harebrained activity in which they would all have to participate, his main concern was that someone would malign him and weaken his position as favorite or, should some society Siegfried appear who knew no fear, perhaps try to usurp it. He claimed that every time Christina escaped his vigilance something terrible happened. And Basualdo, of course, had a highly subjective sense of what constituted "terrible."

Late one hot and bright afternoon about six when Christina and her guests were leaving the lunch table, she announced that she was in the mood to go exploring in the helicopter—not any of the usual haunts, but someplace new, a bit further from Skorpios. Basualdo and Clare came forward, ready for duty. Christina contemplated them for a moment, then said, "You stay here today, Luis. I think Clare looks tired. She should rest and you should stay with her."

Basualdo and Christina exchanged glances. It was one of the rare moments when the delicate matter of who was controlling whom came to the surface, and both knew it.

"Oh, no, Christina, Clare's not tired," Basualdo replied while he appraised the dangers. Such displays of independence did not occur often, but when they did, Basualdo knew, they usually meant trouble. "We're happy to come with you."

"No," Christina said with a hint of firmness. "Take Clare for a nap and we'll see you later."

Basualdo thought for a moment, then decided the matter was not important enough to contest. Christina marshaled three of the other guests and the group headed off to their rooms to prepare for the expedition. Aloft in the helicopter Christina told the pilot to head north along the coast while they discussed possible destinations. Suggestions were offered and rejected. Then someone suggested they visit the Club Méditerranée on Corfu. "Oh, no," said a guest. "It will be full of overexcited secretaries from Düsseldorf."

"Sounds splendid," said a male member of the group.

"Oh, yes," Christina said. "It will be hysterical. Let's go!"

It took about an hour to reach the island as the helicopter swooped and dipped over dark green islands that dotted the brilliant blue water. When they approached Corfu, Christina told her pilot to find the Club Med and determine the best place to land. Although it was close to seven in the evening, the broadest beach still had many bathers, but there were enough empty areas to make a landing feasible, or rather, well mannered; a helicopter had only to roar its rotors over a spot then descend gradually to make its landing intentions clear to the people below. Christina's pilot knew to seek a spot close to whatever appeared to be the center of action, so she would not find herself isolated with no transportation. An additional motive was his employer's liking for the sensation her descents always caused.

The crowds on this beach, unlike the islanders near Skorpios, were unfamiliar with Christina's clamorous arrivals from the skies, and were mesmerized. As the helicopter descended to the beach, all the bathers were on their feet, pointing, shielding their eyes from the late-afternoon sun, asking what it all meant. When Christina and her party emerged from the helicopter onto the warm sand, she waved at the crowd, who responded with applause. Word of her identity was passed from group to group.

They had landed, as hoped, on the Club Méditerranée beach. They asked some bathers the location of the clubhouse and were pointed toward a long, low building on a hill above the beach. They followed a bougainvillaea-lined path up the rise and found a terrace bar overlooking the beach. Settling at a table, they ordered drinks and appraised the parade of near-naked and oil-slick bodies passing in front of them as bathers strolled to the hotel. When the drinks arrived, the Skorpios group began a game of guessing women's occupations by the size and shape of their navels. After a half hour, they left the bar and browsed in two nearby shops. For once Christina bought nothing.

Ready to leave, they strolled down the hill toward the beach, which now had only a few stragglers. As they were crossing the sand to the helicopter, a thin dark-haired boy holding a camera stood in their path. He looked about seventeen and wore a red bikini. With deeply tanned skin and a lithe body, he had the nondescript good looks of thousands just like him who cover Mediterranean beaches from Gibraltar to Algiers. Looking grave, he came up to Christina and, ignoring the others, said, "*Êtes-vous Christina Onassis?*"

She said that she was.

Continuing in French he said, "Would you mind if I had my picture taken with you?"

Surprised, Christina contemplated him for a moment, then broke into a happy smile. "Of course, I would be delighted to be photographed with you."

Still serious, the boy said, "Perhaps we could stand next to your helicopter?"

"Certainly."

They walked to the craft, and silently the boy handed the camera to one of Christina's group with an expression of request.

As they were standing stiffly by the helicopter, the boy suddenly put his arm around Christina's shoulder. Startled and amused, she looked at him. "What's that on your head?" she said.

"It's a yarmulke," he said. "I'm Jewish."

"You're Jewish even when you go swimming?"

"Always," he replied without smiling.

Christina asked her pilot to take a photo of them with her camera. When he was finished, she asked the boy his name.

"Dovi."

"Tell me, Dovi," she said, "how would you like to come to my island."

"I would like to very much sometime."

The others in the group exchanged alarmed glances. The boy was not a type that usually interested Christina. Youth was not an attribute that attracted her. Still, they recognized the signs that she was moving into amatory gear.

"Not sometime, I mean now. Come back with me."

"That is not possible. My clothes, they are up the hill at the club."

"Just come in your bathing suit. We can fix you up with clothes. I'll send my pilot back for your things tomorrow morning."

The boy stared at her expressionless. "All right."

When the group was aboard the helicopter, the motors chugged into action and, slowly, majestically, they rose noisily from the beach. Hera, emulating her husband, had plucked a naked Ganymede from the crowd of earthlings and was transporting him to Mount Olympus.

Around ten o'clock that evening on Skorpios, Eleni rushed up to Basualdo, who was dressed for dinner and reading a newspaper on the loggia of Christina's villa. "Oh, monsieur, monsieur, the most terrible thing has happened."

Basualdo, convinced he should not have let Christina go off without him, said, "What now, Eleni?"

"Madame has come back with a little Jewish boy who has no clothes on."

Basualdo put down his paper and prepared for action. Christina came rushing in. "Oh, Luis," she gushed, out of breath. "It's incredible. I met this fabulous young boy. He's from Marseilles, he's actually from Tunis but his family has moved to Marseilles. His father's a rabbi. Isn't that fantastic?"

Basualdo, who shared with Christina an impatience with unimportant facts, got to the point. "Do you want to go to bed with him?"

"Of course. He's the most adorable thing I've ever seen. I've put him in the room next to the Fraziers. His name is Dovi. He came only in his bathing suit. I want you to lend him a shirt to wear to dinner."

"No pants?"

"He's much thinner than you. I've asked Gilles to lend him a pair. Take the shirt right now. I can't wait to see how he looks cleaned up with his hair combed."

Neither can I, thought Basualdo, as he went into his room and began riffling through his large assortment of shirts, looking for one that hadn't been expensive. To his great annoyance, he couldn't find one, so pulled out an Armani he didn't much care for. When he delivered the shirt to Dovi, Basualdo was as charming to him as possible, saying later, "You never know when someone like that might emerge in a position of power."

At predinner drinks, Christina, who was at her most overweight, looked radiant. Word of the abduction she had staged had reached every chaise longue, guest room, and stall shower of Skorpios in a matter of minutes. Now, as her guests congregated on the terrace, they giggled nervously about Christina's "souvenir" from the tourist island, keeping one eye on the path leading up to the main villa, awaiting his arrival. No one said anything to Christina about the development, but one Frenchman told her in a voice heavy with innuendo that she was looking particularly "ravishing," a slight pun that worked as well in French as English.

Suddenly Dovi was among them. Having lost his way, he had entered the main house through the kitchens, where he had gone to ask directions, and emerged through the living room onto the terrace. Lighting up when she saw him, Christina introduced Dovi to each conversational group as though he were an old friend of the family. Then, to Basualdo's relief, she deposited him with the last cluster of guests she came to and, from then on, seemed to ignore him.

Christina pulled Basualdo aside. "Isn't he beautiful?"

"Not to me. He's a little boy, and so thin . . ." Before Basualdo had a chance to dream up a criminal record, Christina had moved on.

At dinner Basualdo was further encouraged when Christina sat her protégé not with her but at a table that was clearly the "Z" table, made up of children, friends of friends, and others she didn't know what to do with. Dovi's dinner-table conversational thrusts were limited to such blunt requests for information as "Where does she get the money?" and "How much is she worth?"

After dinner, Christina continued to neglect her discovery and focused her attention instead on a number of older guests from Paris. It didn't trouble her in the least that she was leaving to others in her house party the difficult task of making conversation for hours with someone who, in terms of common interests, could have dropped in from Saturn. His last name was Tubrussi, and it was learned that his family had moved from Tunis to Marseilles about five years previously and he was a second-year medical student. His father, although a rabbi, didn't have a proper congregation, and the family was poor. He was the youngest of many brothers and sisters.

As on most nights on Skorpios, Christina continued chatting with the group assembled around her in the living room until about four in the morning. When she rose, the others kissed her goodnight and left for their rooms. She rushed to Basualdo.

"Where is Dovi? I don't see him!"

Basualdo said that he had apparently gone to bed.

"But he can't! I'm crazy about him. I want to see him. Go get him."

Basualdo tried to protest about the hour, that the boy was too young to understand her urgency. Christina cut him off. "Get him. I've got to have him. I'll go to my room and wait there."

Exhausted, Basualdo walked down the hill to Dovi's room and knocked on the door. He knocked again. After a few moments, he opened the door. The room was empty, the bed still made.

He returned to Christina. "Looks like you're out of luck. Somebody's beaten you to it."

"What do you mean?"

"He's not in his room."

"What?" Christina was frantic. "Wake everyone up! We must stop . . ."

Basualdo calmed her down and said he would find Dovi. On a hunch, he walked down toward the beach. As he approached the pool area, he could hear giggles. In the dim light of dawn, he saw Dovi stretched out on a single chaise with his arms around the young daughter of friends of Christina's. Both were dressed.

Making as much noise as a solitary stroller can make, Basualdo strode onto the moonlit terrace. Feigning surprise to discover them there, he apologized for his intrusion but made no move to leave. The girl, fumbling with her blouse buttons, scrambled to her feet and ran off toward the guest wing. Confused and a little drunk, Dovi said he too had to go to bed.

Happy to have averted disaster, Basualdo climbed the path to Christina's pavilion. She was frantic to know what had happened.

"He was with Marie Clare."

"Were they having sex?" she asked without breathing.

"About to."

"What did you do?"

"I made noise and they both ran off in different directions."

"Good. Now go get him."

"But, Christina, you don't know if he's . . . capable."

"You mean 'interested.' You're right. How will I know? I've got an idea. Bring him up here and I'll make some sign to him, put my arm around him or something. If he seems to respond, I'll give you a signal. I'll say, 'Wasn't it a nice day today, Luis?' and you go to bed. If he doesn't respond, I'll say, 'I hope it's a nice day tomorrow,' and you take him back to his room. Then you can get rid of him tomorrow."

Basualdo returned to Dovi's room to find him in bed asleep. Waking him, he said that Christina wanted to see him. The boy said it was too late and he was too tired. Sitting on the edge of the bed Basualdo said, "She likes you."

"I like her too," replied Dovi with no hint that his liking was in the same category as Christina's, or that the weight he gave to Christina's approbation was similar to what it was for Basualdo.

"Come on," Basualdo urged, "we can have some breakfast and conversation. She's waiting for you." Dovi pulled on his borrowed pants and shirt, and manfully followed Basualdo out into the Skorpios daybreak.

Christina greeted him cheerfully, full of pep and chat, no sign that it was five in the morning. Dovi got into the swing of the odd social event and sat beside her on a deep sofa. He declined anything to eat but joined her in a Coke. They made desultory conversation as Christina twisted a strand of her dark hair on a finger, a chronic gesture when she was a teenager but now only seen when she was thinking of two things at once. After the three chatted for a few minutes, Christina placed her hand on Dovi's thigh and stroked it gently.

"Are these Gilles's pants?" she said softly. "They're very nice. They look well on you."

Dovi immediately moved closer to Christina and, her voice catching, she remarked to Basualdo what a nice day it had been.

Three hours later, about eight-thirty in the morning, Christina burst into Basualdo's room. "Luis, wake up. He's fantastic. You said he wasn't attractive. He's a god! Three times in three hours!"

Dovi's clothes were picked up, and for the three days he had remaining in his vacation, Christina was extremely happy. Bacchus had arrived to rescue Ariadne from boredom and grief. Often abandoning the other guests, Christina and Dovi swam, went for afternoon cruises in the *Alexander*, and made frequent love. At meals and the few other occasions when they were with the others, particularly the older group from Paris, she was discreet and paid no more attention to Dovi than to her friends' children. She considered her affair illicit and relished that aspect and what she saw as a need for subterfuge. Of course everyone on the island knew of the joy that had struck their hostess.

Christina spoke by phone to Dovi's father. She wanted to take him to Paris with her and transfer him to a medical school there. The father replied that he could not consider giving up Dovi, who was "*le soleil de la famille.*" He was adored by all, so the family had to stay together. Christina tried another tack. Would monsieur allow her to move the entire family to Paris?

"We are too many."

"How many?"

"Thirteen."

Christina said that would cause no problems. Stunned, Dovi's father said he would consider the proposal.

Later she whooped with laughter to a group of friends who knew her plans. "Thirteen of them? Can you imagine? No family has thirteen people. Do you think they are taking the neighbors?" Christina immediately got on the phone to influential friends in Paris who could help with Dovi's transfer.

When the day arrived for Dovi to leave for Marseilles, Christina said he had to phone her daily. She was going to St. Moritz in a few days and she gave him that number.

"But, madame," Dovi said, "I am a poor medical student. It costs a lot of money to telephone to Switzerland."

Christina whispered something to Eleni, who left and returned almost immediately with a white envelope. Christina handed it to Dovi.

"Here's $10,000. Now you have no excuse not to phone me every day."

"Madame is most generous," Dovi replied formally.

Dovi was sent off by helicopter, which stopped at the Club Méditerranée so he could check out, then took him on to Aktion military airport, from where Christina's jet flew him, alone, to Marseilles.

The next day, Dovi telephoned as promised. Christina was thrilled to hear from him and they spoke for half an hour. The following day Christina, Basualdo, and Clare flew in her jet to St. Moritz, to which she often retreated late in the summer to escape the heat and the routine of Skorpios. When the group was settled in the Villa Cristal, a telephone call came from Dovi. Surely with coaching from his family, who may have decided his new girlfriend was too insane to notice, he called collect.

In order to keep within bounds, and perhaps reduce, her pill dependency, Christina would take her regular dose for two days, then nothing on the third day. Frequently on the nonpill days, she would seek to bolster her mood by traveling to Vienna, Madrid, or whatever place sparked her fancy—and her fancy more often than not would be sparked by a magazine photo or a gossip-column item that reminded her of pleasure she had experienced in a particular place.

Generally these trips would last only a day—she would return home in time for dinner—but this was never certain. On this visit to St. Moritz, when the first of her drug-free days loomed, Christina announced to Basualdo and Clare they were going to Venice for the day; they should be ready to leave by 8 A.M. She also brought her nurse, Véronique, whom she had hired to administer her pills and occasional shots and who was now with her constantly.

Emerging from the Venice airport, Christina and her party boarded a boat taxi. Never one to chat up waiters and the legions of service people who eased her path, Christina took an immediate liking to the driver, a rotund and jovial man about sixty named Robertino, who made constant jokes in splintered English and French that no one understood. Every time Robertino spoke, Christina laughed uproariously and insisted he accompany them everywhere.

Arriving at the Piazza San Marco, Christina told the pilot and Véronique to meet them at the Hotel Gritti at five o'clock, then with Basualdo, Clare, and Robertino she strolled the alleys of expensive shops, where she bought an antique bracelet for Eleni and a glass vase for Madame Michard-Pellisier. Then they boarded Robertino's taxi and headed across the lagoon to the Hotel Cipriani for lunch.

After an excellent meal, Christina decided Venice was wonderful and she wanted to remain there a few days. She had Basualdo telephone the Gritti and book them a suite with two bedrooms, and smaller rooms for Véronique and the pilot. They went for a swim in the Cipriani pool, then had Robertino take them back across the lagoon to the Gritti. Christina went to her room and they all rejoined her at six o'clock for drinks in the Gritti bar.

Settled in the small bar off the lobby, Christina sipped a Coke and gave her attention to the Gritti's piano player. When he played Rodgers and Hart's "My Funny Valentine," Christina turned suddenly grim. The song had depressed her deeply, she told the others, and she wanted to return immediately to St. Moritz. Basualdo was sent to phone the pilot in his room and came back with the information that it was too late to return to St. Moritz. The airport closed at 7 P.M. and it was now 6:30. By the time they got out of the hotel, to the airport, and cleared for takeoff, it would be after 7.

"Well, where can we go?" asked Christina with the panic of an outlaw under sheriff's orders to be out of town by sunset. "I can't stay in Venice."

The airports of large cities remained open later and they discussed possibilities. Rome? No, even more depressing to Christina's mood than Venice. She must leave Italy. They were leaning toward Munich when Christina suddenly had an inspiration. "I know. Let's go to Marseilles and see Dovi!"

There was a chorus of reasons why that was a bad idea. It was too late. Arriving in such an odd manner, Basualdo pointed out, was no way to meet your lover's family for the first time. They would be alarmed, scandalized, frightened. But Christina could not be dissuaded and Basualdo was sent to find out how late the Marseilles airport stayed open.

He came back and told her, glumly, that they had until midnight. "Great," said Christina as she started to rise. "I'm going to my room and phone Dovi. I'll talk to his father and make up some excuse why we're passing through Marseilles." She returned to say that the family had agreed to her visit. Having no luggage, Christina and her party were able to check out of the Gritti quickly and were soon in Robertino's taxi speeding up the Grand Canal to the airport.

They arrived in Marseilles about ten. Clare and Véronique were told to get rooms for them all in the airport hotel and wait there. Basualdo would accompany Christina to Dovi's house. In front of the Marseilles airport they encountered a fresh obstacle: no taxi driver would drive them so late at night to Dovi's neighborhood, one of Marseilles's roughest. Basualdo picked a driver who looked less adamant than the others and worked on persuading him. Pushing Basualdo aside, Christina told the man she would give him double the amount on the meter. When he said no, she said she would triple his fare. He agreed.

Dovi's quarter was a trash-strewn North African slum near the center of the city. When they arrived at the address, Christina pointed to a restaurant across the street that was still open and told Basualdo to wait for her there.

Close to midnight, having dragged four other adults through three countries, spent thousands of dollars on jet fuel, landing fees, hotel rooms, meals, and a bribed taxi driver, a thirty-one-year-old Christina Onassis appeared by herself at her teen-aged lover's door, wearing the clothes she had left St. Moritz in that morning at eight.

Her meeting with the Tubrussi family was as natural and unstrained as her journey had been eccentric. She was greeted warmly by Dovi's father and mother. She met an indeterminate number of brothers, sisters, aunts, and uncles. She was offered wine but took a glass of mineral water instead. The principals settled at a large kitchen table with as many family members as could be seated crowding around, others standing in the background, and talked and laughed until two in the morning.

Christina answered cheerfully the unabashed questions about how many houses she had, how many servants, cars, and fur coats. She spoke frankly about her good fortune in having been left an enormous amount of money by her father. They discussed plans for the family's move to Paris.

Meanwhile, at the restaurant across the street, which fortunately stayed open as long as anyone wanted it to, Basualdo sat trying to gag down a wretched couscous and sour Algerian red wine, thinking that, at $30,000 a month, he was being underpaid. Finally Christina appeared, alone and beaming. A taxi was telephoned, and they returned to the airport hotel.

Several days went by while Christina paid further visits to the Tubrussi family. She and Dovi would then go off to a restaurant for dinner and he would return with her to the hotel. Christina seemed happy to remain in the Marseilles airport hotel indefinitely, while Basualdo, Clare, and the others were growing increasingly bored and eager to leave.

About the third evening, Dovi dealt Christina a blow that the others saw as possible deliverance. It was against his religion, his father had told him, for them to make love since they were not married. He could sleep with her, but they would have to stay on different sides of the blankets; he would be in the bed, she on top. Dovi did not say what tenet of his religion designated him the one to sleep between sheets.

To the dismay of her entourage, Christina did not order the jet readied for departure. For several more days, she would be put to bed by Basualdo and Véronique, Dovi under the covers, Christina on top, with another blanket thrown over her, from which her feet invariably emerged. Although it was still summer, the hotel room was air-conditioned and Christina caught a bad cold. Still she showed no signs of losing heart.

One evening Basualdo, rigid with boredom, violated his own rule about leaving Christina alone and asked her if she would permit him to take their rented car and, with Clare, drive to St. Tropez to dine with London friends who were vacationing there. Christina, who cared about nothing but being with Dovi, said that was fine with her.

Relieved to be away from the platonic love nest, Basualdo and Clare had a delightful evening and didn't return until about two in the morning. Arriving at the hotel, they found a note from Christina. She was fed up with Dovi, she said, and couldn't endure his treatment another minute. She had taken the jet with the others to Paris. She enclosed a 5,000-franc note for two plane tickets. Basualdo and Clare were to join her in Paris the next day.

For Basualdo, who had not traveled by any means but private jet for some time, having to deal with porters and check-in lines was a calamity akin to having to hitchhike to Paris. His resolve never to leave Christina's side was codified into law. Once they were reunited, plans were dropped to move the Tubrussi family to Paris and Dovi's name was never mentioned again.

# 19

....................................................

# FATAL REUNION

.....................................................................................................

*W*hen Christina came together again with her former lover Thierry Roussel, they each filled needs that were particularly pressing in the other's life at the moment, needs that were absent when they had known each other ten years earlier. Hers were emotional, his were of a more concrete nature. Even if Roussel had not been brought to Skorpios in the summer of 1973, he would have eventually come into Christina's orbit. He was an attractive, if not highly visible, member of Paris's *jeunesse dorée*, the swarm of wealthy, pleasure-bent, and well-connected young Europeans into which Christina had thrown herself since resigning as a Los Angeles housewife. After each of her subsequent marriages, it was the group to which she returned and which she saw as a constantly changing pool of potential lovers and husbands.

The summertime affair into which Christina and Roussel had fallen in 1973 had remained for Christina, despite the abrupt ending, one of her fondest memories. He, too, now looked back on it warmly. They had wanted to marry at the time, Roussel later told reporters, but "events" had prevented it. One of the obstructing events was a beautiful Swedish woman named Gaby Landhage, who worked in Paris as a model and a translator and with whom Roussel was living at that time. When word of Roussel's prior involvement leaked out to the press many years later, he altered slightly his version of his affair with Christina. They had developed a strong feeling for each other, indeed loved each other, but the talk of marriage had been instigated, not by them, but by Aristotle Onassis, who decided Roussel would make an ideal husband for his daughter.

When Christina had had her dalliance with Roussel, she was going through a period of random dating and casual lovers. As the young men came and went with a regularity that might have worried some women, Christina gave little thought to the reasons for their disappearance. More often than not, the short duration of her romances was Christina's choice, not the young man's. Her hunger for excitement and new experiences, which gave her a reputation in business for a short attention span, applied to her romantic interests as well. In her love affairs, her natural tendency toward flightiness was reinforced by her father's cruel warning that, because of her wealth, no man would be interested in her for herself alone. Christina turned that cynical prophecy to her advantage by exploiting the parade of would-be suitors before they exploited her.

When Roussel told her he did not want to marry because of his involvement with Gaby Landhage, Christina was crushed briefly, but soon mentally placed him, as she did all her lovers when a mutual attraction did not seem totally spent, in a pleasure-pending file to be drawn on at some future date when circumstances permitted further exploration of the possibilities. Roussel had been unlike the straggle of disco lizards who usually paid court to her, most of them rich young idlers who thought it might be amusing to be richer. Roussel had not been a regular fixture of the *tout Paris* scene, but spent his time pursuing his own, more individualistic amusements. In Christina's judgment, he had more sensitivity, more intelligence, more sense of purpose. She felt sure he, unlike most of her boyfriends, would evolve into a person of substance, would make something of his life. For all these reasons, he had remained in her mind as one of the more noteworthy of her amatory interludes.

In December of 1983, when a chance encounter thrust Roussel back into her consciousness, her life seemed an array of voids—emotional, sexual, directional—and her need for a focus had never been greater. Rather than relishing her rare financial position, she felt herself drowning in the limitless possibilities her fortune gave her. She had had no serious involvement since Nickie Mavroleon, she was desperately lonely, and her overall condition had never been worse. Her weight had climbed to over two hundred pounds, she was taking as many as six Seconals a day, and her love life had slipped into a game of blatantly using the vague promise of unnamed benefits to lure men to her bed. Those contenders with too high a self-view to oblige her in return for an invitation to Skorpios or a morning-after gift she cynically permitted to audition for the larger role to which they aspired, then cast them aside.

The game had begun to bore Christina, who, being Greek, could deal with unhappiness but found boredom intolerable. Increasingly, her only antidote for it was to haul her bulk to a disco and hope to meet a man who was attracted, like Kausov, to fat women. All this was, of course, depressing, and her black moods increased. Watching her disintegration, Basualdo began to worry, not about Christina's state of mind, which he felt was her psychiatrist's responsibility, but about his job. He knew that while she might not look to him for her happiness, she did look to him for *fun* and she was having very little of that. Her need of a lover was so acute he decided to shift from his policy of protective obstruction to one of genteel procurement.

Christina, who had earlier said that she detested England, suddenly announced she wanted to live in London. A large furnished flat was leased near Eaton Square, to which Basualdo began inviting young men he thought might be interested, for whatever reason, in a fling with Christina. When he suggested one bachelor or another to her, Christina, who abhorred any suggestion that she was being "fixed up"—but got angry if she wasn't—invariably quashed the idea. "Not him, he's scum," she would tell Basualdo, or "I wouldn't have that amateur crook in my house." Just as inevitably, she would change her mind after mulling over the proposed candidate and instruct Basualdo to invite the man.

During a dinner party at Christina's London apartment, she decided that one of Basualdo's protégés, a man with a reputation as a cardsharp, whom she had previously rejected as "a slimy hustler," was instead a nice person and wonderfully attractive. Excitedly she informed Basualdo of her attraction and asked him to do something about it. As the party was winding down, Basualdo told Christina to go to her room so that he could "arrange things." Over a brandy

Basualdo told the man of Christina's keen interest, and got back an equally keen expression of lack of interest. Although Christina had not threatened Basualdo with dismissal, a number of recent confrontations made him feel that the present situation represented a crisis for his position. From the pointed way Christina emphasized her desires, he strongly suspected that if he couldn't deliver on this he would be fired.

Basualdo told the man that if he would go to Christina and make her happy, he would personally give him $200,000, an amount that was, according to Basualdo, all the money he had. His flamboyant offer was based on his certainty that Christina would make good on her promise to pay him ten times his salary, $300,000, if she found happiness with a man. If she didn't, he could be out of a job. In Basualdo's eyes, he was not only investing $200,000 to make $300,000, but to keep his $30,000-a-month income as well. Dramatically, Basualdo wrote out the check and handed it to the startled Englishman, who examined it, decided the whole thing was some sort of practical joke, and handed it back. Years later, when Basualdo ran into the man and assured him the check had been good, the man turned ashen, closed his eyes, and said, "Oh my God."

Other zany episodes of Christina's, many as ill conceived as the affair with Dovi, showed the desperation that was short-circuiting her none-too-strong mechanisms of restraint. At a St. Moritz dinner party, she met and took an interest in an Englishman in his early forties, David Davies. He was the cousin of David d'Ambrumenil, who was a popular member of George Livanos's circle and was then insurance agent for much of Christina's fleet. Although Davies was involved with another woman at the time, he responded to Christina's invitation to dine sometime when they were both in Paris. Their first evening together ended up in bed, an experience that Christina ranked as "fantastic." When she asked Davies when they might meet again, he said he was going to Aspen, Colorado, to ski with some friends and suggested casually that she should come too.

Christina jumped at the invitation and, despite warnings from Basualdo and others that Davies was an inveterate womanizer, she flew to America, meeting Davies in the Denver airport. Since he had been invited to stay in the apartment of his friends, he was dashed to see that Christina had arrived with her maid, Eleni, the nurse, Véronique, and a hairdresser. Putting her entourage up in a nearby hotel, Christina moved into the friends' apartment with Davies. The mountain air of Colorado was apparently less inspiring to his libido than that of France, and Davies found himself unable to perform with Christina. After several loveless days, in which it became increasingly apparent to her that he regretted her arrival, Christina, humiliated at her own precipitateness, abruptly returned to St. Moritz by four jet planes, three commercial and one of her own.

At a dinner party Christina gave in Paris some months later, she found herself strongly attracted to a seventy-year-old man from whom she occasionally bought jewelry. Again she had Basualdo inform this guest that he should remain after the others had left, then proceed to Christina's room, where she would be waiting for him. The bewildered jeweler arrived at Christina's bedside to find her naked and feigning sleep. For a while he tried to uphold the honor of France, but with disheartening results. After a time Christina rolled over and buzzed Eleni on the house phone. "Call a taxi, Eleni," she said. "Monsieur Ponchard will be leaving now."

On another evening in Paris, Christina had done some business with Gunther, her helicopter pilot, then asked him to join her group at a disco. As the evening progressed, Christina seemed to be noticing for the first time this employee who had been part of her life for three years. She made her delayed interest obvious to him as well as everyone else in the disco. At the evening's end, Gunther returned with her to Avenue Foch and they went to bed. The next day Basualdo asked Gunther if he fancied the seriously overweight Christina. He replied tactfully that she was not his type.

"Well, why did you go to bed with her then?"

"I was afraid I'd lose my job if I didn't."

The pilltaking grew worse. At a Paris dinner party, Christina was seated next to the very social and elegant Jimmy Douglas, who had lived with Barbara Hutton for a number of years and had settled in Paris. Chatting with Christina, Douglas got on the subject of tranquilizers and Christina remarked that she used barbiturates, and sometimes took as many as six a day (two or three less than Basualdo said she took). Douglas grew excited. "But you mustn't," he said.

"They are worse than cocaine, worse than heroin. They make you crazy. They destroyed Barbara." Clearly annoyed with Douglas's agitation, Christina said, "Look, I don't drink, I don't smoke, I hate all those drugs people take at parties . . . I have to do *something*." She made a point of avoiding Douglas in the future.

Eleni had always worried about her mistress's use of pills and now enlisted Basualdo in a conspiracy to save Christina from calamity. They would find her pill supply—in Paris they were kept in the butler's pantry—and mix into the bottles of barbiturates harmless placebos that looked identical to the potent ones. The ruse appeared to work and the result was that Christina was taking fewer pills than she thought she was. For all her cavalier defiance to people like Douglas and particularly those closest to her, like Eleni and Basualdo, Christina would sometimes throw out a chilling remark that indicated she knew full well the danger in these pills, which had, by most appraisals, killed her mother.

Once, taking her usual afternoon dose, she turned to a friend and said casually, "These things will probably kill me one day."

Still, like most drug-dependent people, she hated hearing the warnings from others and would banish them from her life if necessary to assure that she didn't. A fight over pill taking brought on a near-terminal blowup between Christina and Basualdo. Her old fears that he was blocking her from romantic happiness may also have contributed to the falling-out. And as Christina's mood swings grew worse, Basualdo had increasing trouble dealing with them. Once when he was driving her through Paris, he spoke to her sharply, and she suddenly turned, opened the door, and tried to jump from the car. Since they were moving rapidly through heavy traffic, Basualdo was convinced that, had he not grabbed her, she would have been killed, which, for those brief seconds, seemed to be what she wanted. But even less-dramatic behavior revealed her inner turmoil. She became more and more erratic, and almost daily, nonsensical or wholly imagined matters would send her into very real rages. He thought she had become impossible.

Finally, although he knew how she felt about discussing the forbidden subject of drugs, Basualdo blurted out, "You're taking too many of those damned pills! You're not yourself; you're acting crazy."

Since one of Basualdo's major assets from Christina's point of view was his worldly cynicism and the permissiveness that went with it, his angry lecture was not well received. She began yelling: he was not treating her as a friend, he was against her, and finally, she didn't want him living with her anymore. Even after she calmed down, she remained resolute for a change in her household arrangement. About the same time, Basualdo's stock dropped even further when Christina caught him in a bit of financial chicanery. Hearing that her old friend Rodney Solomon was in a financial tight spot, Christina asked Basualdo to give him £3,000 from her. Basualdo presented Solomon with £1,000 but asked for a receipt for £3,000. Suspecting what Basualdo was up to, Solomon told a friend of his and Christina's about the discrepancy between cash and receipt.

As hoped, word of Basualdo's hustle got back to Christina, who berated him and pushed ahead with her plan to move him, not out of her life—she was too forgiving and sentimental for anything so drastic—but out of her apartment. She wanted him to get his own apartment in London—she would pay for it, of course—and would continue his $30,000-a-month salary, but their lives were to be separate. When she needed him—to help with a dinner, to take her shopping or to a party, to watch a video—she would call him. As always when his unofficial guardianship over Christina was interrupted, Basualdo predicted something terrible would happen to her.

Apart from the specifics of her deterioration, Christina's general outlook at this time of her life was bleak. The fun and excitement of having the fortune at her command had sustained her in the first grim years following her father's death, but now, after five years, she had grown accustomed to the wealth and the instant gratifications it bought. She came to see the money no longer as a source of endless pleasure but as an intensifier of her misery. "If I can't be happy with all I've been given," she told a friend, "something must be very wrong with my fate—or with me." Usually when in the throes of this brand of self-doubt, she would invoke her family's terrible history and place the blame on fate. Now even that rationalization had worn itself out and she was feeling herself to be a very sorry mess.

Exasperated by her chronic unhappiness, her friend Willy Rizzo once exploded, "What's wrong with you, Christina? You have so much, yet you're never content with your life as it is. What is it you want?"

She responded *"Je veux être draguée,"* which can be translated: "I want to be lusted after."

For an over-thirty woman with bad teeth and a serious weight problem, that hope would have appeared to be a prescription for ever-increasing frustration. There were signs, however, that Christina was beginning to realize that her best chance for fulfillment was not in a passionate romance that would sweep her, as Kausov briefly had, away from her degenerate and self-destructive existence, but rather in the more solid gratifications of having a family. She had always considered the raptures of romance to be a necessary first step, but now she wondered if she shouldn't give up on the passion and go directly to the family.

In the midst of this inner turmoil of self-disgust and reappraisal, Christina went to a large party at London's Claridge's and, as she was leaving, ran into Thierry Roussel's father, Henri, in the lobby. Henri Roussel was a prominent member of Paris society with a reputation as a ladies' man. The very reminder of her happy interlude with the handsome Thierry was a much-needed tonic for Christina's battered self-esteem. Henri Roussel told Christina his son had recently broken with a girlfriend, was lonely, and would love to hear from Christina. Those lovers or potential lovers she had placed on hold, her "pending files," especially the rich, good-looking ones, had a way of not remaining pending, of becoming involved elsewhere. When Christina heard that Roussel was not only available but in need of consolation, she grew excited, and the vague outlines of her salvation began to form in her mind. It was, instead, her final destruction.

At the moment, Roussel was in Kenya, where his father had owned a game ranch, visiting friends for Christmas and pursuing a business venture. Christina resolved to make contact with him as soon as he returned to Paris, and went to St. Moritz. As she waited, something at which she had never been good, the idea of taking up again with Roussel burgeoned in her mind. Her recollection of him was of a likable, sympathetic young man. An air of shyness, given his marvelous good looks, had pleased Christina enormously. In addition, he had, she recalled, been a very skillful and resourceful lover.

As a member of a wealthy and social French family, Roussel was immune to the fortune-hunter charge. His money and position meant that Christina's interest in him could not be interpreted as an outright act of defiance against her father's wishes, like Bolker and Kausov, nor oppressively in tune with them, like the very Greek and business-oriented Andreadis. Roussel was rather a member in good standing of the world Christina had made her own—rich, attractive young people who dabbled at enterprise but whose main objective was to have fun.

Christina was viewing Roussel across a decade, to a period that had been more innocent and carefree in both their lives, when she was slender and striking, when love was still exciting and lovers were plentiful. She was also viewing him in the midst of a swarm of decadent and corrupt playboys, compared to whom he took on the beatific glow of a Parsifal. The ten years in which she had not seen him had been the worst years of her life: the succession of deaths in her family, her three marital misfires, her descent into pills and one-night stands. Resuming an affair with Roussel would be a way to expunge those bad years, to start over from the year when disasters began pummeling her family. She decided she could not wait until he returned to Paris. Swallowing her pride, something she did now with greater and greater ease, she phoned his father and obtained the telephone number in Africa. By the time she got Roussel on the phone, she was already in love.

Thierry Roussel had grown up to wealth. His father's family had founded France's largest pharmaceutical company, which had been partially nationalized by the Mitterand government and was now called Roussel-Uclaf. The family retained a 40 percent interest, but Thierry's father, Henri, had sold his share to a brother and had used the proceeds to maintain a life among the very rich with his Kenyan ranch and a sprawling pink villa overlooking the Mediterranean outside of Marbella, the Spanish playground for millionaires and titled bon vivants. Henri had become involved in real estate, a traditional way for those with wealthy friends to parlay their contacts into income. He had sold a vast Marbella estate to Adnan Khashoggi, then said to be the world's richest man. While always managing to maintain his foothold among Europe's moneyed dynasties, Henri Roussel had suffered a number of reverses, and his financial status was considerably less secure than when he had still been an owner of a major French corporation.

His son Thierry had attended one of France's best boys' schools, the exclusive École des Roches, along with the sons of political leaders and the great industrial families. In his teens, Thierry was an odd mix of introvert and extrovert; he could show up at a gathering of friends wearing with nonchalant panache an outlandish new garment—a fur coat or a wild-colored jacket—or he could sink into a sullen appraisal of his surroundings, which many mistook for introversion if not timidity. With either mood, he showed a vigorous and quick intelligence. As he matured, refined features gave him the slightly baby-faced look of the actor Gérard Philipe, but bright blue eyes, a good physique, and a luxuriant head of thick and wavy brown hair marked him clearly as a breaker of hearts. For a time, Roussel made good use of his physical assets and played Europe's most fruitful fields for willing young beauties: Paris, the Riviera, Marbella, and the Greek islands.

Throughout his twenties, he had shown a taste for the costly pastimes of the adventurous rich—helicopter skiing, power boating, falconing, big-game hunting. On occasion, he displayed a propensity for reckless showing-off. One summer on the Riviera, he was in a helicopter that was about to alight on the deck of a friend's yacht and suddenly had an impulse to disembark early. With the aircraft still some thirty feet above the yacht, he climbed from the cab and hung Indiana Jones style from the landing bars as the aircraft descended to about twenty feet, then dropped to the deck of the yacht. Everyone watching was certain he was going to be killed, if not by the fall, then by the helicopter itself. Roussel was delighted with his prank.

In addition to such feats of derring-do, Roussel had also shown a keen interest in making money. As for his expectations, he knew that there would be little family money left when his father died. If there was anything, he would have to share it with siblings. Roussel was resolved to make his own fortune while he still had at least some financial backing to facilitate his schemes. After a stint in the advertising department of Roussel-Uclaf, he had gone on his own to pursue various business ventures; at one time or another he became involved in home furnishings, an advertising agency, a publishing house, and finally a modeling agency—always as the entrepreneur. Despite several flurries of success, none of the businesses were solid moneymakers, most ended up with losses, and he was still looking for the big breakthrough that would secure him in the world of easy affluence to which he had been born.

Regardless of his financial ups and downs, Roussel lived well. In Paris's fashionable Sixteenth Arrondissement, he had a roomy apartment including a huge salon, with white walls and gold *boiserie*. Of the two master bedrooms, in his the luxury was given a he-man flourish with a set of weights and an adjacent sauna. The apartment was maintained by three live-in Moroccan servants, a couple and another man. For weekends, he had the family estate in the Sologne area 160 miles from Paris. Built in the *faux-château* style of the nineteenth century, when France lacked sufficient authentic châteaux to satisfy all the new industrial millionaires, the mansion was formal, gloomy, and full of animal heads shot by various Roussels, including Thierry. The house was also disastrously rundown.

As a self-styled "venture capitalist," Roussel was full of energy and a daring sense of adventure. He was given to flamboyant expeditions and costly gestures, such as chartering a plane to take a group of associates on a business trip to Portugal, then chartering a yacht on which to conduct the business. Once, just for fun, he hired a plane to take some friends to the Riviera, insisting that, en route, the pilot fly low through the Alps, exhilarating some of the party but terrifying others.

Despite his enthusiasm for the things great amounts of money could buy, Roussel was not a snob and constantly showed an above-average interest in other people. When in the mood, he would engage any and all comers—waiters, taxi drivers, boatmen—in lengthy conversations about a wide range of subjects. He would give the person his full attention until he thought he had learned all he could, then abruptly terminate the dialogue. If he suddenly decided the person he was talking with was a villain or a fool, he would freeze him with steely hauteur. With newcomers in his social sphere—a friend's new girlfriend, for example, he was unabashedly curious and would ask endless questions, some quite personal—"How did you guys meet?" "Do you enjoy the same things?" "What is it you like about him?"—flattering the target with his interest but making him or her feel besieged.

Throughout his twenties, Roussel's love for Gaby Landhage was the most stabilizing influence in his desultory life. She was a ravishingly beautiful blonde, with high cheekbones and the finely etched features of a Garbo. She was also, by all accounts, exceptionally good-hearted and kind, an unaffected woman with her feet squarely on the ground in a solid, particularly Swedish sort of way. Despite the recherché Parisian worlds to which her remarkable looks gave Landhage access, her head was not turned by the glamour or high life. Her feelings for Roussel were total and, in the estimation of her friends, unencumbered with extraneous ambitions.

At the time of his reunion with Christina, Roussel was starting a company to build high-speed sporting boats, a somewhat typical enterprise for rich young men who want to make money but have no willingness to be bored doing so. In developing the business he had hired a marine engineer, moving the man and his girlfriend into his own Paris apartment to save on hotel bills. This economy, intermingled with his other wild extravagances, was characteristic of Roussel's free-and-easy style, his casual mixing of business and private life.

Even before they met again, Christina and Roussel's worlds had drawn slightly closer together. Roussel's uncle, a former tennis champion and current backgammon and card player named Jean Noël Grinda, had years earlier married one of Christina's oldest friends, Florence Michard-Pellisier. Had Florence, who had grown up in the same Avenue Foch building as Christina, remained married to Jean Noël, she would have become her childhood chum's aunt. As it developed, she became one of the most scathing and outspoken critics of her former nephew by marriage, Thierry Roussel.

As for Gaby, she had grown tired of waiting for Roussel to marry her and had returned to Sweden, where she enrolled in a management course and a short time later took a job with a cosmetics firm in Malmö. Roussel bought her a modest house there and continued to see her as often as he could. When alone in Paris, he began seeing other women as well, all of them the same type as Gaby: slender blondes. Despite the encouraging information given Christina by his father, his long-time love affair with Gaby was by no means terminated.

There was perhaps a reason why Thierry Roussel did not marry Gaby Landhage at a time when they were both young, affluent, unencumbered, and, as subsequent events proved, deeply in love. In Roussel's world of large fortunes, marriage was used primarily as a strategic device, every bit as much as it is among royal families. This is particularly true with the rich who are in the process of becoming unrich, people who see their eroding social position as a fleeting asset that must be marketed before they sink irredeemably into middle-class ignominy. It is even truer of those in this transitional state who can enter the matrimonial sweepstakes with a son as marketable as Thierry. It was quite possible that his reunion with Christina was brought about, not by a chance encounter of his father's or by one of them contacting the other, but by the first step in a calculated family strategy. Roussel's enemies, whose numbers would grow considerably in the next four years, insisted that the wooing and winning of Christina was, from the very start, a well-planned campaign in which a number of Roussels participated.

Gunar Larsen, the photographer who was the first to employ Gaby as a model in Paris, offered a blunt appraisal of Roussel's treatment of Gaby and his subsequent interest in Christina. "Gaby was not rich enough for the Roussels." Not everyone agreed. A woman who saw a lot of Roussel at the time was convinced he had no need of Christina's money. "I don't think he loved her, but he didn't marry her for the money. He had plenty." Her hunch was that the motive was celebrity and contacts. Since people rarely have any clear idea of their friends' finances, the woman may have meant not that Roussel had plenty but that he *spent* plenty. Or she may have assumed, as many do, that when one shared a last name with a major corporation, abundant money is there somewhere.

More knowledgeable people insisted that in 1983 when he renewed contact with Christina Roussel was deeply in debt, and that Henri Roussel felt that the family's financial decline was approaching the crisis stage. Thierry had sold out his interest in the modeling agency at a loss of between $3 and $4 million. An African land venture he had launched was said to have suffered losses in the tens of millions. "He owed a lot of money to some extremely rough characters," said one close friend of Christina's, "and had no prospects for paying them back." If Roussel was, in fact, weighed down with money worries when he was on his trip to Kenya, for him to receive an unexpected and flirty phone call from an old girlfriend, who also happened to be one of the world's richest women, could only be seen as providential, if not parental, intercession.

Christina's telephone conversation with Roussel in Africa was a great success. As his father had promised, Roussel seemed delighted to hear from her, and they fell quickly into the easy intimacy they had briefly known ten years earlier. For Christina, her lively, amusing conversations with Roussel were a breath of sanity from a more stable, sensible world she had gradually lost. He, in turn, was eager to learn everything about her—whom she had been seeing, the true story of her Russian marriage, how her businesses were going.

As the phone calls between St. Moritz and Kenya became daily events, Christina very quickly opened her heart to Roussel. She told him of her unhappiness, her disillusionment with people, the self-disgust she felt for letting herself deteriorate, for putting on weight, for keeping bizarre hours, having bizarre friends. He reciprocated with confidences about his own fears and concerns. Picking up on her greater disarray and need for counsel, however, Roussel took affectionate command and lectured her on what she must do to straighten herself out.

Perhaps Christina, at the time, was eager for a disciplining guru or perhaps her romantic fantasies concerning her old lover were strong enough to induce her to listen to his lectures. Because of the strength and suddenness of her feelings for him, it was probably a combination of both. Whatever it was, Roussel was permitted a far higher degree of criticism than Basualdo and others close to her, and he was quickly established in her mind as not only one who cared, but also as the instrument for her rehabilitation. She envisioned him as a lover, to be sure—that was all but decided on the phone—but she also envisioned him as a strong influence for regaining her self-possession and making something of her existence.

By the time they met in Paris, Christina had put herself completely in Roussel's hands, and he set diligently to work reassembling the shattered pieces of her life and making Christina whole again. Like everyone else who got close to her, Roussel saw that the pills were a major cause of her confusion and distress, and he launched a campaign to end her reliance on them, which, surprisingly, she accepted. Not only did he go to war with her more glaring failings, he scrutinized every aspect of her behavior and held it up to his own standards for normal womanhood. If anything struck him as odd—whether from neurosis or too much money or both—he worked on its elimination. By this time, most facets of Christina's behavior did not fit Roussel's criteria. He thought it silly, for example, that she needed to be constantly driven by a chauffeur. She knew perfectly well how to drive, he told her, and healthy women in their thirties drove themselves. Her chauffeurs had to go—as did, it turned out, a lot of Christina's friends.

There is nothing unusual about a new husband going at his wife's address book with a ruthless red pencil, but Roussel's cuts, even before he married Christina, were pretty much across the board. If friends had let her get into such deplorable shape, he reasoned with her, they couldn't be much in the way of friends. His bad opinon of her circle was reinforced, in many instances, by firsthand knowledge. But others equally cut off, like her former stepsister Henrietta Gelber, did not know Roussel and were barely aware of Christina's excesses, let alone accomplices in them. Still others whom Roussel insisted Christina drop completely were difficult to cut off because they were very close and old friends. One of these, Florence Grinda, had known Christina since they were girls, was a regular in her present Parisian life, and had been married to Roussel's uncle. Such claims for clemency made no difference to Roussel, who announced publicly that he detested Christina's friends and that they all had to go.

In her previous marriages, Christina had permitted her husbands to call a shot or two, and she played at playing their game, whether it was Los Angeles Housewife, Greek Business Wife, or Heiress Goes to Moscow. But no one ever had any doubt that the game belonged to Christina. Her apparent adaptation to her former husbands' lives was done in highly visible, symbolic ways. Privately, if she experienced a moment's boredom, she would call time out from the game and fly off alone to Paris, Skorpios, or La Jolla. Not even with her

move to Russia was there a sense that she was permanently relin-
quishing her rights as an heiress and replacing them with whatever
life her husband provided. Her lack of commitment to her first three
marriages was ultimately made apparent by the ease with which she
walked away from them. Now, for the first time in her life, Christina
was actually abdicating her spoiled-rich-girl willfulness and subjugat-
ing herself to a higher authority. The sensation was totally new and
it made her as happy as she could remember being.

No sooner were she and Roussel established as lovers than Christina began talking about marriage. At first, Roussel hedged and
Christina told him, she later reported to close friends, she would give
him more money than he had ever dreamed of. He then told her she
would have to lose fifty pounds. His harsh requirement for matrimony became public when Roussel repeated it to an interviewer from
*Paris Match*. While the condition struck many as inconsistent with
the eager-bridegroom image, it confused those who suspected Roussel of fortune hunting; the true fortune hunter would have assured
Christina her extra pounds were adorable. On February 23, 1984,
just two months after her phone call to Kenya, Christina gave a flashy
party at The Palace, then making a comeback as Paris's most popular
disco, and announced her engagement to Roussel.

Almost unnoticed during Christina's romantic euphoria, Roussel
began laying down other odd stipulations. He insisted, for instance,
that Christina move in with him. Although his apartment was luxurious by most standards, it was squalid compared to the apartment
she owned at 88 Avenue Foch, her father's very grand penthouse,
which had been, as much as any place, her girlhood home and which
she had no intention of selling. When she and Roussel began making
specific wedding plans, he agreed to a Greek Orthodox ceremony,
but only if they first had a civil ceremony in his *arrondissement*, the
sixteenth.

Both of these requests were later viewed by Roussel's detractors as
legal ploys to make Christina *more* married to him. In the beady eyes
of French law, there are marriages and marriages. If a woman moves
into a man's home and marries him in his neighborhood, her matrimonial intentions are clearer and she is more his wife than if, for
example, she runs off with him to Las Vegas or Acapulco after a
night of carousing. In a press interview, Roussel spoke of Christina's

arrival into his residence as being "like a student home for vacation," which made the relationship sound more congenial than passionate.

Whatever Roussel's motives for his measured matrimonial program, Christina's state of beguilement was such that she would have agreed, had Roussel wished it, to another Moscow wedding. Her euphoria was so great that she cared about nothing—where she lived, whom she saw, how much of her fortune she gave away. She would do whatever was needed. The impossible had happened. The fate that had crushed the rest of her family had been defied. She was happy—and could see nothing but more happiness ahead.

When she and Roussel were interviewed shortly before the wedding by a *Paris Match* reporter, Christina said, "I simply hope to make Thierry happy. We will try to be together as much as possible —in Paris, in St. Moritz, in Greece. I want to look after my house and begin a family. I think I deserve to be happy." When Roussel was interviewed on his own, he paid lip service to his long-term involvement with Gaby Landhage, which was well known to many people. He told reporters that, when he had fallen in love with Christina many years earlier, her Greek temperament had excited him with its passion and volatility, whereas Gaby had soothed him with her calm and solidity. He made it sound as if he had always been torn between these two women, but that Christina had finally won out in his affections.

In addition to agreeing to Roussel's logistical requests, Christina was succeeding in taking herself in hand. She stopped eating and found the pounds dropping off. She booked herself into her Marbella health clinic, where she underwent a stringent regimen of bouillon, enemas, and hydrotherapy. She cut down drastically on her barbiturate and amphetamine consumption and made heroic efforts to avoid sleeping pills altogether. By March, the month for which they had scheduled their wedding, she looked and felt better than she had in years. She told a friend from Rome, Countess Marina Cicogna, that, because of her great desire to have a baby, she intended to marry Roussel.

"But why do you have to marry in order to do that?" asked her worldly friend.

Christina was shocked, but could only muster a feeble reply that revealed her contradictory sense of propriety: "How would that look to the people in my office?"

In the month prior to the wedding, Christina took Roussel on a number of trips, perhaps to show off her new figure as well as her new fiancé. They spent a few days in New York, where she paid a visit to her former stepmother on Fifth Avenue. Christina was not one to bear grudges—or rather to let grudges stand in the way of formal relationships—and she had no trouble obliging Roussel's curiosity to meet the legendary Jackie with a bury-the-hatchet gesture. Christina was eager to show her critical fiancé that all the people in her life were not café-society trash; some were figures of major, if not historical, importance. She was just as eager to give her former adversary some lessons on what marriage was meant to be by flaunting her prize catch.

Before international café society had caught up with the new relationship, Christina and Roussel were married on the morning of March 17, 1984, in a civil ceremony near Roussel's apartment. After a wedding lunch for intimate friends, they were married for a second time in a late-afternoon service in a Greek Orthodox church. Two hundred and fifty people filled the church, which one guest described as "a sea of black mink." Christina wore a white silk-and-linen suit, picked out by Roussel, which set off her dark good looks, her new figure, and her radiant state. The church service was followed by a dinner for a hundred at Christina's favorite Paris restaurant, Maxim's. Although no one realized it at the time, the lavish and festive party turned out to be Christina's farewell both to a dissolute and aimless life and the friends who abetted it.

# 20

# A UNIQUE ARRANGEMENT

O nce Christina was married to Roussel—her happiness fixed, in place, locked up—some of her old willfulness began to reassert itself. Much as she loved him, she was not skilled at adapting her wants to those of another. In principle, she understood the need for give and take in human relationships; she simply lacked practice. Aggravating the problem, Roussel had a willfulness that matched her own, although it did not emerge immediately.

Major decisions had to be made quickly. Christina wanted to live on Avenue Foch, and Roussel, now that they were married, had no objection to leaving his own flat, but thought it unseemly for them to move into the apartment that all the world knew had been hers and, before that, her father's. Something new, that's what they needed. With the problem-solving facility a half-billion dollars allows, Christina bought another apartment in the building, this one on the fifth floor, and hired her old friend, Atalanta Politis, to decorate it. Roussel was somewhat appeased by this show of making a fresh start, but after a time began to brood that they were still living in Christina's building, No. 88 Avenue Foch, and that, as everyone knew, was Onassis country.

When Christina wished to visit her villa in St. Moritz or fly down to Skorpios for a few days to consult about improvements, Roussel followed dutifully along—at least at first. But as the novelty of his wife's many establishments wore off, he began complaining about these ownership tours, and eventually took to ducking them. His discontent finally erupted into complaints about always living in Christina's homes, and he began agitating for a totally new residence, one free of a vivid history of one-woman rule.

Christina spent a good part of the summer of 1984 on Skorpios, with Roussel coming and going as he looked after his own business enterprises. He quickly came to dislike staying on the island, more even than in Christina's other residences. Since her role as Skorpios's autocrat was so embedded in the reflexes of both Christina and her large staff, Roussel's efforts to appear the island's new co-owner were greeted with blank stares. Rather than feeling like a husband, Roussel was never able to rise above the level of an honored guest, a niche wholly unacceptable to him since it relegated him to the status of a Basualdo.

Before his marriage, Roussel had taken a good amount of ribbing from his friends about becoming "Mr. Onassis." At the time he had borne the gibes with admirable good humor, but the humor evaporated after the wedding. Then, when the name was awarded him, most often by mistake, he was not shy about showing his displeasure. He proved himself increasingly sensitive to slurs on his head-of-the-family role; when they occurred—or when he thought they had occurred—he would eventually reveal a temper every bit as volcanic as Christina's.

Roussel took a hard look at his wife's financial affairs and concluded she was living well below her means. Her income was in the neighborhood of $50 million a year, and she spent about $6 million. He urged her to get rid of the six-seater Lear jet and buy a larger airplane. She ordered a $15 million Falcon 50, which would seat twenty, but which Christina had done over to seat ten in greater comfort. She bought a larger flat in London for close to $2 million. But for their marriage's principal base, Roussel urged that she buy a place in Switzerland, which offered tempting tax benefits. That she already owned a home in Switzerland was brushed aside. It was too isolated, too seasonal, too indelibly Christina's turf. Roussel envisioned a large estate near a major city.

Most men, on marrying a woman with four homes, a yacht, a

helicopter and a private jet, would think they had fallen into something rather special in the way of plutocratic comforts. Roussel was not like most men. He had been born in a milieu of wealth, and now her fortune could be used to satisfy his voracious appetite for the amenities and emblems of status that great wealth allows. Others suddenly finding themselves in possession of a personal jet might find the distinction between a Lear and a Falcon trifling. To Roussel it was the difference between routine luxury and *glory*.

When Christina took delivery of the Falcon, she and a group of friends flew from Paris to Monte Carlo on its maiden flight. Claude Roland was one of those on board and he remembered a frightening moment. "Shortly after taking off, drinks were being served and we were all settling down for a pleasant flight when suddenly there was a sharp smell of smoke and Christina went into a panic. When we actually could see the smoke seeping through the ceiling panels she started screaming, 'Oh, my God, you're all going to be killed and it's going to be my fault!' She really was in a state, but one of the pilots found the problem, which was easily corrected." Although Christina now felt herself to be extremely happy, she still believed that a curse hung over her family. She was terrified that the curse, now focused on her alone, might drag others down with her.

To gratify her husband's wish for a home base substantial enough to build her new marriage on, Christina found an eighteen-room villa outside Geneva in the small town of Gingins. The house, surrounded by ten acres of landscaped gardens overlooking Lake Leman, belonged to the German automotive heir Gunther Sachs, a former husband of Brigitte Bardot. Christina paid Sachs $5 million for the estate and began pouring money into a total overhaul.

After only a few months of marriage, Christina had an additional reason for renovating: she was pregnant. It was thrilling news for everyone concerned. Roussel's mother told the press that her son and all the Roussel family were "drowning in happiness." No one was more ecstatic than Christina herself. Although she had always loved children and desperately wanted to have her own, the time had never been right. During two of her former marriages—to Andreadis and Kausov—she had become pregnant, but had had abortions, knowing that the marriages were mistakes and that she herself was not psychologically steady enough to start a family, perhaps alone.

She had also had abortions during affairs starting with her first lover Danny Marentette.

To Christina, it had always seemed as if there would be plenty of time for all that, but she was now thirty-three and time was running out. Finally married to a man she loved deeply, she felt psychologically stronger and happier than she had thought possible, and she was determined to make this marriage last. Having a child would be the culmination of her triumphant emergence from the chaotic and aimless years following her father's death. Since then, she had completed one-half of the program she had set for herself—the businesses were running smoothly and needed less and less of her attention. The program's second half, finding a man with whom to create a family, had proved far more difficult. But now, after nine years of floundering, that, too, had come about. She told reporters that she hoped the child would be a girl, but if it was a boy, as her husband wished, she would name him Alexander after her brother.

The enthusiasm with which she threw herself into fixing up her new home was a reflection of her happiness. Altogether, she spent $2.5 million refurbishing and decorating the Gingins estate, which was named Boislande. Aside from the usual remodeling and decorating—plus some unusual flourishes like a swimming pool in the living room—she ordered, with her child in mind, a complex security system that would have given peace of mind to a despised dictator. Closed-circuit television was concealed in every room and was monitored twenty-four hours a day. Movements throughout the house were also electronically recorded, and doors in the nursery wing had electronic combination locks like those in nuclear research facilities. Christina's terror of kidnappers was not inherited, but her own. Although her father had received threats regarding Christina and her brother when they were children, he did not show undue concern and allowed his children to grow up without the elaborate precautions that, since the Lindbergh kidnapping, have cluttered the lives of the very rich.

In anticipation of the expected baby, all of Christina's other residences were similarly subjected to substantial renovations; elaborate nurseries were installed in the Avenue Foch apartment, in the Villa Cristal, and on Skorpios. Christina was so eager for this child that her chronic propensity for worry and imagining potential disasters approached a feverish level. With construction crews hard at work fortifying and beautifying her new house, she turned her attention to her own physical condition. At enormous expense, top medical experts in Paris and Geneva were consulted and extraordinary measures for Christina's health and safety were inaugurated. Whenever possible, she traveled by train rather than plane; and when in a car, she never went over thirty miles an hour. Her friend Dominique Rizzo became pregnant about the same time, which escalated the friendship into one of soul-sister inseparability.

In the summer of 1984, during the early months of her pregnancy, Christina experienced worrying symptoms while on Skorpios and was rushed to a hospital in Switzerland. Although the problem turned out to be minor and was easily corrected, the experience was sufficiently frightening for her to settle into a suite in a Geneva hotel to be near skilled doctors throughout her pregnancy, as well as to keep track of the work going on at Gingins. She passed the time selecting upholstery and curtain fabrics and consulting with representatives of Dior, whom she had flown down from Paris to create the baby's wardrobe. Her happiness that she was at last to become a parent with a man she truly loved combined with her limitless resources to produce a slightly mad nesting frenzy.

When Roussel married Christina, he told Gaby Landhage, according to a friend of hers, that their relationship would not be affected. He was marrying, he said, for business reasons. Shortly after the wedding, he made good on this assurance by bringing Gaby back from Sweden and moving her into his former apartment. Since it was a twenty-minute walk from the apartment he shared with Christina, it was possible for him, even when Christina was in Paris, to remain a presence in both households. With Christina's many absences from town—to St. Moritz, to Skorpios, and finally coming to rest in Geneva—and with Roussel's business commitments in Paris, Gaby was very soon seeing as much of her lover as she ever had.

As evidence of the speed with which Roussel resumed relations with Gaby, she became pregnant by him in the fall of 1984, seven months after his marriage to Christina and four months after Christina became aware she was carrying Roussel's child. Perhaps because of Gaby's condition and the burgeoning domestic complications it presaged, Roussel decided that she should return to Sweden, where she had family and friends to assist her. But once she was out of town, Roussel continued his attentions. He was used to having a woman in two different cities, Paris and Geneva, so it made little difference if one of those cities changed. If he was in Geneva visiting his pregnant wife, it was only slightly less convenient to fly to Malmö to see Gaby than to go to Paris, especially as he often made the trip in Christina's jet.

The primary reason for Gaby's move was discretion. In Paris, Roussel was too well known, his marriage to Christina having made him a celebrity. If the new husband of the famous Greek heiress was seen out on strolls with another woman, she pregnant and very beautiful, Parisian passers-by might make certain unwanted assumptions and feel they had stumbled upon a succulent morsel of gossip. Malmö presented far less risk of exposure. Christina and now Roussel often complained of the way in which they were stripped of every vestige of privacy by a rapacious tabloid press. Roussel's marital juggling act, word of which never surfaced despite massive press curiosity, indicated how easy it was to avoid such scrutiny if one sincerely wished.

Far from being an embarrassing accident, Gaby's pregnancy was very much desired, especially by Gaby. Like Christina, she wanted children by the man she loved and felt time was running out for her. Figuring that her ten years as Roussel's lover gave her certain rights, she insisted on having his child, not only because she was determined to be a mother but also because she wanted proof of the permanent commitment that Roussel professed. Inevitably, more and more people grew aware that Roussel was still seeing Gaby, but Christina, preoccupied with her pregnancy and her plans for her child, remained totally, and blissfully, ignorant.

On January 28, 1985, almost three months earlier than expected, Christina gave birth by Caesarean section to a baby girl, whom she named Athina for her mother. After a worrying few days, the child's vitality took hold and she rapidly became robust and healthy. Christina was in transports of happiness. She was a mother at last and she had given her father, now dead ten years, his first grandchild. Barely out of the hospital, she began talking about having more children.

A nine-man security staff was hired at Gingins, three as round-the-clock bodyguards for the baby and six more to patrol the grounds. There were also three shifts of nurses to serve the baby's every need. Even with all this assistance, Christina was an obsessive mother and spent most of her daughter's waking moments with her. She also lost control in showering treats on her child. As Athina outgrew her baby clothes, Christina spent $25,000 outfitting her at Baby Dior and would spend a similar amount each year thereafter. She would install a private zoo at the estate at Gingins and another at the estate outside Paris she rented for weekends.

Perhaps because of Christina's obsession about her daughter, Roussel's absences became more frequent and she began to complain about them. One time when the couple was in Paris, he checked into a hospital with mysterious stomach pains. Christina turned to her friend with the most extensive experience in her distresses, Luis Basualdo. When she married Roussel, she had terminated Basualdo's salary, but maintained regular telephone contact with him, defying a prohibition imposed by Roussel. She implored Basualdo to come to Paris to keep her company. "I'm so unhappy, Luis," she said. "My husband doesn't want to be with me. He won't sleep with me. You've got to come and keep me company."

After flying to Paris, Basualdo was housed in the apartment she owned on the first floor of the Avenue Foch building, and his $30,000 a month salary was resumed. He found that Christina was severely depressed, and had sunk back into overeating. He did what he could to cheer her up, including taking her to bed a few times. When Roussel heard that Basualdo was back in residence on Avenue Foch, his stomach pains disappeared and he came briskly out of the hospital. But after reflecting that the development might make Christina less needful of his attentions, he decided to be cordial about it and welcomed Basualdo with a phone call. This was for the sake of form. Roussel had instructed Christina to make sure there were no encounters between him and Basualdo, even chance ones.

When Basualdo was joined by Clare, Christina, with her old companions in residence, soon slipped into her former ways. As soon as she knew Roussel would not be home, she would invite Clare and Basualdo to her apartment for dinner, and they would stay up late into the night watching videos. About 3 A.M. on one of these occasions, Christina took a sleeping pill while still in front of the television in anticipation of going to bed. She fell asleep on a sofa and, seeing her eyes closed, Basualdo also fell asleep. He was jolted awake by horrendous screams. Christina had awakened and, finding Basualdo asleep, went into a rage. She was paying him an astronomical amount just to keep her company and he had the gall to sleep in front of her.

Basualdo's lapse brought to the surface all her feelings of rejection and the pain of her predicament. Married less than a year, she found herself alone so often she was forced to pay an old friend to watch television with her. And even heavily bribed, the friend was unable to remain awake in her presence. At another time Christina would have laughed at Basualdo's dereliction or ignored it altogether, but coming at this particular moment, it provoked the most ferocious tantrum. She screamed and ranted. They didn't give a damn about her. No one did. Eleni was called and eventually calmed her and, with the help of some more pills, got her to bed.

Then Roussel would turn up and the bad, lonely stretches were forgotten. In March of 1985, Christina threw a first-wedding-anniversary party on Skorpios, flying in several planeloads of friends for a festive weekend. Among the guests was her former husband Sergei Kausov, whose fortunes continued to flourish in London. Christina had kept up friendly relations with Kausov since their divorce in 1979 and often had dinner with him when she was in London. For a wedding present, Kausov had sent her a new Mercedes sedan, which he thoughtfully renewed each year thereafter. As a tribute to his successor's first year with Christina, and perhaps to show his ex-wife he had picked up a broad repertoire of rich-man's gestures, Kausov imported a troupe of Greek folk dancers to the island to entertain the party after dinner.

During the performance, Christina was at first delighted by the entertainment, but as the energetic and joyous dancing went on and on, she turned to the person next to her and said, "Are they ever going to stop?" This sour note revealed the edginess behind the weekend's air of forced gaiety. For all the high spirits and congratulatory mood, as well as Roussel's efforts to charm even the blacklisted, there was a pervasive undercurrent of gloom to the celebration as guests wondered what exactly they had flown across Europe to celebrate. Almost everyone present knew about Roussel's other home, except, of course, Christina.

Rumors began appearing in the press that all was not well with Christina's marriage to Roussel. Europe's glossy media, particularly the very popular picture magazines, had grown starved in recent years for the kind of international superstars who had proliferated in Europe in the fifties and sixties and who had provided a steady supply of circulation-boosting copy. No one had come along to replace the Grace Kellys, Brigitte Bardots, and Sophia Lorenses, who could be counted on to have a baby, file for divorce, or step from a limousine, thus keeping readers involved with the world of high glamour. The ranks of café-society charismatics continued to shrink until Princess Caroline of Monaco and Christina were about the only two whose most innocuous activities were deemed by editors to be of endless public interest.

Even when nothing much was happening, photographers were posted at the entrance to 88 Avenue Foch when Christina was in town to be ready in case she should choose to electrify Europe by going out to a restaurant or a disco. Considered equally newsworthy was the addition, or loss, of a few pounds; her weight was monitored with the thoroughness accorded the Paris Bourse. Now, with the unmistakable signs of actual news, the press went berserk. If Christina was spotted with a slight look of annoyance on her face, it would be interpreted as proof her marriage was over. Christina took all this in stride, but Roussel, whose nerves were already strained by the complex commuting schedule of his captain's paradise, exploded with anger that his domestic arrangements, even the half that were known to the public, should cause such widespread interest.

His exasperation did not help relations between him and Christina, and arguments over his absences grew more frequent. He told her she was difficult and exhausting to live with and that he needed time to himself. Not limiting his complaints to private conversations with Christina, in a surprise move he gave an interview to a reporter for

*France Soir*, in which he said he was "scandalized" by the irresponsible press reports of trouble in his marriage. In June of 1985, to show what a happy couple he and Christina were, he invited a team of reporters and photographers from *Paris Match* to visit them at their Gingins villa to record for its readers the conjugal happiness that abounded there and perhaps put an end to the baseless speculations about separation and divorce.

As Roussel showed the press people around the sumptuous estate —including the miniature zoo, which had just been installed for the five-month-old Athina—there seemed to be an assumption that the sheer luxury of it all was proof of the couple's contentment. When Roussel and the on-site inspection team were joined by Christina, they could see she was pointedly embarrassed and ill-at-ease, perhaps because of the weight she had regained since her wedding, which put her once again in the two-hundred-pound area. By now Christina was accustomed to talking with reporters and they were accustomed to her. On this occasion, however, they could see that she was not, as she usually was, outgoing and unguarded. Christina answered their questions cautiously in a deliberate attempt to convince the skeptical that, although she and Thierry had problems like every couple, theirs was a completely solid marriage. Roussel eagerly agreed. The reporters were invited to return the next day to take pictures of Athina.

The next morning, having breakfast at their hotel, the *Paris Match* team was stunned to receive a phone call from Roussel. They were not to return to the villa, he told them. He was divorcing Christina. If anything could conjure up a picture of, not domestic tranquillity, but two strong-willed individuals at war, it would be suffering a marital collapse in the middle of a press conference called to deny such a possibility. Roussel stormed off to Paris. A few days later, an article appeared in *Match* that was an unsparing portrait of the horrors of living with Christina—her erratic moods, her willful impulses, her bizarre hours, even her obsession with her child. Nowhere in the article was Roussel quoted directly, but the information was specific and accurate enough to leave little doubt, particularly to Christina, that the reporter had talked at length with her husband.

It was so obvious that the article was based on derogatory information about Christina only Roussel could supply that it came to be seen as an open letter from a husband at the end of his rope, beseeching his impossible wife to mend her ways. It might also have been seen as an attempt to enlist public sympathy by a man who had never intended to remain in the marriage and who was preparing his next move. Such an open use of the press to air personal squabbles was considered infra dig among the people in Christina's and Roussels' world. When a good friend of Christina's asked her how she felt about this breech of good form, she replied that she thought his crying to the press was "childish."

On this occasion, Roussel and Christina patched up the quarrel and were soon seen out and around together. But their battles and reconciliations soon became a pattern that went on for many months. A couple with a half-dozen residences to storm off to is under far less pressure to resolve differences than the couple who must crawl into the same bed no matter how angry they are with one another. Similarly, when a husband has a second wife to run to for comfort, it reduces the motivation to reconcile with the first. Unsolicited assistance in the peacemaking efforts came from Roussel's family, who, with the first news of a separation, would bombard Christina with phone calls telling her how sorry Thierry was, how much he missed Christina, how he was too proud to ask forgiveness. Never suspecting ulterior motives, she would respond to these efforts, and her anger at Thierry would subside. Invariably, Christina would cajole Roussel into returning to her, usually with a promise of a sizable chunk of money. When they had first married, there was a gift to him of $20 million to place his businesses on a more solid footing. Now there were additional gifts of $5 and $10 million, usually presented in the form of peace offerings.

During the summer of 1986, a little over two years after her wedding, Christina was in Paris and received a phone call from her uncle George Livanos saying he was in Paris and wanted to speak with her. Could he come to her apartment? She saw her uncle frequently, but usually in groups, dinner parties, or when skiing in St. Moritz. For him to request a private interview usually meant unpleasant family news or business problems.

Arriving at Avenue Foch, Livanos was grim-faced and clearly dreaded the errand for which he had come. Before she learned about it in some other way, he said, he had to tell her that her husband was deeply involved with another woman. Christina was stunned. She acknowledged that she and Thierry had been fighting a lot, but that was nothing more than the acting-up of the two spoiled children she knew that they were. She had almost come to view the spats as evidence of their compatibility. Wasn't Thierry her soulmate? Didn't she listen for hours to his problems as he listened to hers? Hadn't he been her mentor in straightening herself out? Livanos had more to tell her. Thierry's affair was not a mere fling, but a long-standing relationship with a woman of some character and substance. The worst of it was that she had recently had a child by him.

Still in a daze a day later, Christina received a jocular phone call from her second husband, Alexander Andreadis, who was now re-married and living in London. "That husband of yours is quite a guy," he gloated. "Two wives and having kids with both of them!" When Christina berated him for his cruelty, Andreadis insisted that he had assumed Christina knew all about it; it was, after all, common knowledge as far away as London.

After struggling with her conscience, Florence Grinda, somewhat belatedly, decided she too had to break the news to Christina. For several days Christina was in a state of shock. In the first period of floundering bewilderment, she made a frantic effort to find Basualdo, who, during a few weeks of domestic calm in Christina's household, had been dismissed and told to stand by for future assignments. She tracked him down in Florida, where he had gone to play polo.

"Luis," she said, highly agitated, "Thierry has another wife! Some woman he's been seeing for years. They have children. I just found out. I want you to go to Malmö—it's in Sweden. I want you to rent a car and find the house where she lives and take pictures. I want pictures of the house, but I also want pictures of her and the baby if you can get them."

Basualdo grumbled. It was too far and what was the point? Christina was insistent. Not only would she pay his expenses, Christina assured him, she would pay his full monthly salary of $30,000, even if it only took him a day or two. As soon as Basualdo could get away from Palm Beach, he flew to Stockholm, rented a car, and drove down the coast to Malmö. He found the house without much difficulty, but saw no sign of life. After hanging around Gaby's neighborhood for two days, he was overcome with the futility of his mission

340 ··· CHAPTER TWENTY

and was at the point of approaching the door, knocking, then clicking the camera until the door was slammed. Finally, when the weather turned warm and sunny, a stunning blond woman appeared, carrying a baby, and settled on a chair in the front garden. From her beauty, he was confident she was Gaby. He managed to snap a few pictures without being discovered, then flew to Paris to show them to Christina.

While Basualdo was on his espionage mission, Roussel returned to the Avenue Foch, and Christina immediately confronted him with what she was now hearing from others with oppressive regularity. Her friends, upon learning that the existence of her husband's other family was known to Christina, had been lining up to prove their friendship by telling her the painful news. Invariably they would insist that their failure to tell her earlier had been due to their dread of wounding her rather than to poor gossip pipelines.

Faced with Christina's accusations, Roussel admitted their truth and added a devastating detail she had not heard. Gaby was expecting another child. Having known it would all come out sooner or later—he had managed to keep it from Christina for a remarkable two years—he was prepared for this scene. Calmly, he told Christina that he had been Gaby's lover for a decade and had strong feelings of obligation to her. Gaby now realized that she was getting older and she, like Christina, wanted children, and she wanted them by the only man she loved. Roussel felt he owed her this. Also, he could not consider abandoning her now that another of his children was on the way; it would be too cruel. Naturally, if Christina felt this was cause for divorce, he would acquiesce without a murmur.

Christina was flummoxed. The elaborate and extremely costly life she had built around her love for Roussel was suddenly reduced to a farce. Not only had the marriage lasted less than two years, it now appeared to have been a sham from the start. Although Roussel insisted that he and Gaby were estranged at the time that he and Christina had married, Christina was hearing a lot of evidence to the contrary. In the wreckage the news made of her life, she looked around for some redeeming aspect to what appeared to be another ghastly mistake, another disastrous lowering of her self-protective guard against being used. Her attention quickly focused on her daughter. The marriage may have been false, her friends as false as

Roussel claimed, her fortune a perilous chimera, but Athina was real. Athina made her happy. Athina made it all worthwhile.

And Roussel was not just another man who had tricked her and exploited her. He was Athina's *father*. In a near mystical, very Greek way, that gave Roussel an unassailable status in her life. And as she grew more accustomed to the hideous reality of his betrayal, this view of him grew stronger. The man who had given her the most precious thing in her life was entitled to special rights and dispensations. In addition, he continued to be entitled, she apparently came to feel, to special claims on her money.

Christina's agonizing struggle to think her way through her marital nightmare to some semblance of a sane posture was strongly affected by one overriding fact: she was still powerfully in love with Roussel, perhaps even more so since learning of his split allegiance and his offer to walk away from their marriage. Christina made a mental shift in the way she regarded Roussel. He was still her husband and her lover, but he was first and foremost Athina's father. Relieved that Christina was not slamming the door on their relationship, Roussel assured her of his deep love for her and their child. In speaking of his other involvement, he relegated it, in the grand tradition of double-dealing husbands, to a lower level of human bonding. With one child by Gaby, and another on the way, he could not belittle the affair altogether, but he depicted it as little more than a kindness done for an old friend. Christina and their daughter would always hold, he assured her, the principal place in his heart.

Christina's friends were startled to see that she would submit to continued misuse by Roussel now that she knew of his other family. They were unaware of the consoling, self-exonerating lies she was hearing and which she desperately wanted to believe. Although the basic facts of the situation had their own irrefutable eloquence, Christina managed to reject the dreaded conclusion to which they pointed and accepted Roussel's characterization of his other life.

At first, the realization that all her friends had known of Roussel's second family merely added to Christina's pain and humiliation, but in a curious way the common-knowledge aspect of the situation reversed itself in her mind and made it easier for her to accept. Her strained logic ran: "If my friends and those who loved me all knew what was going on and managed not to fall apart, why should I?" She even began joking about the grotesque situation, telling one friend that she was now an Oriental wife, who had to learn to accept her husband's concubine.

After mulling it over, Roussel decided that he had to divorce Christina. It was not fair to her, he said, now that everyone knew about Gaby and his two children. Nothing would change between them, he assured her, but for appearances' sake it would be better if they were no longer man and wife. He probably had been listening to the advice of lawyers. The birth of a second child by another woman would have greatly reduced his legal standing as a husband in the eyes of French law. One child could be dismissed as an awkward accident, but *two* suggested long-range family planning, and that would stretch even French tolerance too far. Divorce proceedings were begun and Roussel made good on his promise to remain in the life of Christina and Athina.

The decision to divorce would have seemed to reduce, if not eliminate altogether, Roussel's hold over Christina. A man in Roussel's position, with a rich wife desperately in love with him, can use the threat of divorce as a lever to bring the wife to heel, to obtain from her what he wants. But Christina was not to be so fortunate. Even when they divorced, Roussel knew that another fear would enable him to control Christina. More than anything else in the world, she now dreaded his marrying Gaby, and she pleaded with him not to do that. Now, whenever they disagreed about anything or she refused him something he wanted, Roussel merely had to evoke this terrifying possibility and Christina would quickly give in to him.

# 21

# LOVE AT ANY PRICE

*I*n May of 1987, Roussel's divorce from Christina became final. The cash settlement was modest; Roussel had no desire to inject a note of finality into his financial dealings with Christina. As promised, he continued to see her regularly—speaking with her often by phone when away on trips and, when in Switzerland, visiting her villa almost daily. He continued to take an interest in her problems, just as he relied heavily on her sympathetic ear to listen to his. Despite all that had happened, the same closeness existed between them that had begun with the phone chats from Paris to Kenya. Although most of his attention was now going to Gaby and his business enterprises, Roussel remained the dominant influence in Christina's life. With both of them once again single individuals as Roussel wished, Christina undertook an audacious strategy. In perhaps the most curious twist in an already strange three-way arrangement, she decided to befriend Gaby.

Christina could have been forgiven for hating her rival, even wishing her harm. She might have viewed Gaby as a ruthless poacher in her home, a wanton destroyer of her happiness. But oddly, Christina put no blame on Gaby for anything that had happened. Because of the chronology of Roussel's affair with Gaby, Christina had a salve to her wounded feelings that most betrayed wives lack. Since she had come along after Roussel was involved with Gaby, she could view herself as the one who stole Roussel away, an interpretation that made her the marauding seductress rather than the abandoned victim. That interpretation also gave Roussel a moral foothold, however precarious, in that he had not strayed in the classic bored-husband pattern but was loyally adhering to a prior commitment.

Whatever prop to the various egos involved that twisted reasoning provided, it enabled Christina to view Gaby with more sympathy. Bearing her no ill will, Christina gradually elevated Gaby's position in her mind until her former husband's mistress came to enjoy the respect and special status of a family member. Just as Roussel, as the father of Christina's child, was honored—and forgiven everything— so was Gaby honored as the mother of two of his children. Christina struggled to use this biological credential to untangle her own knotted emotions and to harness the more positive ones into a constructive course of action.

When Roussel rented a modest house for Gaby not far from the estate at Gingins, enabling him to keep tabs, as he had in Paris, on both his families, Christina put up no objections. Not content with merely acquiescing to Gaby's proximity, Christina announced that she wanted to meet her. Making a friend of Gaby would surely please Roussel, perhaps throw him off guard, and it was certain to relax the tension inevitably caused in a three-sided relationship. After lengthy deliberations with Roussel and others, Christina devised a plan for the meeting, one she hoped would cause the least discomfort for all concerned. She would invite Gaby to a small dinner party at a restaurant in Geneva, only eight or ten guests, enough to defuse the awkwardness of the first encounter, but not so many as to prevent the two women from becoming acquainted.

Roussel was pleased with Christina's plan. Gaby, on the other hand, was baffled and wary. Having come this far with Roussel's program, however, she accepted the invitation in the friendly spirit in which she hoped, and had been assured, it had been offered. One of the other guests recalled that Christina had phoned them all the day of the dinner and instructed them on how to behave. "She insisted that we all be nice to Gaby. Under no circumstances were we to misinterpret the reason for the dinner and to snub her. If we failed to be friendly and gracious, we would have Christina to answer to."

The night of the dinner, Christina was in particularly high spirits and looked better than she had for some time. When Gaby arrived at the restaurant, she appeared frightened and ill-at-ease. The only one in the group known to her was Roussel, who was working so hard at appearing upbeat and nonchalant that he paid little notice to the mother of two of his children. Not Christina. She sat Gaby one male guest away, as close as convention allowed, and in every possible way tried to make her feel comfortable. Whenever Gaby spoke, Christina unceremoniously stopped listening to whomever she had been conversing with and turned her attention to Gaby. She left little doubt she considered Gaby her guest of honor, which provided an ironic contrast with Roussel's coolness toward her. The others at the table, as per instructions, used their considerable powers of charm to make Roussel's mistress feel she was among friends.

By the end of the evening, Gaby was a bit less on guard but still perplexed by the kindness being showered on her by the woman whose life she was disrupting. It was not, however, until the two women met again a few days later at Christina's lakeshore estate, to which Gaby was invited with her two children, that all tension evaporated as the shared concerns of motherhood relegated Roussel's domestic legerdemain to an insignificant, almost irrelevant, place. Determined as Christina was to make Gaby her friend for strategic reasons, the Swedish woman's gentle nature and her obvious pain at the situation won Christina completely, and a genuine friendship grew up between them.

Gaby and her children became regular visitors to Boislande, which had been converted into a child's dream of enchantment—with the playgrounds, walk-in zoo, miniature Land-Rover, indoor swimming pool, and rooms full of Fisher-Price toys. Gaby's two children proved delightful and well behaved; they were also thrilled at the private fun fair their mother had found for them. Christina's sense of protocol, which could be jettisoned in many situations but would come over her resoundingly in others—was brought into full play by her awareness that these two blond and healthy infants were her beloved Athina's brother and sister.

Christina went to considerable effort to provide her daughter with playmates her own age, scouring the hills around Geneva for suitable children, and setting up an elaborate network of recruitment to corral them to her home. With Gaby's family, however, Christina was able to present her daughter not just with prop playmates but with a real, live baby brother and sister. What could be better? In her typical response to anything that touched her emotions, Christina began lavishing expensive gifts on Gaby's children and, of course, on Gaby herself. So frequent did the visits of Gaby and her children become that a columnist erroneously reported that Christina, Roussel, and Gaby were all living together, presumably in some sort of *grand luxe ménage à trois*.

Gratified by the unexpected development in the complex life he had created for himself, Roussel started spending more time at Christina's Gingins villa, often without Gaby. He was touched by the noble way Christina had accepted his having-it-all arrangement. He was also resolved to spend as much time with his daughter Athina as with his other two children. When in Switzerland, he would pass the afternoon playing with Athina, then remain for a quiet dinner with Christina. After dinner, however, he would always return to Gaby, pointing to the fact that she was alone while Christina was surrounded with people—her household staff, bodyguards, nurses, and usually a few house guests.

Christina accepted this as she accepted everything else. Miraculously, Roussel continued to make her feel as though she were number one in his affections, that their relationship was the official, serious one, Gaby merely a prior obligation he did not have the heart to abandon. When her friends raised eyebrows on hearing of Roussel's declarations, Christina would pathetically cite the flimsiest evidence of his devotion. If at the dinner table Roussel placed his hand over hers, she would pull a friend aside later and say, "I hope you saw that. See how much he loves me?" On no more hard evidence than that he had fathered her child and dropped in to see them from time to time, Christina still considered Roussel her husband.

From the start of the marriage, Christina's relatives were alarmed about the large pieces of her fortune that were reportedly being transferred to Roussel. The top executives of Christina's companies, mostly Greek men who had devoted their lives to building the Onassis empire, were equally dismayed. In addition to the normal concerns that she was dissipating her inheritance, perhaps throwing good millions after bad, there was a chauvinistic concern that these hard-earned Greek assets were falling, without a struggle, into foreign hands. The most informed estimates placed the total amount she gave him at $50 million, a figure that became common knowledge quite quickly. It would be considerably more before her death. Christina herself confided to an old and close friend that the final amount was $73 million.

While still married to Christina, Roussel aggravated her family's concerns by making statements to the effect that he was no longer content with handouts to refuel his own businesses, he wanted a major say in managing Christina's interests. His own record of business success would have been sufficient to send a chill through the corridors of Olympic Maritime, where the feeling was that he had gone through the Roussel fortune and now wanted to finish off the Onassis one as well. As his credentials as a dutiful husband deteriorated, the threat grew more ominous.

None of Christina's former husbands had attempted such a power play, which to her family and the Greek men running the empire was carrying café-society hijinks too far. The concerned parties knew that, in the end, the only thing that stood between the fortune and Roussel's announced ambition to manage it was Christina herself, a line of defense that gave them little comfort. Her grandmother Arietta Livanos, whose disdain for marriage with non-Greeks had only grown over the years, once remarked to a friend, "My poor Christina can never separate her money from her emotions."

A good part of George Livanos's motive in revealing to his niece the truth about Gaby had been his hope that awakening Christina to the extent of her husband's deceit would stop the drain on her Onassis-Livanos fortune. On the contrary, Christina continued to give Roussel large amounts almost on demand. Sometimes she balked and there would be heated words, ending usually with his storming off and remaining incommunicado until Christina, dreading a break or, even worse, news of his marriage to Gaby, tracked him down and gave him what he asked. A woman who was known to be a very soft touch to friends pleading the most frivolous needs— one couldn't afford St. Moritz that winter, another needed a new fur coat—Christina was a pushover when the man she loved was suffering over business emergencies.

For the most part Christina's relatives and close friends avoided saying anything to her against Roussel, but on one occasion the family's low opinion was placed squarely before both Christina and Roussel. They were sitting at a nightclub table in St. Moritz when Christina's cousin Constantine Niarchos asked her to dance. Christina said she was tired.

"Oh, come on, Christina," Niarchos said, fixing Roussel with his eye. "At least it won't cost you fifty million."

Roussel lunged at Niarchos. Others intervened and peace was restored. Painful as such incidents were for him, Roussel could turn them to his advantage by refusing to have anything to do with Christina's family. If he sensed someone in her world was critical of him, and by this time almost everyone was who had survived the earlier purges, they were immediately persona non grata when he was around. Since she wanted him around as much as possible, the offending friend found himself or herself shut out completely. As for friends like Florence Grinda, about whom Roussel felt he had hard evidence that she was campaigning against him, he placed Christina on the honor system, and forbade her to see Grinda at any time.

Aside from extracting large sums in return for not marrying Gaby, Roussel continued to manipulate Christina in other ways. Her friends were stunned to hear that, for the first time since she had inherited the island, Christina was not planning to spend her summer on Skorpios. The reason cited was the difficulty of making the approachable island as secure from kidnappers as she had made the estate at Gingins. There was some reason for such a fear. The Greek police had gotten hold of a terrorist hit list and informed Christina that her name was at the top. But a close Paris friend insisted that this had nothing to do with her decision to abandon Skorpios. "It was because Thierry had told her he wouldn't go there," the woman said, "nothing else."

Since the French Riviera was his favorite summertime haunt, Christina leased a large place there for the summer. But even this substantial concession failed to win Roussel's regular attendance. The story started circulating that Christina was paying Roussel $100,000 for every night he spent in the Riviera villa. While it was perfectly within Christina's repertoire of inducements to make such an offer—the checkbook had long been her first reflex in dealing with frustration—the story was probably apocryphal for the simple reason that $100,000 a night was insignificant compared to the millions Roussel was obtaining from Christina while sleeping where he wished. On the other hand, Roussel may have pleaded lost revenues from his business interests if he dallied in the south of France when he should have been tending to his affairs in Paris. If that was so, the money may have been offered in the nature of compensation for business time lost rather than the cash-for-cuddles some columnists suggested.

It was also possible that Christina, angered at the brevity of a Roussel visit after having given him a large sum, may have tossed off a sardonic remark about how much the visit had cost her, based perhaps on her own quick calculations of her recent advances to him, only to have the line misinterpreted as a statement of literal fact by a Christina watcher ravenous for scurrilous particulars. Such press reports infuriated Roussel. His outraged denials inevitably focused on the letter of the accusation. He may have failed to acknowledge, even to himself, that its underlying thrust was true, that money was what had brought him into Christina's life and money was what was keeping him there.

If Roussel's plan in marrying Christina had been to give her a year or two of happiness then depart with his businesses in more solid financial shape, there was nothing so heinous in such a scheme, assuming he had a fondness for her and enjoyed, or didn't mind, making love to her occasionally. These squalid little transactions go on all the time among the rich and the would-be rich. In playing these high-level bedroom games, however, there is a wild card that can appear without warning to dislodge such corrupt but innocuous arrangements and turn the urbane comedies into tragedies. That is when the person used falls deeply in love with the user.

When that calamity struck Christina, Roussel's mildly naughty game turned vicious. The positive aspects of his relationship with Christina—the love-making, the companionship, the fun—became for her agonizing reminders of the happiness that was being withdrawn and that had probably never been rightfully hers. The schemer had lost control of the scheme, which had started harmlessly, and found himself viewed no longer as a sly operator but as a sadistic villain. Half-hearted efforts to extricate himself from the now hideous situation caused added tortures to Christina. Even his kindness caused pain.

Had Christina, after a year or two of marriage, followed her usual

pattern of sliding into a bored affection for her partner, no harm
would have been done by Roussel. She would have had a period of
conjugal happiness, followed by the outlay of an easily replaced slice
of her fortune, and she would have come away with a new confidant
in her stable of men who had desired her, with whom she had been
intimate, and for whom, because they had once lusted after her, she
would always hold a special affection. This had been the resolution
of her marriages to Kausov and, to a degree, to Andreadis. With
Roussel, she would also have come out of it with what she most
wanted: a child. Everyone would have been happy. But by falling
deeply in love with Roussel, Christina threw the game out of control
and set loose emotional havoc.

Roussel could have resolved the dilemma in one of two ways: nur-
tured Christina with handouts of attention that were all the more
painful for the manifest pity that inspired them, or brutally broken
off the relationship in the hope that no contact would have acceler-
ated the healing process. Roussel chose the former path, which was
mandated to a degree by the daughter they shared. Had he not continued to extract money from his ex-wife, however, it would have
been easier to believe that concern for Christina played a part in his
decision.

Aside from Christina's family, another spectator was deeply affected
to see Christina heaping riches upon a man who was making her
profoundly unhappy. It was Luis Basualdo, who was stung that, after
doing so much for Christina, he was coming away with so little.
While he knew he had enjoyed for a number of years a sinecure that
others considered unbelievable good fortune—being paid lavishly for
flying around the world with Christina, skiing in St. Moritz, sum-
mering on Skorpios, eating and drinking like a prince—he knew, too,
the humiliating demands of his position, the workday that lasted
until 4 A.M., the tantrums directed at him more than others because
of his employee status, the need to feign amused merriment when
he was rigid with boredom. Her last two husbands, Kausov and now
Roussel, were leaving their brief tours of duty rich men. After suffering more at the hands of Christina's whims and moods than either of
them, Basualdo, whom she had once wanted for a husband, might

now be leaving her world with nothing. At the same time, his irreplaceable source of income would be cut off.

When she first fell in love with Roussel and sent Basualdo away, he felt little concern, knowing that her involvements never lasted very long. But this business with the Frenchman appeared to be different, their strong involvement lingering even after the divorce. Christina seemed to be changing, maturing perhaps. Or maybe motherhood, in opening up new life possibilities, had shut off others. There was no doubt that Christina seemed to be moving permanently away from her self-destructive former life that Basualdo, more than anyone else, personified.

For whatever reason, their friendship was not as strong as it once had been. When they were together, they bickered more often than previously and Christina seemed less amused by his cynical view of the world. Basualdo saw himself on the way out, and he was coming away empty-handed. Adding to his concern were his less than bright prospects. His divorce from Lucy Pearson had been ugly, making a powerful enemy of her father and his former sponsor, Lord Cowdray, and he was persona non grata in quarters of England that might, before the Pearson scandal, have been congenial havens.

Although most of his living and pleasure expenses had been paid, he had saved little from his hefty monthly salary from Christina. When left on his own, he still felt obliged, for reasons of personal pride as well as habit, to operate on the Onassis level. If he had to cross the Atlantic, he wouldn't consider flying any other way than first class. A restaurant had to be three stars; it was not his nature to eat at Le Burgerking and bank the $30,000. He viewed his salary and the high living as the benefits a lover or a husband would have enjoyed during their tenure. Like a used-up husband, he was about to be cashiered. The time had come to think about a settlement.

A near-farcical incident that occurred in Christina's Villa Cristal in St. Moritz shortly before she had married Roussel presaged the darker financial drama between Basualdo and Christina that was to unfold shortly. Unable to ski because of a case of the flu, Christina was propped up in bed going over bills and initialing the ones she wanted paid. Pausing over one, she adjusted her reading glasses, then went into a rage. A bill from the Palace Hotel, where she had installed Basualdo and Clare as her guests, was thousands of dollars higher than she expected. Reading through the itemization, she discovered that Basualdo had ordered, among other amenities designed for visiting rajahs, daily room deliveries of caviar and champagne.

Always generous to those she sponsored, Christina could turn on them abruptly if she felt her generosity was being exploited. Rarely was there a middle ground of wounded coolness; she would suddenly switch from loving benefactress to raging, wrathful prosecutor. Phoning Basualdo at the hotel, she swore and yelled at him for about ten minutes. Apologetic at first, Basualdo turned angry himself when she remained unmollified by his promises to discontinue abusing room service. Defiantly, he asked what she could do about it? The charges had already been made on a bill she had guaranteed. Christina knew what she could do about it. She could, she roared, withhold his salary, then hung up. Basualdo, deeply stung by Christina's attack, happened to be in particular need of his salary at that moment and was reluctant to be docked $30,000 for his snacks. In a fury, he jumped into his Porsche and roared the short distance to the Villa Cristal. When he arrived, the butler greeted him at the door and told him Madame Onassis was ill and could not see anyone.

Benjamin Clutterbuck, an English friend, who was staying with Christina at the time, recalled what happened next. "A group of us were sitting in the living room and we could hear Luis push his way into Christina's private quarters. There he was met by the second line of defense, her maid, Eleni, who started crying, 'Oh, monsieur, monsieur, madame est malade. Vous ne pouvez pas déranger madame.' From the bedroom we could hear loud voices, then a scream from Christina followed by Eleni's voice, saying, "Laissez madame tranquille! You must not hurt madame, monsieur!" Finally, Luis emerged from the bedroom and, to our astonishment, triumphantly brandished a check for $30,000."

In Basualdo's version of this incident, he added that Christina first miswrote the check, either from her confusion or perhaps from trying to write while in a hammerlock, then put that check aside on the bed and wrote another. When Christina handed him the rewritten version, he took it, but also picked up the first check and managed to get both checks honored.

There were conflicting versions of a far more serious misappropria-tion of Christina's funds, this time more than a million dollars. By Basualdo's account, Christina, while still married to Roussel, gave Basualdo two large checks—one for $700,000 and one for $500,000, and instructed him to use them to set up a bank account in Austria. The purpose was to enable her to make large payments, without Roussel's or her accountants' knowledge, to various individuals—primarily her former stepbrother James Blandford and her Aunt Merope's lover-companion, whom Christina had "borrowed" to ac-company her on several trips. The money could also be used to pay other obligations Christina preferred to keep secret, such as the bills of the New York doctor who supplied Christina with barbiturates and amphetamines.

Ever since Christina's forcible abduction of James Blandford at the Paris airport for drug treatment, an action few could see as anything but a bold and selfless effort to rescue her former stepbrother from self-destruction, he had been threatening to sue Christina for sizable damages. A large chunk of the Austrian money was, according to Basualdo, a discreet payoff to Blandford. As she requested, Basualdo set up the bank account, then, instead of dispensing the money to the people designated, gave Blandford a token $60,000 and kept the rest for himself. His feeling was that "she owed it to me." The other side, the Onassis interests, said simply that he forged the two checks and that Christina knew nothing about it.

Both versions agreed on the most damaging fact—that Basualdo walked away with $1.2 million that had not been intended for him. No matter how large the amount or how complex his relationship with Christina, that would be considered by most people and most legal systems as theft. But while admitting to having taken the money, Basualdo relied heavily on the distinction he made between keeping funds entrusted to him to dispense to others as opposed to the outright raid on his employer's bank account that his accusers alleged—perhaps because, under most legal systems, forgery is more unequivocally a crime.

Basualdo claimed that he had diverted the money from one of Christina's expenditures he considered harebrained and unnecessary to a payment to himself that he considered merited. Hadn't Christina felt sufficiently ashamed of the outlays to set up a secret account?

Also, that the money in question was, by his version, payment for services rendered made it more reasonable for him to cut himself in on the financial expressions of gratitude.

Basualdo had a further justification, which he offered somewhat half-heartedly. "Christina often told me that if she found happiness with a man, she would pay me $300,000, but once she told me she would pay me ten times my annual salary. That would be $3 million. I never took the promise seriously, but here she was married to Roussel, madly in love with him. I thought I was entitled to something."

Blandford would deny any part in the scheme. He remembered that he and Basualdo were taking a trip to Spain, where Basualdo had promised to introduce him to, perhaps fix him up with, brewing heiress Daphne Guinness. Driving out of St. Moritz, Basualdo stopped at Christina's bank, then returned to tell Blandford they had to make a small detour before proceeding to Spain. He had a banking errand to execute in Landeck, Austria. Arriving in Landeck, Blandford waited in the car while Basualdo went into a bank. After a time, Basualdo returned and said the manager had never met a marquess and wanted an introduction to Blandford. Obligingly, Blandford entered the bank and was asked to show his passport—to verify he really was as exalted as he claimed, Blandford later supposed. He professed total ignorance that Basualdo's "banking errand" had been to open an account using three-quarters of his name—the first three parts of "Charles James Spencer Churchill."

If Blandford's version was self-serving and he was, rather, a co-conspirator in the enterprise, he could find some exoneration in that it took place at a time in his life when he was so out of control on heroin that, among other stunts, he was arrested in England for breaking into a pharmacy and once suggested to a friend of Christina's that they burglarize her St. Moritz villa for her collection of Fabergé eggs. He had also slapped a policeman who was trying to arrest him. But even Basualdo had a stake in Blandford's appearing innocent; it would have seemed odd for him to collaborate in the theft of the money if a large portion of it was intended for him, as Basualdo claimed.

Also casting doubt on Basualdo's version that Christina had instigated the secret account was the fact that she was the one who called attention to the missing money. She had requested funds from her account in her St. Moritz bank, Crédit Suisse, and was told that it was almost empty. Aware that she had not used the account in many months, she knew immediately something was very wrong. An audit quickly revealed the recent transfer of $1.2 million to the Austrian bank, and a few inquiries with the two banks involved left little doubt in her mind that Basualdo was behind the business. She denounced him to the authorities.

If Christina had instigated the account as Basualdo claimed, she would have been hypocritical in the extreme to throw her old friend into serious trouble with the law over a special service *she* had requested of him. It was also unlikely that even Basualdo would relish being converted by this scenario into the G. Gordon Liddy of the Corviglia Club. Neither was there any evidence that Roussel or her accountants—the individuals the secret account was intended to deceive, according to Basualdo—had veto power over the way in which she spent her fortune. Christina certainly did many odd and extravagant things in the interest of keeping peace, not just with her husband but with close friends and her executives as well, but had she believed herself obliged to pay James Blandford or anyone else a large sum of money, it was unlikely she would have felt the need for secrecy to do so.

Over the years, Christina had grown philosophical about attempts to defraud her, since it occurred with such regularity by everyone from shopkeepers to close friends. She cared little, not only because she was indifferent to the money involved, but because her sympathies more often than not went out to the person reduced to cheating. Her frequent compliance with friends' requests for money to help them out of tight spots was not because she believed all the hard-luck stories—she never checked them out—but because she was made uncomfortable by the others' need to demean themselves by asking for money—the more far-fetched the reason, the more demeaning. Her speed at obliging requests for cash was also a function of her guilt at having so much.

When she discovered the fraud involving Blandford and Basualdo, two of her closest friends, Christina's mood was quite different. Aware of the enormous drain on her fortune caused by her emotional servitude to Roussel, she had exhausted her store of tolerance for extraneous losses. She wasted no time on behind-the-scenes ma-neuvers, but promptly hired Interpol to gather enough evidence to make possible a successful prosecution. With the detective agency's findings, as well as the two canceled checks, Christina proceeded against the pair, as did the Austrian bank involved.

Laying hands on Basualdo presented problems. Shortly after Christina's discovery of her missing money, he had been arrested in London on a two-year-old drunk-driving charge for which he had failed to show up in court. The matter was settled when he paid a modest fine, but as he was leaving the court he was detained by two detectives, who said he was wanted by the Austrian police in connec-tion with a bank fraud in Landeck. Until the extradition papers ar-rived, the police demanded his passport. Now a U.S. citizen, he handed over his American passport, then was permitted to leave the station.

Basualdo claimed this incident marked the first knowledge he had of any money problem with Christina, but he was sufficiently alarmed by the development to flee the country. He took Clare out for a farewell dinner, then the next morning, using his old Argentin-ean passport, which he had retained, boarded a plane for Buenos Aires—his home, to be sure, but also an extradition-proof refuge for fugitive felons.

When the Austrian authorities tracked him down, he at first stuck to the story that the bank account had been set up at Christina's request for payments to be made elsewhere, but when evidence was produced that traced the money to him, he admitted having taken it on the grounds that he believed he was entitled to it. When it was pointed out that this excuse was available to anyone who ever took money, he cut off all further ethical discussions by announcing that he no longer had the money. He had lost it, he regretted to say, through bad investments. He maintained that any further action was pointless. The Austrian authorities were not so easily put off, but Christina was. She dropped charges and, eventually, forgave him.

Basualdo would later grow heated at any version of this episode that deviated from his own: that Christina gave him the money to give to others and he kept it. To him, as well as to the authorities, that was far less reprehensible than planning a fraud, forging checks, lifting money from a bank account where it was sitting idle. About the central fact, that he misappropriated money from Christina, he was nonchalant, almost smug. Sometime later he was with a group of Christina's friends who were discussing the $200,000 she had given her maid Eleni when she left, she thought for good, for Moscow, only to ask for the money's return when her marriage to Kausov collapsed.

"Did Eleni return it?" asked one of the group.

"Every penny," said Basualdo.

"Good God," said another young man. "I would have told her I lost it in bad investments."

"When they came after me, that's what I did tell her," Basualdo said quietly, clearly referring to his own custody of some of Christina's money.

Although Christina was highly suspicious that her former stepbrother was implicated in the Austrian bank scam, she met with him on a social basis in London in hopes of learning more about what had happened. At dinner in London, they discussed the problem, but when they had exhausted this subject, Christina fell into her favorite pastime with Blandford, reminiscing about their childhood days at Lee Place. It was clear, however, that her usual relish for this sport was missing. Until the money problem arose, Blandford had been for Christina a reminder of one of the few happy periods in her life. When in the company of Blandford or his sister Henrietta, Christina could indulge her passion for nostalgia without the usual need for editing out the pain and humiliation. But Blandford was no longer one who triggered only pleasant associations. He had joined the vast battalion of figures in Christina's life who were either guilty or suspected of abusing her friendship for profit.

This was a bad period for Christina on money matters. Although she justified the enormous outlays for Roussel as nothing less than the price for her happiness, she was increasingly aware of how little happiness she was getting for her money. The Basualdo business had stung her deeply. Then she was angered and hurt when she heard rumors that one of her oldest friends had sold candid snapshots of a fat Christina and her guests on Skorpios to a German magazine for $60,000. On top of this, she was hit with what she considered a financial betrayal from another quarter: the Doderos. Marina's father was ill and not expected to live. He was determined that, before he died, he would repay the loan that Christina had made to save the family business. Rather than being delighted to get her money back —in all likelihood the only one of her loans ever repaid—Christina was furious.

When Marina Dodero had pleaded with Christina in Lenox Hill hospital to give her $4 million, Christina had lent her the money at no interest on the proviso that Marina and her husband make themselves available to her, Basualdo style, when she wanted them. Now, after four years, the loan was being repaid—without interest. But during the intervening four years the Doderos had felt as free as they ever had to decline Christina's "invitations" to stay with her—more often pleas not to leave her. She felt they had reneged on the agreement, and therefore owed her the interest. When the check for $4 million arrived with no mention of interest, Christina exploded and launched a lawsuit to recover the money she felt she was owed.

Although Christina could be incredibly extravagant with her money, even profligate, she was not stupid about it. She knew that $4 million could easily earn $400,000 a year, considerably more, in fact, than she had paid Basualdo. The four years of the loan would bring the interest to $1.6 million, too much money to wave off as a gesture between friends, and enough money, surely, to expect something in return (although it would have meant that in addition to the money she was giving Roussel, she was spending close to a million a year to keep her closest friends adequately attentive). More important to Christina than the Doderos' truancy was her feeling that they had made a deal and not lived up to it. She was losing Basualdo over a bitter money fight; she might as well lose the Doderos too.

The case ended up in a Greek court, where the Doderos dutifully appeared. On the steps of the Athens courthouse, however, they encountered Christina. Marina, seeing her dearest friend arriving for battle, burst into tears and threw her arms around Christina, who also burst into tears. While lawyers watched unhappily, the two women cried and hugged and begged each other's forgiveness, and the matter was forgotten.

After a number of blowups and reconciliations, relations between Roussel and Christina were cordial going into the summer of 1988, when she leased the magnificent Villa Trianon in St.-Jean-Cap-Ferrat on the Riviera. The house—an imposing, baronial affair with formal gardens stretching to the sea—was almost as grandiose a showplace as her father's Château de la Croe just a few miles along the coast at Antibes and three decades into Christina's past. De la Croe had been Aristotle Onassis's debut residence in Europe, and it was sadly fitting that his daughter would make a similarly outsize Riviera palace her last new residence.

The mansion had been rented, of course, to please Roussel, who considered the Riviera his bailiwick. Also to please Roussel was Christina's new figure, over which she had suffered an unusually difficult springtime stint at the Marbella health clinic. Once she and Athina and the usual large staff were settled in Villa Trianon, Roussel was in frequent attendance, and he and Christina were closer than they had been in months. Seeing them together so frequently, friends talked of remarriage, a rumor that Christina did nothing to squelch. She also confided to friends her eagerness to have another child by Roussel.

Although willing to oblige, Roussel had a problem. While insisting he loved Christina, he made little secret that he was unable to perform sexually with her. Even that breakdown, which she regarded as temporary, did not discourage her. She persuaded her ex-husband to create a sperm bank from which she, with medical assistance, would make withdrawals at the most propitious time of each month. As a token of appreciation for this friendly gesture, she gave Roussel a $165,000 Ferrari. She also told him that if she had another child by him, she would give him $10 million.

Her plan, which seemed to make Christina happy, surely marked the most pathetic point of her fixation on Roussel. She was reduced to bribing the man she loved with expensive gifts, not for his attention, his love, his body, but for a small quantity of his semen, which was inserted into her mechanically, by trained technicians, in a cold, clinical setting. Rather than wounding and humiliating Christina, with her strong sexual and romantic nature, it gratified her to have the cooperation of Roussel in the goal of making another child.

"Could he want this if he did not want me?" she asked her friends, many of whom inwardly said, "Why not?" Also, another child would place her on a maternal par with Gaby. Christina closed her eyes to everything but the childbearing aspect of the arrangement and felt closer to Roussel than she had in some time. To celebrate this upturn in her sliding hopes, Christina decided to throw a large, sumptuous party at her new villa.

As plans unfolded for the event, it began to take on the importance of a major society wedding. There would be a circus-sized marquee on the lawn for dancing, a full orchestra, armies of caterers, butlers, footmen, and 250 guests, many flown in from London, Paris, New York, and Los Angeles. Throwing herself into the arrangements with childlike excitement, Christina came up with many individualistic touches, most of which emphasized the party's theme: she and Thierry were together again.

Cocktail napkins and match books were printed with "Christina and Thierry." A photographer would thoroughly record the party, the photographs to be mounted later in small hardcover books and mailed to each guest. On the red silk cover would be inscribed "Villa Trianon" and the party date. Inside the front cover would be a photo of Christina and Roussel, the happy couple. On the following pages would be three or four photos of the guests who received each book. This thoughtful touch would keep three secretaries editing photographs for several days. Christina said she was giving the party for Roussel, but the souvenir book left little doubt that the event was planned to mark an important milestone: Christina's reconciliation with her husband.

As the day of the party approached, Christina and her large staff were in a dither of excitement, which produced a sad effect. A house guest who had arrived from Argentina for the event noticed trucks arriving during the day to unload cases of Dom Pérignon and other costly provisions, only to see the same cases being loaded that evening into private automobiles parked at the villa's service entrance. One afternoon he noticed a small white truck delivering some huge tins of caviar. Suspecting that wholesale theft was in progress, he asked Christina over cocktails that evening if he could have some caviar. She spoke to her butler, who returned with a tiny dollop of Beluga caviar on a piece of toast.

"Is this all I get?" the guest asked. "I really have a taste for caviar tonight."

Christina sent her butler back to the kitchen only to have him return shamefaced. "There is no more caviar, madame," he said. The guest, who knew that pilferage is a chronic problem of the rich, felt that in the Villa Trianon in the preparty confusion world records were being set. But he also felt Christina's elation at the moment was too fragile to deal with such irrelevant problems, so did not mention it.

The party was a smashing success. The night was soft and balmy, the summertime Riviera at its best. The Villa Trianon, which on an ordinary day would have been residence enough for Marie Antoinette, was now decked out as a glimmering, gardenia-scented monument to limitless wealth. Liveried attendants crowded the entrance, waiting to dispose of the arriving Bentleys and Mercedeses. Towering floral arrangements lined the grandiose entrance hall, through which guests were lured by orchestra music coming from a rear terrace where cocktails were being served. Stone steps led to the lawn and on to the dance floor toward the sea, where round tables were set with ducal silver, crystal, and china, and where twinkling hurricane lamps echoed the coastal lights that shimmered across the Gulf St. Jean.

As Christina and Roussel greeted guests on the rear terrace, she appeared vivacious and elated. A slight puffiness to his face and a fatigue around his eyes tarnished the movie-star perfection of his looks. They were no longer beauty and the beast of Christina's fat days, but rather a handsome young couple who would not be young much longer but who seemed too content to care. As the guests streamed in, Christina's excitement increased until she was almost giddy. Total amnesty having been granted to all the banished friends, the party seemed to have included everyone she had ever liked. Florence Grinda, Claude Roland, Gilles Dufour, Basualdo—all the exiles showed up to see in the flesh the two people about whom they had spent the last year or two speculating, gossiping, worrying.

For Christina, receiving her guests on the terrace was fulfilling the party's primary purpose: to show her world that she had pulled herself together, now looked terrific, and with the man she loved at her side, their three-year-old daughter safe on the villa's upper floor with her nanny and bodyguards, she had managed to reassemble the total happiness she had felt on her wedding day. Dancing went on until nearly dawn, with Christina showing her usual exuberance and tirelessness. A breakfast of scrambled eggs, red caviar, and champagne was served around four o'clock, after which guests began to leave, drunkenly aware they had been to a memorable Riviera event that clearly had been a high point in the life of their famous and adversity-prone friend.

The next morning Christina was up by 10 A.M., running through the sprawling villa, hurrying the workers who had come to clear away the party debris. There was a reason for her urgency. At 1 P.M. Gaby and her two children were arriving for a week's stay. Fearing Gaby would be hurt not to have been included, Christina had ordered that all traces of the party be removed by the time she arrived. The close friends who had been put up for the night had been informed they had to leave by noon, and Christina hectored staff and guests alike not to leave around any evidence, such as souvenir menus, party balloons, or the daily newspapers with accounts of the event. Even the large flower arrangements were lifted into trucks and sent to the local hospital.

Christina's concern for concealing the party from Gaby was based on consideration, to be sure, but her conspiratorial secrecy also made her feel as though she had a legitimacy in Roussel's life her rival lacked. For Christina, having had Thierry serve as host for the lavish party, parading arm in arm their happy togetherness before two hundred friends, validated their relationship, proclaimed its preeminence, and relegated Gaby to a back-street, morning-after status.

But if Christina's main purpose in giving the party had been to show herself triumphant to a group she knew considered her a victim, its secondary purpose had been to remind Roussel of the rich enchantments her billionaire's wand could conjure up. Relying as always on what she saw as her greatest asset, her money, Christina sought to overwhelm Roussel with its capabilities. She knew his weaknesses. Still, to use it to intimidate Gaby would not, in Christina's mind, be playing fair.

Satisfied that the villa would soon be free of any evidence of the previous evening's excitement, Christina found a copy of the newspaper she had saved because of a particularly good photograph of herself and Roussel on the front page, then headed upstairs to her bedroom to show it to him. On the large balcony adjoining the master suite, she found Roussel sitting at a breakfast table reading a Paris paper and sipping coffee in the bright sun that bounced from the sea and sparkled through the cool cypresses.

Looking grave, Roussel asked Christina to sit down. Since awaking that morning, she had been looking forward to rehashing the party with him, and now she launched into a story about one of the guests drunkenly insulting another. Roussel cut her off. There was something important he had to say to her. He had arrived at a difficult conclusion. He could not continue with Christina in this way. Everything was over between them. He was going to marry Gaby and make a life with her. Pleading illness when Gaby arrived, Christina stayed in her room and cried for two days, Eleni never leaving her side.

A few weeks later, all the guests who had attended the gala party received a small package in the mail. They opened it to find a slim book exquisitely bound in crimson silk with stiff pasteboard pages, white and gilt-edged. Inscribed on the cover in gold letters was "Villa Trianon, August 8, 1988." On the first page was a color photograph of Christina and Roussel taken on the estate's lawn the night of the party. Arms around each other, they were both smiling and radiant. In the opulent setting of great beauty and luxury, they appeared two of the gods' favorites, a young man and woman—handsome, rich, vital—two people who had exactly what they wanted.

# 22

# ENDING WHERE IT BEGAN

Christina's friends were bewildered when they learned of her sudden enthusiasm for Argentina. She had just spent close to $8 million creating a Swiss home for herself and her daughter and, for changes of scene, she maintained four other residences in Europe, always staffed and ready for her arrival. Much as she loved Europe, particularly France and England, she also enjoyed an occasional visit to New York or Southern California. What was Argentina all about?

In the opinion of her intimate friends, it was all about Roussel. Christina liked Buenos Aires, to be sure. She had many friends there, particularly the Doderos. She relished the social life and she liked the reverse seasons, which enabled her to swim in the winter. For the family-oriented Christina, Argentina also had a sentimental attraction; it was where her father had started the Onassis fortune. And ever since her five-day idyll in the pampas with Basualdo, the country had taken on romantic associations for her, a tantalizing mix of past experience and future possibilities. Perhaps because of her Mediterranean looks, she seemed to win more attention from men here than in Europe, making her feel sexy, *draguée*. Reinforcing that agreeable impression, Buenos Aires held out a specific romantic prospect. Marina's brother, Jorge Tchomlekdjoglou, whom she had known since they were teenagers, had visited Christina in Europe the previous year, and their friendship had taken an amorous turn. Frequent phone conversations had made Christina anxious for a prolonged reunion to explore this intriguing new prospect.

But it was her feelings about Roussel that superseded all other motives for exploratory trips to Argentina. In addition to whatever other attractions Buenos Aires might have had for her, it was very far from Roussel, Gaby, their children, their love for each other, their pity for her. In Christina's desperate obsession with her former husband, she had kept a grip on hope by believing his explanations for his unhusbandly behavior: he felt responsible to Gaby and owed her allegiance; he had obligations toward his children by her; Gaby was alone, Christina had so many in her life; he was cursed with loving two women at the same time. In spite of his inability to prove it to her sexually, he loved Christina, she was his soulmate, Athina was his legitimate child.

In defiance of the evidence, Christina grasped at these excuses for his life with another woman and shut out the possibility that the money she continued to lavish on him might have prompted the tortured explanations and motivated his reluctance to end their relationship. All she received from him was lengthy phone conversations and the visits, which were more in the nature of the visits a young man might make to a favorite aunt. To everyone but Christina, it was clear Roussel had finished with her and was living with Gaby and the other two children.

With Christina's dogged acceptance, he might have maintained the ludicrous charade. But with her spectacular Thierry-Christina party at the Villa Trianon, she overplayed a meager hand and precipitated a speedy conclusion. So overcome was Roussel at the hypocrisy of the second wedding party as well as the false signal it was sending to their world (one guest later said, "It was understood that they would remarry"), he waited until the next morning to tell Christina he could no longer keep up even the pretense that she required.

With this declaration, the entire superstructure of her hopes, so flimsily supported with misrepresentations about himself and Gaby and, for Christina, with blandishments, lies, hand pats, and fatherly scoldings, now crashed into a devastating awareness of how irrelevant she was to Roussel's happiness, how onerous it was for him to maintain even a ceremonial relationship with her. She no longer could escape what everyone had been trying to tell her: she was letting him make a fool of her. When she was told that an agent for Roussel had made a deal with *Paris Match* to sell them photographs of the Villa Trianon party, the party she had hoped would consolidate their relationship, when Roussel appeared to have found a way to profit from the event, she couldn't miss the ironic summing-up of that relationship. The sudden clarity of vision did nothing to lessen the love she felt for Roussel, but it gave her the self-protective impulse that has saved others trapped in hopeless loves: flight.

According to one of her closest friends, "Christina was as in love with Roussel as ever, but she was sick of the whole situation and had to get away." If her interest in Tchomlekdjoglou blossomed into a new affair, that would be ideal, but in her state of beleaguerment and confusion it would be enough if Argentina could provide much-needed surcease.

Another move she made toward recovery and a new life was a major change in her body. Regardless of how many pounds she had been able to shed with diets and stints at her high-priced clinics, she had never had much success in reducing her massive thighs. So she decided to have them reduced surgically. For weeks after the operation, Christina was confined to a wheelchair in the Clinique Valmont in Switzerland, a pathetic exhibit of the desperate lengths to which her needs drove her and which her wealth made possible. Perversely, a woman who spent millions each year to avoid discomfort, boredom, and frustration suffered a lengthy hospital stay, considerable pain, and additional scars in an attempt to accomplish what nature denied.

Planning to stay only a few days, Christina flew to Buenos Aires on the 19th of October 1988 to attend the fortieth birthday party of Marina Dodero. At a cost of $15,000, she had her secretary purchase three round-trip first-class tickets on Aerolineas Argentina—for herself, Eleni, and Atalanta Politis. In Buenos Aires, Christina was officially the guest of the Doderos, but took a $1,000-a-day two-bedroom suite on the sixth floor of the Alvear Palace, a luxurious hotel about three blocks from the Doderos' apartment. The main purpose of the suite was to provide a place for the endless phone calls to Europe that would tie up the Doderos' lines and make the most generous host nervous. Her plan was to take part in the celebrations for Marina's birthday, spend time with Tchomlekdjoglou, and if things worked out as she hoped, perhaps look around for an apartment.

After the tearful reconciliation on the courthouse steps in Athens, Christina was closer to the Doderos than ever and generally slept each night at their apartment, often in the same bed with Marina. After the loneliness of the abandoned wife, Christina cherished the intimacy and the sense of family she felt when she was in the Doderos' home. For her part, Marina worked assiduously to make her "little sister" forget the pain of the Roussel débacle. She mapped out a heady social schedule for Christina and, thrilled at the flirtation between her best friend and her brother, made every effort to fan this spark into a conflagration.

"Christina was intrigued by Jorge," said Basualdo. "She was intrigued because she couldn't figure him out. She knew he liked women, but he had never been married and that puzzled her."

With her own history of rocky marriages, Christina's fascination with a man who had remained outside the fray was understandable. Genial and self-assured, Tchomlekdjoglou had been born in Greece, but had grown up in Argentina. He had dutifully taken over the family textile business—the business Christina's $4 million loan had saved—and good-naturedly trailed along in his sister's frenetic social life. In Buenos Aires society, he was a popular extra man.

To Christina, Tchomlekdjoglou showed a father's strength and self-possession while at the same time placing himself completely at her service, accommodating her every whim. After only a few days in his company, her enthusiasm for Tchomlekdjoglou mounted to the customary all-consuming nature of her infatuations. She wanted to be with him constantly, even going to his office during the day; she would throw herself on his sofa and read magazines while he transacted business. In the evening they went everywhere as a couple. When Tchomlekdjoglou refused to take her to a starchy diplomatic reception on the grounds that their arriving together would cause gossip, Christina threatened to walk into moving traffic unless he agreed to take her.

Her growing involvement with Tchomlekdjoglou did not push all thoughts of Roussel from Christina's mind. On the phone with intimates in Europe, she hounded them with questions about Roussel. Had they seen him? Heard anything about him? Seen anything in the papers? Dominique Rizzo tried to distract her by turning the conversation to Tchomlekdjoglou. In one phone conversation, Dominique, who relished Christina's candor, was exasperated by her lack of it in talking about her romance with Tchomlekdjoglou. "Come on, Christina, are you sleeping with him or not?"

"Maybe I made love to him once," Christina replied as though thinking of something else.

Her curious response suggested that, for once in Christina's love life, sex was not the primary point of an involvement with a male. Here was a man who made her feel cared for, pampered, safe. They had fun together, he made her laugh, and he was clearly a good person. To a degree Christina had entered into the flirtation with an ulterior, somewhat cynical motive. Tchomlekdjoglou was nice, a companion, a brother—but not the dream lover Roussel had been. She began to see in that a clue to her perpetual problems with men. She had always been looking for the idealized lover rather than a *husband*, clinging—stubbornly, romantically, childishly—to the notion that they should be one and the same. Now, as she became increasingly involved with Tchomlekdjoglou, Christina felt herself falling victim of her own game. But she rather liked the feeling.

Tchomlekdjoglou and Marina began to notice welcome changes in Christina. For the first time in recent years, she was extremely outgoing and interested in everything. Tchomlekdjoglou looked on in amazement at a dinner one night to see Christina engrossed in a weighty theological discussion with a clergyman. She also looked better than she had for some time. During her stay at the Clinique Valmont, dieting and surgery had reduced her weight by almost sixty pounds, which had enabled her to bring to Buenos Aires a trunkful of Saint Laurent and Chanel dresses that for years had been little more than wistful reminders of a lost slimness. Across from her hotel, she found a hairdresser she liked very much, a *simpatico* man named Andrea, who bubbled with intriguing suggestions for glamorizing her. Sweeping into the parties Marina lined up, in her couturier clothes and flashing expensive jewelry—on two occasions she wore her $2 million diamond pendant—she was instantly the center of attention.

Nowhere was this more apparent than at Marina's elaborate and highly publicized fortieth birthday party. For this, the Doderos had assembled fifty of Buenos Aires's richest and finest, many of whom arrived with bodyguards for dinner and dancing at Le Club, the successor to Régine's as the city's most fashionable disco. When Christina entered the party, the orchestra abruptly stopped the song they were playing and launched into the "Zorba" theme as all eyes turned to her. Christina had not enjoyed herself so much in years—since falling in love with Roussel, in fact.

At the end of each day in Buenos Aires, Christina phoned Athina, catching her shortly after she awoke, and they would discuss her daughter's plans for the day. Then, in the morning, Christina would phone the villa at Gingins to get a report from her daughter on the day's activities and to say goodnight. Christina would also converse with Athina's nurse, insisting on full reports on Athina's meals, how she slept, her behavior, her moods—even her regularity. At least once a day she spoke with Roussel—plans for Athina's fourth birthday party were a major topic of conversation—and she frequently had long chats with Dominique Rizzo and other close friends.

By now, the European press had tuned into Christina's Argentinean frolic and was giving full coverage to her spirited reemergence from motherhood and tragic love. Always curious about press comments about her, Christina was now obsessed with them. In addition to the clipping service she often hired to send whatever was printed about her, she urged friends in London and Paris to mail to her anything they saw, fearing the professional clippers might miss something.

Her concern, of course, was not that Europeans learn about her social whirl, but that one European learn about it. During her phone conversations with Roussel, she gushed on about the fun she was having, the attentions being lavished on her, stressing what a devoted friend and amusing companion she had found in Tchomlekdjoglou. But even with this good-times propaganda barrage, Christina was delighted to know that every time her ex-husband picked up a magazine he was hit with picture spreads of the new slim, glamorous, carefree Christina.

Part of Christina's new Argentinean enthusiasm was a subsidiary plan, one that had nothing to do with Roussel or Tchomlekdjoglou.

She was eager to trace her father's origins in the city and had, with the help of her Onassis cousins and a woman journalist friend, made up a list of still-extant places that he had frequented. When Athina arrived, Christina told reporters, she would take her daughter to visit them all and try to talk with people who had known her father, if only casually. While this search for family roots was partly motivated by the strong nostalgic side of Christina's nature, it now became more serious than her love for reminiscing, for poring over scrapbooks to frantically, pathetically seek a happy memory.

Ever since the death of her brother, Christina had brooded about her family's bent for tragedy. Her outburst at Alexander's graveside, "What is happening to us?" had caused her to replay continually the chain of calamities, to which she coupled her own inability to find happiness, in an attempt to find a cause that made sense to her. Her father believed he had found it; he was being punished for his hubris in marrying Jackie. But this did not satisfy Christina. Since she had been doggedly against that marriage, the gods could not consider her a collaborator, yet she was being punished, too. Perhaps in the 1920s vestiges of Buenos Aires—the theaters, restaurants, and cafés her father frequented as a poor, ambition-consumed Greek immigrant— she could find an explanatory clue, some mystery-piercing "Rosebud," to the grim fate that had stalked every Onassis—and now had only her left to torment.

With each day in Buenos Aires, however, she felt more and more detached from that curse. She could feel her spirits rising and an optimism for the future returning. In the evenings, she threw herself into the social maelstrom with the people she liked best, the rich pleasure seekers who make up the society of every city. Among them there were invariably men and women of accomplishment, men like her father, for example, but the *sine qua non* of admittance was not accomplishment but a lot of money. How you got it—whether by talent, brains, inheritance, or theft—was unimportant. This was the milieu that Christina preferred, not because she venerated money so much, but because *they* did. Above anything else, society venerated *being rich* and she was better at it than any of them. They shared the same interests—clothes, jewels, beautiful homes—but more than that, among them she was a queen. In fact that was what Marina called her, Reina. Having at least as much insecurity as the next person, Christina thrived on such ego-bolstering deference.

It did not trouble her in the least that her wealth and nothing else was the reason all of Buenos Aires was throwing itself at her feet. Throughout Christina's life, but particularly since inheriting her fortune, so many of the people around her, regardless of how affluent or respectable, had turned out to be shameless money grubbers. Experience had left her with few illusions about those whom she found close to her.

In the first six months the fortune was hers, both her stepmother and her husband had asked for $20 million. Money had been the guiding principle in her mother's and her Aunt Artemis's efforts to marry her off. Money ruined her friendship with Basualdo and nearly ruined the equally close one with Marina Dodero. Money attracted countless lovers who had no interest in Christina herself, but who played along for the benefits and ended up hurting her badly. She had repeatedly lavished money on the one man she had loved above all others and he had repeatedly asked for more. Money was the underpinning to even her most innocent involvements, such as with her beloved Sunbun. Money brought litigious battles with her uncle Stavros Niarchos and her cousin Nicos Konialidis. Every time she contemplated with affection a husband, lover, relative, or friend, money kept popping up like some hideous funhouse clown and mocked the recollection.

Money had been her curse and her salvation. To her the world was peopled with money-obsessed connivers. She played with them, she fell in love with them, she married them—how could she be blamed if she at least surrounded herself with those who amused her? But over the years, her attitude evolved from such passive resignation to active collaboration in this fate. Increasingly her insecurities had caused her to require a certain degree of money awe in her friends, until she could no longer delude herself that she craved people in her life who were indifferent to her wealth. When as a guest on Skorpios Basualdo had shown insurrectionist signs of such indifference, she had brought him back into line with an enormous salary. When Roussel threatened to leave her, she threw additional millions at him. Her money, she knew, was the cause of her problems, yet she also had come to see her money as the only way out of them.

· · ·

Whenever Christina appeared in public during her visit to Buenos Aires, she was besieged with reporters, who invariably asked if she was thinking of establishing a residence in Argentina. She answered that she was. For Christina, shopping for terraced penthouses and rolling estates provided the excitement that playing dress-up does for children, enabling them to see themselves now in this role, this setting, now in that. But with her wealth Christina could at any moment call a halt to the fantasy and say, "Wait. I *will* be this king, this queen, or the owner of this mansion, this penthouse, this ranch. Prepare the papers." If she bought a place in Argentina, spent money outfitting it, then changed her mind, there would be far less bother in selling it than in not having a house ready when she wanted it.

In an interview for a local magazine, Christina enthused about how much she loved Buenos Aires, and offered such momentous revelations as the number of Cokes she drank each day (between fifteen and twenty) and her greatest weakness (chocolate). She confirmed that she was bringing her daughter to live in Argentina. When the interviewer slyly asked her why she was so often seen entering an apartment building on Avenida Montevideo, she replied forthrightly, "Because Jorge Tchomlekdjoglou, Marina's brother, lives there."

As her visit progressed, the notion of settling in Argentina became less and less a fantasy. Christina had now decided she was in love with Tchomlekdjoglou. He made her agree to cut her use of pills by two-thirds. She solemnized this promise in church in return for his promising to reduce his weight. But as their romance was taking a serious turn, he made it clear to Christina that he would not leave Argentina. She insisted to him that, to be with him, she would move there most happily. She would buy an apartment in Buenos Aires and a country place as well. An *estancia* with dogs and horses would be a healthy, normal place for Athina to grow up. Knowing how addicted Christina was to the excitements of Paris and St. Moritz, Tchomlekdjoglou was skeptical. "Would you sign an agreement," he asked her half jokingly, "to limit the time you spent in Europe to two months a year?" Christina assured him she would.

Brushing aside all such concerns, she saw no reason why they should not get married right away. Tchomlekdjoglou found her impulsiveness unsettling. "Look, Christina," he told her, "I'm not like you, getting married every other year. To me it's a very important step." She insisted that she had changed completely; she was no longer the flighty, headstrong girl of the past. Wasn't she still in love with Roussel, he asked? She respected him as the father of her child and as a friend, she replied, but as for loving him, that was completely finished. Tchomlekdjoglou persuaded her to return to Europe as scheduled, wait six months, then if she still felt the same way, they would get married.

On the 24th of October, Christina returned to Europe. Phoning Tchomlekdjoglou three and four times a day, she immediately began begging him for permission to return. At first he held firm to his cooling-off scheme, always responding to her pleas by reminding her of her precipitate nature and the history of marital mistakes to which it had led. She was a new Christina, she insisted; her last marriage had cured her of her romantic weaknesses. She got Eleni to telephone him with additional testimony to the massive improvement in her mistress's stability. Finally, at the end of the first week of November, Tchomlekdjoglou relented, and Christina made plans to leave for Buenos Aires two days later with her daughter and Eleni. On the day of their departure, however, Athina developed a middle-ear infection from swimming in the living-room pool at Boislande and could not travel. Christina would not wait. As soon as Athina was well, her nurse could accompany her on the flight to Buenos Aires.

On the 9th of November, Christina kissed Athina goodbye and, with Eleni, returned to Buenos Aires. Although Tchomlekdjoglou was as pleased to see Christina as she was to see him, he still urged that they proceed slowly with their plans to marry. Since they were once again together, Christina was able to control her impatience. With Tchomlekdjoglou at her side, she threw herself once again into the frenzied social activities of the Doderos' world. Every morning she had Andrea dress her hair and took his suggestion to streak it blond. The effect was dramatic and becoming. She looked at some lavish apartments in town, and decided on an exquisite place with a $2 million price tag, only to be dashed when the owners changed their mind about selling it. With a real-estate agent she planned a tour to inspect a number of country estates that had come on the market.

On Thursday evening, November 17, Christina returned to her hotel from a party and went to bed. Unable to sleep, she startled hotel employees by appearing in the lobby at 4 A.M., casually dressed but her feet bare. When asked if she needed anything, she lifted the headset of her Sony Walkman from one ear and said, no, she was just going out for a walk. In a city where, even during the day, many wealthy citizens will not venture into public without a bodyguard, the prospect of one of the world's richest women wandering alone through the streets in the middle of the night brought fervent pleas from the hotel staff for her to reconsider. Polite but unswerving, Christina pushed her way through the revolving doors. About two hours later, she returned, still listening to her Walkman and, bidding the lobby personnel goodnight, went to her room. The next day, which was warm and sunny, she complained to Eleni of feeling cold.

Early Friday afternoon, the Doderos picked Christina and Eleni up at the Alvear Palace and they drove, ahead of the weekend traffic, thirty-seven kilometers to the northwest of Buenos Aires to the Tortugas Club, an exclusive country club with some 150 satellite villas on its grounds. Tchomlekdjoglou owned a villa there, which he turned over to his sister and brother-in-law and their guests, he sleeping in an adjacent guest house. Tortugas had tennis, swimming, polo, and everything to attract the younger and flashier elements of the Buenos Aires affluent. During the drive Marina told Christina about the barbecue planned for that evening, who would be there, the food that was being served.

Arriving around five in the afternoon, Christina was shown to her room, where Eleni unpacked the few things she had brought for the three-day visit. Christina was eager to phone Athina, invariably her first impulse when she arrived anyplace, but was dismayed to discover that the Tortugas telephones were unable to make international calls. Marina had a hairdressing appointment in the nearby village of Tortugitas and suggested to Christina she come along and call Athina from the telephone office there.

The village was a quaint but scruffy community that had not yet caught up with the veneer of affluence the Tortugas Club had brought the area. At the telephone office, Christina was once again frustrated when she was told she could make an international call only during weekday office hours; they were now into the weekend.

Christina pleaded with the operator, but resisted resorting to saying her name and insisting that the flow of the world's oil supply depended on her getting through to her tanker fleet. Having ascertained that calling Switzerland was possible from the telephone office, simply a violation of the rules, Christina would not relent.

Suddenly putting it together, the harassed operator looked at her and asked, "Are you Christina Onassis?" When Christina said she was, the operator immediately placed the call and pointed Christina toward a booth. Her secretary in Gingins answered and within two minutes Christina was talking happily with Athina. The picture is haunting. In a poor village in rural Argentina, in a dirty, bad-smelling public telephone booth, one of the world's wealthiest women had her last conversation with her child, the only fully loving human bond she had ever known, a bond that had nearly saved her.

At the barbecue that evening, Christina was in good spirits, not the frenzied elation that often came over her when having a good time, the chemically heightened euphoria that so often collapsed into burned-out depression. Instead of the frantic joy she usually craved, she experienced an unfamiliar contentment, based on being with her closest friends, with a man she was coming to value more and more, and in a pleasant country setting, ideal for savoring the fragrant spring evening. After the hearty feast of charcoal-broiled Argentinean beef, the group returned to the Doderos' villa and Christina suggested they all stay up for a while and talk. Marina and Alberto, no strangers to Christina's all-night talkathons, pleaded exhaustion. They made plans to take a swim with Christina the next morning after breakfast, then kissed their guest goodnight. At Christina's suggestion, she and Tchomlekdjoglou took a stroll through the club's gardens, then he retired to his quarters. About one-thirty Christina went alone to her room.

The next morning around ten, Marina expressed surprise to Eleni that Christina was not yet up. She knew that Christina liked to rise early at Tortugas and indeed had asked that they all take an after-breakfast swim together. Knowing of the problems Christina had sleeping, Eleni urged that her mistress not be disturbed. But feeling something was not right, Marina went into the bedroom and returned to say that Christina was out of bed and the bathroom door was closed. She was probably taking a bath. Eleni said that was not possible; Madame never took her bath until she had had her coffee. They looked at each other, then at once rushed to Christina's room and entered the bathroom. In a tub with about two inches of water, they found Christina slumped naked, her knees bent and her head bent down on them. Marina became hysterical and started screaming for help. Eleni knew immediately that her beloved mistress was dead.

Assumptions were inevitably made about the sudden and unexpected death of a rich woman who was known to be a substance abuser. Not only did the worldly gossips of international society immediately assume an accidental or deliberate overdose, medical and civil authorities were almost as quick to jump to similar conclusions. To establish that a death was unnatural or even accidental, however, authorities are obliged to produce some evidence. In the death of Christina, there was none. That did not rule out either an accidental or deliberate overdose, but it turned out to be impossible to establish either with any certainty.

The official report of the investigation into Christina's death, which was slow in coming, said that it had been accidental, the result of an acute pulmonary edema of the lung, which had produced a heart attack—precisely the cause given for Tina Onassis's equally mysterious death fourteen years earlier. But this impressive medical phrase merely described the patient's condition at the time of death: the lungs had filled with fluid. It left open the question of what caused the lethal fluid to fill the lungs. One possible cause of pulmonary edema is an overdose of barbiturates, which was generally accepted to have caused Tina's pulmonary edema.

Obscuring the facts of Christina's death were a series of mistakes made at the time by the Doderos, who later admitted that they were not thinking rationally, a lapse that many people found understandable. Initially, they sought assistance from the attendant at a first-aid station on the club grounds, losing valuable time before a bona fide doctor was brought to the scene. There was never a chance of saving Christina, but the delay further obfuscated the cause of death. When the doctor began asking questions that the Doderos felt were scandal-prone, they ordered him to leave the premises before he had had a chance to examine Christina's body thoroughly.

Adding to the confusion, the angry doctor later raised the possibility that Christina's hosts had tampered with items in her room, items such as pill bottles that might have thrown light on the disaster. Later, an empty vial was found not far from Christina's bathtub, but it had contained amphetamines, not a drug one would take in the middle of the night to sleep—or to kill oneself. If there was tampering —whether it was done by the Doderos, Eleni, or someone else— it was done in all likelihood not to destroy evidence but rather to protect Christina's privacy. Destroying evidence, unfortunately, was the net effect.

Much more conclusive would have been unduly high levels of barbiturates in Christina's body. Judge Juan Cardinali in Buenos Aires, where Christina's body was taken some four hours after it was discovered, was notified of an unresolved cause of death and officially ordered an autopsy. His order made public the news of her death, and headlines of the catastrophe screamed from newspapers around the world. A second judge, Alberto Piotti, was placed in charge of an investigation into the question of a pill overdose, and he forbade the removal of the body from the country until his investigators had time to run the necessary tests. A search of her hotel room in Buenos Aires turned up forty-two different medications, but only the diet prescription had been taken with her for the weekend at the Club Tortugas. Within twenty-four hours, the examiners had all they needed and a judicial release was signed granting permission for Christina's body to be taken back to Europe.

The official report of Judge Alberto Piotti stated that drugs had not caused Christina's death. Insignificant traces of amphetamines were found in her body and *no* barbiturates. Indeed, in a private conversation with a family friend, Greek Orthodox Archbishop Chrysoulakis, Christina had told the churchman that for the first time "in her life" she was able to sleep without the help of pills. After a careful evaluation of the test results and the interviews with everyone around her at the time of her death, it was announced that there was no evidence of either a deliberate or accidental overdose. Nor was there any evidence of foul play. Judge Piotti's report added that the investigators did not know what had caused her death.

Knowledgeable friends knew that, in addition to her long-time use of barbiturates and amphetamines, her wild weight fluctuations had placed substantial strains on her heart. She had recently lost nearly fifty pounds in a two-month period. It was also theorized that the futile injections of Roussel's spermatozoa may have had heart-weakening effects. To varying degrees and from a variety of causes, there seemed little doubt that Christina's heart—so abused by herself and, in a different sense, by many others—had given out.

In a surge of long-dormant religious feeling, Christina had attended the Greek Orthodox church in Buenos Aires the week before she died and had taken communion, her first in many years. She had later had lunch with Archbishop Chrysoulakis and told him of her plans to buy a home in Argentina and to marry Tchomlekdjoglou. Like everyone else, he reported that Christina had seemed in particularly high spirits and optimistic about the future. She requested that the archbishop say a special mass in memory of her father, mother, and brother the following Sunday. She told Marina she wanted to give a gift to Archbishop Chrysoulakis's church and did Marina think $100,000 was enough. The mass was held as Christina wished, but the archbishop sadly included her in those commemorated.

Within hours of finding Christina, Marina telephoned the news to Roussel, who made immediate plans to come to Buenos Aires, although arrangements had already been set to have the funeral in Greece. She also telephoned Atalanta Politis and Dominique Rizzo, both of whom were devastated. Late Sunday morning, a puffy-eyed Roussel arrived in Buenos Aires and went immediately to Christina's suite at the Alvear Palace. Encountering there Christina's friend Mercedes Zavalia, whom he had known in Europe, he fell into her arms and sobbed uncontrollably. Roussel was particularly horrified at the rumors of suicide, insisting that in his conversation with Christina the day before her death she had seemed in particularly high spirits. Mercedes confirmed Christina's upbeat state of mind, as did everyone who had been with her in Argentina. Further undermining suicide theories was the absence of any note, nor was there anyone who could claim to have heard a despairing remark from Christina.

The tabloid press would later make much of Christina's having written a new will shortly before leaving on her first trip to Buenos Aires, implying she planned to end her life in Argentina. But with a little examination, this evidence of intention fell apart. For some time Roussel had been after Christina to reduce an enormous bequest she had made to George Livanos, on her theory that part of her inheritance came from her mother, that is to say the Livanos family. Roussel had successfully persuaded her to increase the amount that went to Athina.

Although the circumstances of rewriting the will struck outside observers as odd—she took a room at a Geneva hotel, just a few miles from her estate, and handwrote a five-page document—others close to Christina insisted that this impulsive manner of disposing of a half-billion dollars was thoroughly consistent with the way she did everything. About to embark on two lengthy airplane journeys—to and from Argentina in less than a week—Christina had adequate reason to bring her will up to date. Even with the apparent spur-of-the-moment nature of the revision, it constituted poor evidence of intent to commit suicide, especially when the will was written before the *first* brief trip, a trip from which she returned to Europe well and healthy.

The rumors of suicide were understandably hideous for Roussel. He was aware that everyone who knew him and Christina, as well as the readers of the gossip press, felt he had treated her abominably and that she had suffered enormously over him. If it were to appear she had taken her own life in grief over him, he would be transformed from a dashing heartbreaker to a life-taker monster. He would go through the rest of his days hated and despised. And in all probability, had she, apart from appearances but in actuality, destroyed herself, it would have been more than *he*, not his image, could bear. He was not an icy sociopath, totally lacking in conscience. And he had been sincerely fond of Christina. The evening of his arrival in South America, Roussel sat alone in the Greek Orthodox church. In front of him in an ebony casket Christina's embalmed body was laid out. She was dressed in white, a single red rose placed in her white, translucent hands, her face made up with her own cosmetics. Roussel sat for an hour in the empty church crying softly as he prayed for Christina's soul and, surely, his own.

With her death, the dislike of Roussel that had been smoldering among Christina's friends, moved toward open hostility. Roussel exacerbated the trend with the funeral arrangements, which he now took over. Her old friends—many having flown to Athens from such distant places as New York and Argentina—were admitted to the funeral services, but found themselves unwelcome at the burial on Skorpios. Unlike the unwieldy throngs that had arrived on the island for Onassis's interment, only about fifteen people were permitted to make the short journey across the water from Nidri for Christina's.

This insult caused a hardening of feelings toward the man many felt had speeded Christina's death by his heartless and cruel treatment, feelings that had spread beyond her circle of intimates to the large public who followed her joys and vicissitudes in the glossy magazines. As Roussel had entered the church in Athens, rude jeers and whistles were heard from the crowd. One woman spat at him and there were shouts of *skatapedo* ("son of a shit") and *dolofone* ("killer"). With such venomous epithets in the air and a brush fire of rancor spreading among those closest to her, Christina was laid to rest in the Skorpios chapel beside her father, mother, and brother. The Onassis name, for fifty years synonymous with the most blessed of humans, was no more. The curse that she believed haunted her family had claimed its last victim.

In the grand tradition of keeping Greek shipping fortunes together, Christina left everything, with the exception of a few relatively small bequests, to her daughter. Skorpios, the Avenue Foch apartment, and the Villa Cristal were to be retained until Athina was old enough to decide whether or not she wanted to keep them. Still only three when Christina died, Athina was spared the terrible news and was told instead that her mother had gone on an exceptionally long trip to find her another brother and sister. On the Monday following Christina's death, with Roussel in Argentina, Athina, with her nurse and her two bodyguards, took a commercial flight to Paris. She was met by her grandfather, Henri Roussel, who put Athina in his dark blue Mercedes and drove her to his country house in the Loire Valley, where Roussel's sister, Christine de Luynes, was waiting to look after her.

The reason cited for this abrupt move was that Athina's nurse,

Monique, was too distraught by the tragedy to look after the child alone. Others saw it as an immediate assertion by the Roussel forces of parental rights, a move calculated to forestall a custody battle. Accustomed by her mother to impulsive shifts from one residence to another, Athina saw nothing strange about being suddenly snatched from her home in Switzerland to her grandfather's house. As Christmas approached, the Roussels did what they could to keep the press from the little girl, their human booty, and to distract her from her mother's absence.

After Athina's, the largest bequest in Christina's will was a lifetime income to Roussel of $1.4 million, provided Athina's annual income did not drop below $4.5 million. It was a remarkable piece of generosity to one who had caused Christina much grief and appalled many of her friends, none of whom were left anything, although some later said that Christina had led them to believe they would be. The most knowledgeable of these friends, knew, however, that the annual income to Roussel, who had not been mentioned in any of the nine previous wills Christina had drawn up since coming into her fortune, was Christina's way of assuring that his two children by Gaby would always be well provided for even if he went through the millions she had already given him.

The only other substantial bequests were to long-time Onassis officers Stelios Papadimitriou, Apostolos Zambelas, and Paul Ionnides, who received $2 million apiece. These three men would serve as trustees of Athina's inheritance along with Roussel and Theodore Gavrilides, a lawyer for the Onassis companies. Christina's two most faithful servants, Eleni and her husband, Jorge, were each left $200,000. Many were surprised that Christina's uncle George Livanos or any other representative of her mother's family were not included in the group that would oversee Athina's upbringing, but that may have been at Roussel's insistence. His influence was apparent throughout the five-page handwritten document.

As it emerged that Roussel intended to take over Athina's rearing completely, members of the Onassis group, who during Christina's life had made no secret of their hostility to him, were dismayed. Many believed that, from the beginning of her involvement with him, the romance had been a conspiracy of the entire Roussel family, particularly Thierry's father and sister. Convinced of these machinations, Onassis friends and business associates had watched with increasing dismay as Christina continued to lavish large helpings of the Onassis fortune upon him. Now it all appeared to be falling under the control of the Roussels. There was talk of a legal struggle, but the resigned conclusion of one trustee—"He is her father and that's that"—came to be shared by everyone in the Onassis camp.

Friction over minor matters, however, cropped up constantly between Roussel and the other trustees, as when they complained of his excessive use of "Athina's" jet—news stories had appeared describing airborne champagne parties—but such points of discord were quickly and privately resolved. One of the trustees telephoned Jorge Tchomlekdjoglou in Buenos Aires and said, "We've all got to stop speaking badly about Roussel. He is, after all, the father of Ari's only grandchild."

In a public display of the paternal obligations he was intent on assuming, Roussel announced that he planned to rescue his daughter from the armed fortress Christina had built for her in Gingins and would instead move her into a more modest house he and Gaby were building in Switzerland. A year after Christina's death, Roussel and Gaby settled on a village further along the shores of Lake Geneva, Lussy-sur-Morges, where he bought an estate and set out to renovate it. Athina would be raised there like other children, not with nannies, nurses, bodyguards, boatmen, and animal trainers, but with a mother, father, sister, and brother. He added that he and Gaby would marry eventually (which they did in Villeny, France, on May 12, 1990, eighteen months after Christina's death, a cheerful Athina in attendance, with the traditional Greek garland of flowers crowning her head).

Given Roussel's behavior toward Christina and his suspect motives, a number of Christina's friends sadly acknowledged that Athina might conceivably be facing a saner, more promising future than she would have had if her mother had lived. None of them felt Christina was a bad parent; Roussel was not stretching the truth much in calling his former wife a "perfect mother." But Christina's restlessness, her world fame, and jet-tycoon style all loomed as sizable threats to Athina's enjoying a normal childhood. In addition, Christina's volatile emotions (which Athina had inherited), as well as the wounded psyche with which she attempted to deal with the world, would have lessened the chances of her providing her daughter with a stable and trauma-free upbringing. No matter how much mother love and costly coddling she lavished on Athina, she might well have ended by inflicting the same sort of pain-racked and disorienting childhood she herself had endured.

Whatever Roussel's transgressions, he seemed to have found a stabilizing anchor in Gaby—an anchor he may have needed as much as Christina needed one—and he seemed intent on atoning for whatever wrong he had done Christina by doing right by their daughter. The tragedy had netted Athina a little brother and sister and perhaps, sad to say, a mother who did not bring to the job of child rearing the emotional scars of thirty-seven years of turmoil, lovelessness, and pain. As for Roussel and the wrongs he did Christina, he may not have been evil so much as lethally selfish.

In the last years of her life, Christina had been gradually selling off her fleet, with the aim of withdrawing from the shipping business altogether. By the time of her death, she owned only twelve ships. In April, 1990 Athina's trustees, in a package deal netting $130 million, sold her last three tankers, thus marking the end of the Onassis family's three-quarters of a century involvement with the transport of crude oil. The ships had made them extremely rich, but the money had brought far more grief than pleasure. The decision to divest was based on sound business considerations, but few would have been surprised if superstition also played a part.

On her eighteenth birthday, Athina will come into her tankerless fortune, which by then should have grown to over a billion dollars. If she should not live to be eighteen, the entire fortune would in all likelihood go to Roussel. Her chances for a normal life looked dim when, shortly after Christina's death, a London tabloid offered £10,000 to anyone who could produce a new photograph of the world's richest infant. This opening shot in the war between Athina and a curious world conjured up visions of swarms of *paparazzi* conniving their way to the girl—disguising themselves as deliverymen, climbing walls, bribing servants, ambushing schools—anything to get her picture.

The badgering Christina received from the press was far down on the list of problems that finally defeated her. In fact, she discovered, perhaps too late, that the assaults on her happiness came from peo-

384 ··· CHAPTER TWENTY-TWO

ple on the welcome side of her estate walls. Athina will undoubtedly know the same friendly perils. No matter how sane and level-headed the parenting of Roussel and Gaby, no matter how tempering to her personality the healthy competition she gets from her brother and sister, no matter how much high-tech protection she is given from marauding journalists, Athina's prospects for a happy life are precarious for the same reason her mother's were: she possesses in vast quantity something everyone who comes near her wants.

# ACKNOWLEDGMENTS

Because secrecy was desired by several of my most helpful sources, rather than omitting from a list of names those to whom I was especially grateful. But this, I feared, would serve little purpose but to register ingratitude to the many

Early in my research for this book, I learned what an odd quest I faced. Several of the first sources I contacted told me I must speak with Luis Basualdo, Christina's close friend and paid companion for a number of years. They assured me that without help from Basualdo, I could not fully depict Christina or her bizarre life. Adding to his allure as an interviewee, they also told me that his friendship with Christina had hit a snag when she accused him of embezzling $1.2 million from her.

All my efforts to find Basualdo failed. Phone numbers for him in Paris, London, and New York were defunct. I heard he had returned to Argentina, but some diligent international sleuthing on my part could uncover no trace of him there. I moved on to other aspects of Christina's life.

Some months later, a screenwriter friend who had been in Palm Beach working on a script about polo told me he had overheard a locker room conversation in which some Argentinean players were talking and joking about Christina. One boasted that he had gotten $1.2 million out of her. My friend had the phone number of one of the players. I called, explained my mission, then asked as casually as possible if one of his teammates was named Luis Basualdo. "Oh, yes," came the answer, "He's here and is a good friend of mine."

In fact, Basualdo had just returned to Argentina and it was many more weeks and many phone calls that never got beyond "Ola!" before I found him. When I did, he turned out to be, as billed, extremely knowledgeable, insightful, witty, and, in all of his stories that I was able to double-check, accurate and truthful. I began to wonder, however, if this method of tracking sources would become a pattern: identifying them not by their names but by the amounts they had extracted from Christina.

The pattern that did develop was quite different—winning the help of primary sources who wished to remain anonymous. At the time, it was uncertain who would get custody of Christina's daughter, Athina, and some who had been closest to Christina were fearful of saying anything that might estrange them from the winning faction, thus cutting them off from their friend's only child.

Because secrecy was desired by several of my most helpful sources, I considered acknowledging no one rather than omitting from a list of names those to whom I was especially grateful. But this, I realized, would serve little purpose but to register ingratitude to the many others who made valuable contributions to this book.

So, with particular thanks to my unnamed deep throats, I would also like to thank Baron Alessandro Albrizzi, James Lee Auchincloss, Luis Basualdo, Victoria Bolker, Lady Sarah Churchill, Amanda Clapperton, Benjamin Clutterbuck, Rod Coupe, Julie Davis, James Douglas, Gilles Dufour, Dominick Dunne, Tasso Fondaris, Nicholas Gage, Lady Henrietta Gelber, Judith Kazantzis, Daniel Marentette, Kyle Morris, Nigel Neilson, June Oberio, Nicholas Papanicolaou, Dominique Rizzo, Willy Rizzo, Claude Roland, Countess Aline de Romanones, Muriel Slotkin, Nadia Stancioff, Jorge Tchomlekdjoglou, Baroness Fiona Thyssen-Bornemisza, Virginia Vanocur, Princess Diane von Furstenberg, Countess Christina Wachtmeister, Susan Warner, and Frank Zachary.

Finally, I would like to express fervent thanks to Fred Hills and Burton Beals, my editor and alter-editor, and Daphne Bien, the Simon & Schuster support group that has seen me through my biographies of both Lillian Hellman and Christina Onassis—two very singular and elusive women.

# INDEX

# About the Author

William Wright is the best-selling author of *Lillian Hellman, The Von Bülow Affair, Pavarotti,* and *Heiress: The Rich Life of Marjorie Merriweather Post.* He lives in New York City and Bucks County, Pennsylvania.